"Doesn't holiness mean that God st. Ayars, Bounds, and Friedeman answer that God's holiness and graciousness are inextricably linked. By providing a careful survey of how holiness is understood both in the Old and New Testaments and by orthodox theologians from different eras and denominational backgrounds, the authors point us to a holy God who invites us to come as we are so that we can become like him. This book both uplifts and challenges us to accept this invitation by leaving a life of mediocrity and compromise to embrace a life of holiness."

Mark R. Teasdale, E. Stanley Jones Professor of Evangelism at Garrett-Evangelical Theological Seminary

"John Wesley was convinced that God had raised up the Methodists to 'spread scriptural holiness throughout the land.' In many modern expressions of Christianity, a concern for holiness has been neglected—not only within evangelicalism generally but also within much of the Methodist tradition. This book seeks to recapture the vision of the Wesleys, showing that the doctrine is grounded in Scripture as well as the deep and broad Christian tradition. It will be a blessing to both fellow Wesleyans and Reformed Christians who will find much with which they can heartily agree."

Thomas H. McCall, Tennent Professor of Theology at Asbury Theological Seminary

"With careful attention to the biblical, historical, and doctrinal material, Ayars, Bounds, and Friedeman make a powerful case for recovering the importance of holiness as a real possibility in the Christian life. Although the authors are confessionally Wesleyan, this book reaches across traditions, inviting all to reflect on this crucial matter."

David Firth, tutor in Old Testament at Trinity College Bristol

"This readable, concise, and scholarly book on Christian sanctification is a 'three-in-one' approach, including contributions from biblical, historical, and systematic theology. The earlier chapters present a strong case that the Wesleyan approach to this doctrine has solid foundations in Scripture and the historic teachings of the church. The systematic chapters present an informative account of variations within the Wesleyan tradition. This is necessary reading for all within the tradition and a helpful primer for all pastors, teachers, and laity across the church."

Thomas A. Noble, professor of theology at Nazarene Theological Seminary

"The heart and soul of all good Wesleyan theology, the doctrine of holiness, has been neglected for too long. This new work by a team of established Wesleyan scholars is a monumental first step toward a recovery of holiness not only as a doctrine but also as a way of life. A must-read for all who hunger and thirst for God."

Jason E. Vickers, William J. Abraham Professor of Theology and Wesleyan Studies at Baylor University

"This is a most welcome book. Its great strength is in its comprehensiveness. It shows how the Bible lays the foundation, how the church has built on that foundation over its history, and then how we can think about the concept in ways that are philosophically and theologically sound. The final section on the theology of holiness is especially to be commended; Bounds has done a great service in making the subject both comprehensible and compelling. Both those who do believe in holiness and those who don't should read this book. Both will be helped."

John Oswalt, visiting distinguished professor of Old Testament at Asbury Theological Seminary

"The quest for Christian perfection in the twenty-first century is as fresh as it was in biblical history. These distinguished Wesleyan scholars have given a detailed biblical, historical, and systematic theological witness to the doctrine of entire sanctification. The authors provide a serious case for the 'middle way,' or a new appeal for the message that so distinguishes biblical Christianity. Their ability to trace the witness to holiness in every segment of the Bible and in divergent historic Christian traditions endears this book to a wide readership. This is an extremely important resource for those seeking deeper Christian experience and for those seeking deeper theological appreciation of entire sanctification as a biblical truth."

Robert K. Lang'at, bishop of Africa Gospel Church, Kenya

"This long overdue and thoroughly accessible volume describes with perfect clarity both the scriptural basis for and the practical manifestations of holiness doctrine. It will encourage individual believers to claim the privilege of a growing relationship with Christ, and it is just what the church needs to minister more effectively in a hurting world. I recommend it without reservation."

Kenneth Hodder, national commander of The Salvation Army

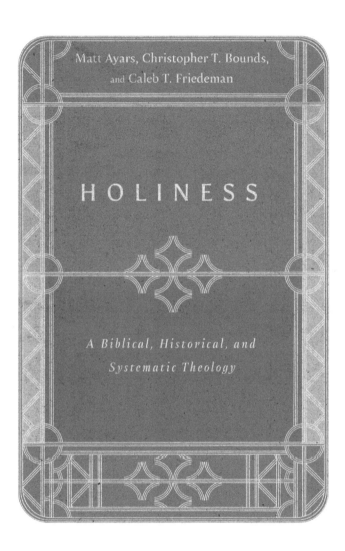

Matt Ayars, Christopher T. Bounds,
and Caleb T. Friedeman

HOLINESS

A Biblical, Historical, and
Systematic Theology

ivp
Academic
An imprint of InterVarsity Press
Downers Grove, Illinois

InterVarsity Press
P.O. Box 1400 | Downers Grove, IL 60515-1426
ivpress.com | email@ivpress.com

©2023 by Matthew Ian Ayars, Christopher Todd Bounds, and Caleb Travis Friedeman

InterVarsity Press® is the publishing division of InterVarsity Christian Fellowship/USA®. For more information, visit intervarsity.org.

The publisher cannot verify the accuracy or functionality of website URLs used in this book beyond the date of publication.

Cover design: David Fassett

Interior design: Daniel van Loon

ISBN 978-1-5140-0230-8 (print) | ISBN 978-1-5140-0231-5 (digital)

Printed in the United States of America ∞

Library of Congress Cataloging-in-Publication Data
A catalog record for this book is available from the Library of Congress.

30   29   28   27   26   25   24   23 | 13   12   11   10   9   8   7   6   5   4   3   2   1

To John Oswalt,

who has inspired us and a generation of

Wesleyan-holiness leaders to boldly proclaim the

message of Scriptural holiness.

CONTENTS

Part Four

"MAY THE GOD OF PEACE SANCTIFY YOU ENTIRELY"

A Theology of Holiness

ACKNOWLEDGMENTS

WE WOULD LIKE TO EXPRESS our deep gratitude to all those who have helped us to bring this volume to completion. The present book began as a project with the Francis Asbury Press. However, as we worked on it and saw the deep need for a book like this, we realized that it might be beneficial to have a publisher with a wider reach. The Francis Asbury leadership agreed and graciously allowed us to pursue publication with IVP Academic instead. We would like to thank the Francis Asbury leadership—and particularly then-president Ron Smith—for their selflessness in this regard. We are also grateful to Jonathan Morgan, Brian Shelton, and Jerome Van Kuiken, who provided testimonials regarding the need for this book in our proposal to IVP Academic. A number of scholars reviewed parts of the manuscript and provided feedback: Rick Boyd, Scott Engebretson, Chris Lohrstorfer, Jonathan Morgan, Matt O'Reilly, John Oswalt, Jerome Van Kuiken, Murray Vasser, and Jason Vickers. We are grateful to these for their time and valuable insights. Any errors that remain are, of course, our own. Finally, we would like to express our gratitude to IVP Academic for accepting this project; we could not have asked for a better publisher to work with. In particular, we would like to thank our editor David McNutt for his guidance, encouragement, and perceptive feedback at every step from proposal to publication.

ABBREVIATIONS

ANF   *The Ante-Nicene Fathers.* Edited by Alexander Roberts and James Donaldson. 1885–1887. 10 vols. Peabody, MA: Hendrickson, 1994.

BDAG   *Greek-English Lexicon of the New Testament and Other Early Christian Literature.* Edited by Frederick W. Danker, Walter Bauer, William F. Arndt, and F. Wilbur Gingrich. 3rd ed. Chicago: University of Chicago Press, 2000.

HALOT   *The Hebrew and Aramaic Lexicon of the Old Testament.* Edited by Ludwig Koehler, Walter Baumgartner, and Johann J. Stamm. Translated and edited under the supervision of Mervyn E. J. Richardson. 4 vols. Leiden: Brill, 1994–1999.

NPNF[1] *The Nicene and Post-Nicene Fathers,* Series 1. Edited by Philip Schaff. 1886–1889. 14 vols. Repr., Grand Rapids, MI: Eerdmans, 1983.

NPNF[2] *The Nicene and Post-Nicene Fathers,* Series 2. Edited by Philip Shaff and Henry Wace. 14 vols. Grand Rapids, MI: Eerdmans, 1983.

TDNT   *Theological Dictionary of the New Testament.* Edited by Gerhard Kittel and Gerhard Friedrich. Translated by Geoffrey W. Bromiley. 10 vols. Grand Rapids, MI: Eerdmans, 1964–1976.

WJW   *The Works of John Wesley.* Edited by Thomas Jackson. 14 vols. Grand Rapids, MI: Baker, 1978.

INTRODUCTION

THE WORLD IS HUNGRY for God. Everywhere we look, we find people seeking a person, object, or experience to satisfy their desire for the transcendent, the sublime, the *other*. Yet as Blaise Pascal observed, "This infinite abyss can be filled only with an infinite and immutable object; in other words by God himself."[1] But how will the world find the holy One who alone can fulfill its deepest need? According to Scripture, the primary way that the world encounters God is through the people of God—the redeemed bearers of the divine image who fill creation with God's glory by living holy lives that imitate God's own life.[2] Holiness, then, is not merely a matter of personal piety; it is a matter of missional urgency. And what we believe the Bible teaches about holiness will inevitably shape how we live in relation to God, to other believers, and to the world.

So holiness is important. But what *is* it? Scripture portrays holiness above all as a divine attribute: God is holy (Lev 11:44-45). Indeed, God is the holy One, the one whom the seraphim call "holy, holy, holy" (Is 6:3). As we will see in part one of this book, the Old Testament depicts Yahweh's holiness as his otherness, his distinctness from both pagan deities and sinful humans. Yet Scripture also teaches that people, places, objects, and times can become holy through relationship with the holy One. The doctrine of holiness, then, addresses both what it means for God to be holy and how

---

[1]Blaise Pascal, *Pensées*, trans. A. J. Krailsheimer, rev. ed. (London: Penguin, 1995), 45 (§7.425).
[2]Parts one and two of this book discuss this point at length, but some of the key passages are Gen 1:26-27; Ex 19:5-6; Is 43:10, 12; and Acts 1:8.

humans and other elements of creation can share in God's holiness. The present book focuses on holiness in the divine and human spheres but touches on other dimensions of holiness as necessary. Scripture uses a wide range of words and concepts to describe what it looks like for humans to participate in God's holiness (bearing God's image, being faithful to the covenant, living wisely, being God's witnesses, etc.). A theology of holiness, then, must deal not only with biblical occurrences of "holy" and related words but also with the diverse ways that Scripture develops the concept of holiness.

As followers of a holy God, Christians *should* be holy. But *can* we be holy with any sort of completeness and consistency? One popular answer to this question is that Christians can become more holy as they walk with Christ but that they will always sin daily in word, thought, and deed. Indeed, for many this is the obvious biblical answer to the question. But there is another perspective—namely, that God can sanctify believers to the point that they are wholly devoted to him and can live lives of joyful obedience free of willful sin. Within Christian theology, this latter view is often associated with the eighteenth-century evangelist and theologian John Wesley and his doctrine of entire sanctification or Christian perfection. However, Wesley did not invent this idea. In developing his doctrine of entire sanctification, Wesley was actually recovering a much older view of the Christian life with roots reaching all the way back to the church fathers and, we would argue, to Scripture itself. Unfortunately, many Christians both inside and outside of the Wesleyan tradition do not understand this view of holiness or the biblical, historical, and theological basis for it—hence the need for the present book.

We are Wesleyan scholars who are ordained in Wesleyan denominations and currently serve in Wesleyan academic institutions. In our preaching and teaching, we have seen the need for a book that treats the Wesleyan doctrine of entire sanctification or Christian perfection from the perspectives of biblical, historical, and systematic theology in a single volume. The present book aims to fill this need. We have tried to write it in a style that is accessible to serious laypeople, undergraduate students, and pastors, but with enough footnotes to be appropriate for graduate students. Our overarching thesis is that the Wesleyan doctrine of entire sanctification or Christian perfection is well-grounded in Scripture, well-represented in the Christian tradition, and consistent with classic Christian teaching. Yet while we have written this book from (and in some sense for) the Wesleyan tradition, we believe that the doctrine of holiness it presents is something all Christians should affirm precisely because it is biblical, has precedent throughout the Christian tradition, and coheres with orthodoxy.

This book is divided into four parts, each containing three chapters. Each part has a primary author, as indicated below:

- Part One: "Be Holy Because I Am Holy": Holiness in the Old Testament (Ayars)
- Part Two: "Be Perfect as Your Heavenly Father is Perfect": Holiness in the New Testament (Friedeman)
- Part Three: "Let Those of Us Who Are Perfect Think This Way": Holiness in Christian History (Bounds)
- Part Four: "May the God of Peace Sanctify You Entirely": A Theology of Holiness (Bounds)

All the authors gave input on each chapter, but we retain first-person singular pronouns (I, my, me) throughout to recognize the primary authors.

The final chapter of part four ("The When and How of Holiness") discusses different understandings of entire sanctification within the Wesleyan tradition and outlines what we believe to be the most biblically faithful and theologically coherent version of the doctrine: a neo-holiness "middle way." Within the Wesleyan tradition, there are three major positions on when and how believers experience entire sanctification or Christian perfection:

- The "shorter way"—Christian perfection now by total conse-cration and faith
- The "middle way"—Christian perfection by seeking until you receive
- The "longer way"—Christian perfection by a long process of continual growth

The "shorter way" is exemplified in the American holiness movement, which flourished in the nineteenth and twentieth centuries and continues to the present. With the holiness movement, we affirm that Scripture presents entire sanctification as the normative Christian life and that believers should expect to receive it sooner rather than later (contra the "longer way"). However, the holiness movement has sometimes taught that believers can simply decide when to be entirely sanctified, essentially reducing entire sanctification to entire consecration. In our view, this grants too much to human ability and too little to the divine initiative in entire sanctification. We argue that the holiness movement's view of entire sanctification as the normative Christian life needs to be recontextualized within a "middle way" perspective that recognizes the priority of divine grace in entire sanctification. According to this view, believers should give everything to God and seek him expectantly for Christian perfection until he sanctifies them entirely. We offer this neo-holiness "middle way" as a fresh articulation of holiness theology that upholds the biblical vision of entire sanctification as the normative Christian life alongside the equally biblical truth that entire sanctification is an act of God.

Part One

"BE HOLY BECAUSE I AM HOLY"

Holiness in the Old Testament

1

HOLINESS IN THE PENTATEUCH

AS THE OPENING CORPUS to the Christian canon, the Pentateuch is foundational for understanding holiness.[1] To arrive at how the rest of the Bible conceptualizes holiness, one must first go through the Pentateuch. The Pentateuch establishes the theological (and historical) framework for Scripture's telling of the single narrative of God's rescue of the creation, which includes a robust introduction to the biblical notion of holiness and its role in the greater salvation narrative.

So, how does the Pentateuch conceptualize holiness? This chapter demonstrates that the Pentateuch first understands holiness as "otherness." The seventh day of the creation is holy because it is *different* from the other six days (Gen 2:3). It is distinct. Furthermore, applied to both God and people, to be "holy" means to be set apart. God is holy in that he is qualitatively different from the false gods of Israel's neighbors, and his life is different from human life. In distinction from human life, God is eternal, immutably good, he transcends the creation, and he is sovereign. God's people are set apart in that when they are faithful

---

[1]Starting here and continuing to the end of the section on Genesis, I develop some of my earlier studies at https://mattayars.com/holiness-in-genesis-otherness-and-the-image-of-god-restored/.

to obey the commands of the Pentateuch (i.e., covenant stipulations), their entire way of life is different from that of the other peoples of the world.

In what way are God's people holy? What makes them different from the nations around them? As the Pentateuch sees it, *holy* is synonymous with the restoration of the image of God via covenant faithfulness. In short, when God's people are faithful to the covenant (i.e., holy), they resemble him; they are bearers of the divine image. The definition of *holy* as the divine image restored via covenant faithfulness flows out of a new-creation motif running through the controlling narrative of the Pentateuch (and the rest of the Bible). We will see that the fall of humanity results in God's good creation regressing back to chaos, and the need for a new creation—and particularly a new humanity—arises. In relationship to the new-creation motif, God's holy people—Israel—are the representative head of the new creation. We will further see below that the two dominant themes of the Pentateuch are: (1) people and (2) land. More particularly, Israel is the new Adam (i.e., image-bearer), and the Promised Land is the new Eden (i.e., the shared living space of God and humanity). With this new-creation motif at play in the narrative, the overarching purpose of the restoration of the image of God (i.e., holiness) is for the glory of God to fill the creation. As the new Adam multiplies, the divine image that glorifies God fills the creation. This means that when God's people are holy, they are not only set apart as they embody the divine image; God's original intent for the creation is also restored.

GENESIS

Genesis sets the tone for how the rest of the Scriptures conceptualize holiness. Genesis can be divided into two main parts: chapters 1–11 and 12–50. The first section (1–11) comprises pre-history, including the story of the origins of the cosmos, humanity, sin, and God's creation-rescue mission. The second section (12–50) is also about origins, namely, the origins of God's chosen people, starting with the patriarchs Abraham, Isaac, and Jacob. Genesis is loud and clear on three ideas that are foundational to holiness:

1. The creator is the one, true, and good God who is utterly other than the deities of ancient Israel's neighbors in both nature and act.

2. God's original purpose for the creation is to fill it with his glory through the multiplication of humanity, his image-bearing vice-regents.

3. God's rescue plan will be accomplished through Abraham and his family.

The otherness of God. Is the tragedy of human life all there is? Are conflict, suffering, betrayal, corruption, and death the beginning, middle, and end? Creation myths of the ancient Near East consistently answer "yes" to all these questions.[2] Furthermore, in such accounts, an unending cycle of existential and ethical brokenness characterizes the human condition and the lives of the gods. Like humans, the gods of the ancient Near Eastern pantheon are subject to fate and live by their own ethical standards. Dennis Kinlaw describes the worldview of the ancient Near East in this way:

> The reality is that the divine world is a reflection of the human world, not visa [*sic*] versa. This also means that since everything came out of the same womb, there is a certain continuity in everything. . . . There is a certain continuity of both the divine realm and the human/nature realm with each other and with the primordial realm, since everything came ultimately from that primordial womb.[3]

In other words, non-biblical worldviews conceptualize deities after the human image and the divine existence in the likeness of the human condition. For humans and gods alike, conflict, suffering, and death—which all result from moral relativity—are all there is.

---

[2]See John N. Oswalt, *The Bible Among the Myths: Unique Revelation or Just Ancient Literature?* (Grand Rapids, MI: Zondervan, 2009), esp. 21-85.

[3]Dennis F. Kinlaw and John N. Oswalt, *Lectures in Old Testament Theology* (Wilmore, KY: Francis Asbury, 2000), 79.

Genesis 1 opposes this pagan view of the world with a resounding, "No!" Furthermore, this "no" is at the heart of holiness in the Pentateuch. Genesis announces that the creator's existence is utterly different from human existence. Unlike the gods of Israel's neighbors, God's life is not a mirror image of human life. Genesis 1 makes the unique claim that God is (1) sovereign (i.e., all-powerful), (2) one (i.e., there are not many Gods), (3) transcendent (i.e., not continuous with the created world), and (4) good. Genesis 1 proclaims that the creator is the one, true, good God. This is not only a dramatic departure from the way ancient Near Eastern peoples viewed the world (both invisible and visible); it is also the fundamental starting point for understanding reality and, more specifically, human existence.

Forming and filling the creation: The vocational image of God. The otherness of God is not the only good news of Genesis 1. Genesis 1 also announces that the tragedy of human existence is *not* what God intended. He desired for humanity—and by extension the entire creation—to share in *his* "other" life of light, order, self-giving love, joy, and peace. This is accomplished through conformity to the divine ethic. In a word, God's life, unlike the human condition, is one of *shalom*.[4] It lacks nothing. It is whole and absent of strife. Furthermore, God created humanity in his image and with a vocation to *multiply and fill the cosmos with his* shalom *life*.

This vocation is highlighted in the forming and filling motif of Genesis 1. The first three days (days 1-3) of the creation are forming days, and the last three days (days 4-6) are filling days. This pattern is fleshed out in all six days of God's creating activity. God's forming and filling come to a climax on the sixth day when he creates humanity. In Genesis 1:26, God creates humanity in the divine "image" (*tselem*) and "likeness" (*demut*) and subsequently commands humanity to (1) multiply and (2) rule over the creation. As the creator's image-bearing vice-regents are faithful to their vocation, the cosmos

---

[4]The Hebrew word *shalom* means "perfect balance" or "peace."

will be filled with God's glory. Life, order, freedom, justice, love, and *shalom* are to reach the ends of the earth as humanity is faithful to its vocation. All of this comes together with the single purpose of glorifying God. This is the image-bearing vocation of humanity. As G. K. Beale writes, "[God's] special revelatory presence does not fill the entire earth yet, since it was his intention that this goal be achieved by his human vice-regent, whom he installed in the garden sanctuary to extend the garden boundaries of God's presence worldwide."[5]

Yes, the glory of God fills the creation (Is 6:3; Ps 19:1; Rom 1:19-20), but it is the multiplying of his image-bearers that brings the glory of God's personal presence to the creation. This God-glorifying, image-bearing vocation of humanity as described in Genesis 1 establishes the goal of holiness. The goal of holiness is special, personal revelation of the glory of God.

Excursus: The Sabbath is holy. The first occurrence of "holy" is in Genesis 2:3: "Then God blessed the seventh day and made it holy, because on it he rested from all the work of creating that he had done." Here, it is the seventh day of creation—the Sabbath—that God blesses and sanctifies. The second half of the verse provides the rationale for God's blessing and sanctifying the Sabbath: "for in it he rested from all his work which he created." In other words, the seventh day is *distinct* (i.e., set apart) from the other six days because on this day God rested, while on the other days he was actively creating. There is a distinction here between two types of days: (1) workdays and (2) rest days. All the other days comprise life-creating activity, yet the seventh day is one of rest from that activity.

While there is a qualitative difference between the six workdays and the Sabbath, these two categories of days share something in common: both support the generation and flourishing of life. The generation and sustaining of life are central themes of Genesis 1–2. In these two chapters, God creates life and systems that enable that

---

[5]G. K. Beale, *The Temple and the Church's Mission: A Biblical Theology of the Dwelling Place of God,* New Studies in Biblical Theology 17 (Downers Grove, IL: IVP Academic, 2004), 138.

life to flourish. In Genesis 1, God first creates habitations in which life can flourish (days 1-3), then fills those habitations with inhabitants (days 4-6). He then commands those inhabitants to propagate more life (Gen 1:22, 28). God's command to the first humans to cultivate and care for the creation is integral to the theme of the generation and flourishing of life. This theme also comes through in Genesis 2 where God's creating activity comes to a climax with breathing the breath of life into Adam (Gen 2:7). The theme of life also resonates with the declaration that the tree of life was in the midst of the garden (Gen 2:9) and with Eden's rivers as the source of life flowing from the garden to generate and nourish life in its surrounding lands (Gen 2:10-14). Altogether, God's good creation as he intended it is perfect and complete when teeming with self-propagating life.[6]

It is clear how six days of work to cultivate the creation generate life, but what about the day of rest? What do life and the flourishing of life have to do with the holiness of the Sabbath, and particularly rest? The creation cycle is incomplete without rest because life cannot be properly sustained without balancing work with rest. The Sabbath protects life by guarding humanity against being absorbed in work. Henri Blocher writes:

> Now what is the meaning of the Sabbath that was given to Israel? It relativizes the works of mankind, the contents of the six working days. It protects mankind from total absorption by the task of subduing the earth, it anticipates the distortion which makes work the sum and purpose of human life, and it informs mankind that he will not fulfill his humanity in his relation to the world which he is transforming but only when he raises his eyes above, in the blessed, holy hour of communion with the Creator. . . . The essence of mankind is not work![7]

---

[6]This is also emphasized through the fact that death is the consequence of violating God's rules (Gen 2:17; 6:6-8, 13).

[7]Henri Blocher, *In the Beginning: The Opening Chapters of Genesis* (Downers Grove, IL: InterVarsity Press, 1984), 57.

In sum, rest is required for life to flourish, even when cultivating the creation is the primary human vocation. Being absorbed in work ultimately hinders the flourishing of life.

An obsession with work also distorts human meaning and witness to the nature of the creator. The human vocation to cultivate and have dominion over the creation is one aspect of being created in the divine image. God is the model for human life in working six days a week and resting one. The Sabbath is a reminder that humanity's identity is not entirely wrapped up in work. Just as the creator is more than the work he does, so is humanity. This day of rest, then, points to a reality about God and humanity. The consequence of the divine image-bearers failing to observe the Sabbath not only thwarts the sustaining of life, it also distorts the witness to the nature of the creator.

The risk of the tyranny of work exponentially increases because of the consequences of sin in the garden in Genesis 3. As a result of their disobedience, God pronounces a curse against Adam and Eve (Gen 3:16-19). Eve's consequence is that she will have pain in child-bearing (Gen 3:16). Adam's consequence is that he will have pain in cultivating the earth because the earth is now cursed (Gen 3:17-19). For both of them, bringing forth and sustaining life will be risky, onerous, burdensome, and painful due to their rebellion. Together as divine image-bearers, their vocation to generate and sustain life is one means by which they faithfully embody the likeness of God. In obeying the command to multiply and have dominion over the creation, they participate in the life-generating and sustaining activity of the creator. However, it is precisely at this place of faithfully fulfilling their image-bearing vocation that they are cursed. The curse means that generating and sustaining life will be much more difficult and demand much more effort. This demand heightens the risk of the tyranny of work.

Perhaps more importantly, the curse of Genesis 3 also thwarts humanity's witness to the nature of the creator. In Genesis 1–2, God delights in his work, unlike the creator deities of the pantheons of the ancient Near East and unlike humanity laboring under the burden of the curse. It is by strife, struggle, risk, betrayal, and pain that the creation comes about in all other ancient Near Eastern creation myths. In the biblical origin story, God is utterly unchallenged in creating. God's sovereignty comes through in the formulaic declaration of, "And God said, 'Let there be X...' and it was. And it was evening, and it was morning. Day X." It is that simple. God wanted it to happen, so it did. Creation comes about as a result of his unchallenged and perfect will, and he took delight in it. It was good. No other deity forced his hand. It was just as he intended, and life flourished. Now that humanity has rebelled, however, they look more like the ancient Near Eastern gods who are burdened by work and who must struggle to keep death at bay. Humanity was supposed to delight in their work, and in doing so, to reflect the creator who delighted in his work. Now it is not so. When they rest, however, they still bear witness to the creator, who also rested.

The life-preserving function of the Sabbath is heightened, then, when mapped onto the curse in Genesis 3. The Sabbath is the day on which the curse of toil is lifted. It is the day that brings relief from the curse. While the burden of strenuously fighting back death mark all the other days, the Sabbath is marked by life and peace. Moreover, when the image-bearers make the Sabbath holy by observing it, they continue the witness that they, like God, are more than the work they do.

Egyptian slavery is the epitome of human life absorbed in work culminating in death, which is why as we move forward in the story of the Pentateuch, the Sabbath is also mapped onto the Egyptian deliverance event.[8] Slavery in Egypt is a case study of what happens when the will of the creator is ignored. A calendar with a day of rest at its center has special meaning for a nation delivered from

---

[8]Interestingly, nearly half (47) of the total OT occurrences (111) of *shabbat* are in the Pentateuch. More than half (25) of the Pentateuch occurrences are in Leviticus.

generations of slave labor. Immediately following their deliverance from Egypt, God gave Israel an entirely new calendar that is centered not on work, but on rest. Redemption from a life of slavery means the reintegration of rest into the life of God's people for the flourishing of life as patterned after the creator in Genesis 1. With the Sabbath in place, the vocation to work returns to its proper place and meaning. Put another way, when Sabbath is in place, the vocational aspect of the image of God in humanity is redeemed and God's perfect creation is restored. With the image of God restored, so is the witness to God's character via humanity. This reality surrounding the sanctity of the Sabbath is a picture of what will come in the Sinai covenant.

When we map the Sabbath onto the human vocation of Genesis 1–2, the curse of Genesis 3, and deliverance from Egyptian slavery, we can see why the Sabbath plays a crucial role in the holiness manifesto in Leviticus.[9] Leviticus 23:3 says, "Six days shall work be done, but on the seventh day is a Sabbath of solemn rest, a holy convocation. You shall do no work. It is a Sabbath to the Lord in all your dwelling places" (ESV). The Sabbath marks Israel as not only God's possession, but also a means of relief from the curse that is the tyranny of work that culminates in death. God's holy people live according to the model of Eden where humans faithfully bear God's likeness, work is kept in its proper place, life flourishes, and God's will for the creation is fulfilled.

In sum, the Sabbath is not merely holy because it is a day of rest distinct from other working days. Sabbath is blessed and holy (i.e., qualitatively different) because it is a linchpin for fulfilling God's will for the creation, specifically regarding the generation and flourishing of life and for humans to give a proper witness to his nature and character. When humans are absorbed in work, it leads to death, the distortion of the image of God, and a fatal departure from God's

---

[9]*Shabbat* ("Sabbath") occurs thirteen times in Leviticus (Lev 16:31; 23:3, 11, 15, 16, 32; 24:8; 25:2, 4, 6).

will for his creation. When humans keep work in its proper place by leaving room to rest, it leads to life. This Sabbath day, then, is qualitatively *different* from all other days. Beginning with the sanctification of the seventh day, we can safely say that holiness is *qualitative otherness.*

The fall: Abdication, moral autonomy, idolatry, regression to chaos, and death. Genesis 2 recounts how God places Adam and Eve in the Garden of Eden and commissions them to work and keep it. He instructs them that they may freely eat from the trees in the garden except for the tree of the knowledge of good and evil because they will die if they do (Gen 2:16-17). In the chapter immediately following, the serpent accuses God of lying to Adam and Eve (Gen 3:4) to convince them to eat the forbidden fruit. The serpent explains that the consequence of eating the forbidden fruit is not that they will die but that they will become like God. Believing the serpent's lies, Adam and Eve eat the forbidden fruit. In doing so, Adam and Eve go from innocent obedience to a state of guilty disobedience and are expelled from God's presence.

When viewed through the wide-angle lens of Genesis 1, the fall becomes much more than human disobedience needing punishment. The fall is, first and foremost, humanity's abdication of its image-bearing vocation. Rather than filling the earth with God's glory by ruling over the creation in his likeness, humanity's progenitors give themselves over to the temptation of doing things their own way at the expense of fellowship with the creator. The forbidden tree's name indicates that in disobeying God's prohibition, Adam and Eve are deciding for themselves what is good and evil. That which God has called "bad," Adam and Eve have called "good." This is moral autonomy. Moral autonomy, however, is not part of humanity's vocation. God alone has the special right and privilege of moral sovereignty and authority. When created beings decide independently from the creator what is right and wrong, ethical relativity enters the creation, and chaos and darkness reign in a world in which people do what is right in their own eyes (Judg 21:25) precisely because the proper order and function of the creation is programmed according to God's definitions of good and evil. Because God's ethical profile is built into the ordering of the cosmos, and the creation is dependent on him for proper function and well-being, turning away from ethical behavior as defined by God results in regression back to the chaos of the watery abyss. Furthermore, breaking fellowship with the creator of life results in death.

The failure to recognize the creator as God is a failure of worship. It is an act of idolatry. Proper worship is one of the natural outcomes of holiness. Misplaced worship by way of idolatry results in the unraveling of the cosmos. The unraveling of the cosmos is what Genesis 4–11 is all about. As the story progresses after the fall, sin escalates to cosmic proportions. Evil becomes the standard. The brokenness of human life becomes, in a word, "common." Genesis 6:5-6 says, "The LORD saw how great the wickedness of the human race had become on the earth, and that every inclination of the thoughts of the human heart was only evil all the time. The LORD regretted that he had made human beings on the earth, and his heart was deeply troubled."

This is what precipitates the flood. The flood returns the creation to the state of watery chaos and darkness that was present in the *tohu wabohu* (often translated "formless and empty") of Genesis 1.[10] Before God brought light, order, and life into existence, there was formlessness and emptiness. It was, as it has been translated, "desert wasteland."[11] In bringing life to the creation, God separated between the waters above and the waters below (Gen 1:6-8). The flood undoes this separation as "all the springs of the great deep burst forth, and

---

[10]For a thorough explanation of this phrase in its philological context see Victor P. Hamilton, *The Book of Genesis: Chapters 1-17*, New International Commentary on the Old Testament (Grand Rapids, MI: Eerdmans, 1990), 108-9; David T. Tsumura, *The Earth and the Waters in Genesis 1 and 2: A Linguistic Investigation*, Journal for the Study of the Old Testament Supplement Series 83 (Sheffield: JSOT Press, 1989).

[11]Hamilton, *Genesis: Chapters 1-17*, 108.

the floodgates of the heavens were opened" (Gen 7:11). In other words, sin returns to the world to this lifeless wasteland. Life cannot be sustained without absolute morality. What became common in the world was utterly different from God and his intentions for the cosmos. By God's grace, the waters recede, and the dry land emerges once again from the chaos with Noah as the representative head of the new humanity (Gen 9:1-5).

It only takes a few verses for things to go sour with humanity yet again. By wrongly consuming the vine, Noah follows in the footsteps of Adam and Eve. With Ham's sin (Gen 9:20-29), the cycle of sin starts all over again, and evil runs amuck in the post-flood creation just as it did prior to the flood. The rebellion of humanity comes to a climax in the story of the Tower of Babel (Gen 11). The Tower of Babel symbolizes humanity's rebellious autonomy and self-sufficiency that is ultimately motivated by fear and lack of trust. In a word, the Tower of Babel is a symbol of idolatry. The people of Babel congregating in one place is the opposite of what God intended (Gen 1:28). God's vision of the human vocation was for them to spread out over the creation and for God to share that space with them. The story of the Tower of Babel tells us that humanity is opposed to God's intention for humanity and creation. God does not give up on his creation-redemption plan. God judges Babel by dividing the people and dispersing them and launches an entirely new plan to redeem creation.

The patriarchal narratives: The new Adam, election, and covenant. To get his project of filling the earth with his relational presence back on track, God will enter into a covenant with one who will become a new, faithful image-bearer, a prefiguring of the new Adam who trusts him and worships him alone. By grace, God chooses Abraham and his family as the representative head of the new humanity. God promises Abraham that blessing will come to the world through his descendants.[12] At the

---

[12]Gen 12:1-3; 22:18; Is 51:1-5; Lk 1:72; Acts 7:1-8; Rom 4:1-25; 9:6-8; Gal 3:7-9.

center of God's promises to Abraham are land and family. In short, God's *shalom* will return to the creation through Abraham's family.

Soon after Abraham goes out from Ur, God seals his promises to Abraham with a covenant (Gen 15). The importance of intimate fellowship between God and humanity in the creation-rescue mission is highlighted in the fact that covenant is the instrument through which God's redemption comes to the world. The Hebrew word for *covenant* (*berit*) means "agreement" or "alliance."[13] Animal sacrifice was an essential part of covenant-making in the ancient Near East. The blood sacrifice in covenant-making is rooted in the concept of fictive kinship in ancient Near Eastern patriarchal culture.[14] Covenants originally served to create conceptual family bonds between people, like marriage or adoption. The blood sacrifice symbolized that even though two parties were not of the same bloodline, they would exist together as if they were, thereby creating an imaginary shared bloodline between them. This is the most intimate of bonds. It is a symbol of two becoming one.[15] It is also an act of formal oath which essentially declares, "May God do so to me if I break this covenant."

Thus, when God makes a covenant with Abraham in Genesis 15:17-18, he binds himself to Abraham in the most intimate way possible. In this account, God promises to be faithful to Abraham and then instructs Abraham to sacrifice five animals and separate the halves of the carcasses. After Abraham does this, he falls into a deep sleep. While sleeping, Abraham has a vision of God's presence passing between the divided carcasses. In passing between the carcasses, God is sealing his promise to Abraham. His

---

[13]*HALOT* 1:157-59.

[14]See Sandra L. Richter, *Epic of Eden: A Christian Entry into the Old Testament* (Downers Grove, IL: IVP Academic, 2008), 69-91.

[15]For a helpful discourse on metaphors for salvation in the scriptures that highlight the level of intimacy God desires with humanity, see Dennis F. Kinlaw, *Let's Start with Jesus: A New Way of Doing Theology* (Grand Rapids, MI: Zondervan, 2005), 47-70.

passing between the carcasses symbolizes that if he does not uphold his promise, he is subject to the punishment of death. He is making a familial promise to Abraham and thereby declaring his loyalty to Abraham.

The patriarchal narratives that make up the remainder of Genesis affirm God's loyalty to Abraham and Abraham's faith in God. God fulfills his promise to Abraham and Sarah, and Isaac is born (Gen 21). The testing of Abraham's faith comes to a climax in Genesis 22 when God instructs Abraham to sacrifice Isaac, his one and only son. This story highlights that Abraham lives by the conviction that God is God, and he is not, that God alone decides what is good and evil. Abraham, as the representative head of the new humanity, is walking in fellowship with God and worshiping God alone. This is what God intended from the beginning. What God has with Abraham is what the Garden of Eden was supposed to be about. In Abraham's relationship with God, the restoration of Eden is prefigured.

As the story continues, God's faithfulness to Abraham is affirmed as the Abrahamic promises pass on to Isaac, Jacob, and Joseph. In all the successes and failures of the patriarchs, God proves faithful to his promise to Abraham in the multiplication of his family and the acquisition of land.

Genesis 50:19-20 summarizes the book's central theme: God is sovereign and trustworthy. Forty-nine chapters after the creation account, Genesis reminds the reader that while it seems as if the cosmos is unraveling, the creator is the one, true God who is powerful enough to rescue the creation.

Trust is the foundation for the divine-human relationship and the basis for God's life to fill the creation through humanity. Genesis 15 gives us a clear example of justifying faith. In this story, God promises a sterile Abraham and Sarah the impossible: innumerable offspring. Abraham *believed* in God. He trusted God. He had confidence that God would make good on this promise. This faith is the basis for the restored relationship with the holy creator, and being reconciled to the holy One is at the heart of holiness. As image-bearers, humanity was made to be in relationship. Being estranged from the creator makes them less than human. Being reconciled to God repairs the image; it restores that which is at the heart of humanness: personhood. Trust is the foundation for a reconciled relationship.

Exodus

Genesis establishes the context for understanding who God is, what it means to be human in the creation, and God's plan to rescue the creation through Abraham's line. In Exodus, the new-creation motif that began with the patriarchs in Genesis becomes more robust as Israel—the new humanity—emerges out of the chaos of Egypt by way of the Red Sea, and the tabernacle is constructed as the microcosm of the new creation. Exodus depicts Israel as the new humanity headed toward the Promised Land, the new Eden. Land, then, is a central theme in Exodus and the remainder of the Pentateuch.

Deliverance from Egyptian slavery: The new Adam needs a new land. The good news is that Abraham's family (the representative head of the new creation) has mushroomed into a nation. The bad news is that they hardly live in the *shalom* of Eden. The ground was cursed as a result of human rebellion in Genesis 3. The theme of holy land is the promise of the reversal of that curse. God's promise of family has been fulfilled, but not the promise of land, for Abraham's descendants are enslaved in Egypt. Out of his loyalty to Abraham, God commissions Moses to bring Abraham's family out of Egypt so that they can inherit the land that God had promised (Gen 12:1-7; Ex 2:23-24). Against the backdrop of Genesis 1, Egyptian slavery exemplifies the condition of humanity under the tyrannical reign of sin and death. As is evidenced in the story of baby Moses' rescue from Pharaoh's death decree, Pharaoh, like death and the chaos of the watery abyss, will not have the final word. God can reach into human life and break the cycle.

The story of the burning bush (Ex 3) introduces the theme of God's faithfulness to fulfill his promise of holy land. In the narrative, God appears to Moses in the burning bush, and the word "holy" appears for the first time in Exodus when God says, "Do not come near, take your sandals off your feet, for the place on which you are standing is holy ground" (Ex 3:5). In Genesis, there was a holy day (Gen 2:3). Here, however, we have "holy ground" (*'admat-qodesh*). This "holy ground" anticipates the land that God has set apart for Abraham's descendants. The new Adam—the holy people—needs a new, holy land to inhabit with the creator. What is unusual is that this holy ground is in the desert. As Victor Hamilton notes,

> Normally, then, the wilderness is the antithesis of holiness. They go together like oil and water. The one thing that can transform common, unholy ground into extraordinary, holy ground is a theophany, a (spectacular divine manifestation). And if God can transform unholy ground by the glow of his presence, might he not also be able to transform an unholy life? What God can do with the *'ădāmâ*, might he not also do with the *'ādām*?[16]

This land is holy because it is set apart from the cursed space of the created order as the place where God's special presence rests. Once again, it is the place where the curse on the ground (Gen 3:17) is lifted. Moses, and later Israel, are invited into that special space.

So, why must Moses remove his shoes? One possibility is that shoes are made from animal carcasses and are therefore unclean and not permissible in God's presence. Another option is that it was customary in ancient cultures to remove footwear when invited into a home out of respect for the host. To apply the priestly law code at this point in the narrative would be anachronistic, so it seems that the latter interpretation is the more likely. This view harmonizes with the controlling new-creation motif. Even as the new Adam,

---

[16]Victor P. Hamilton, *Exodus: An Exegetical Commentary* (Grand Rapids, MI: Baker Academic, 2011), 49.

Israel is a foreigner in God's presence, meaning that they do not yet know God personally, and that personal relationship, once again, is at the heart of holiness as the restoration of the divine image. As the story continues, it becomes evident that Moses does not know God, although he knows of God. Moses says, "Suppose I go to the Israelites and say to them, 'The God of your fathers has sent me to you,' and they ask me, 'What is his name?' Then what shall I tell them?" (Ex 3:13). God goes on to reveal the divine name: "I AM WHO I AM. This is what you are to say to the Israelites: 'I AM has sent me to you'" (Ex 3:14). Once again, Moses and YHWH—like Israel and YHWH—are not acquainted. YHWH will make Israel his own and invite them to live in his land as guests. More specifically, their indwelling will depend on their covenant faithfulness. They are not entitled to this land. This land is where YHWH, and none other, reigns. Moses removes his shoes as the first guest invited into God's holy habitation on earth.[17]

The unusual divine name attests to God's holiness.[18] While there is no shortage of conjecture over the meaning of the phrase "I AM WHO I AM" (*'ehyeh 'asher 'ehyeh*), Sarna is correct that "either it expresses the quality of absolute Being, the eternal, unchanging, dynamic presence, or it means, 'He causes to be.'"[19] In other words, God *is utterly different* from everything in the creation. He does not change, he is eternal, he is not restricted by time and space, and he is in no way dependent on created things or beings.[20]

Israel must first be delivered from Egyptian slavery to get to the holy land. God loosens Pharaoh's grip on Abraham's family through

---

[17]The practice of entering God's presence barefoot is upheld later in the priesthood where the only part of the priest's body that is to be uncovered when entering the tabernacle is the feet.

[18]For more on the theology of the placement of the divine name see Sandra Richter, *The Deuteronomistic History and the Name Theology*, Beihefte zur Zeitschrift für die alttestamentliche Wissenschaft 318 (Berlin: De Gruyter, 2014); Carmen Joy Imes, *Bearing God's Name: Why Sinai Still Matters* (Downers Grove, IL: IVP Academic, 2019).

[19]Nahum M. Sarna, *Exodus*, The JPS Pentateuch Commentary (Philadelphia: Jewish Publication Society, 1991), 17-18.

[20]For a more detailed discourse on the theology of the divine name, see John Goldingay, *Old Testament Theology, Volume 1: Israel's Gospel* (Downers Grove, IL: IVP Academic, 2003), 332-43.

plagues. In the plagues that lead up to the climactic Red Sea crossing, we hear echoes of the creation account from Genesis 1. As the plagues wreak havoc on Egypt, God demonstrates his sovereignty, oneness, and transcendence once again by making a mockery of the false gods of the Egyptian pantheon. It all comes to a climax with the division of the Red Sea. Israel emerges out of the Red Sea just as light, life, and order emerge from the watery chaos of Genesis 1, just as Adam emerged from the dust, just as Noah came out of the ark, Abraham came out of Ur, Isaac out of Sarah, and baby Moses out of the Nile River. This is a re-creation event. Israel is the new Adam. Immediately after God subdues the chaos in Genesis 1, he makes a covenant with Adam and Eve, his image-bearing vice-regents (Gen 1:28). Likewise, after the Israelites come out of the Red Sea as the new humanity, God makes a covenant with them (Ex 24:3-8). God is making Israel his family of priests who share in his likeness.

The Mosaic law and the profile of the image of God. The new-creation motif continues in the giving of the Mosaic law at Sinai and the building of the tabernacle. God frames the covenant law code within this motif. He says, "Now therefore, if you will indeed obey my voice and keep my covenant, you shall be my treasured possession among all peoples, for all the earth is mine; and you shall be to me a kingdom of priests and a holy nation" (Ex 19:5-6). God is pointing out that

1. Israel is to be different from the nations as he is different from deities of the ancient Near Eastern pantheon (i.e., "a holy nation"); and

2. their covenant faithfulness will serve as testimony to his existence by embodying the moral character of God (i.e., "a kingdom of priests"). If the world wishes to have a part in YHWH, it must have a part in Abraham.

God gives Moses the covenant stipulations in the Ten Commandments at Sinai (Ex 20). Then Moses conducts the blood covenant ceremony between God and Israel (Ex 24). In creating the covenant between God and Israel, Moses dashes blood on the altar and the

Israelites. This is reminiscent of God's covenant with Abraham in Genesis 15. As Israel becomes God's people, they are mandated to look like him. This is nothing short of the image of God restored through covenant faithfulness. This is holiness. The people of Israel are to conform to the ethics of the one, true God in their love of God and each other.

The profile of God's image is encoded in the covenant stipulations. His character is revealed in the quality of life he demands of his people. God prohibits adultery because he is faithful. He prohibits murder because he loves life and honors his image in humanity. God prohibits false testimony because he is honest and true. God commands the Israelites to leave behind a portion of the harvest for the poor and treat foreigners well because he is compassionate. Each of the 613 commands of the Pentateuch underscores an attribute of God that he shares with his image-bearers. Behaviors, thoughts, desires, and attitudes that conflict with God's character result in a regression toward chaos. When people lie, cheat, steal, and murder, the cosmic order breaks down because such behavior violates the character built into the ordering of the cosmos. However, when God's people obey his commands, they embody his image in the creation, and he is glorified. Their faithful obedience to his ethical code out of a heart posture of pure love and fellowship is an act of worship. They obey, like Abraham, because they trust him. Where there is a lack of obedience, there is a lack of trust and worship.

The Hebrew word that best summarizes God's holiness regarding ethics is *hesed*. The various English translations for this unique Hebrew word include: "steadfast love" (ESV, NRSV) and "kindness" (ESV, NIV). More specifically, in *hesed* is the sense of deep, steadfast loyalty that characterizes familial bonds.[21] It is loyalty that is driven by intimate love. Grace is a critical concept that plays a part in this kind of love. Family members are not bound to one another because

---

[21]*HALOT* 1:336.

of material benefit (i.e., something earned) but out of affection and devotion. This word is first used in the Bible to describe Abraham's servant's affection and faithfulness to Abraham when Abraham commissioned him to find a wife for Isaac (Gen 24:12). Even though Abraham's servant is not Abraham's blood relative, his affection for Abraham is as if they were blood relatives. Abraham's servant is faithful to Abraham just as family members are faithful to one another regardless of personal gain or changing life circumstances. This *hesed* describes God's posture toward humanity and is the blueprint behind the profile of the image of God codified in the law.

As Israel is to be like God in his *hesed*, their way of life as prescribed by the law makes them utterly different from their neighbors. Israel is to be different not simply for the sake of being different but for bringing life and order—and subsequently God's glory—to the creation. Israel's call to holiness serves to restore God's original intent to the creation. When Israel is faithful to the covenant, the nations can see who the people of God are. Consequently, God calls Israel to be different from its pagan neighbors as God is from the pagan deities.[22] In fulfilling their image-bearing vocation, Israel is to embody the character of God, who is categorically different from the pagan gods and their human worshipers. Israel is called out of the chaos and darkness of the broken world of human rebellion and moral relativity (typified in Egypt) to live in the Promised Land, where moral absolutes reign under the leadership of the one, true God. With holiness, proper worship of the one, true God is restored. Christopher Wright says,

> In Old Testament terms, being holy did not mean that the Israelites were to be a specially *religious* nation. At heart, the word "holy" . . . means *different or distinctive*. Something or someone is holy when they get set apart for a distinct purpose in relation to God and then are kept separate for that purpose. For Israel, it meant being different by reflecting the very different God that YHWH revealed himself to

---

[22]See Ps 115.

be, compared with other gods. Israel was to be as different from other nations as YHWH was different from other gods.[23]

The tabernacle: A microcosm of the new creation. As a part of the covenant stipulations, God instructs Israel to build a tabernacle (*mishkan*) so that he can fill it with his presence and glory (Ex 26–31). Here we have the Genesis 1 forming and filling motif once again. The tabernacle is constructed as God's special place of residence, just as creation was intended to be in Genesis 1. The tabernacle (and its later articulation, the temple) is a microcosm of the creation which was the original tabernacle (Ps 78:69), and it is to be a holy place where God can dwell among humanity in his glory.[24] *Holy*, which has appeared only six times between Genesis 1 and Exodus 24, occurs nearly fifty times in Exodus 25–40. This demonstrates a direct connection between God's holiness and his presence, as these chapters are singularly focused on the construction of the tabernacle. Most of the holiness language in these chapters refers to the "holy place" within the tabernacle.[25] God's presence is holy and being in that presence demands holiness. If "holy," in at least one sense, means "set apart," then God—the holy One of Israel—cannot mix with that which is unholy. God is holy, so the world that has been profaned by sin would be utterly consumed in his holy presence. How will unholy people get into God's holy presence? More to the point of holiness, how can an unholy people be reconciled to share in God's life-giving, holy presence that is made manifest in the tabernacle? Leviticus answers that very question.

LEVITICUS

Leviticus continues the story of the exodus by taking a deeper dive on the divine-human relationship. Leviticus answers the question of

---

[23]Christopher J. H. Wright, *The Mission of God's People* (Grand Rapids, MI: Zondervan Academic, 2010), 123, emphasis original.

[24]For an in-depth description of the tabernacle as a microcosm of the cosmos, see Beale, *The Temple and the Church's Mission*, 29-80.

[25]Ex 26:33, 34; 28:29, 35, 36, 43; 29:30.

how all-holy YHWH can share an earthly residence with Israel—a
sinful people living in a sinful world. In short, Leviticus explains
how God can sanctify people and places. The priesthood and the
sacrificial system, which Leviticus unpacks in painstaking detail, is
the answer. As such, Leviticus can be divided into at least two main
parts: chapters 1–10 (the way to the holy One) and chapters 11–27
(the way to holiness).[26]

*An object lesson in holiness: The priesthood and sacrificial
system.* In a way, the priesthood and sacrificial system can be viewed
as an elaborate object lesson on holiness and sin.[27] This object lesson
makes several things clear:

1. God is perfectly pure; in him there is no deficiency, defect, dis-
   honesty, corruption, or death; he is morally perfect and purely life.

2. People are utterly sinful; sin is pervasive in that it touches every
   human and every aspect of human life.

3. Sin is organic and contagious; it never remains localized; it always
   spreads to infect the whole.

4. Sin always leads to death; it does not stop until it has taken the life
   of its host.

5. God's presence does not tolerate sin. God's purity and holiness
   obliterates sin when it comes in contact with it; it is dangerous for
   sinful people to be in God's holy presence.

6. Even though sin is serious and powerful, God can sanctify
   the impure.

7. God expects his people to be holy as he is holy.

The holiness code that is laid out in Leviticus, then, details a
partial antidote for the powerful disease of sin. It explains the mechanics of temple rituals and regulations as the means for alleviating
the sin problem to enable sinful people to share in God's holy life
and thereby restore God's original purposes for the creation (i.e.,

---

[26]Norman Geisler, *A Popular Survey of the Old Testament* (Grand Rapids, MI: Baker, 1977), 66.
[27]Cf. Gal 3:24.

divine-human cohabitation). Considering these characteristics of sin, Israel's call to holiness in Leviticus encompasses every aspect of their social, religious, and familial lives and leaves no room for tolerance for the deadly disease that sin is.

Leviticus not only explains the mechanics for temple rituals; it also explains the rationale behind Israel's call to holiness. The rationale is wrapped up in the recurring phrase "be holy for I am holy." This phrase serves as the preamble to the details of the holiness code (cf. Lev 11:44, 45; 19:2, 24; 20:7, 26; 21:6, 8; 23:20) and is best interpreted as "be holy *because* I am holy." The repetition of the phrase in Leviticus is a reminder that Israel is to relentlessly embody God's character and to pursue pathways to connect to their holy God and maintain relationship with him. They are to be different from their neighbors as YHWH is different from the deities of the ancient Near East. They are to embody the *image of God* as was always intended for humanity. Furthermore, the repetition of the phrase means that God's holiness demands purity. In his holiness, it would be contradictory to his character to tolerate corruption of any sort. As is evident through the sacrificial system, a part of his holiness is his mercy and grace which makes provision for sanctification in lieu of annihilation.

Often paired with the command to be holy is the phrase, "I am the LORD your God." This phrase—which also introduced the Ten Commandments (Ex 20:2; cf. Deut 5:6)—evokes the memory of Israel's miraculous redemption from Egyptian slavery in tandem with the call to holiness. This means that Israel is not called to mindlessly imitate YHWH, but to imitate their covenant God *out of a sense of gratitude, love, and devotion to their deliverer*; they are to reciprocate his *hesed.* As Wenham states, "Under the covenant the people of God were expected to keep the law, not merely as a formal duty but as a loving response to God's grace in redemption."[28]

---

[28]Gordon J. Wenham, *The Book of Leviticus*, New International Commentary on the Old Testament (Grand Rapids, MI: Eerdmans, 1979), 251.

Leviticus 19 provides numerous concrete examples of how the command to "be holy as I the Lord God am holy" applies in everyday life. These commands correspond to various attributes of the character of God. Human holiness as it reflects God's holiness as described there includes the following:

Table 1.1. Human behaviors in Leviticus that correspond to God's attributes.

Human behavior	Attribute of God's character
Honor your parents (19:3)	Respects persons
Keep the sabbath (19:3)	Loyal, faithful
Don't make idols (19:4)	Loyal, faithful
Leave some of the harvest for the marginalized (19:9-10)	Compassionate, generous
Don't steal (19:11a)	Honest
Don't lie (19:11b)	Honest
Don't swear by my name falsely (19:12)	Honest
Don't oppress or rob neighbors (19:13)	Just
Don't curse the deaf or cause the blind to stumble (19:14)	Just
Don't hate your brother in your heart (19:17)	Loving

The holy life as described in this chapter comes to a climax in verse 18: "You shall not take vengeance or bear a grudge against the sons of your own people, but you shall love your neighbor as yourself: I am the LORD."

The holiness of God and the need for atonement. According to Leviticus, there are degrees of holiness (and cleanliness) and likewise varying degrees of consequence for a lack of holiness. More specifically, there are three zones of proximity to God's presence, each being further from the previous: (1) holy (2) clean, and (3) unclean. The rationale for this is that because God is morally perfect, his presence in a fallen world has conditions and consequences. Leviticus 10 recounts the story of God killing two of Aaron's sons because they offer unauthorized fire in the temple.[29] This story illustrates that God's holiness is dangerous and not to be violated. This

---

[29]Cf. 2 Sam 6:6-11.

point is further underlined in the stipulation for the high priest to be adorned with bells and pomegranates when entering the holy of holies "so that he will not die" (Ex 28:31-35).

The operative notion here is that God's moral perfection and divine power are inextricably linked. When fallen human beings with imperfections and moral deficiencies encounter an infinitely moral and pure being, there is an overwhelming sense of terror.[30] Beyond teaching the seriousness of sin, this aspect of God's holiness is why atonement via the sacrificial system is needed. It is also why the priests, who are regularly near the presence of God, must take special care in carrying out their service in the temple.

The sacrificial system: Already, but not yet. At this point in the biblical narrative, there is an "already, but not yet" aspect to God's cohabitation with Israel. While the tabernacle and Israel represent the restoration of Eden, this representative head of the new creation is still located within the time and space of the fallen cosmos. Israel, as the new humanity, is called to live a life that is holy, pure, and set apart from the world that is pervaded by sin. Israel's holiness, however, is exposed to the contagious profane of the fallen world. It is inevitable that they will come in contact with the unclean. One of the purposes of the sacrificial system and atonement is to make provision for this. Atonement is how Israel maintains eligibility to be in God's holy presence. The sacrificial system and atonement are undergirded by the expectation that God's people be *perfect* as he is perfect.

The sacrificial system also provides a means for resolving the on-going sin-guilt problem of Israel. Inherited from Adam is the proclivity to turn inward, to not trust God, to worship the creation rather than the creator. Israel's ongoing sin problem is not limited to behaviors, thoughts, attitudes, and desires but extends to their very nature. Through the sacrificial system, God, out of grace, provides a means for those who have committed sin to love and worship

---

[30]Cf. Is 6:1-7.

him with all their heart, soul, mind, and strength to dwell in his presence. Oswalt writes:

> Notice very carefully that the sacrifices are not for those who unintentionally sin and later think better of it. Neither are they for those who want to enter into a relationship with God. No, the sacrificial system is for those who are already in a relationship with God, those who are committed to living a life like his, and who are enjoying a sense of his presence with him.[31]

This means that the sacrificial system is *instrumental*. It serves the greater aim of divine-human fellowship, which puts God's intentions for the creation back on track. Through the sacrificial system God can manifest his heavenly reign on earth once again, and Eden can be restored.

Holiness, judgment, and atonement. But how does the sacrificial system mend the relationship between humanity and God? What is the rationale behind vicarious suffering and penal substitution that is at the heart of the sacrificial system? Inseparable from God's "otherness" is his justice. As already noted, God created the cosmos in a way that it is governed by moral principles. It follows that when the principles are broken there are consequences. This is required for order to be maintained. Thomas Oden writes,

> The just God does not casually say at one moment to humanity: "when you eat of it you will surely die" (Gen 2:17), only at the next moment to set aside the penalty after the transgression. *The holiness of God required a penalty for sin*, just as promised, otherwise there would be no way to count on the moral reliability of God's word. Lacking penalty for sin, the moral order is jeopardized.[32]

For the relationship to be restored between God and humanity, there must be acknowledgment and rectification of guilt. God does not forgive people because they ask forgiveness; he forgives

---

[31]John N. Oswalt, *Called to Be Holy: A Biblical Perspective* (Nappanee, IN: Francis Asbury, 1999), 29.
[32]Thomas C. Oden, *The Word of Life*, vol. 2, *Systematic Theology* (San Francisco: Harper & Row, 1989), 350, emphasis original.

because a sacrifice has been made on their behalf. To forgive without penalty would be a violation of his character. In sum, "God demonstrates his holiness in judging sin."[33] As is detailed in Leviticus, the blood of the sacrifice purifies as the sacrificial animal takes the place of the worshiper in paying the consequence or punishment for sin that is demanded by the holiness of God (i.e., substitutionary atonement). As the sacrifice is put forth in the place of the worshiper, the worshiper is cleansed of his sin-guilt (i.e., expiation). As the worshiper is cleansed by the substitution, the wrath of God is appeased (i.e., propitiation), and *shalom* between God and people is restored. Expiation and propitiation together are what constitute "atonement" (*kippur*).[34]

But in what sense does atonement cleanse? Atonement is the provision that is made for the impure to share life with the pure by way of "covering," "removing," or "blotting out" the contaminate. Why is it that the shedding of blood blots out sin? Once again, it has everything to do with the nature of sin. Informed by Genesis 3, sin can be generally defined as the refusal to live according to God's plans and purposes. Rebellion against God means breaking fellowship with the Life-Giver, and, therefore, separation from God, who is life itself. Death is the natural result of being separated from God as the giver of life. Atonement is the reversal of this consequence. Blood sacrifice is what is required to restore fellowship with God because blood is symbolic of life (Gen 9:4; Lev 17:11; Deut 12:23). Only life— symbolized in blood—can blot out death.

The notion of atonement is best illustrated in the ritual practice and observance of the Day of Atonement (Lev 16). James L. Mays accurately describes the Day of Atonement as "the climax and crown of Israel's theology of sanctification."[35] The Day of Atonement was the

---

[33]Wenham, *Leviticus*, 22.

[34]Is 52:13–53:12; Rom 3:23-26; 2 Cor 5:21; Gal 3:10, 13; Col 2:13-15; 1 Pet 2:24; 3:18.

[35]James L. Mays, *The Book of Leviticus; the Book of Numbers*, Layman's Bible Commentary (Atlanta: John Knox, 1977), 52.

mechanism through which God offered provision to cleanse Israel from all its sin and defilements. Allen P. Ross writes, "The revelation of the removal of sin and defilement is also clearly presented here in the scapegoat. All the sins of the people were confessed and transferred to the victim, which was then led outside the camp. All sin was completely removed by this substitute."[36] The scapegoat carrying the people's sin to the wilderness is symbolic of sin being sent to the place of the curse, the place of death.

The blood of the sacrifice sprinkled on the ark of the covenant is also significant. Inside the ark are the Ten Commandments, which summarize the covenant stipulations. The meaning of blood sprinkled on the ark of the covenant has two prongs. On the first prong is the acknowledgment of worshippers that they have violated the covenant and that the consequence for covenant violation is death. On the second prong, the blood sacrifice satisfies the requirement of death due to their rebellion against God. As the ark symbolizes the place of God's presence with his people, this ritual demonstrates that this restored fellowship is only possible with the blotting out of sin-guilt from God's people (expiation), and the satisfaction of the covenantal stipulations and the wrath of God (propitiation). The animal sacrifice is a substitute for God's people in satisfying the consequence of rebellion against God, which is death.

So, with atonement, *life blots out death*. Life symbolized in blood accounts for death by covering it and making it possible to restore fellowship with God. Furthermore, the ultimate outcome of fellowship restored between God and his image-bearers is that God's plans and purposes for creation are restored.

Nevertheless, where does the oneness (i.e., unmixed nature) of God come into play in the broader schematic of atonement? God is pure life and there is no death in him. Should death come into his presence, it is consumed because life "purges" death. A worshiper

---

[36] Allen P. Ross, *Holiness to the Lord: A Guide to the Exposition of the Book of Leviticus* (Grand Rapids, MI: Baker Academic, 2002), 314.

who is a mixture of death and life that enters God's pure-life presence will be consumed. Death, however, is purged from a worshiper whose sin has been covered with life blood. The covering of sin-guilt with blood, then, restores the creation to God's overall purposes for life and the flourishing of life through the eradication of the contamination that is death.

While atonement comes through God's prescribed ritual, it is not magical or mechanical. The prophets abhor such a thought (Is 1:10-15). In the pagan view, where all things are at least potentially continuous with one another, an appropriate ritual seals the continuity of the worshiper with the sacrifice. Thus, what is done to the sacrifice is done to the worshiper, thereby achieving the desired result of the worshiper escaping the god's ire. Here the attitude of the worshiper is of no consequence. In the Bible, the sacrifice is understood to accomplish nothing in itself. Rather it symbolizes the changed relationship between YHWH and the worshiper in which YHWH extends gracious forgiveness, and the worshiper signals his or her acceptance of that grace through repentance, faith, and complete devotion. The giving of the sacrifice symbolizes that spiritual reality. If it does not, the sacrifice is not only worthless but counterproductive.

Last, the sacrificial system, along with the purity laws, communicates the severity of sin. For starters, sin always leads to death. This is why death is required to regain access to the presence of God. Sin, intentional or not, is fatal and to be avoided at all costs. Sin is also contagious and pervasive. We see this is the requirement for cleansing and purity laws. For example, lepers are required to be quarantined (Num 5:2). Sin has no place among God's people. Because of the pervasive nature of sin, Israel's devotion must be wholehearted. If God requires an absence of sin, then he in turn requires an undivided heart.

NUMBERS

Numbers continues the story of God fulfilling his promises of land to Abraham. As the people of Israel make their way across the wilderness to inherit the gift of land, God's holy presence goes with them. During the journey, two primary dynamics related to holiness are revealed: (1) Israel has a stubborn heart, and (2) Israel is the chosen nation through whom God will rescue the world. Israel's stubbornness foreshadows the unending cycle of disobedience in the rest of the story of the Old Testament, and this cycle flags up the problem of the sinful condition that the law of Moses is unable to resolve.

Israel as a blessing to the nations affirms once again the missional aspect of the image of God restored in humanity with the goal to witness to and glorify the one, true God. God decided that his creation-redemption project would unfold in the world *through Abraham.* Abraham was to be the conduit through whom the nations would receive blessing (Gen 12:3). This point is affirmed in Numbers 22–24 in the stories of Balaam. In short, Balaam, a pagan prophet, is instructed by king Balak to pronounce a curse against Israel. In his instructions, Balak uses language that recalls Genesis 12. He says, "Now come and put a curse on these people, because they are too powerful for me. Perhaps then I will be able to defeat them and drive them out of the land. For I know that *whoever you bless is blessed, and whoever you curse is cursed*" (Num 22:6, emphasis added). As Balaam sets off to do as instructed by his king, God sends an angel to stop him from pronouncing the curse. In place of the curse, Balaam pronounces an oracle in favor of Israel (Num 23:7-10). Once again, this story illustrates that Israel is the chosen people through whom God's redemptive work will manifest in the world for all nations.

Interestingly, another message of Numbers is that, regardless of Israel's special status among other nations before God, their faithfulness to the covenant is still required for the success of God's redemption plan. Election, in other words, is not license for lawlessness. As the Israelites wander through the wilderness and fail to uphold the law, they are still cursed. Israel's repeated stubbornness anticipates its downward spiral of rebellion as recounted in the historical books and the Prophets and as predicted in Deuteronomy.

Before moving to Deuteronomy, however, Aaron's priestly blessing (Num 6:22-27) also illuminates thinking about holiness in Numbers. The priestly blessing reads, "The LORD bless you and keep you; the LORD make his face shine on you and be gracious to you; the LORD turn his face toward you and give you peace." The blessing emphasizes the Lord's face. This is *relationship* language. Being in the presence of God is the same as being "before his face" (*liphne*). What God is saying is that Israel, as his chosen and blessed people, lives in reconciled relationship with him, and that very relationship is founded on the grace of the holy One of Israel. Furthermore, the fruit of that reconciled relationship is peace restored and the fullness of human life as God always intended it.

DEUTERONOMY

Deuteronomy brings the Pentateuch to a close with Moses' retelling of the law to the new generation of Israelites as they are poised to inherit the Promised Land. Moses not only reminds Israel of the covenant stipulations but also encourages them to be faithful to the covenant so that they will experience God's blessing. A lack of faithfulness, Moses says, will result in God's curse on them and their expulsion from God's presence.

The prohibition of idolatry as well as the missional nature of holiness via covenant faithfulness is wrapped up in the so-called Shema in Deuteronomy 6:4, which says, "Hear [*shema*], O Israel, the LORD our God the LORD is one." This verse captures in a single statement the core theological value undergirding holiness as it has been understood from the very beginning of the narrative in Genesis. God's people are set apart from their neighbors as they embody the truth that God is one, sovereign, and transcendent.

In the ancient codices from which the original Hebrew Old Testament is translated, the last letter of the first word (*shema*) and the last consonant of the last word (*ehad*) of Deuteronomy 6:4 are enlarged. Those Hebrew letters are *'ayin* and *dalet*. When read together, these two consonants create the Hebrew word meaning "testimony," or "witness" (*ed*). What does this mean? It means that adherence to the law *testifies* to the nature of the one, true God through conformity to God's ethical standard as set forth in the law code. When the prescribed behavior and heart posture described in the law code are applied, God's moral standard for humanity as the ordained authority over the creation becomes visible to the world. Israel, in other words, is the window through which the world can see what the creator God is really like. Israel is God's representative on earth. They are his image-bearers. They are the true Adam, as this was the goal for all of humanity through the gift of the image of God in the garden. This is the frame for understanding the phrase "walk in obedience to him . . ." that recurs throughout Deuteronomy.[37] Through complete obedience to the covenant stipulations, Israel conforms to the image of God as God always intended for humanity.[38]

The Shema is immediately followed by this: "Love the LORD your God with all your heart and with all your soul and with all your strength" (Deut 6:5). The repetition of the word "all" (*kol*) before "heart," "soul," and "strength" captures the Shema's emphasis on *complete devotion*. Because YHWH alone is God, there is no room for divided hearts. Exclusive worship of the faithful, loving creator who is transcendent yet immanent demands steadfast loyalty. The hearts—or "will"—of his followers should not be split between YHWH and Baal, nor should their souls or strength. The call to holiness is a call to undivided devotion.

Deuteronomy is an appropriate conclusion to the Pentateuch as the new-creation motif comes through once again. Deuteronomy echoes Genesis 1–2 when God placed humanity in the garden. Just as God created Adam and Eve and placed them in the garden to work and keep it, Israel stands on the banks of the Jordan River

---

[37]Deut 5:33; 8:6; 10:12; 11:12; 19:9; 26:17; 28:9; 30:16.
[38]Certainly, this does not intend to exclude other readings of the image of God, including substantive, relational, functional, and royal interpretations.

ready to inherit Canaan as the new Eden to work and keep. If they heed his commission to work and keep the garden, they will keep fellowship with God. If they rebel against him, they will be expelled from his presence and die. This resonates strongly with God's commands about not eating of the tree and the curse of expulsion for infidelity in the form of idolatry. In fact, God predicts Israel's infidelity. In Deuteronomy 31:16-18, God says to Moses,

> You are going to rest with your ancestors, and these people will soon prostitute themselves to the foreign gods of the land they are entering. They will forsake me and break the covenant I made with them. And in that day I will become angry with them and forsake them; I will hide my face from them, and they will be destroyed. Many disasters and calamities will come on them, and in that day they will ask, "Have not these disasters come on us because our God is not with us?" And I will certainly hide my face in that day because of all their wickedness in turning to other gods.

The historical books and the Prophets tell the story of the fulfillment of this prediction. As the story unfolds, the cycle of sin and rebellion continues in various forms and with very little exception. Moses' prediction clues us in to what the historical books and the Prophets will fully disclose and that is that the problem of sin is not merely a matter of "dos" and "don'ts," but a problem with the diseased nature of humanity. Thankfully, the historical books and the Prophets not only reveal this problem that the Mosaic law is unable to resolve but also reveal God's solution: a *new* covenant.

2

HOLINESS IN THE HISTORICAL BOOKS AND THE PROPHETS

HOLINESS AS OTHERNESS in the historical books and the Prophets continues to spin on the axes of (1) God's sovereignty and (2) *hesed* as the signature communicable character attribute of YHWH as set forth in the Pentateuch. The sovereignty of God is repeatedly demonstrated through the refrain of his *lordship over the nations* in both the historical books and Prophets. The *hesed* of YHWH is witnessed in his unshakable faithfulness to Israel even during their ongoing disobedience. At the center of Israel's holiness in the historical books and the Prophets is the restoration of the human vocation as image-bearing vice-regents over the creation, which comes about because of covenant faithfulness. Both YHWH's holiness and Israel's holiness unfold within the new-creation motif that was launched in the Pentateuch.

The sections below explore the key motifs and turning points within the narrative as it picks up where Deuteronomy left off. In the historical books, we will consider the theme of holiness as pertains to *the organic nature of sin and the sinful condition* as revealed in Judges, and *God's expectation for reciprocal hesed from his image-bearers* in Samuel and Kings. We will see in the prophetic literature that God plans to redeem the creation and Israel through a new covenant that will be administered by and through the Davidic Messiah and will be marked by the indwelling of the Holy Spirit. The indwelling of the Holy Spirit will address not only the problem of sinful behavior but also the sinful condition itself.

HISTORICAL BOOKS

The historical books tell the story of Israel's conquest and colonization of Canaan (Joshua), the period of the judges (Judges and Ruth), the establishment of the monarchy, the rise of David as the model, image-bearing vice-regent (1–2 Samuel), and the unraveling, destruction, and exile of the northern and southern kingdoms (1–2 Kings to Esther).[1] The historical books, then, end with Israel's return to a cursed land in the form of exile. This frame for the historical books advances the metanarrative of creation, sin, and recreation as it was introduced in the Pentateuch.

Through the course of events, Israel temporarily experiences regional hegemony under king David's leadership. David proves himself as a true image-bearer in his loyalty to YHWH during times of distress (1 Sam 18–2 Sam 4). God honors David's devotion with a promise to establish an eternal kingdom with David's heir as the eternal, messianic king (2 Sam 7). The northern and southern kingdoms, then, crumble against the backdrop of God's promise of a Davidic redeemer to come. In Joshua–Kings, the Deuteronomic formula declares that absolute devotion to YHWH necessitates the strict prohibition of idolatry and calls for justice in human relationships.

Joshua: Complete dedication. Joshua picks up where Deuteronomy left off as it recounts the story of Israel inheriting the Promised Land. God's promise to Abraham of family has been fulfilled in Egypt, and now, under the leadership of Joshua, the

---

[1]Unless otherwise stated, "Israel" refers to the collective people of God as opposed to the northern kingdom exclusively.

promise of land will be fulfilled. In Joshua, the holiness of God constitutes the basis for his covenant faithfulness to Abraham and Israel as well as his capacity to make Canaan the new Eden. God's holiness is also the reason for his standard of complete dedication in Torah obedience.

The book of Joshua can be divided into two parts: Joshua 1–12 and Joshua 13–24. The first half of the book recounts Israel's conquest of Canaan, and the second half details the distribution of the land among the Israelite tribes. The major themes of the book are (1) the sovereignty of YHWH over all people; (2) the faithfulness of YHWH to his promises; and (3) complete dedication as the natural outworking of exclusive monotheism.

The sovereignty of YHWH over all people. In Joshua, YHWH miraculously enables a nation of wilderness-born slaves to conquer experienced warlords, and he does it with ease. In the opening chapters of Joshua, God reiterates to Joshua that Israel's success in acquiring Canaan will not come as the result of skilled warfare, but of complete obedience to YHWH. God is unlike the gods of Canaan and Egypt in that he can easily and freely dispose of other gods and peoples as he chooses. The sovereignty of YHWH is further underlined in the story of the circumcision of all males prior to going into battle (Josh 5:1-9). Strangely, God commands Israel that they use their swords on themselves before using them on the Canaanites. The circumcision of Israel's soldiers just before battle does not exactly put them in an optimal combat condition. It's counterproductive, yet God demands it. The point of the story, once again, is that victory depends on complete obedience to YHWH and his covenant stipulations, not on strong, able-bodied soldiers and technologically advanced weapons. YHWH, not Israel, is the divine warrior who fulfills his promises.

This point is further accentuated in the short account of Joshua being confronted by a warrior angel prior to embarking on the conquest of Canaan. Joshua asks the angel, "Are you for us or for our enemies?" (Josh 5:13). The angel's response is, "Neither . . . but as commander of the army of the LORD I have now come" (Josh 5:14). What we see here is that this battle is not one of flesh and blood and military strategizing as much as it is a cosmic battle for YHWH's redemption of the fallen cosmos. This event also recalls Genesis 3 where God places a cherubim at the entrance of Eden to guard humanity's access to God's presence. Israel's conquest and colonization of Canaan is a microcosm of the restoration of Eden. Like Moses, Joshua must take off his shoes, for he is entering holy ground when entering Canaan (Josh 5:15). This is a reminder that Canaan is not for the Canaanites, nor for Israel; it is for YHWH. This is Eden restored.

This emphasis on the lordship of YHWH reinforces sovereignty as one of the four pillars of God's holiness (i.e., monotheism, sovereignty, transcendence, and ethics). God is unlike the gods of the inhabitants of Canaan in that they are subject to forces outside of their control. God is not. The gods of the Canaanites are under the lordship of YHWH, and YHWH is under the lordship of none. He is utterly different than they are. He is set apart.

The faithfulness of YHWH to his promises. The faithfulness of God is the framing theme of the entire book of Joshua. The very reason for the conquest and colonization of Canaan is God's promise to Abraham. He promised Abraham both land and family. He has given Abraham family, and now his family is to inherit the gift of land. God, in taking Canaan from its original inhabitants and giving it to Israel, is proving good to his word. In a word, God is *hesed*. Furthermore, God's devotion to Abraham and Israel sets him apart from other deities and from people. People and their gods lie, cheat, steal, and commit adultery. This is not true of YHWH. His promises are good. Not only are his promises good, but he is also faithful when Israel is not. Israel was rebellious in the desert. They repeatedly violated the covenant stipulations. Even so, God keeps his word to Abraham through the gift of Canaan.

Complete dedication. Just as God is faithful, Israel is to be faithful. As the new Adam, Israel is expected to reciprocate YHWH's *hesed* as the divine image-bearers. The theme of complete dedication is one of the major points of theological and literary unity across the book of Joshua. We first see this theme in Joshua 1, where God commissions Joshua to succeed Moses as Israel's leader. In that commission speech, God reminds Joshua that the key to his success is complete obedience to the Torah:

> Only be strong and very courageous, being careful to do according to all the law that Moses my servant commanded you. Do not turn from it to the right hand or to the left, that you may have good success wherever you go. This Book of the Law shall not depart from your mouth, but you shall meditate on it day and night, so that you may be careful to do according to all that is written in it. For then you will make your way prosperous, and then you will have good success. (Josh 1:7-8)

The most striking example of complete obedience in Joshua is God's command that Israel completely destroy the inhabitants of the land. God requires that the land be entirely purified, not just tidied up a bit for tolerant cohabitation with pagans. James Hamilton summarizes the underlying theology to this command well in stating that

> the ban on the Canaanites heralds the infinite majesty of the justice of Yahweh, whose holiness demands perfect loyalty, whose worth is such that anything less than absolute allegiance defiles unto death. The conquest of Canaan enacts the glory of God's justice against those who look to worthless things to be for them what only God can be for them. This justice against the inhabitants of Canaan is intended to deliver Israel from the deleterious influence of idolaters and give them the land that has been promised. Yahweh commissioned Adam and Eve to "fill the earth and subdue it" (Gen 1:28), and in Joshua 18:1, the sons of Israel assemble in Shiloh and "the land was subdued before them."[2]

---

[2]James M. Hamilton Jr., *God's Glory in Salvation Through Judgment: A Biblical Theology* (Wheaton, IL: Crossway, 2010), 141-42.

As the Israelites arrive on the scene, they are rescuing the creation from its total depravity. Their arrival in the land is a representation of a new era characterized by the ethics of the Torah and the extermination of corruption and tyranny. The Israelites—unlike the Canaanites—have at the center of their governing laws God's character and by extension his system of ethics. The image that we get in Joshua with the colonization of Canaan is the bringing of light to darkness and order out of chaos. This is a rescue story, and it's not a partial rescue; it's a complete rescue.

With this in view, the book of Joshua is framed by the new-creation motif. In the opening chapters of Joshua, Israel, the representative head of the new humanity, is poised to inherit the Promised Land, the representative head of the space of the new creation. In Genesis 1, God created out of chaos, and he will do it once again, but this time in Canaan. The darkness of Canaan that faces Israel before they conquer the land is not a physical one as much as it is one of the pagan inhabitants' moral depravity. Like the dry land emerging from the water in Genesis 1 (and Gen 8), and like Israel's departure from Egypt through the Red Sea, Israel will emerge from between the waters of the Jordan River as they move into the new-creation space of the Promised Land. Likewise, the book ends with the distribution of the land among the Israelite tribes. This echoes the forming and filling motif of Genesis 1. In the conquest the new creation is formed, and in the colonization the land is filled. Joshua moves God's creation-redemption project one step further with the restoration of Canaan to the Edenic state.

Judges: The sinful condition, moral relativity, chaos, and the need for a king. Judges recounts the tragic story of Israel's downward spiral into near annihilation because of sin. The downward spiral is driven by repetition of the following formula: (1) Israel sins; (2) God judges Israel by giving them over as slaves to neighboring peoples; (3) Israel cries out for help; (4) God raises up a military hero (i.e., a "judge"); (5) through divine empowerment, the hero delivers Israel from their enemies; and finally (6) there is peace in the land. With the repetition of each cycle, however, things get worse. The gradual decline results in an all-time low for Israel. By the end of the book, the tribe of Benjamin is nearly wiped out entirely, and the level of the human depravity caused by sin is on full display.

Within its literary-canonical context, the book of Judges tells us that Israel was *not* successful in eradicating tyranny from Canaan. The last verse establishes the rationale for the monarchy: "In those days there was no king in Israel. Everyone did what was right in his own eyes" (Judg 21:25; cf. 17:6). This verse also prepares readers for God's next move in redeeming humanity and the creation. He will find a vice-regent in the form of a king who is a loyal image-bearer. This vice-regent will fulfill God's promise to the woman of a seed who will crush the head of the serpent (Gen 3:15).

Judges is concerned with holiness in that it reveals the seriousness of sin and its effects. Sin is a downward spiral that is lethal not only to the individual but also to the entire community. Sin is never static; it is organic and always spreads to infect the lot. Judges demonstrates the outworking of what happens when people fail to heed the command of complete dedication.

The book of Judges makes it clear that humanity not only has a sinning problem; it has a *sinful condition* problem. Israel, even with the law in hand, cannot help but sin. They repeatedly fall to the temptation to worship their neighbors' idols. This is epitomized not only in the Israel's repeated apostasy but also in the gradual decline of the moral standing of the judges themselves, who are the ironic heroes of the story. Samson, for example, exemplifies the problem of sin. Israel's hero is one who blatantly and arrogantly violates not only the law but also his Nazarite vow. At the end of the Samson story, the judge's only act of obedience results in his death. In Samson we see that even the heroes define for themselves what is right and wrong.

Judges also demonstrates that sin is synonymous with moral relativity, which always regresses to chaos. Each one doing "what was right in his own eyes" results in a complete unraveling of the fabric that holds healthy human existence together. Anything less than exclusive monotheism is idolatry and, by extension, moral relativism. When people follow the command of "Do what thou wilt" as opposed to "You shall have no other gods before me," everything reverts back to the *tohu wabohu* of Genesis 1.

The big question facing readers at the end of Judges is, "Can and will God keep his promises to Israel when they suffer from what seems to be a terminal disease? Can the human condition thwart God's ability to fulfill his promises?" The remainder of the historical books answer precisely this question, and the answer is *yes*. God will fulfill his promises through his chosen king. He can because he is sovereign, and he will because he is *hesed*.

Samuel: Human arrogance, humility, and holiness. The book of Samuel recounts the establishment of the Davidic monarchy, which becomes the seedbed for the hope for a messianic figure who will be the fulfillment of God's mission to redeem the creation. The story begins with David's rise to power, and 2 Samuel details David's reign as God's chosen king. The dominant theme of 1–2 Samuel is that God *exalts the humble and humbles the exalted*. This theme is highlighted at the beginning and end of 1–2 Samuel in both Hannah's prayer (1 Sam 2:1-10), and David's song (2 Sam 22–23). This theme runs through the narrative of 1–2 Samuel with the downfall of the house of Eli and the rise of Samuel's leadership (1 Sam 3:19-21), the downfall of Dagon before the ark (1 Sam 5), the downfall of Goliath and the rise of Israel (1 Sam 17), the downfall of Saul and the rise of David, and ultimately the downfall of the Philistines and the rise of Israel to regional hegemony under David's kingship.

The foolishness of self-exaltation. The message of God exalting the humble and debasing the proud is that human pride in the face of the *mysterium tremendum* ("awe inspiring and overwhelming

mystery") is foolish. Those whom God exalts are those who recognize that God is not rivaled, that he is sovereign, and he alone
defines good and evil. One true test of holiness is humility. This
comes clearly into focus through the above examples of God exalting the lowly and debasing the exalted. God brings down Eli and
his sons because they do things their own way (1 Sam 1:11-17), God
tears the kingdom from Saul when he performs an unlawful ritual,
and God brings down the giant who defies YHWH the Lord of hosts
(1 Sam 17:45).

David's holy hesed. Despite the book's title, the main character in
the book of Samuel is David. David's rise to power does not come
easily. Saul, David's predecessor, attempts to kill David out of
jealousy. This keeps David on the run. Despite Saul's many attempts
on David's life, David remains loyal to both YHWH and Saul. David's trust in YHWH is proven as he constantly faces powerful adversaries. David's loyalty flags him up as a model image-bearer. He
has *hesed* for Saul the same way that YHWH has *hesed* for Israel.
David is a proper embodiment of the character of YHWH (2 Sam
3:8). He is holy in his *hesed.*

King Saul dies at the close of 1 Samuel, and at the start of 2 Samuel
David is made king of Israel. At this time the political and religious
center is moved to Jerusalem. As the newly crowned king, David
ends any doubt that he is YHWH's chosen king by decisively de-
feating Israel's enemies. In doing so, he accomplishes what Joshua,
the judges, and Saul failed to do before him. David's coronation is a
pivotal moment in the bigger narrative. In David, God's promises to
Abraham and Israel have been fulfilled. Israel—as the representative
head of the new creation—is living free from pagan oppressors in
God's presence in the Promised Land.

Marking this turning point in the story is God's covenant with
David (2 Sam 7). God promises that God will establish an eternal
kingdom and that David's heir will be the eternal chosen king, the
Messiah. God says to David in 2 Sam 7:12-14, "When your days are

over and you rest with your ancestors, I will raise up your offspring to succeed you, your own flesh and blood, and I will establish his kingdom. He is the one who will build a house for my Name, and I will establish the throne of his kingdom forever."

This Davidic covenant is the root of the belief that God will fulfill all his promises to redeem humanity through a king in the lineage of David and in the likeness of God. In this promise to David is the hope for a solution to Israel's ongoing sin problem. Israel gaining regional hegemony under David's faithful leadership prefigures the future kingdom. In the story of David, then, we encounter an image of what the divine-human relationship was always meant to be: *a holy people being led by a holy king as image-bearers who reign over the land in the likeness of God*. Sadly, David too falls into temptation (2 Sam 11), but he does so against the backdrop of hope for an eternal kingdom in which a king—who is yet to come—will be entirely loyal to YHWH. Eden will be restored in the Messiah.

Second Samuel ends the way it begins, with the song of one who has been exalted (first Hannah, now David). At the same time, the closing chapter details God's punishment of David for a census he conducted. Apparently, this census was done out of David's arrogance. David, like the other kings, exalted himself. By closing on this note of David's error, the book prepares for the sad saga of the divided monarchy, the string of unfaithful kings, and Israel ultimately being taken into captivity. Things are going to get worse before they get better.

Kings: YHWH is the only true God. The books of Kings begin with the transition of the kingdom from David to Solomon and end with the Babylonian exile. Through the course of the narrative, the kingdom moves steadily downward from the point of flourishing to eventual destruction. The downward turn, while foreshadowed from the beginning of the narrative, starts with Solomon's idolatry and polytheism (1 Kings 3:3), which is a departure from his father's faithfulness to exclusive monotheism. From Solomon onward, the people of Israel wrongfully integrate local deities into their worship, a direct violation of the covenant stipulations founded on exclusive monotheism. Israel's inability to break away from idolatry explains the gradual decline of the united monarchy into a divided monarchy and eventually into exile.

A key theme in Kings is that YHWH *is the only true God*. This marches directly in step with the dominant theme of exclusive monotheism that was launched back in Genesis 1 and functions as the theological bedrock for the entire Old Testament, and the cornerstone for the Old Testament's thinking about holiness. In Kings in particular, YHWH is set apart (i.e., holy) from the gods of Israel's neighboring states. As in Joshua and 1–2 Samuel, Israel's success in victory over opposing armies is recognition and worship of YHWH as the one, true God. Further still, YHWH is the one, true God in the sense that he is not only the patron deity of Israel, but the God and creator of all nations.

Kings emphasizes that YHWH is the one, true God through a recurring reference to Israel's unlawful "high places." Deuteronomy stipulated that God's people are to have *one place of worship* to reflect the essential oneness of God (Deut 12:5). The Israelites violated this command by following the model of their pagan neighbors by building temples (i.e., "high places") throughout the territory. The multiplicity of temples signals the multiplicity of the gods. As the books of 1–2 Kings go through the various lists of kings and their notable successes and failures, we find that many of them "failed to take down the high places."[3]

The Elijah and Elisha narratives underscore this point. The message of exclusive monotheism comes to a climax in the story of Elijah and the prophets of Baal in 1 Kings 18, where Elijah shows up Baal's prophets by calling down fire from heaven after Baal's prophets fail miserably. The irony in the story is that Baal is the storm god. If

---

[3] 1 Kings 3:2, 3, 4; 11:7; 12:31, 32; 13:2, 32, 33; 14:23, 15:14; 22:43; 2 Kings 12:3; 14:4; 15:4, 35; 16:4; 17:9, 11, 29, 32; 18:4, 22; 21:3; 23:5, 8, 9, 13, 15, 19, 20.

there were any god who should be able to send a firebolt from heaven to ignite a pile of wood, it would be Baal. After a theatrical attempt, Baal's 450 prophets fail, and onlookers are left underwhelmed with the absent, powerless deity. After the prophets give up on Baal, Elijah steps onto stage and immediately calls for water—during a drought—to be poured on the wood so as to demonstrate the power of YHWH. Elijah then calls to heaven, and immediately a pillar of fire consumes the soaked wood. This, like the exodus and like the conquest of the Promised Land in Joshua, puts God's glory on display. YHWH is the one, true God. The story comes to a climax in 1 Kings 18:39: "And when all the people saw it, they fell on their faces and said, 'The LORD, he is God; the LORD, he is God.'" This verse summarizes the goal of Elijah's ministry: to demonstrate that YHWH is the one, true God and to return God's people back to exclusive monotheism, which is the foundation for holiness.

Directly related to the demand of exclusive worship is the consequence for failing to do so. The books of 1–2 Kings end with the Babylonian exile. This is a return to the slave state which characterized Israel's existence prior to the covenant at Sinai. Israel's failure to conform to the covenant stipulations by doing what is right in their own eyes sends them back into the *tohu wabohu*. There is hope, however. As the prophets will remind us, YHWH made a promise to David that a messiah would come and restore God's glory to the creation via Israel. God is willing to save the creation because of his *hesed*, and he is also *able* to save the creation because he is the one, true God.

THE PROPHETS

The prophets offer a theological commentary on the unraveling of the kingdom. The vast majority of the content in the prophets consists of oracles of judgment due to Israel's covenant infidelity. Through the prophets, God repeatedly warns Israel that judgment will befall them if they are not faithful to the covenant. Scattered

throughout the oracles of judgment are oracles of hope and a reminder that God—out of his *hesed*—will be faithful to his promises
to both Abraham and David. God will fulfill his promises to
Abraham to redeem the creation through a new Adam born from
Abraham's family. This head of the new creation will not only be
in the likeness of Adam but also David. This is the Messiah. The
Messiah will be the pinnacle of God's faithfulness to redeem his
original design for humanity as well as the entire creation. The
Messiah will be the true Adam who faithfully bears the divine
image as God's vice-regent over the creation and will administer
a *new covenant* in which the law of God will be written on the
hearts of his people. This new covenant will address not only the
problem of sinful behavior but also humanity's sinful state. The
basis of YHWH's faithfulness is his holiness; his *otherness* as the
one who is sovereign, transcendent, and good (i.e., *hesed*). He is
sovereign to the point of directing the course of events in human
history so as to fulfill his promises. He can redeem Israel and will
do so, because he is unmatched in power and unwaveringly
faithful. Since an overview of all of the prophets is beyond the
scope of this project, we will focus on the major prophets: Isaiah,
Jeremiah, and Ezekiel.

Isaiah and the holy One. The holiness and power of YHWH are
at the center of Isaiah's rich and integrated theology. This is most
evident in Isaiah's favorite title for YHWH: "the holy One of Israel."
For Isaiah, the God of Israel, more than anything else, is *holy*.[4] Isaiah's holiness-centered theology likely comes from his vision in the
temple in which the seraphim sing to one another "*Holy, holy, holy*
is the LORD Almighty; the whole earth is full of his glory" (Is 6:3,
emphasis added). This vision is the point of departure for the
prophet's thinking about YHWH, holiness, sovereignty, sin,
judgment, redemption, the people of God, and servanthood, all of

---

[4]For more discussion of the title "the Holy One of Israel," see John Oswalt, *The Holy One of Israel:
Studies in the Book of Isaiah* (Eugene, OR: Cascade: 2014).

which are key themes that tie the book together. Commenting on the title, "the holy One of Israel," John Oswalt writes:

> He [God] was not merely a superhuman, as were the pagan gods, nor was he a great "grandfather in the sky." He was of a completely different order from his creatures. . . . But it was not merely God's ontological otherness which captured Isaiah's thinking. In fact, the primary characteristic that set this God apart from humanity, made him holy, was his moral and ethical perfection. Thus Isaiah's response to his vision of God was "I am unclean" (6:5). This uncleanness was not merely ceremonial, as the words "unclean lips" testify. Before the presence of this moral and ethical perfection the prophet knew that the whole issue of his life and that of his people were defiled and corrupt. Their problem was not that they were finite before the Infinite or mortal before the Immortal or partial before the Complete. Their problem was that they were morally filthy before the Morally Pure. This is nowhere clearer than in 5:16: "The Lord of Hosts is exalted in justice, and the Holy God is sanctified in righteousness." The primary mark of God's holiness is his moral and ethical purity.[5]

Isaiah's robust theology of holiness is wrapped up in the structure of the book of Isaiah as a whole, which can be divided as follows:

- Chapters 1–5: introduction to the prophecy—judgment and hope
- Chapter 6: a vision of the holy One of Israel
- Chapters 7–39: oracles of judgment—trust in the holy One
- Chapters 40–66: oracles of hope—new creation, atonement, and redemption

Within this literary structure of the book, the first two sections (chaps. 1–5 and chap. 6) establish the theological framework within which the content of the remaining chapters unfold.

---

[5]John N. Oswalt, *The Book of Isaiah, Chapters 1–39*, New International Commentary on the Old Testament (Grand Rapids, MI: Eerdmans, 1986), 33.

Isaiah 1-5: Introduction to the prophecy—judgment and hope.
Isaiah 1–5 introduces the prophecy and is characterized by the two
themes of *judgment* and *hope*. One the one hand, Israel is "a people
laden with iniquity, offspring of evildoers, children who deal cor-
ruptly! They have forsaken the Lord, they have despised the holy
One of Israel, they are utterly estranged" (Is 1:4). On the other hand,

> It shall come to pass in the latter days that the mountain of the house
> of the Lord shall be established as the highest of the mountains, and
> shall be lifted up above the hills; and all the nations shall flow to it, and
> many peoples shall come, and say: "Come, let us go up to the mountain
> of the Lord, to the house of the God of Jacob, that he may teach us his
> ways and that we may walk in his paths." For out of Zion shall go forth
> the law, and the word of the Lord from Jerusalem. (Is 2:2-3)

This two-pronged theme appropriately introduces the book because *each of these themes is the major theological motif for half of the
book*. Oracles of judgment make up most of chapters 7–39, oracles
of hope chapters 40–66. The question facing readers coming out of
the introduction is *how will Israel move from judgment to hope?* How
can God's people go from sinners to saints? Chapter 6 answers that
question. The story of the prophet's vision and commissioning serves
as a concrete example of what that looks like to move from judgment
to hope and is the key to the theological interpretation of the book.

Isaiah 6: A vision of the holy One of Israel. Isaiah's vision takes
place in the Jerusalem temple where the prophet sees YHWH seated
on a throne that is high and lifted up, and the train of his robe and
smoke fill the temple while the temple doorways tremble. Mean-
while, the seraphim sing to one another, "Holy, holy, holy." This
vision undoes the prophet. The moral purity of YHWH forces
Isaiah to his knees in repentance. The prophet cries out, "'Woe to
me!' . . . 'I am ruined!' For I am a man of unclean lips, and I live
among a people of unclean lips, and my eyes have seen the King,
the Lord Almighty" (Is 6:5).

YHWH responds to Isaiah's confession by forgiving his sins. Isaiah says, "Then one of the seraphim flew to me with a live coal in his hand, which he had taken with tongs from the altar. With it he touched my mouth and said, 'See, this has touched your lips; *your guilt is taken away and your sin atoned for*'" (Is 6:6-7, emphasis added). Immediately after Isaiah's sins are forgiven, he hears the call of YHWH looking for a messenger to send to God's people. The now-pure prophet volunteers himself for service.[6]

This chapter is the key to the interpretation for the book as a whole and particularly to Isaiah's robust theology of holiness. What Isaiah experiences in his vision is precisely what all of Israel needs to experience in order to move from judgment to hope. Like Isaiah, Israel needs to see God in his power and holiness, be moved to repentance, be cleansed from sin, and be sent out as a faithful servant with a message to bear to the world. That is, the prophet's witness of transformation from rebellious sinner to faithful servant is not only Isaiah's story, but Israel's as well. The call to holiness is ultimately aimed at testimony to the power and holiness of YHWH and is rooted in a clear vision of who he is. This testimony, then, is the means by which the nations turn to Zion for deliverance (Is 2:2-4). If Israel responds to the call to holiness, it will bear witness to the fact that YHWH is the one, true God. Israel's holiness is the means by which the glory of the YHWH is laid bare for all to see.

Isaiah 7–39: Oracles of judgment—trust in the holy One. Moving from chapter 6 to chapter 7, readers encounter a story about a test of faith.[7] The central character of the story is Ahaz, king of Judah.

---

[6]Many interpreters have debated the placement of the events in the sixth chapter of Isaiah's prophecy. Most stories of prophetic calling in the writing prophets are placed at the start of the book. With Isaiah, however, the prophet's calling comes after five chapters of oracles. A compelling case can be made that the events of Isaiah 6 are placed thematically rather than chronologically. For a thorough treatment of the question of how this chapter functions in its literary context, see Oswalt, *Isaiah: Chapters 1–39*, 171-76.

[7]In these sequences we have stories full of kings, including the kings of Judah (Uzziah, Jotham, Ahaz and Hezekiah), the king of Israel (Pekah), the king of Syria (Rezin), and the king of Assyria (Sennacherib). All these human kings are set in contrast with the true king YHWH who is

This story is aimed to answer the question, Will the king be like the prophet in his conviction, repentance, trust, cleansing, and servanthood? Will Ahaz be another case of transformation from sinner to saint through exclusive commitment to the holy One of Israel?

The plot of the story is that Ahaz (and Judah with him) is under threat of invasion from their neighbors to the north (Israel and Syria). Ahaz and the people together are afraid (Is 7:2). Ahaz is checking the city's water supply when God sends Isaiah to him to tell him not to be afraid, but to trust in the holy One of Israel. Does Ahaz respond to the call to faith? Sadly, he does not. Ahaz fails to trust in YHWH and calls on the violent, pagan Assyrians for help. Ahaz, who represents all of Judah, needs a lesson in who God is and why he merits *trust*.

The vast majority of Isaiah 7–39 is exactly that—*a lesson in trust.* The bulk of this section consists of oracles of judgment against the nations (Is 13–27). For the holy One of Israel to be able to pronounce authoritative judgment over the nations of the world makes one thing clear: YHWH is not only the God of Israel, but the God of all. He is not like the patron deities of Israel's neighbors. He and his power are not limited to geographic regions and to certain people. The holy One of Israel is the creator God of the cosmos. To trust in the gods of the other nations is foolish when the God of all nations has made you his own. *Exclusive faith in YHWH is the basis of moving from judgment to hope.* Isaiah witnessed the absolute sovereignty and holiness (i.e., the *mysterium tremendum*) of YHWH in chapter six; now Judah needs to see the one whom Isaiah saw through the prophet's message.

One of YHWH's unique attributes that Isaiah regularly points out is that he is the orchestrator of history and can predict the future (Is 14:26-27). He, unlike the pagan gods, can foretell what the future will hold. It is only when people get a clear view of YHWH that they can

---

revealed to the prophet in Isaiah 6. Compared to the One Holy One, these kings are nothing. YHWH is the king of Israel and the nations.

understand the folly of idolatry. A point of climax in this view of YHWH's orchestration of history is the fulfillment of Israel's mission to the nations in Isaiah as we saw in Isaiah 2:2-5. What Isaiah prophesies there is a clear vision of the big picture of the fulfillment of YHWH's faithfulness played out. Israel, in their covenant faithfulness (i.e., holiness) is a faithful witness to the nature of the one, true God. Oswalt writes, "If Zion is to be the means of declaring God's glory to the earth in his Torah, then clearly it is God's glory that must fill Israel."[8] And, as a result, "God's ultimate purpose is that the nations should know and worship him, and Israel is the instrument by which that purpose will be accomplished."[9]

After the case for the holiness and sovereignty of YHWH is laid out, Isaiah 7–39 closes with another test in faith. Have Judah and her king been listening to the word of YHWH through the prophet? Now that they have had their lesson in faith, will they fail again? In the first test, Ahaz failed. This time it is Hezekiah, Ahaz's son and successor, whose faith will be tested. Hezekiah is in a similar position to that of his father in Isaiah 7. Hezekiah, like Ahaz, is being threatened by his pagan neighbors. Ahaz was under threat of Israel and Syria, two relatively small nations whose power was waning at the time. Hezekiah, however, is being threatened by the all-powerful and violent Assyria. Hezekiah is standing in the exact same place where Isaiah confronted Ahaz in chapter 7 when Isaiah tells him, "Do not be afraid . . . behold I will put a spirit in him, so that he shall hear a rumor and return to his own land, and I will make him fall by the sword in his own hand" (Is 37:5-6). Will Hezekiah be like his father and fail to heed the word of the prophet and put his faith in the holy One of Israel? The answer is *no!* Hezekiah goes to the temple

---

[8] John N. Oswalt, "The Nations in Isaiah: Friend or Foe; Servant or Partner," *Bulletin for Biblical Research* 16 (2006): 43.

[9] John N. Oswalt, "The Mission of Israel to the Nations," in *Through No Fault of Their Own: The Fate of Those Who Have Never Heard*, ed. W. V. Crockett and J. G. Sigountos (Grand Rapids, MI: Baker, 1991), 92.

(like the prophet himself in Is 6) and pleads to YHWH for assistance. YHWH responds with this:

> Therefore this is what the Lord says concerning the king of Assyria: "He will not enter this city or shoot an arrow here. He will not come before it with shield or build a siege ramp against it. By the way that he came he will return; he will not enter this city," declares the Lord. "I will defend this city and save it, for my sake and for the sake of David my servant!" Then the angel of the Lord went out and put to death a hundred and eighty-five thousand in the Assyrian camp. When the people got up the next morning—there were all the dead bodies! So Sennacherib king of Assyria broke camp and withdrew. He returned to Nineveh and stayed there. One day, while he was worshiping in the temple of his god Nisrok, his sons Adrammelek and Sharezer killed him with the sword, and they escaped to the land of Ararat. And Esarhaddon his son succeeded him as king. (Is 37:33-38)

Unlike Ahaz, Hezekiah wisely puts his trust in the holy One of Israel for Judah's deliverance. Hezekiah, like the prophet, sees God for who he is in his holiness and his power.

The book of Isaiah, however, does not end there as one might expect based on Hezekiah's success. Even though Hezekiah had a moment of success, it was not enough to avoid exile. Isaiah 38–39 tells the story of Hezekiah's arrogance that leads to judgment and ultimately to the fall of Judah. Yes, Hezekiah was faithful, but not unwaveringly so. His heart was divided, and it resulted in destruction. Exile, however, will not have the last word.

Isaiah 7–39, then, affirms repeatedly that YHWH is holy in that he is the sovereign creator who is far superior to the deities of Israel's neighbors. It also affirms that human humility and trust in the holy One of Israel is key to membership among God's people. Failure to repent and believe in the face of the holiness of God will lead only to destruction.

Isaiah 40-66: Oracles of hope—new creation, atonement, and redemption. The central question facing Isaiah's exilic audience in

Isaiah 40–66 is, How will the cycle of sin be broken? Even though Hezekiah was faithful for a moment, he ultimately lived out the heritage of human arrogance that he inherited from his father and his before him. Hezekiah's experience is the experience of all of us: faithfulness, but with a divided heart. How will the endless cycle of sin end? Isaiah 40–66 answers that question. The problem is not just that people keep sinning but also that God's original image-bearers have a *sinful condition*. But as the sovereign over the creation, God is powerful enough to *create humanity anew*.

As such, the theme of new creation is especially present in Isaiah 40–66.[10] The basis of the prophet's message of YHWH's ability and willingness to deliver them from their Babylonian exile—a symbol of humanity's exile from the Garden of Eden and the presence of God—is the holy One's power to create from nothing. Isaiah encourages them to be mindful that as the one, true God stood alone on the stage of the creation at the start of it all, his oneness, sovereignty, and transcendence are enough for their deliverance today.

But how will that work? What are the mechanics of redemption from exile to return to Eden? How will people go from being arrogant rebellious sinners to servants of the holy One? According to Isaiah, this new creation comes through *atonement*. The famous servant song of Isaiah 52:13–53:12 epitomizes this. As God's people undoubtedly raise the question in exile, "How will he break the cycle of ongoing sin?" the prophet responds with the song of the obedient servant who will suffer in the place of the people. Through the unprecedented atoning work of one whose heart is *not* divided, one who is holy and entirely faithful to God, the hearts of God's people will be made new. They, like the servant, will become completely obedient.

This servant is the one that was promised in Isaiah 7–39. He is the Emmanuel of Isaiah 7:14. He is the child on whose shoulders the

---

[10]Is 41:17-20; 42:9, 15-17; 43:19; 44:3-4, 27; 45:7, 12-13, 18-19.

government will rest, the one called wonderful counselor, mighty God, everlasting father, and prince of peace (Is 9:6). He is the righteous one who is to come forth from the stump of Jesse, and on whom the Spirit of the Lord rests, who wears a belt of righteousness (Is 11:1-5). This is the one in whom the human vocation as the image-bearing vice-regents over the creation will be restored; this is the servant of the holy One, the Messiah.

The role of the Holy Spirit is key in the fulfillment of the Messiah's ministry. As Isaiah 40–66 is preoccupied with hope for redemption, one of the pieces of evidence of a redeemed people is *righteousness*.[11] The question was raised in the historical books, "How can a sinful people fulfill the commands of the covenant?" Isaiah offers the Holy Spirit as the answer to that question.[12] Isaiah 42:1-4 says,

> Behold my servant, whom I uphold, my chosen, in whom my soul delights; *I have put my Spirit upon him*; he will bring forth justice to the nations. He will not cry aloud or lift up his voice, or make it heard in the street; a bruised reed he will not break, and a faintly burning wick he will not quench; he will faithfully bring forth justice. He will not grow faint or be discouraged till he has established justice in the earth; and the coastlands wait for his law. (Emphasis added)

Particularly noteworthy here is the connection between the Holy Spirit and righteous leadership. This echoes the human vocation set forth in Genesis: to fill the creation with the glory of God through vice-regency in God's image.[13] While the servant of YHWH in this passage is normally interpreted as the Messiah, we also see the Spirit poured out on all of God's people in Is 32:14-17, which says,

> The fortress will be abandoned, the noisy city deserted; citadel and watchtower will become a wasteland forever, the delight of donkeys, a pasture for flocks, till the Spirit is poured on us from on high, and the desert becomes a fertile field, and the fertile field seems like a forest.

---

[11]Is 45:8, 13, 24; 46:13; 48:18; 51:5, 7; 53:11; 54:14; 56:1; 58:8; 59:17; 60:17, 21; 61:3; 62:1-2.
[12]Cf. Joel 2:28.
[13]Cf. Is 11:1-5.

The Lord's justice will dwell in the desert, his righteousness live in the fertile field. The fruit of that righteousness will be peace; its effect will be quietness and confidence forever.

In this segment of text there is a direct correspondence between the Spirit-filled people of God and life and order in the creation. This, once again, alludes to the purposes of creation and the human, divine-image-bearing vocation introduced in Genesis. When people are filled with the Spirit (i.e., holy), the creation is as it should be. When fellowship with God is restored through Spirit-indwelling, what was lost in Genesis 3 is restored. The loss of the personal presence of God as a result of humanity's rebellion against God was the cause of image becoming twisted, or distorted. When that presence is restored through the Holy Spirit, the image is healed.[14]

Jeremiah: Holiness and judgment. Jeremiah takes the holiness narrative one step further with his prophecy of a *new covenant.* Isaiah made it clear that yes, God will be faithful to his promises to Abraham; yes, his promises will be fulfilled through the *hesed* of his Messiah; and yes, the human sin problem can be resolved through atonement. *What Jeremiah adds is that all this work will be wrapped up in a new covenant that will fulfill the promises of the first covenant.* This new covenant will do what the first covenant was not capable of—namely, to restore to humanity the image-bearing vocation that God intended for them from the very beginning.

As noted in the previous chapter, the covenant was the means through which God's creation-redemption project was to manifest in the world. More specifically, we noted that "holiness" was synonymous with the restoration of the image of God via faithfulness to the covenant stipulations. We said that the profile of the *imago Dei* was encoded into the laws of the Pentateuch, which means that when God's people obeyed the 613 commands of the Pentateuch,

---

[14]Reading the Old Testament as Christian Scripture thus allows one to affirm the distinct personhood and activity of the Holy Spirit.

they would look like what God always intended humans to look like as image-bearers. We also said that when Israel was faithful to the covenant, they would fulfill their vocation as the representative head of the new creation. The ultimate goal of the covenant was to redeem God's plan to fill the creation with his glory through the multiplication of the image-bearing vice-regents. So how would this new covenant be different?

According to Jeremiah 31:31-34,

> "The days are coming," declares the Lord, "when I will make a new covenant with the people of Israel and with the people of Judah. It will not be like the covenant I made with their ancestors when I took them by the hand to lead them out of Egypt, because they broke my covenant, though I was a husband to them," declares the Lord. "This is the covenant I will make with the people of Israel after that time," declares the Lord. "I will put my law in their minds and write it on their hearts. I will be their God, and they will be my people. No longer will they teach their neighbor, or say to one another, 'Know the Lord,' because they will all know me, from the least of them to the greatest,'" declares the Lord.

Jeremiah's prophecy states that this new covenant will "not be like the covenant I made with their ancestors when I took them by the hand to lead them out of Egypt" (Jer 31:32). So, is there something wrong with the first covenant? Why is there need for a new covenant? Did God give them a faulty mechanism for restoring his purposes to humanity and ultimately the creation? Much has been written in response to these questions and there is not sufficient space here to offer an exhaustive treatment of the issue. However, an attempt can be made to answer these questions, at least in part, from Jeremiah's description of the new covenant. Before looking at the differences between the first and second covenant, however, let us look at the similarities.

First, both covenants result in, "And I will be their God, and they shall be my people" (Jer 31:33b; Ex 6:7), meaning that fulfillment of the covenant stipulations is aimed at marking off people who belong to YHWH. Second, the *law* is still the heart of the content of the covenant, as Jeremiah says, "I will put my *law* within them" (Jer 31:33c). So, with both covenants there is the law of YHWH that results in God's people embodying the image of God.

So, what is the big difference between the two covenants? The difference is that with the new covenant the law will be *internal*, as Jeremiah says, "I will put my law within them, and I will write it on their hearts" (Jer 31:33c). Inherent to this prophecy is an awareness that the first covenant does not remedy the inner twistedness of humanity. The first covenant which was given at Sinai is external. God's people need the law of God not to be written on tablets of stone but on the tablet of the heart. This imagery signifies that what humans need is a *new nature*. Conforming to God's moral code starts with the heart. It is not only behaviors that need managing; it is the entire person that needs reborn. This is the very same point of the new-creation motif which ties the narrative together. Holy people are a new creation. F. B. Huey writes,

> What was needed, as God revealed through Jeremiah in this passage, was not another covenant renewal but an internal transformation of the people based upon the divine provision of complete forgiveness. These would be the provisions of what the Lord referred to here as a "new covenant," which he promised to institute with Israel and Judah in days to come to replace the one made at Sinai (11:1–17). This new covenant relationship would not be "skin-deep" and subject to the waywardness of the people but "heart-deep" and permanently enduring.[15]

Ezekiel: Vigilant holiness for his name's sake. As a priest (Ezek 1:3), Ezekiel is naturally concerned with the holiness of God and consequently the sin of the people. Ezekiel's commission as a prophet to Israel comes during the exportation to Babylon. The timing of

---

[15]F. B. Huey, *Jeremiah, Lamentations*, New American Commentary 16 (Nashville: Broadman & Holman, 1993), 280-81.

Ezekiel's calling is inextricably linked to his message: *there is hope for rebellious Israel's relationship with YHWH to be restored.* Anything short of complete compliance to the covenant stipulations requires judgment because of God's holiness.

Lord of all nations. Ezekiel, like Isaiah, also emphasizes the lordship of YHWH over all nations. God is not merely Israel's national patron deity; he is the sovereign creator over all. This is pointedly the case with the debasement of king Nebuchadnezzar. Like the Assyrian princes, Nebuchadnezzar is merely an instrument in the hands of the holy One of Israel to accomplish his purposes (Ezek 21:19-23; 30:25). This point also comes through in the vision of the chariots and the mobility of the prophet himself. As a priest-prophet, Ezekiel goes with God's people into captivity. The role of the priest as an intermediary between God and his people is not done away with post-judgment. God will go with them and meet them where they are in the *tohu wabohu* of exile.

Ezekiel's temple vision offers us a commentary on the holiness of God and his lordship over all the nations (Ezek 8-11; 40-48). The new temple is the culmination of the story as it was launched in Genesis 1. God will form and fill a new-creation space and cohabit that space with a new-creation people, and that cohabitation is dependent on exclusive worship of YHWH. The simple fact that this image of redemption comes in the form of a temple by the pen of a priest accentuates *holiness.* This is a sacred place that is set apart for a sacred God who is worshiped exclusively by a sacred people.

Sovereignty, sin, and holiness. Ezekiel, like Isaiah, understands the robust nature of God's holiness as it relates to other divine attributes. Ezekiel 20:41-43 details the interconnectivity between the sovereignty of God, testimony, awareness of sin, and the holiness of God:

> I will accept you as fragrant incense when I bring you out from the nations and gather you from the countries where you have been scattered, and I will be proved holy through you in the sight of the nations.

Then you will know that I am the Lord, when I bring you into the land of Israel, the land I had sworn with uplifted hand to give to your ancestors. There you will remember your conduct and all the actions by which you have defiled yourselves, and you will loathe yourselves for all the evil you have done.

It is clear in this passage that YHWH's holiness is linked with his ability to redeem from exile. This feat can be likened to Israel's deliverance from Egypt. God demonstrates his power over the nations and their deities through Israel's redemption from Egyptian slavery. Likewise, God will demonstrate his power and holiness once again, but this time in the form of redeeming from exile. It is likewise explicit in this passage that exposure to the holiness of YHWH brings an overwhelming awareness of the sinful condition (Ezek 20:43), and that this redemptive act will serve as a witness to God's sovereignty and holiness. Israel's redemption from exile will show both Israel and the nations that YHWH is the only one worthy of exclusive worship as the one, true God.

The exaltation of YHWH. Another recurring theme in Ezekiel is that YHWH will redeem Israel for *his own sake.* Ezekiel repeatedly points out that God's saving activity will demonstrate that YHWH is God. The phrase "and they shall know that I am the Lord" occurs dozens of times in Ezekiel, and the expression that God will deliver Israel "for the sake of" his reputation occurs repeatedly. This theme parallels what we find in Genesis regarding the glory of YHWH filling the entire creation. This language is also Exodus language. Ezekiel sees the return from exile as a second exodus. This is the point of creation and, especially, humanity. The redemptive work of YHWH will glorify his name and will culminate in the restoration of the image of God in humanity.

The Holy Spirit. Holiness in Ezekiel culminates in the prediction of the people of God being filled with the Holy Spirit in order to restore Eden and glorify God. Ezekiel 36:25-29 says,

I will sprinkle clean water on you, and you will be clean; I will cleanse you from all your impurities and from all your idols. I will give you a new heart and put a new spirit in you; I will remove from you your heart of stone and give you a heart of flesh. And I will put my Spirit in you and move you to follow my decrees and be careful to keep my laws. Then you will live in the land I gave your ancestors; you will be my people, and I will be your God. I will save you from all your un-cleanness. I will call for the grain and make it plentiful and will not bring famine upon you.

Here the prophet discusses God's solution not only to the guilt of sin but also to the condition of sin. Freedom from the guilt of sin is provided for in the sacrificial system via substitutionary atonement. Israel's persistent disobedience has revealed, however, that the sinful condition—not simply sinning—is the problem. We learned from Genesis that humans were made for fellowship with God. Adam and Eve's rebellion in the Garden of Eden caused the loss of that divine-human fellowship, resulting in a distorted, or damaged image. The only way the damaged human nature can be repaired and the problem of sinning resolved is *through the restoration of God's presence*. Ezekiel prophesies that God will remedy this problem by putting his Spirit in humanity, curing the sin condition caused by the loss of the divine presence.

CONCLUSION

Holiness in the historical books and the prophets is consistent with the Pentateuch's conceptualization of holiness as *otherness* as well as *the restoration of the image of God*. God is *different* from the patron deities of the peoples living in Canaan prior to the conquest, he is *different* from the deities of Israel's neighbors (namely, the Phil-istines) during their inhabitation of the Promised Land,[16] and he is especially *different* from the lifeless gods of Israel's captors in Assyria

---

[16]YHWH's superiority to the Philistines' deities is pointedly demonstrated in the ark narrative in 1 Sam 4–6.

and Babylon. Contrary to ancient Near Eastern religion and worldview, Israel does not end up in exile because YHWH is inferior to the deities of their captors. Israel ends up in exile *because YHWH is superior to those so-called deities.*[17] Israel ends up in exile *because of God's holiness*, and God puts the lesser "gods" to work in carrying out his plan for human history. Furthermore, to allow Israel to remain in his holy presence during their rebellion against him would be contrary to his nature. Just as it was with Adam and Eve in Eden, Israel is expelled from the Promised Land because of their infidelity and by extension their failure to fulfill the human vocation of divine image-bearing.

The historical books and the prophets also highlight that Israel's sin problem is not simply a matter of human behavior. As Moses prophesied in Deuteronomy 31:16-18, Israel continues to repeat the cycle of sin epitomized in idolatry. While there are a few moments of success in faithfulness to the covenant, the overarching theme is Israel's ongoing disobedience and infidelity. This cycle of sin demonstrates that the problem of sin in Israel—as a representation of all of humanity—resides in *human nature*. And, as the prophets point out, human nature cannot be changed by a covenant in the form of an external law code written on tablets of stone. A change of human nature can only come about by way of an internal transformation. Israel's problem cannot be resolved through a physical, exterior circumcision. What Israel needs is a circumcision of the heart. Rather than the moral code of God written on tablets of stone, Israel needs the divine image implanted on the center of their very being. This calls for what is ultimately revealed in the New Testament: a resurrection, a new Adam.

This new Adam, we learn from the prophets, is the Messiah. In the Messiah all of God's promises are fulfilled. The Messiah is the

---

[17]See 2 Chron 36:15-18; Is 10:5-11; 28:11; 41:2; 44:28–45:7; Jer 1:14-15. YHWH's sovereignty over the nations is also affirmed in the various oracles against the nations found in many of the prophetic books. Cf. Is 13–27; Jer 46–51; Ezek 25–32; Joel 2:18–3:21; Amos 1:2–6:14; Obad 1:1-15; Jonah; Nahum 1:9–3:19; Zeph 1:7–3:20.

fulfillment of faithfulness of God to Adam, Noah, Abraham, Israel, and David. He is the one who will redeem the divine image in humanity. He is the model of holiness and means for the sanctification of humanity. Because of his faithfulness, the image of God will go out and carry the personal presence of God to the ends of the earth.

3

HOLINESS IN THE WISDOM LITERATURE

Is holiness in the Old Testament strictly a matter of conformity to the 613 commands of the Pentateuch? The Wisdom literature of the Old Testament (Job–Song of Songs) tells us that there is more to it. By standing on the shoulders of the Pentateuch and the call for exclusive worship of YHWH, the Old Testament Wisdom literature extends the application of holiness beyond religious life and the temple into the arena of everyday activities. Yes, holiness is about life in the tabernacle and religious practice (Leviticus), but it is also about the art of living a life that honors God in casual circumstances and everyday relationships; holiness shapes how we carry out the mundane activities of life at home and work. The Wisdom literature details the working out of covenant faithfulness in everyday life and in worship.

The Wisdom literature also explains why some human behaviors make for a good life and others do not. Wise people the world over have observed that some behaviors work and others do not. The question is, Why? The Wisdom literature says that the reason certain behaviors work and others do not is because the creator—the holy One of Israel—has made the world this way.

JOB, PROVERBS, AND ECCLESIASTES: MONOTHEISM AS THE BASIS OF WISDOM, ETHICS, AND HOLINESS

As we noted in previous chapters, the ancient world was a lot like the modern world in that it was pervaded with pluralistic moral relativity. Everyone did what was right in their own eyes because that was the life that the gods modeled. We also said that in contrast to this, it is only in a world in which there is one, true God that there can be peace (*shalom*) that extends from absolute truth and ethics that transcend time, space, and culture. This very idea of transcendent monotheism (i.e., one, true God who is not continuous with the creation) is the major philosophical underpinning of the concept of holiness as otherness.[1] We further said that because YHWH is the one, true God, he is unlike the gods of the ancient Near Eastern pantheon and humans. YHWH is unlike the gods and people in many ways, but two of the most important points of distinction are (1) his transcendence and (2) his uncompromising faithfulness (*hesed*).

God's ethical otherness as summed up in the Hebrew word *hesed* is the basis of Israel's otherness (i.e., holiness). Israel, as the new humanity, was to embody the image of God as characterized by *hesed*. The fact that Israel's God was different meant that they too had to be different. They were to embody *hesed* because YHWH is characterized in terms of *hesed*. They were to live by a different standard than the nations of the world. As we said earlier, the temple life with all its rituals and demands was an elaborate object lesson that taught this very point: that YHWH is holy, and Israel is called to be holy. The painstaking details of proper sacrifices, festival observance, and food laws reminded YHWH's people that they were to be set apart because God was holy. They were to be a nation of priests.

---

[1]See chapter one (on the Pentateuch) for more information on the monotheistic worldview of the ancient Israelites.

Holiness as conceptualized in the books of Job, Proverbs, and Ecclesiastes rests on the foundation of these ideas. At the most fundamental level, the Wisdom literature of the Old Testament *presupposes an absolute ethic that is only possible within a worldview framed by transcendent monotheism.* If there is not one, true God, then there is no basis from which we can draw standards for the treatment of persons. Without a single ethical standard there is no such thing at all as right or wrong, or better or worse; there is only *relativity.* There is my truth, and there is your truth. This means that Israel's monotheism is the only view of the world in which claims can be made about one way of life being better than another way of life. Any worldview that is not rooted in monotheistic revelation *must* forfeit all moral claims and propositions. It is the single, transcendent measuring rod of the life of the one, true God that makes statements like the following possible: "Lazy hands make for poverty, but diligent hands bring wealth" (Prov 10:4). The suggestion that an impoverished life is inferior to economic health is only possible because there is a single standard against which to measure all things.

Furthermore, the life prescribed for humanity in Proverbs is one that is holy and pleasing to YHWH. The list of behaviors that Proverbs prescribes can also be seen as a supplemental catalog to the life of holiness as described in the Pentateuch. We said before that holiness in people is the restoration of the image of God that in turn fulfills the creation's purpose to glorify God. This all presumes that God designed human life to be carried out in a certain way and that this way is good. Wisdom is a matter of marching in step with the way that the creator God designed the world according to his character and will. Seen this way, holiness and wisdom are intimately related.

Another related but different point of connection between wisdom in Proverbs and holiness is that wisdom results from an awareness of sin. Proverbs, like the Pentateuch, *reveals* holy living. Most people do not think of themselves as fools. The book of Proverbs, like the Pentateuch, offers readers an honest look in the mirror to assess how they fare against honorable and wise character. With the purpose of polishing the rough edges of human behavior and revealing the natural tendencies of the sinful condition, Proverbs provides many maxims such as:

> If one gives answer before hearing, it is folly and shame. (Prov 18:13)

> When words are many, transgression is not lacking, but the prudent are restrained in speech. (Prov 10:19)

> Fools show their anger at once, but the prudent ignore an insult. (Prov 12:16)

> Precious treasure remains in the house of the wise, but the fool devours it. (Prov 21:20)

The book of Proverbs affirms that managing resources prudently, working hard, listening well, being prudent, generous, and gracious all play a key part in the holy life. More to the point, such a life glorifies God by bringing the divine image to fulfillment in people. In short, wisdom is the working out of the covenant life in the practicality of everyday circumstances and relationships. Proverbs assumes that the very character of God himself is worked into the fabric of the universe and that conformity to God's definitions for human behavior results in a better human existence.

The book of Proverbs also praises those who seek wisdom. Seeking wisdom is virtuous. Proverbs 1:2-6 says,

> For gaining wisdom and instruction; for understanding words of insight; for receiving instruction in prudent behavior, doing what is right and just and fair; for giving prudence to those who are simple, knowledge and discretion to the young—let the wise listen and add their learning, and let the discerning get guidance—for understanding proverbs and parables, the sayings and riddles of the wise.

Likewise, it is bad to ignore wisdom and embrace folly:

> Wisdom cries aloud in the street, in the markets she raises her voice; at the head of the noisy streets she cries out; at the entrance of the city gates she speaks: "How long, O simple ones, will you love being simple?

How long will scoffers delight in their scoffing and fools hate knowledge? If you turn at my reproof, behold, I will pour out my spirit to you; I will make my words known to you. Because I have called and you refused to listen, have stretched out my hand and no one has heeded, because you have ignored all my counsel and would have none of my reproof, I also will laugh at your calamity; I will mock when terror strikes you, when terror strikes you like a storm and your calamity comes like a whirlwind, when distress and anguish come upon you." (Prov 1:20-27 ESV)

The point is that it is good to embrace and recognize human limitations and to respect the boundaries that God has put into place for human existence. Seeking knowledge stems from an awareness of the deficiencies of human self-reliance. This is summarized in the famous statement from Prov 1:7: "The fear of the LORD is the beginning of knowledge, but fools despise wisdom and instruction." In short, YHWH alone is God. Ecclesiastes expresses the same sentiment:

I perceived that whatever God does endures forever; nothing can be added to it, nor anything taken from it. God has done it, so that people fear before him. That which is, already has been; that which is to be, already has been; and God seeks what has been driven away. (Eccles 3:14-15)

Fear God and keep his commandments, for this is the whole duty of humanity. (Eccles 12:13b)

Ecclesiastes, like Proverbs, claims that human life as God intends it begins by recognizing that YHWH is God and people are not. In a phrase, humble faith is the starting point to a happy and holy life.

If something must be fully comprehensible to be true, then God must be fully comprehensible; and if God is fully comprehensible by creatures, then he cannot be "God" by definition. This way of thinking raises human reason to the point of full comprehension of all things, which undermines *faith*. Another implication of this is that God and humanity are equal. This is precisely why faith and wisdom alike require a degree of mystery. God is one who is beyond human comprehension, and this is one of the things that makes him different. Mystery is a necessity in a world that is created by One who is far superior to his creation. This is *faith*. Faith takes us *outside* of ourselves—faith takes us beyond the realm of our own human experiences and certainties. The limitations of the human mind necessitate faith, and living within boundaries is what exclusive monotheism is all about; it is likewise what holiness is all about. Faith itself is a witness to the incomparability and incomprehensibility of the one, true God. He is set apart in that he is beyond the bounds of human thought.

The Pentateuch's conceptualization of holiness as the fulfillment of the image of God through covenant faithfulness is at the heart of the biblical notion of wisdom. More specifically, morality and ethics as constituted in the covenant law code are the cornerstone on which the very notion of wisdom itself stands.

JOB AND THE EXISTENCE OF EVIL: THE TEST OF FAITH

One of the greatest dilemmas facing monotheists in a fallen world is the existence of evil. This is the problem that the book of Job addresses, and it is related to the concept of holiness as *otherness*. How could it be that evil exists in a world created by an all-powerful creator who is good? The book of Job answers this question with a story. The book tells the story of Job, a righteous man who *seems* to suffer meaninglessly. He loses his wealth, his family, and his health. The bulk of the book records Job's painful conversations with his friends in search for an answer to his unmerited affliction and agony. Job is trying to reconcile his experience with the existence of a sovereign and good God.

Sovereignty means that you get what you want (i.e., one is all-powerful). No one can contend with a sovereign, and a sovereign gets their way. If God is truly sovereign, and evil exists, then it must follow that he wishes it to exist. Human reasoning leads us to two possible solutions to this line of argumentation: either (1) God is not sovereign or (2) God is not good. There is another possibility, and that is that human reasoning is limited and is therefore unable to resolve the dilemma of the existence of evil in a world created by a sovereign and good creator. This is precisely the answer the book of Job offers. God says to Job, "Where were you when I laid the earth's foundation? Tell me, if you understand. Who marked off its dimensions? Surely you know! Who stretched a measuring line across it? On what were its footings set, or who laid its cornerstone—while the morning stars sang together and all the angels shouted for joy?" (Job 38:4-7). God goes on to say, "Brace yourself like a man; I will question you, and you shall answer me. 'Would you discredit my justice? Would you condemn me to justify yourself? Do you have an arm like God's, and can your voice thunder like his?'" (Job 40:7-9).

Job answers with this:

> I know that you can do all things; no purpose of yours can be thwarted. You asked, "Who is this that obscures my plans without knowledge?" Surely I spoke of things I did not understand, things too wonderful for me to know. You said, "Listen now, and I will speak; I will question you, and you shall answer me." My ears had heard of you but now my eyes have seen you. Therefore I despise myself and repent in dust and ashes. (Job 42:2-6)

The point here, once again, is that God is God and people are people. People cannot compare with God. To suggest that things unexplainable are distasteful to people is to likewise diminish the majesty and fullness of God.

Walking in step with Ecclesiastes, the solution that the book of Job offers is that human reason is limited, and this is where faith comes in. Once again, Job reminds us that God and his ways cannot be reduced to the limitations of human reasoning. This in turn means that for people to hold that God is both sovereign and good while affirming that evil exists in the world means to be irrational from a humanistic standpoint. It means that there must be some mystery, something that humans cannot fully understand. Faithfulness to YHWH means submitting the most valuable human asset (reason) to the bar of God's sovereignty. Once again, as relates to holiness, it means admitting that God is God and humans are not. God is *other* than humanity. This is the opposite of what we saw in Genesis 3 when Adam and Eve ate from the tree of the knowledge of good and evil. By deciding independently from God what was good and evil, they were making themselves equal to God. So, once again, the book of Job is an appeal to the importance and challenge of the practice of exclusive monotheism.

At the heart of Job is a reminder that the humble life of faith is one that fully embraces the lordship of YHWH as the one, true God. This full embrace of or submission to the lordship of YHWH is intrinsic to holiness. It is complete devotion, steadfast faith, and trust. Humble faith is prerequisite for the art of living a life that honors and glorifies God. Humble faith, like holiness, is a testimony of the wise who know their place in a vastly mysterious world. The life of faith is one that recognizes and happily accepts boundaries that mark off God's intention for a happy and healthy human existence. It is a life that promotes and sustains the *shalom* life of God.

THE PSALMS: PRAYER, WORSHIP, LORDSHIP, AND HOLINESS

Psalms is the praise book of God's covenant people. Yes, the book of Psalms contains prayers,[2] laments,[3] wisdom psalms,[4] royal psalms,[5] processional hymns,[6] psalms of trust,[7] thanksgiving songs,[8] and much more. Collectively, however, Psalms is a book of praise. This is evident in the Hebrew title of the book, *tehillim*, which means

---

[2] Ps 17; 86; 142.
[3] Ps 3–7; 9–10; 12–14; 17; 22; 25–28.
[4] Ps 1; 19; 37; 49; 50; 73; 78; 112; 119.
[5] Ps 2; 18; 20–21; 45; 72; 89; 101; 110; 144.
[6] Ps 15; 24; 120–134.
[7] Ps 11; 16; 23; 27; 62–63; 91.
[8] Ps 30; 32; 34; 40; 75; 107; 116; 118.

"songs of praise."[9] This means that even the other genres within the book are ultimately classified as worship, as they are part of the collective *tehillim*.

But what does worship have to do with holiness? Everything. Worship is the fulfillment of holiness as it is confessional. Through the Psalms, worshipers proclaim their allegiance and faithfulness to YHWH as the one who is worthy of their worship as the one, true God. As set forth in the Pentateuch and affirmed again and again in the historical books and the prophets, YHWH is the one, true God who is entirely sovereign, transcendent, and immanent. None compete with him or restrict him. Therefore, YHWH alone merits worship. He is the only one to whom people submit themselves in a posture of awe as a response to the holiness of God. When the creation—and humans in particular—confess the exclusive lordship of YHWH, the world is as it was meant to be from the very beginning. Worship is the proper human response to the moral purity and ontological otherness of God. James L. Mays sums it up perfectly:

> The One Hundredth Psalm says, "Know that the Lord is God." That is, by the acclamation of your joyous praise, acknowledge and declare that the one who has named himself by the sacred tetragrammaton, whom the scriptures pronounce Adonai and our versions translate as Lord, that one is God, the only God, the one of whom alone the predicate of God may be used, the one who in his identity defines and preempts the noun "god." And the confession is completed by declaring, "Adonai made us and we are his, his people and the sheep of his pasture." That is, the psalm adds to the confession the most central activity which gives content to the name, the salvation-story.[10]

---

[9]Furthermore, many of the psalms contain the title "song" (*shir*; Ps 18; 28:7; 30; 33:3; 40:3; 42:4; 45; 46; 48; 65; 66; 67; 68; 75) or "hymn" (*tehillah*; Ps 119:171; 145; 147:1; 148:14), and the book closes with an exuberant shout of praise for the kingship of YHWH (Ps 145–150).

[10]James L. Mays, *The Lord Reigns: A Theological Handbook to the Psalms* (Louisville, KY: Westminster John Knox, 1994), 65.

As noted earlier, the purpose of humanity is to fill the creation with the glory of God. When Adam and Eve fell, they abdicated this responsibility as image-bearing vice-regents over the creation. As rebels against God, they no longer glorified him. They failed to recognize YHWH as the one, true God. They became morally relative, pluralistic polytheists (making themselves equal with God). They created for themselves a world in which everything is the same. No one and nothing are set apart. Everything is continuous and common. When humans worship YHWH, however, the human vocation as God-glorifying image-bearers is restored. The people of God are the ones who confess their exclusive allegiance to YHWH in worship. The outworking of holiness in people is worship. When people praise YHWH, the human vocation is fulfilled. This means that the saints—those who are sanctified—are those who truly worship.

Prayer, the presence of God, and holiness. The historical context and literary shape of the Psalter reveal a further connection between the Psalms and holiness. The book of Psalms is divided into five "books":

- Book 1: 1–41
- Book 2: 42–72
- Book 3: 73–89
- Book 4: 90–106
- Book 5: 107–150

These five books of the Psalter reflect the five books of the Pentateuch.

As tradition attributes the book of Psalms to king David, it is understood that while the Pentateuch is a book of instruction given to Israel by Moses, the Psalter is a book of instruction given to Israel by David. The Midrash on the Psalms states:

> As Moses gave five books of laws to Israel, so David gave five Books of Psalms to Israel, the Book of Psalms entitled Blessed is the man (Ps

1:1), the Book entitled For the leader: Maschil (Ps 41:1), the Book, A Psalm of Asaph (Ps 73:1), the Book, A Prayer of Moses (Ps 90:1), and the Book, Let the redeemed of the Lord say (Ps 107:2). Finally, as Moses blessed Israel with the words Blessed art thou, O Israel (Deut 33:29), so David blessed Israel with the words Blessed is the man. (Midr. Pss. 1:1)[11]

The Psalter speaks to a time in which there was no temple. How does this reality reconcile the fact that the temple is a major controlling theme that spans the book of Psalms?[12] More specifically, what happens when there is no temple? How can one worship God in his presence when there is no temple? How can Israel access the presence of YHWH after the temple has been destroyed? Could God truly be with them without the temple, and if so, how? The Psalter's answer to that question is prayer and worship.

The five books of the Pentateuch provide stipulations for the priesthood and rules for regulating how Israel accessed God's holy presence. The Psalter, then, is a handbook for experiencing God's presence, not through the temple, but through prayer and worship. With the destruction of the temple, the Psalms offer an alternative solution for experiencing God's presence. In short, if you are in the Psalms, you are in the temple. The psalmist says it perfectly in Psalm 22:3: "You are holy, enthroned on the praises of Israel."

If the book of Psalms is a means for getting into the holy presence of God, then by extension it is a means of sanctification. If God's people are going to be transformed by the holy presence of God, and prayer is the door to that presence, then prayer is a means for conforming to the holy image of God. Mays writes,

---

[11] William G. Braude, *The Midrash on Psalms*, 2 vols., Yale Judaica Series 13 (New Haven, CT: Yale University Press, 1959), 1:49-50.

[12] Most if not all the Psalms are imagined having a place in the life of worship in the temple. This is evidenced in the liturgical nature of many of the psalms (Ps 24; 118; 136), certain psalms being attributed to temple musicians (Ps 42–49; 50; 73–83; 84–85; 87–88), as well as Old Testament references to hymns being sung in the temple (1 Chron 15:16-19; 2 Chron 20:19). This temple is synonymous with motifs in the Psalms related to God as refuge/protection, Zion, and the holy hill. See also Ps 5:7; 11:4; 18:6; 27:4; 29:9; 48:9; 65:4; 68:29; 79:1; 138:2.

"Means of Grace" is a term used recurrently in the Christian tradition for regular and established ways in which divine grace is offered and received. The list of means has usually included the sacraments, reading scripture, and prayer. These psalms composed as prayers of need, gratitude, and trust have provided on the most important resources in the disciplined use of means of grace. The prayer psalms are both scripture and prayer. Everything that we know about their role in the life of faith across the centuries is a record of their significant value.[13]

The Psalms as a means of grace is also what Psalm 1 is all about. Psalm 1 is a contrast between the righteous and the wicked. According to Psalm 1, the righteous person meditates on the law of the Lord day and night (1:2b). The word *law* (torah) here refers to the book of Psalms in its five-part correspondence to the Pentateuch. This means that Psalm 1 is telling readers that people who are righteous (i.e., faithful to the covenant, holy) meditate on the book of Psalms. Considering the historical context during the time in which the Psalter was finalized, Psalm 1 is telling its exilic or post-exilic audience that even though there is no longer a temple, you can still be faithful to the covenant (i.e., holy), and the way is through praying the Psalms.

There is yet another crucial temple-centric dynamic in the Psalter. Each of the five books within the Psalter also corresponds to a particular time during Israel's history.[14]

- Book 1: United monarchy under David
- Book 2: United monarchy under Solomon
- Book 3: Divided monarchy
- Book 4: The exile
- Book 5: Return from exile and restoration of the temple

---

[13]Mays, *The Lord Reigns*, 40.

[14]For more details on the canonical shape of the Psalter, see Nancy deClaissé-Walford, Rolf A. Jacobson, and Beth LaNeel Tanner, *The Book of Psalms*, New International Commentary on the Old Testament (Grand Rapids, MI: Eerdmans, 2014), 21-38.

With this, there is a movement from being far from the temple to gradually moving closer to the temple. This movement climaxes in Psalms 145–150 (the so-called Little Hallel), which celebrates the final return to the fullness of the presence of God. As the reader progresses through the Psalter there is gradually less lamentation and more praise. This is representative of movement toward the temple and the exuberant joy that results from being in the presence of YHWH.

What is the significance of this? In light of what we have said in previous chapters about the temple as a microcosm of the new creation and Israel as the new humanity, the Psalter is subtly telling the story of the restoration of Eden. When humans return to the presence of God and worship him, God's purpose for the creation is fulfilled. As Israel worships in YHWH's presence, they recognize him as the one, true God and thereby fulfill the human vocation of glorifying God.

Devotion to the king(s). The themes of temple and kingship fit naturally together as the temple is the place from which the king reigns. We see this in Psalm 2, which with Psalm 1 serves as the introduction to the Psalter. Psalm 1 tells the reader that the key to covenant faithfulness is prayer. Psalm 2, which is a royal psalm celebrating the coronation of the messianic king, declares that faithfulness to God and his anointed king (*mashiah*) is yet a second aspect to covenant faithfulness. To be holy, one must be completely devoted to the one that God has anointed King of the world. This is much like the call to exclusive monotheism that resounds throughout the Pentateuch, the historical books, and the prophets.

This raises a rather obvious question for the exilic audience: "How can one be faithful to a messiah when there is no king?" Psalm 2 is an affirmation to the exilic and post-exilic community that God will be faithful to fulfill his promise to make David's heir the everlasting king of the cosmos.[15] Psalm 110 says,

---

[15]For more on reading the Psalms messianically, see Gordon J. Wenham, *The Psalter Reclaimed: Praying and Praising with the Psalms* (Wheaton, IL: Crossway, 2013), 81-101.

The LORD says to my Lord: "Sit at my right hand, until I make your enemies your footstool." The LORD sends forth from Zion your mighty scepter. Rule in the midst of your enemies! Your people will offer themselves freely on the day of your power, in holy garments; from the womb of the morning, the dew of your youth will be yours. The LORD has sworn and will not change his mind, "You are a priest forever after the order of Melchizedek." The Lord is at your right hand; he will shatter kings on the day of his wrath. He will execute judgment among the nations, filling them with corpses; he will shatter chiefs over the wide earth. He will drink from the brook by the way; therefore he will lift up his head.

Remember that in 2 Samuel 7 God promised David that the Messiah would come from David's family. The Israelites, who are in exile under the reign of a pagan king and country, are naturally asking the question, "Will God be faithful to his promise to David?" Psalm 2 answers that question with a resounding "Yes!" In fact, this theme of God's faithfulness to the Davidic covenant is at the center of the Psalter. Strategically placed throughout the book are royal psalms reminding Israel that God has not forgotten his promises and he will remain faithful because of his holy *hesed*.

Israel is not only called to be loyal to the Messiah but also to God as king. God as king is arguably the central theme of the Psalter as it holds together the Psalter's themes of worship, temple, and lordship.[16] This is what Psalms 93–99 are all about. Psalm 93 is a wonderful example. It reads,

> The Lord reigns, he is robed in majesty; the Lord is robed in majesty and armed with strength; indeed, the world is established, firm and secure. Your throne was established long ago; you are from all eternity. The seas have lifted up, Lord, the seas have lifted up their voice; the seas have lifted up their pounding waves. Mightier than the thunder of the great waters, mightier than the breakers of the sea—the Lord on

---

[16]For an excellent case in support of the reign of YHWH as the central theme of the book of Psalms, see Mays, *The Lord Reigns*.

high is mighty. Your statutes, Lord, stand firm; holiness adorns your house for endless days.

These verses remind Israel that even though their circumstances indicate that God is no longer in control and that he has abandoned them, nothing could be further from the truth. God still reigns. He is not like other so-called deities. He is not restricted to geographical regions, and he does not have to battle with other gods to maintain control of his people. If his people suffer, it is often because they have violated the covenant. And, even when they have abandoned the covenant, he has not. He is utterly faithful no matter what. He is holy.

Hesed. The *hesed* of YHWH is also central in the Psalter. We see this in the repeated refrain of Psalms 118 and 136: "for his steadfast love endures forever" (*ki le'olam hasdo*). The phrase "steadfast love" is the ESV's translation of the word *hesed* (Ps 117:2). The placement of these psalms is crucial to their interpretation and to the theme of *hesed* within the broader scope of the Psalter.

Psalms 113–136 are a collection of psalms dedicated to the commemoration and celebration of Israel's deliverance from Egyptian slavery. Psalms 113–134 in particular are psalms dedicated to each of the three Jewish pilgrimage festivals as detailed in the Pentateuch. Psalms 113–118, also known as the Egyptian Hallel, are sung to commemorate Passover (Ex 12); Psalm 119 is sung to commemorate Pentecost (Ex 26); Psalms 124–130, also known as the Songs of Ascent, are sung to commemorate the Feast of Tabernacles (Lev 23). Psalms 135–136, then, are the capstone of these psalms that celebrate God's saving activity in the life of Israel. Particularly noteworthy is that this collection is placed within book five of the Psalter. Book five addresses the return from exile. The careful placement of these pilgrimage festival psalms in book five creates an intentional connection between Israel's deliverance from Egyptian slavery and their deliverance from Babylonian exile. Further still, the placement of Psalms 118 and 136 as *hesed* psalms indicates God's saving activity among his people is key to his *hesed*. In other words, even when Israel is not faithful, God is faithful, which sets him apart.

In sum, what we see is, once again, a direct link between the *hesed* of God and the otherness (i.e., holiness) of God. YHWH, unlike humans and other gods, is entirely and eternally faithful and powerful to save. Psalm 135, which celebrates the otherness of YHWH among other nations and deities and precedes Psalm 136 (the great *hesed* psalm), says,

> I know that the Lord is great, that our Lord is greater than all gods. The Lord does whatever pleases him, in the heavens and on the earth, in the seas and all their depths. He makes clouds rise from the ends of the earth; he sends lightning with the rain and brings out the wind from his storehouses. . . . The idols of the nations are silver and gold, made by human hands. They have mouths, but cannot speak, eyes, but cannot see. They have ears, but cannot hear, nor is there breath in their mouths. Those who make them will be like them, and so will all who trust in them. (Ps 135:5-7, 15-18)

We also find *hesed* in Psalm 51. In the first verse David appeals to God's *hesed* as the basis for forgiveness. Verse 1 says, "Have mercy on me, O God, according to your steadfast love; according to your abundant mercy blot out my transgressions." David is saying, "Even though I have not been faithful, please be faithful to me according to your *hesed*." In his failure to be faithful to the stipulations of the covenant, David is appealing to God's unwavering faithfulness as the basis of his forgiveness. Reflecting the controlling narrative of the Psalter, David also makes the connection between God's *hesed* and the restoration of the divine presence. Psalm 51:10-12 says, "Create in me a pure heart, O God, and renew a steadfast spirit within me. Do not cast me from your presence or take your Holy Spirit from me. Restore to me the joy of your salvation and grant me a willing spirit, to sustain me."

These verses summarize what holiness as the image of God restored in humanity is all about. David first asks for God to create a new heart for him. The Hebrew word used here for "create" (*bara'*) is the same verb used in Genesis 1:1 where God "created the heavens and the earth." The subject of this verb is always God. In other words, only God can *bara'*. David, then, is asking God to do something only God can do. David is asking for God to do a Genesis 1 work in his heart. This is new-creation language.

David goes on to ask God to "renew a steadfast spirit within me" (Ps 51:10). Synonyms for the Hebrew word translated "steadfast" (*kun*) are "firm," or "right." This word marches right in step with the concept of *hesed*. David is asking that God help him be unwavering in his faithfulness just as God himself is. David is asking for the restoration of the divine resemblance. David wishes to be as faithful to YHWH as YHWH is to him.

David pleads, "Do not cast me from your presence or take your Holy Spirit from me" (Ps 51:11). Here, David recognizes that covenant infidelity means being removed from the divine presence. David knows the story of Adam and Eve. He knows that in his sin he has written his own moral code and therefore rebelled against the lordship of YHWH who is the one, true God. David has become an idolater. Such behavior means losing out on the privilege of enjoying the life-giving divine presence that fosters the divine image in people. David does not want what happened to Saul to happen to him.

Finally, David repeats the request for the restoration of a willing spirit. This phrase is parallel to the "right spirit" we saw previously. Again, David is asking for the divine likeness in the form of faithfulness to be restored. Psalm 51, then, is a reminder that holiness as the restoration of the image of God in humanity depends on YHWH's *hesed* as well as recognition of wrong-doing and repentance. It also makes the direct connection between the image of God in humanity in the form of *hesed* faithfulness.

Lamentation and holiness. Many of the psalms are laments, or requests for God's help in life-threatening circumstances. Psalm 22 is a perfect example of this kind of psalm. In Psalm 22, David expresses his trust in YHWH considering his unbearable suffering. The degree of his suffering is evident in the strong language he uses to describe his crisis. For example, Psalm 22:1-2 says, "My God, my God, why have you forsaken me? Why are you so far from saving me, from the words of my groaning? O my God, I cry by day, but you do not answer, and by night, but I find no rest."

These verses accentuate the gravity of David's situation. Things could not be any worse. He has been betrayed and mocked to the point of causing him to lose all strength and desire to live. David is completely undone. Yet in the midst of his agony, David remains faithful, as he later declares:

> Yet you are enthroned as the holy One; you are the one Israel praises. In you our ancestors put their trust; they trusted and you delivered them. To you they cried out and were saved; in you they trusted and were not put to shame. . . . Yet you brought me out of the womb; you made me trust in you, even at my mother's breast. From birth I was cast on you; from my mother's womb you have been my God. Do not be far from me, for trouble is near and there is no one to help. (Ps 22:3-5, 9-11)

We see that interwoven into David's dire circumstances are his declarations of trust and hope in YHWH. Even though it seems as if YHWH has abandoned him (Ps 22:1), David knows that YHWH is trustworthy and able to save him. It is not by accident that Jesus cites Psalm 22:1 while on the cross (Mt 27:46; Mk 15:34). Jesus is citing Psalm 22 to identify himself with David as the messianic king. Just like David was entirely faithful in the midst of suffering, so will Jesus be faithful. This true, tested faithfulness to YHWH is what holiness is all about. It reflects YHWH's very *hesed* faithfulness. When God's people are faithful to YHWH as the one, true God like Jesus and David are faithful, the image of God is restored.

What does this have to do with holiness? If holiness is wrapped up in faithfulness to the lordship of YHWH, then that faithfulness is ultimately tried in the face of persecution and suffering. The psalmist is a model of perseverance and devotion to YHWH in even in the most difficult of circumstances. These psalms answer questions such as, Will you remain faithful if it doesn't make sense? Will you completely devote yourself to YHWH even though it may seem as if he's not working on your behalf? Will you be faithful even when you are surrounded by enemies, plagued with sickness, and confused (Ps 22)? Those who are holy are those who are faithful no matter what. When they are faithful no matter what, they reciprocate God's *hesed*. They embody his very image in the world, which testifies to his majesty and dominion.

Love and Holiness: Song of Songs

The Wisdom literature comes to a close with Song of Songs. Song of Songs is a love song that makes the love between a husband and wife analogous to God's love for his people. As Tremper Longman III writes, "'Kiss me and kiss me again, for your love is sweeter than wine' (1:2). With this passionate expression, the Song of Songs opens. The woman expresses her intense desire to be in the intimate presence of her man. As we read on, we encounter not only expressions of desire and passion but also the rapturous sighs of their union."[17]

Song of Songs reminds us that the holiness of salvation extends beyond the suzerainty-vassal treaty covenant metaphor and the courtroom metaphor. The relationship between YHWH and Israel is even more intimate than can be expressed in the adoption metaphor. Song of Songs reminds us that the YHWH-Israel covenant is like a *love relationship*. Yes, holiness can be likened to a people's exclusive loyalty to their beloved monarch, or even a child's bond to a parent and honoring the reputation of the family legacy by living by the values and norms of the family. And yes, holiness means loyalty to YHWH and righteous living that honors and glorifies God, but only love is powerful enough to inspire the kind of devotion to

---

[17]Tremper Longman III, *Ecclesiastes and Song of Songs*, Cornerstone Biblical Commentary 6 (Carol Stream, IL: Tyndale House, 2006), 341.

YHWH that will not waver amid adversity. This is *hesed* loyalty. This is the kind of loyalty that YHWH offers his people. It is a commitment that does not depend on circumstances or quid pro quo. It is like a parent's love for a child. Better yet, it is the incomparably deep love that spouses share. As this *hesed* kind of loyalty exists between God and Israel, the image of God in humanity is restored, God is glorified, and holiness is at the center of it all.

Furthermore, like a marriage, the holy love of salvation is *covenantal*. As already noted, at the heart of the Old Testament concept of covenant (*berit*) is a *legally binding agreement*.[18] The marriage covenant, however, is more intimate. According to Genesis, the marriage covenant is two becoming one flesh (Gen 2:24). This means an absence of incompatibility. There is unity with distinction. This is *at-one-ment*. This is a faithful union that is more intimate than the adoption metaphor. Like a marriage covenant, this relationship between God and his people is consensual and exclusive (monogamous). Not infrequently in the Old Testament, the prophets liken Israel's disobedience in the form of idolatry to adultery. Israel's mandate as God's covenant people was for an exclusive love affair with YHWH. YHWH was to be Israel's one God, and Israel was to be YHWH's one people that he chose for himself.

Also, like marriage, holy love is monogamous. YHWH and Israel's relationship, once again, is exclusive. The first commandment of the covenant stipulations is to have no other God but YHWH. This is much like a marriage covenant. Being YHWH's people meant that he had exclusive access to them and them to him (i.e., "a kingdom of priests").

Finally, and most poignantly, the nuptial metaphor reminds us that this relationship between YHWH and his people is of a certain kind of love. This is not a relationship of tolerance, or simple professional collegiality. This relationship is *not only* like the relationship

---

18*HALOT* 1:157. See also Gen 21:27, 31:44; 1 Sam 23:18; 1 Kings 5:26.

between a judge and the one declared innocent. This relationship is comparable to a love that is passionately romantic. There is a sense of *excitement and mystery* that defines the relationship. The romantic relationship between husband and wife illustrates God's relationship with his people in that the passion for the other creates a sense of *remoteness from everyday life.* In other words, this love is so strong that it and it alone can break the individual free from the captivity of the fallen, broken, corrupt, tyrannical, and fear-pervaded human existence. Only this love can melt the frozen heart of people, and the melting of this heart results in an entirely new creature altogether. This is much like Thomas Chalmers's famous expression "the expulsive power of a new affection."[19] This love is so intense, so powerful, that it has the ability to shift the point of orientation for everyday living from self to God. And this is why the nuptial metaphor for the saving covenant relationship with God is so essential for holiness. This is not only *why* but also *how* holiness is more than simple obedience. Holiness, as Song of Songs reminds us, brings us into a whole new world oriented around a single, exclusive love and passion for our creator.

CONCLUSION

In conclusion, what we find in the Wisdom literature is an approach to holiness similar to what we encountered in the Pentateuch, historical books, and Prophets, but also different. At the core, the Wisdom literature affirms that holiness is about complete dedication to the lordship of YHWH. He is the one, true God who alone merits worship and obedience. What the Wisdom books add is a human element to complete obedience. Yes, holiness is about covenant faithfulness to the 613 commands of the Pentateuch, but at the heart of that obedience is the very fulfillment of what it means to be human. It is as Craig Bartholomew puts it: "As the close link between

---

[19]Thomas Chalmers, *The Expulsive Power of a New Affection*, Crossway Short Classics (Wheaton, IL: Crossway, 2020).

the Spirit, creation and re-creation suggests, the work of the Spirit in redemption is not to produce religious cranks, but to open our humanity and to enable us to become what God always and by creation intended us to be: his fully human image-bearers."[20]

Holiness is not about robotic conformity. The Wisdom books remind us that the holy life is the fulfilling and eternally satisfying life, that the only way to be fulfilled in this life as creatures made by YHWH is in a faithful love relationship with the creator. It is only when people are fully committed to YHWH that they are fully human and can enjoy the wonderful, satisfying life that God always intended for his creation.

Understanding holiness in the Old Testament begins with understanding that God is transcendent and *hesed*. These qualities make him utterly different (i.e., *qadosh*) from the deities of the ancient Near Eastern pantheon. Those deities are made in the image of humanity; they are morally corrupt and entirely dependent on external forces for their existence. God is the eternally loving I Am. Furthermore, because God is *hesed*, he is *personal*. As the transcendent God of love, he made humanity in his image with the goal of fellowship with them. The outworking of that goal means that humanity would fill the creation with the glory of his loving relational presence. As humanity is fruitful, multiplies, and fills the earth, the creation is filled with God's image-bearers. When humanity lives as God intended them to live, they share in his holiness. Being holy as God is holy means being faithful in bearing God's image.

Humanity's rebellion against God, however, resulted in the loss of the holy, life-giving divine presence. The loss of that presence yielded the corruption of the divine image in humanity. Losing God's presence means a deep distortion of the human condition because it is missing the critical element for which it was created: God's holy, personal presence.

---

[20]Craig G. Bartholomew, "The Wisdom Literature," in *A Biblical Theology of the Holy Spirit*, ed. Trevor J. Burke and Keith Warrington (Eugene, OR: Cascade, 2014), 33.

The Old Testament does not leave us there, however. God promises that he will restore what was lost when Adam and Eve rebelled against him. He will establish his presence with humanity once again. He begins to fulfill that promise through a covenant with Israel. That covenant stipulated a dwelling place for God's holy presence, and that Israel obey the law code, which is a profile of his very image; a profile of the image of God that was marred. Israel's chronic faithlessness paired with the elaborate object lessons that are built into the covenant stipulations teach a pointed lesson: humanity cannot help but sin because their condition has been corrupted by the absence of God's presence.

In response to this, God, through his prophets, promises that his internal presence will be restored to them through his Spirit (Ezek 36:27) and that a messiah will make it all possible (Is 52:13–53:12). Heading into the following chapters on holiness in the New Testament, we end with this observation from John Oswalt:

> The Old Testament closes on a rising note of hope. Surely God had not brought them all this way to leave them in their sin and despair now. Surely that long history of promise and fulfillment could not end like this. God *was* the King of the whole universe and surely he would make his kingdom manifest in the world. God's covenant was the way of life and surely he would bring that covenant to fulfillment. He had promised to pour out his Spirit on all flesh in the last days and usher in a new era of justice and righteousness in which his people *would* be able to live the life he called them to. The true anointed one (Messiah) would appear, a king who would care more for his people than he did for himself. He would be the messenger of the covenant, who would purify his people with fire. He would make God's Spirit available to all, and the promises of Isaiah 60–62 would become a reality.[21]

---

[21]John N. Oswalt, *Called to Be Holy: A Biblical Perspective* (Nappanee, IN: Francis Asbury, 1999), 100, emphasis original.

Part Two

"BE PERFECT AS YOUR HEAVENLY FATHER IS PERFECT"

Holiness in the New Testament

4

HOLINESS IN THE
GOSPELS AND ACTS

AS WE HAVE SEEN IN PART ONE, the Old Testament is essential for understanding holiness. In it, we meet YHWH, the holy One, and discover his glorious desire to make humans holy as he is holy. Yet the Old Testament also exposes the depths of human sin, and as its story draws to a close, we find that Israel—the servant whom YHWH called to be his light to the nations—has rebelled against YHWH and is itself in the dark. The Old Testament thus leaves us with a pressing question: Can humans really be holy? Or are we doomed to constantly repeat the Adam-Israel cycle of sin?

Over the next three chapters, we will see that the answer to this question is one of the central concerns of the New Testament. We begin with the Gospels and Acts. If you were to ask most Christians what these books have to say about holiness, I suspect you would receive two answers: (1) Jesus *is* holy and (2) we *should be* holy. But the central question that we are after—the question raised by the Old Testament—goes a step further: *Can* we be holy? (And if so, how?) Since together the Gospels and Acts make up more than half of the New Testament and there is no hope of surveying even a fraction of what each book has to say on this matter, we will instead focus on two areas: (1) holiness and the life of Jesus and (2) holiness in the words of Jesus.[1]

HOLINESS AND THE LIFE OF JESUS

If we want to know what it means to be truly human, then we must—as Dennis Kinlaw put it—"start with Jesus."[2] I emphasize this point because many Christians have approached the issue of holiness by beginning with a preconceived notion of what it means to be human (e.g., to be human is to sin) and have therefore set Jesus aside as an interesting exception to the rule. But this will not do. If Jesus was fully God *and* fully human, then the life that he lived must shape how we think about what humans can be by God's grace.

So, what can we learn about holiness from the life of Jesus? I would like to explore the answer to this question through the Gospel of Luke and its sequel, Acts. Luke's two-volume work provides an excellent starting place for thinking about holiness and the life of Jesus for two reasons: (1) Luke emphasizes the work of *the Holy Spirit* in Jesus' life, and (2) Luke connects Jesus' Spirit-filled life to the life of the church through his second volume.

Jesus and the Holy Spirit in the Gospel of Luke. Luke presents Jesus as a real human—one who is born, grows up, is tempted, has emotions, suffers, and dies on a cross. But Luke also presents Jesus as a human whose entire existence is initiated and empowered by the Holy Spirit. Luke first mentions Jesus directly in Gabriel's birth announcement to Mary.[3] The angel tells the startled Galilean girl, "You will conceive and give birth to a son, and you are to call him Jesus. He will be great and will be called the Son of the Most High.

---

[1] For a more extended study of holiness in the Gospels, see Kent Brower, *Holiness in the Gospels* (Kansas City, MO: Beacon Hill, 2005).

[2] Dennis F. Kinlaw, *Let's Start with Jesus: A New Way of Doing Theology* (Grand Rapids, MI: Zondervan, 2005); cf. Thomas H. McCall, *Against God and Nature: The Doctrine of Sin*, Foundations of Evangelical Theology (Wheaton, IL: Crossway, 2019), 208.

[3] Jesus is mentioned indirectly in Lk 1:16-17, where Gabriel tells Zechariah that John will go before the Lord God to prepare the people for him.

The Lord God will give him the throne of his father David, and he will reign over Jacob's descendants forever; his kingdom will never end" (Lk 1:31-33). To a young Jewish woman like Mary, Gabriel's mention of a child descended from David who would be called God's Son and reign over an unending kingdom would have had a clear implication: this child that she was to bear would be the Davidic Messiah, God's promised king who would deliver Israel.[4]

Mary responds, "How will this be . . . since I am a virgin?" (Lk 1:34). Gabriel replies, "The Holy Spirit will come on you, and the power of the Most High will overshadow you. So the holy one to be born will be called the Son of God" (Lk 1:35). Mary will conceive this child not through a human father but by the power of the Holy Spirit. But what is the significance of this virginal conception? For many, the answer is that the virginal conception somehow makes Jesus God. However, Christian theology has traditionally affirmed that Jesus is fully God because he is the eternal Son of God who became human. And while the virginal conception may be fitting for the incarnation, it does not seem to be strictly necessary for it.[5]

But if the virginal conception does not make Jesus God, what does it do? Luke hints at an answer in the latter part of the verse: "So the holy one to be born will be called the Son of God." Luke here links Jesus' virginal conception to his status as Son of God. Somehow, Jesus' status as the Son of God is a result of his manner of conception. But how? The connection becomes clearer if we read on to Jesus' genealogy (Lk 3:23-38), where Luke says that Jesus was descended from "Adam, the son of God" (Lk 3:38). This is the first time that Luke has used the phrase "son of God" since Luke 1:35, where it described Jesus, and the parallel is instructive. Just as Adam was created solely by God in his image and likeness (Gen 1:26) and was

---

[4]On the Davidic promise, see 2 Sam 7:12-16; 1 Chron 17:11-14; Ps 2:1-12; 89:3-4, 20-37; 110:1-7; 132:11-12; Is 9:6-7.
[5]Oliver D. Crisp, "The 'Fittingness' of the Virgin Birth," in *God Incarnate: Explorations in Christology* (London: T&T Clark, 2009), 77-102.

therefore God's son,[6] so now Jesus is conceived of a virgin apart from any human initiative and so will be called God's Son. The virginal conception, then, marks Jesus out as a new Adam, a new human created solely by God's initiative. Jesus is thus the Son of God not only in the sense that he is the Messiah (God's solution to the Israel problem) but also that he is a new Adam (God's solution to the broader human problem).[7]

Luke gives us a first glimpse of Jesus' obedience to the Father when Jesus is twelve years old. Jesus' family, following their normal custom, goes to Jerusalem to celebrate Passover. On the way back, Mary and Joseph accidentally leave Jesus in Jerusalem and, upon discovering their mistake, rush back and find Jesus in the temple three days later, conversing with the teachers. When Mary (probably more than a little perturbed) asks Jesus, "Son, why have you treated us like this?" (Lk 2:48), Jesus replies, "Why were you searching for me? . . . Didn't you know I had to be in my Father's house?" Jesus submits to his parents and obediently returns to Nazareth, but Luke has given us a foretaste of things to come: Jesus is God's Son in a unique sense, and this relationship takes priority over other relationships and desires.

In the body of the Gospel, Luke continues to show how Jesus lives a Spirit-empowered life of obedience to the Father as a real human. Three elements in particular characterize Jesus' Spirit-empowered existence in Luke: (1) prayer, (2) resistance to temptation, and (3) ministry in the mode of Isaiah 61.

Luke recounts that at Jesus' baptism the Holy Spirit descends on him like a dove, and the Father speaks from heaven: "You are my Son, whom I love; with you I am well pleased" (Lk 3:22). Here we

---

[6]On the connection between likeness/image and sonship, see Gen 5:1, 3. Cf. G. K. Beale, *A New Testament Biblical Theology: The Unfolding of the Old Testament in the New* (Grand Rapids, MI: Baker Academic, 2011), 401-2; J. R. Daniel Kirk, *A Man Attested by God: The Human Jesus of the Synoptic Gospels* (Grand Rapids, MI: Eerdmans, 2016), 391; Philo, *On the Virtues*, 203-4.

[7]Luke elsewhere presents Jesus as divine Lord (see esp. Lk 1:16-17, 43, 76; 24:52; Acts 2:17-21, 33, 36-38), so when applied to Jesus, "Son of God" must ultimately refer to an ontological relation that distinguishes Jesus from the Father within the being of God.

see the Father and the Spirit expressing their approval of Jesus at the outset of his ministry. Luke, however, has added one element to the story not found in the other Gospels: between the baptism and the Father and Spirit's affirmation, Luke notes that Jesus is *praying*.[8] Luke's version thus emphasizes not only the Father and Spirit's approval of Jesus but also his posture of dependence on and communion with them.

With the Father's words "You are my Son" resounding in our ears, Luke now moves to Jesus' genealogy. As noted above, in the genealogy Luke traces Jesus' origins all the way back to "Adam, the son of God" (Lk 3:38). So, Jesus and Adam are both sons of God, but what sort of Son will Jesus be? Will he fall as the first human did?

Luke answers this question in the following story. "Jesus, full of the Holy Spirit, left the Jordan and was led by the Spirit into the wilderness, where for forty days he was tempted by the devil. He ate nothing during those days, and at the end of them he was hungry" (Lk 4:1-2). Here, at Jesus' weakest point, Satan approaches with three temptations: (1) turn a stone into bread, (2) worship Satan in exchange for authority over the kingdoms of the earth, and (3) jump from the highest point of the temple. In each case, Jesus resists and responds by quoting God's Word.[9] Luke's point in all this is that *Jesus, the Son of God, succeeds where Adam, the son of God, failed.* Luke encourages this Jesus-Adam contrast in two ways: (1) he places the genealogy between the baptism and temptation so that "Adam, the son of God" is the last phrase that one hears before the temptation begins and (2) he arranges the temptations so that the devil's taunts, "If you are the Son of God . . ." occur in the first and last temptations (Lk 4:3, 9; cf. Mt 4:1-11).

But *how* does Jesus resist Satan? At first glance, the answer might seem simple: Jesus is God. True, but Jesus is also fully human. So, let

---

[8] Cf. Mt 3:16; Mk 1:10.

[9] This detail becomes even more interesting in light of the Jesus-Adam parallel, for Adam and Eve sinned when they failed to trust God's Word (Gen 3:1-6).

us be more specific: how does God, who has become human, resist Satan?[10] Luke answers this by bookending the temptation with references to the Holy Spirit. Before the temptation, Luke notes that Jesus was "full of the Holy Spirit" and "was led by the Spirit into the wilderness" (Lk 4:1). And after the temptation, Luke says that "Jesus returned to Galilee in the power of the Spirit" (Lk 4:14). The implication? Jesus has triumphed over Satan by the power of the Spirit. However, Satan is apparently not finished, for Luke concludes the temptation with an ominous note: "When the devil had finished all this tempting, he left him *until an opportune time*" (Lk 4:13, emphasis added). We will return to this point below.

In Jesus' baptism, genealogy, and temptation, we have observed two of the elements that for Luke characterize Jesus' human existence: prayer and resistance to temptation. The third element emerges a few verses on. Toward the beginning of his ministry, Jesus goes to the synagogue in his hometown of Nazareth on the Sabbath and stands up to read. Someone hands him a scroll of Isaiah, and he unrolls it and reads,

> The Spirit of the Lord is on me,
>   because he has anointed me
>   to proclaim good news to the poor.
> He has sent me to proclaim freedom for the prisoners
>   and recovery of sight for the blind,
> to set the oppressed free,
>   to proclaim the year of the Lord's favor. (Lk 4:18-19; cf. Is 61:1-2)[11]

Jesus rolls up the scroll, hands it back, sits down, and declares, "Today this scripture is fulfilled in your hearing" (Lk 4:21). Jesus

---

[10]Christian teaching affirms that Jesus was sinless, and one of the main arguments for Jesus' sinlessness is that Jesus would not sin because he is God, and "God does not will contrary to God's will" (Thomas C. Oden, *The Word of Life*, vol. 2, *Systematic Theology* [Peabody, MA: Hendrickson, 2008], 254). I do not wish to dispute this but simply to inquire *how* it is that (i.e., by what means) Jesus does not sin despite the fact that he is human.

[11]On the differences between Lk 4:18-19 and Is 61:1-2 LXX, see Darrell L. Bock, *Luke 1:1–9:50*, BECNT (Grand Rapids, MI: Baker Academic, 1994), 404-5.

identifies himself as the Isaianic servant of the Lord who is anointed by God's Spirit to proclaim and enact God's deliverance for Israel and the rest of the world.[12] What is important here is that the Spirit anoints the servant for a *purpose*: to proclaim good news to the poor, to set the oppressed free, and so on. And Jesus claims this Spirit-anointed vocation as his own. Thus, what we see in the life of Jesus (as in the OT) is that *holiness is missional.* The life that the Holy Spirit produces is not merely one of personal piety; it is also one of kingdom ministry.

Jesus' performance in the Nazareth synagogue is more than pomp and circumstance, for in the following stories we find him ministering in the mode of Isaiah 61. In a synagogue in Capernaum, he casts out a demon who hails him as "the holy One of God" (Lk 4:31-37). Afterward he heals Peter's mother in law, and that evening he heals many who are sick and casts out numerous demons (Lk 4:38-41). Asked to stay, Jesus declares, "I must proclaim the good news of the kingdom of God to the other towns also, because that is why I was sent" (Lk 4:43), recalling the servant's mission in Isaiah 61:1.

Jesus' Isaiah 61-themed ministry continues throughout the Gospel. Indeed, when John the Baptist sends his disciples to inquire about whether Jesus is "the one who is to come" (Lk 7:20), Jesus replies using the language of Isaiah 61 to describe his ministry: "Go back and report to John what you have seen and heard: The *blind* receive *sight*, the lame walk, those who have leprosy are cleansed, the deaf hear, the dead are raised, and the good news is proclaimed to the poor" (Lk 7:22). The human life of the holy One is, therefore, irreducibly missional—one that is poured out for "the least of these."

Yet while Jesus' life is missional, it is not the life of some self-made man simply rushing around Galilee getting things done. Jesus continually relies on the Father and the Spirit to provide power and

---

[12]On the speaker of Is 61:1-2 as the servant-Messiah, see John N. Oswalt, *The Book of Isaiah: Chapters 40–66*, New International Commentary on the Old Testament (Grand Rapids, MI: Eerdmans, 1998), 562-63.

direction for his mission. Luke demonstrates Jesus' dependence on the Father and the Spirit by accentuating the role of prayer in the life of Jesus.[13] We have already seen how Luke emphasizes prayer at Jesus' baptism (Lk 3:21). As Jesus' popularity grows, he regularly withdraws to pray (Lk 5:16; 6:12), and Luke alone mentions Jesus praying before other key events such as Peter's confession (Lk 9:18; cf. Mt 16:13; Mk 8:27), the transfiguration (Lk 9:28-29; cf. Mt 17:1; Mk 9:2), and teaching the Lord's Prayer (Lk 11:1; cf. Mt 6:7).[14]

Prayer and temptation both come to a climax for Jesus in the garden of Gethsemane. As we saw above, Luke closes his account of the temptation by noting, "When the devil had finished all this tempting [*peirasmon*], he left him until an opportune time" (Lk 4:13). Jesus' trial in the garden of Gethsemane likely constitutes this opportune time, for here the language of "temptation" (*peirasmos*) appears twice (Lk 22:40, 46) and Luke notes that Jesus' agony was so great that his sweat "was like drops of blood" (Lk 22:44).[15] Jesus, however, responds with prayer (Lk 22:41, 44-45) and submits to the will of the Father by going to the cross. Once again, the new Adam succeeds where the first Adam failed.

The cross, however, is not the end of the story: God raises Jesus on the third day, vindicating him over and against the verdict of his enemies and of death itself.[16] Yet the resurrection is not just good news for Jesus; it is good news for all humans. Jesus' blood inaugurates a "new covenant" (Lk 22:20; cf. Jer 31:31) in which "repentance for the forgiveness of sins will be preached in his name to all nations" (Lk 24:47). Here Jesus' new-Adam vocation comes full circle, for whereas Adam achieved death for all humans through his rebellion

---

[13]Lk 3:21; 5:16; 6:12; 9:18; 9:28-29; 10:21; 11:1-4; 22:32, 41-42, 44-45; 23:34, 46. For Jesus praying in the other Gospels, see Mt 6:9-13; 11:25-26; 14:23; 19:13; 26:39, 42-43; Mk 1:35; 6:46; 14:32, 35-36, 39; Jn 11:41-42; 12:27-28; 17:1-26.

[14]Jesus also prays for Peter to withstand temptation in Lk 22:32.

[15]*Peirasmos* also occurs in Lk 8:13; 11:4; and 22:28.

[16]On the significance of Jesus' resurrection, see N. T. Wright, *The Resurrection of the Son of God*, Christian Origins and the Question of God 3 (Minneapolis: Fortress, 2003), esp. 719-38.

against God, Jesus offers life to all humans by his faithful obedience to God. As Paul would later put it, "For as in Adam all die, so in Christ all will be made alive" (1 Cor 15:22).

So, what can we learn about holiness from Jesus' life? Jesus shows us that to be *truly* human is—in contrast to the first Adam—to live a Spirit-initiated and -empowered life wholly committed to God. In other words, to be truly human is to be holy. What does holiness look like in a human life? Luke emphasizes at least three elements: (1) praying continually in dependence on the Father and the Spirit, (2) resisting temptation, even to the point of death, and (3) ministering in the mode of Isaiah 61. But is this sort of life possible for any human besides Jesus? Luke answers this question in his second volume.

The Holy Spirit and Jesus' witnesses in Acts. Luke introduces Acts by saying, "In my former book, Theophilus, I wrote about all that Jesus began to do and to teach" (Acts 1:1). By describing his Gospel (the former book) as all that Jesus began to do and to teach, Luke implies that Acts recounts what Jesus continued to do and to teach, both directly and through his Spirit-filled witnesses. Luke therefore indicates from the outset that the "acts" of Jesus' followers that his second volume narrates are inherently Jesus-shaped—an extension of Jesus' life and mission.

Acts 1:8 strengthens and develops the link between the life of Jesus and the lives of his followers. Jesus tells his disciples, "You will receive power when the Holy Spirit comes on you; and you will be my witnesses in Jerusalem, and in all Judea and Samaria, and to the ends of the earth." Acts 1:8 constitutes the blueprint for the rest of the book, for when the Holy Spirit comes on the disciples at Pentecost, their witness begins in Jerusalem (Acts 2:1–8:1), spreads to Judea and Samaria (Acts 8:1–11:18), and continues toward the ends of the earth (Acts 11:19–28:31). Two aspects of this verse are key.

First, Jesus says that the disciples will receive power "when the Holy Spirit comes on you." The disciples' witness will be produced not by human striving but by the empowering presence of God's Spirit.

But there is also something deeper going on. The Greek verb here is *eperchomai*, and in the entire New Testament there are only two places where the Holy Spirit is said to *eperchomai* someone/thing:

> The Holy Spirit *will come on* [*epeleusetai*, from *eperchomai*] you, and the power of the Most High will overshadow you. So the holy one to be born will be called the Son of God. (Lk 1:35)

> You will receive power when the Holy Spirit *comes on* [*epelthontos*, from *eperchomai*] you; and you will be my witnesses in Jerusalem, and in all Judea and Samaria, and to the ends of the earth. (Acts 1:8)

Luke has created a parallel between the conception of Jesus and the origin of the church. But why? Let us recall the significance of the virginal conception: it marked Jesus out as new Adam, a new human being whose existence was solely due to God's initiative. And, as we have seen above, Jesus' Spirit-initiated and -empowered life constitutes a new way of being human—one of wholehearted dependence on and obedience to God. So the point seems to be this: *just as the Spirit came on Mary to conceive Jesus—a new Adam, the Spirit now comes on Jesus' disciples to conceive the church—a group of people who will (like Jesus) manifest a new way of being human.* Thus, the Holy Spirit's coming means not only empowerment but also transformation; the Spirit will change the disciples so that they are able to live a new, Jesus-shaped life.

Jesus' words "you will be my witnesses" (the second aspect) underscore this point, but from an Israel angle. "You will be my witnesses" alludes to Isaiah 43, where YHWH declares to Israel, "You are my witnesses" (Is 43:10, 12). But in Isaiah there is a problem: Israel is a blind and deaf witness (Is 43:8). They have become like the idols they have worshiped and are unable to testify to the nations that YHWH alone is God.[17] Isaiah foresees a twofold solution to this problem: (1) the suffering servant will atone for the sins of many

---

[17] Is 6:8-10; 8:16-9:2; 42:6-7.

through his sacrificial death (Is 52:13–53:12), and (2) YHWH will pour out his Spirit on Israel, transforming them from a wilderness into a fruitful field (Is 32:15; 44:3). In other words, in order for Israel to become the witnesses that YHWH desires, the same Spirit who empowered the life of the servant-Messiah (Is 11:2; 42:1; 48:16; 61:1) must also come on them. Against this backdrop, the significance of Jesus' words comes into focus: the Spirit will come on the disciples— a microcosm of Israel—and transform them to be the Messiah-shaped witnesses YHWH always desired for Israel to be.[18]

The coming of the Spirit (predicated, of course, on Jesus' death, resurrection, and ascension) therefore provides the antidote to the Adam-Israel problem. The Spirit will empower Jesus' disciples to manifest a new way of being human that is dependent on and obedient to the Father and simultaneously renew Israel's mission to be a light to the nations (which had been sidetracked because Israel succumbed to sin as Adam did). Jesus' Spirit-filled witnesses therefore continue his mission not only in the sense that they do things in his name (which is true) but also that their Spirit-initiated and -empowered lives are an organic extension of his Spirit-initiated and -empowered life. This ontological link is why Jesus can say to Saul, "Why do you persecute me?" (Acts 9:4) when Saul is persecuting the *church*.

But perhaps I have been playing fast and loose with a few phrases in Acts 1:8. Is there any hard evidence that in Acts the Holy Spirit transforms the disciples to live Jesus-shaped lives? Yes. Recall that three elements characterized Jesus' Spirit-filled life in the Gospel of Luke: (1) prayer, (2) resistance to temptation, (3) ministry in the mode of Isaiah 61. These three elements also characterize the lives of Jesus' Spirit-filled witnesses in Acts.

---

[18]Note that Jesus' twelve apostles (whose number will be replenished by Pentecost) mirror the twelve tribes of Israel. Luke also mentions that the group of disciples awaiting the Holy Spirit numbered "about a hundred and twenty" (i.e., 12 x 10), which may further suggest that they symbolize Israel.

Prayer is central to the life of the early church in Acts. One of the first things Luke tells us about the believers post-Pentecost is that they "devoted themselves to . . . prayer" (Acts 2:42). A few verses later, Peter and John heal a lame beggar as they are going up to the temple "at the time of prayer" (Acts 3:1). This gets them into hot water with the Jewish leaders, and when they are released, we find the believers praying once again (Acts 4:24-31). And these examples are no exception. Jesus' Spirit-filled witnesses pray incessantly throughout Acts, imitating the life of their Spirit-filled Lord.[19]

The Holy Spirit also empowers Jesus' witnesses to resist temptation. We must recall that *peirasmos*, the Greek word often translated as "temptation," can also mean "testing" or "trial." While Luke does not provide a wealth of insight into the internal temptations that Jesus' followers certainly experienced (e.g., to be prideful or to lust), he does recount many temptations/trials that test their resolve to continue proclaiming the good news about Jesus. We may think here of Peter and John being arrested, dragged before the Jewish leaders, and warned "not to speak or teach at all in the name of Jesus" (Acts 4:18), of Stephen being stoned by the Sanhedrin for testifying about Jesus (Acts 7:57-60), of Paul persecuting Christians (Acts 8:3; 9:1-2), or of Paul himself suffering for the sake of Jesus' name (Acts 9:15-16; cf. 14:22). Indeed, at the end of his third missionary journey, Paul describes to the Ephesian elders how he "served the Lord . . . in the midst of severe testing [*peirasmōn*] by the plots of my Jewish opponents" (Acts 20:19). But despite intense temptations and trials, the church presses on. Thus, Jesus' Spirit-filled witnesses not only pray like their Lord; they also resist temptation like him.

Ministry in the mode of Isaiah 61 is also central to the lives of Jesus' followers in Acts. In his post-Pentecost summary, Luke says that the believers "sold property and possessions to give to anyone who had need" (Acts 2:45). The Holy Spirit produces such generosity

---

[19]E.g., Acts 6:4, 6; 7:59; 8:15, 24; 9:11, 40; 10:9; 11:5; 12:5, 12; 13:3; 14:23; 16:25; 20:36; 21:5; 22:17; 28:8.

among the believers that a few chapters later Luke notes that "there were no needy persons among them" (Acts 4:34; cf. Deut 15:4). The church's compassion toward widows is apparently so significant that by Acts 6 the apostles have to appoint seven deacons to serve in this area. The Spirit also empowers Jesus' followers to heal the physically sick and free those oppressed by demons throughout Luke–Acts.[20] And, of course, wherever Jesus' witnesses go, they "proclaim good news" (Is 61:1)—the good news that people can be saved in the name of Jesus. Thus, for the early Christians as for Jesus, holiness—the life that the Holy Spirit produces—is ultimately missional.

Acts therefore presents the life of the church as being Jesus-shaped.[21] Just as the Holy Spirit came on Mary to conceive Jesus—a new Adam, the Holy Spirit now comes on Jesus' disciples to conceive the church—a group of people who will manifest a new way of being human that is inherently Jesus-shaped. All of this, of course, fulfills God's original intent—that humans would multiply his image and fill creation with his glory—and underlines God's faithfulness to his Abrahamic promise to bless the nations through Israel.

The overarching movement of Luke–Acts therefore might be described like this: The holy One becomes incarnate as the human person Jesus and lives, dies, rises, ascends, and pours out the Spirit so that we might be like him. Or, to paraphrase Irenaeus, Jesus became what we are so that we might become what he is.[22] And while the connection between Jesus' life and the life of the church is particularly strong in Luke–Acts because these two books share an author, this is ultimately the storyline of Matthew, Mark, and John as well, for in the New Testament canon the book of Acts functions as the sequel not just to Luke but to all four Gospels.

---

[20]E.g., Acts 3:1-10; 5:15-16; 8:6-7; 14:9-10; 16:16-18.

[21]The three elements noted above constitute only a small portion of the parallels between Jesus in Luke and believers in Acts. For a fuller discussion, see James R. Edwards, "Parallels and Patterns between Luke and Acts," *Bulletin for Biblical Research* 27 (2017): 485-501.

[22]Irenaeus speaks of "our Lord Jesus Christ, who did, through His transcendent love, become what we are, that He might bring us to be even what He is Himself" (*Against Heresies* 5, pref. [*ANF* 1:526]).

So what can we learn about holiness from the life of Jesus? In the first place, humans can be holy. Jesus is, of course, the ultimate example of this. However, if Luke is to be believed, Jesus' holy life and mission continue through the lives of his followers. How can Jesus' followers be holy? In the same way Jesus was—their existence is initiated and empowered by the Holy Spirit. What does holiness look like? It looks like the life of Jesus—a life of Spirit-filled, wholehearted obedience to God characterized by prayer, resistance to temptation, and ministry in the mode of Isaiah 61.

HOLINESS IN THE WORDS OF JESUS

Our study of Jesus' life (and, by extension, the life of his witnesses) in Luke–Acts has suggested not only that humans can be holy but also how this is possible and what holiness looks like in a human life. We now turn to holiness in the words of Jesus. If Jesus himself envisions holiness as being possible for his followers, then we will have strong biblical grounds for thinking that this is indeed the case. We will focus on three passages, one each from Matthew, Mark, and John.

The Sermon on the Mount (Mt 5–7). The Sermon on the Mount is arguably the most beloved and influential of all Jesus' teachings. One would be hard-pressed to find a three-chapter section of the Gospels (or, indeed, of Scripture as a whole) that has been more commented on and cited throughout history. Yet the Sermon also contains some of Jesus' most intense ethical teaching, and this has led many interpreters to attempt to tone down or evade its high demands.[23] One interpretative tradition in Roman Catholicism, for example, divides the Sermon's teaching into "precepts" that are necessary for average Christians and "counsels" that are necessary for

---

[23]See Jonathan T. Pennington, *The Sermon on the Mount and Human Flourishing: A Theological Commentary* (Grand Rapids, MI: Baker Academic, 2017), 2-14. Pennington's study has stimulated much of my thinking on the Sermon, and while I disagree with him on some points (e.g., the translation of *teleios*), the overarching thrust of my discussion here is indebted to his work.

those who wish "to achieve perfection and the higher calling" (e.g., clergy).[24] Martin Luther famously interpreted the Sermon as an impossible ideal (part of the "law" in his law-gospel dichotomy) meant to make people realize their inability to keep it and fall on Christ for grace.[25] Other interpreters, however, have been more optimistic about the Sermon's commands. Jonathan Pennington, for instance, notes that "broadly speaking, in the patristic period, both in the East and West, the Sermon was *not* perceived as problematic."[26]

These divergent interpretations alert us to the fact that the frame within which one interprets the Sermon is as important as the individual commands themselves. "Love your enemies" (Mt 5:44) can mean very different things depending on whether one interprets it as an impossible ideal, a command for the spiritually elite, or a real possibility for normal Jesus-followers. In what follows, I will not attempt to provide an interpretation of the whole Sermon (to do so would require a book in itself) but will rather discuss how Matthew frames the Sermon and explain the meaning of one command that is particularly relevant to our present topic: "Be perfect . . . as your heavenly Father is perfect" (Mt 5:48).

The Sermon on the Mount, which constitutes the first of Matthew's five teaching blocks (Mt 5–7; 10; 13; 18; 24–25), occurs just after Jesus begins his ministry. After Jesus calls his first disciples, Matthew notes that "Jesus went throughout Galilee, teaching in their synagogues, proclaiming the good news of the kingdom, and healing every disease and sickness among the people" (Mt 4:23). Jesus' ministry attracts large crowds, and this provides the occasion for the Sermon: "Now when Jesus saw the crowds, he went up on a mountainside and sat down. His disciples came to him, and he began to teach them" (Mt 5:1-2). Thus, the immediate audience for the Sermon is Jesus' disciples, but Jesus' message also seems intended to draw in

---

[24]Pennington, *Sermon*, 5.
[25]Pennington, *Sermon*, 5.
[26]Pennington, *Sermon*, 4, emphasis original.

the crowds. Indeed, at the end of the discourse we find the crowds marveling at Jesus' teaching (Mt 7:28-29). Matthew therefore frames the Sermon as a kingdom-oriented, disciple-creating exhortation: Jesus teaches his disciples what it means to live in light of God's coming kingdom and simultaneously invites the crowd into this new life as well.

Jesus introduces the Sermon with the Beatitudes (Mt 5:3-12): "Blessed are the poor in spirit," "Blessed are those who mourn," and so on. The Greek word for "blessed" is *makarios*, which might also be translated as "happy," "fortunate," or "flourishing."[27] In the Old Testament and Jewish literature outside of the Bible, such statements occur frequently in Wisdom literature as descriptions of the good life.[28] The Beatitudes, then, are "invitations to the kind of life that will experience flourishing."[29] But this creates a paradox, for at first glance none of the things that Jesus commends as the good life seem to be desirable. (Happy/fortunate/flourishing are the *poor* in spirit, those who *mourn*, the *meek*?) It is for this reason that Jesus explains each *makarios*-statement with a "for" statement. These explanations are of two sorts: (1) affirmations that the kingdom of heaven belongs to such people (Mt 5:3, 10) and (2) promises of future rewards for them (Mt 5:4-9, 12). In short, the life described in the Beatitudes is the good life because it is founded on the unshakable reality of God's kingdom. And Jesus does not merely commend this life to his disciples; he lives it himself. Jesus mourns, grieving the things that grieve God (Mt 23:37-39). Jesus is meek (Mt 11:29), submitting to his Father's will (Mt 26:36-46). Jesus is merciful (Mt 9:27-30). Jesus is persecuted because of righteousness (Mt 26:47–27:56). Pope John Paul II therefore rightly calls the Beatitudes "a sort of *self-portrait of Christ*."[30]

---

[27] BDAG, 610-11; for "flourishing," see Pennington, *Sermon*, xv, 54.

[28] E.g., Ps 1:1; 2:12; 31:1; 32:11; Prov 3:13; 8:34; 28:14; Eccl 10:17; Job 5:17; Wis 3:13; Sir 14:1-2, 20.

[29] Pennington, *Sermon*, 54.

[30] *Veritatis Splendor* §16, emphasis original. The text is available at www.vatican.va/content/john-paul-ii/en/encyclicals/documents/hf_jp-ii_enc_06081993_veritatis-splendor.html. Cf. E. Stanley Jones, *The Christ of the Mount: A Working Philosophy of Life* (New York: Abingdon, 1931), 27: "This

By introducing the Sermon with the Beatitudes, Jesus seems to imply that the Sermon is a gift, not merely a rigorous to-do list. Jesus is inviting current and would-be disciples to live in light of God's coming kingdom—to live the sort of life that he lives. This kingdom-oriented life may initially appear to be anything but happy/fortunate/flourishing because it requires sacrifice and suffering in the present. Yet it is the good life because it is lived in light of God's end-time reign—the ultimate reality—that has begun with Jesus' ministry. We therefore cannot evade the Sermon's commands by writing them off as impossible ideals or optional accessories. No, if we wish to be Jesus' disciples, the solution is not evasion but transformation. We must live into the reality of God's dawning end-time reign.

Jesus begins the body of the Sermon by discussing his relationship to the OT: "Do not think that I have come to abolish the Law or the Prophets; I have not come to abolish them but to fulfill them" (Mt 5:17). He goes on to tell his disciples, "Unless your righteousness surpasses that of the Pharisees and the teachers of the law, you will certainly not enter the kingdom of heaven" (Mt 5:20). While "righteousness" in Scripture can refer to a status that God credits to someone, here it refers to human behavior (note the ethical commands that follow in Mt 5:21-48). The righteousness that Jesus' disciples must have is thus a lived-out righteousness. But how can they possibly exhibit a greater righteousness than the Pharisees and the teachers of the law? Jesus explains by providing six examples of this greater righteousness in relation to the law that clarify in what sense he fulfills the Law and the Prophets (Mt 5:21-48).[31] In each, Jesus begins with a scripture or a contemporary Jewish teaching ("You have heard that it was said . . .") and then provides his own teaching ("But I tell you . . ."). In general, Jesus *intensifies* and *internalizes* the law, showing the heart behind it. For example, Jesus teaches that "You shall not

---

is not a sermon—it is a portrait, the portrait of Jesus himself, and of the Father and of the man-to-be."

[31]Pennington, *Sermon*, 120.

murder" (Ex 20:13) prohibits not only murder but also the ungodly anger that lies at its root. Similarly, "You shall not commit adultery" (Ex 20:14) rules out not only sexual relations with someone other than one's spouse but also lustful thoughts.

Jesus' climactic sixth example focuses on love for others (Mt 5:43-48). True to form, Jesus begins by quoting the existing teaching: "You have heard that it was said, 'Love your neighbor and hate your enemy'" (Mt 5:43). The first part of the teaching, "Love your neighbor," is a direct quote of Leviticus 19:18, which we met in Leviticus as part of the holiness code. However, while a number of Old Testament passages describe individuals as hating their enemies or the wicked (e.g., Ps 119:113; 139:21-22), no Old Testament passage commands hatred for one's enemy. Thus, the second command seems to refer to a contemporary Jewish teaching outside the OT.[32]

Jesus goes on to provide his own teaching: "But I tell you, love your enemies and pray for those who persecute you" (Mt 5:44). Why? Because this is how God loves: "He causes his sun to rise on the evil *and* the good, and sends rain on the righteous *and* the unrighteous" (Mt 5:45, emphasis added). Indeed, to love only those who love you is to behave no better than a tax collector or pagan (Mt 5:46-47). God's children must embody a higher sort of love.

Jesus concludes by saying, "Be [*teleioi*], therefore, as your heavenly Father is [*teleios*]" (Mt 5:48). Jesus' words recall YHWH's command in the OT, "Be holy, for I am holy" (Lev 19:2; cf. 11:44-45; 20:26). However, instead of "holy" (*hagios*), Jesus uses the word *teleios* (*teleioi* is the plural). I have left this word untranslated for the moment for two reasons. First, *teleios* is a notoriously difficult word to render adequately in English, and it seems best to acknowledge this up front. Second, leaving *teleios* momentarily untranslated reminds us that whatever virtuous adjective we put here, the command is a rigorous one. "Be good as your heavenly Father is good" or "Be

---

[32]For examples of Jewish teaching on hating one's enemies, see 1QS I, 9-10; IX, 21-22; Josephus, *Jewish War* 2.139; Sifra Qedoshim pereq 4 on Lev 19:18.

kind as your heavenly Father is kind" would be equally challenging. The real difficulty, then, is not *teleios* but the fact that Jesus is commanding his disciples to be like God.

But what does *teleios* mean? We will be meeting this word again in coming chapters, so it is worth spending some time getting to know it here. The foremost lexicon of New Testament Greek gives four senses for *teleios*:[33]

1. Meeting the highest standard ("perfect")
2. Being mature ("full-grown, mature, adult")
3. Being a cult initiate ("initiated")
4. Being fully developed in a moral sense ("perfect, fully developed")

To determine which of these meanings is most likely in Matthew 5:48, we must examine the immediate context and how Matthew uses the word elsewhere. In Matthew 5:48, the comparison to God ("Be [*teleioi*] . . . as your heavenly Father is [*teleios*]") seems to rule out the first three senses above. It is unlikely that Jesus commands his disciples to imitate God's absolute perfection (how could they do so as finite humans?), and to speak of God as mature or a cult initiate simply seems odd. The fourth sense, however, provides an excellent fit. Matthew 5:43-48 is about loving others, a decidedly moral issue, and Jesus here exhorts his disciples to imitate God in loving their enemies, a model of moral completeness that contrasts markedly with the deficient teaching about hating one's enemies.

Matthew 19:21, the only other place where Matthew uses *teleios*, also supports understanding *teleios* in terms of moral completeness. The instance in 19:21 occurs in Jesus' dialogue with the rich young man:

"Teacher, what good thing must I do to get eternal life? . . ."

"If you wish to inherit eternal life, keep the commandments."

---

[33]BDAG, 995-96.

"Which ones? . . ."

"You shall not murder, you shall not commit adultery, you shall not steal, you shall not give false testimony, honor your father and mother, and love your neighbor as yourself."

"All these I have kept." . . . "What do I still lack? . . ."

"If you want to be perfect [*teleios*], go, sell your possessions and give to the poor, and you will have treasure in heaven. Then come, follow me." (Mt 19:16-21)

This is a textbook example of the fourth sense above. In a dialogue about keeping commandments (a moral issue), the man asks, "What do I still lack?" and Jesus replies, "If you want to be [*teleios*] . . ." In other words, if the man wishes to be fully developed (or lacking nothing) in a moral sense, then he must divest himself of his possessions and follow Jesus. Matthew also links this passage with Matthew 5:43-48 by having Jesus quote Leviticus 19:18 ("Love your neighbor as yourself"), the very passage that Jesus begins with in Matthew 5:43, as one of the commandments that the man must keep. (Matthew is the only Gospel writer to do this.)

Teleios in Matthew 5:48 should therefore be understood as "being perfect in the sense of not lacking any moral quality."[34] Jesus is commanding his disciples to imitate God's moral character, particularly in loving even their enemies. However, two questions remain.

First, how should one translate *teleios*? The standard English translation is "perfect" (e.g., ESV, NIV, NLT, NRSV). Yet some interpreters shy away from "perfect" because they wish to avoid the notion of absolute flawlessness, preferring "whole" or "complete" instead.[35] In my view, this is a mistake for two reasons: (1) "Whole" and "complete" cannot bear the moral freight that *teleios* requires here. (2) "Perfect" has a wide range of meanings beyond "flawless." *Merriam-Webster*, for

---

[34]Johannes P. Louw and Eugene A. Nida, eds., *Greek-English Lexicon of the New Testament: Based on Semantic Domains*, 2nd ed. (New York: United Bible Societies, 1989), §88.36.
[35]E.g., Pennington, *Sermon*, 70, 203-4.

example, gives eight general definitions for "perfect," most of them with multiple subcategories. Definition 1a is "being entirely without fault or defect" (the absolute flawlessness that some interpreters are keen to avoid). However, definitions 1b and 3b are "satisfying all requirements" and "lacking in no essential detail," respectively.[36] Either of these would fit *teleios* in Matthew 5:48. Indeed, we use "perfect" to mean something other than "flawless" on a regular basis. "What a perfect baby!" does not communicate that the child is beyond improvement but rather that it is everything that a baby is supposed to be. Similarly, "This has been a perfect evening" does not mean that one's date could not have somehow been better, only that it was everything one had hoped for.

Second, is Jesus' command possible? By framing the Sermon as an invitation to kingdom-oriented living, Jesus implies that the answer is yes; it makes little sense to invite someone into a way of life that they are unable to live. Furthermore, Matthew 5:48 concludes Jesus' teaching on the greater righteousness in relation to the law that is required if one wants to enter the kingdom of heaven, so inasmuch as Jesus thinks that anyone will enter the kingdom of heaven, it must be possible by God's grace.

In sum, while at first glance the Sermon might seem to be an impossible ideal or instructions for the elite, upon closer examination it appears to be something far better: an invitation to a new kind of life—a life lived in light of God's kingdom, a life that looks like Jesus' life. Against this backdrop, the Sermon becomes not a demand but a gift that opens our eyes to the life of flourishing that is possible for those who follow Jesus. And at the center of Jesus' vision for kingdom-oriented life is this command that is also a promise of what can be: "Be perfect . . . as your heavenly Father is perfect," or, as Leviticus put it, "Be holy, for I am holy."[37]

---

[36] *Merriam-Webster's Dictionary*, s.v. "perfect," www.merriam-webster.com/dictionary/perfect.

[37] John Wesley observes that "every command in holy writ is only a covered promise." He goes on to say, "Does he command us then . . . to be 'holy as He is holy?' It is enough: He will work in us this very thing: It shall be unto us according to his word" ("Upon Our Lord's Sermon on the Mount, Discourse 5," *WJW* 5:314). I owe this reference to Murray Vasser.

The greatest commandments (Mk 12:28-34). The sort of perfect love that Jesus commands in Matthew 5:43-48 also figures prominently in his teaching on the greatest commandments. When Jesus disputes with the Sadducees about the resurrection, one of the teachers of the law is impressed with Jesus' answer and asks him, "Of all the commandments, which is the most important?" (Mk 12:28). This is an understandable question. As R. T. France notes, "Given that there are, according to scribal reckoning, 613 separate commandments in the five Books of Moses (R. Simlai [c. 250] in b. Mak. 23b), the question of priority could not be avoided. . . . There was a natural desire for a convenient summary of the law's requirements, a single principle from which all the rest of the Pentateuch was derived."[38]

Jesus answers, "The most important one . . . is this: 'Hear, O Israel: The Lord our God, the Lord is one. Love the Lord your God with all your heart and with all your soul and with all your mind and with all your strength.' The second is this: 'Love your neighbor as yourself.' There is no commandment greater than these" (Mk 12:29-31). Jesus gives the teacher of the law more than he asked for, outlining not only the greatest commandment but also the second greatest commandment. According to Jesus, the greatest commandment is Deuteronomy 6:4-5, which begins the Shema. As we saw earlier in this book, this passage draws together both YHWH's uniqueness that is the foundation of holiness and Israel's undivided devotion to YHWH that is at the heart of what it means for them to be holy. Devout Jews likely recited the Shema twice daily, so Jesus' selection would have been familiar to the teacher of the law.[39] However, whereas Deuteronomy 6:5 mentions three aspects of a person that are to be wholly devoted to YHWH (heart, soul, and strength), Jesus mentions four (heart, soul, mind, and strength). Since the threefold expression in

---

[38]R. T. France, *The Gospel of Mark: A Commentary on the Greek Text*, New International Greek Testament Commentary (Grand Rapids: Eerdmans, 2002), 477, citing Babylonian Talmud Shabbat 31a as an example (cf. Babylonian Talmud Horayot 8a).

[39]For early witnesses to the twice-daily recitation, see Josephus, *Antiquities* 4.212; Letter of Aristeas 160; 1QS X, 10. For the Shema as part of this recitation, see Mishnah Berakhot 1.1-5.

Deuteronomy was already a way of referring to the whole person, this is not a major change, but it may indicate an emphasis on "the intellectual faculty as a key element in God's service."[40] (Indeed, this seems likely given that the questioner is an expert in the law.) Jesus draws his second greatest commandment from Leviticus 19:18, which we saw above both in the holiness code of Leviticus and in Matthew 5:43. Interestingly, both Old Testament passages command not only love but a certain sort of love ("with all your heart . . . soul . . . mind . . . and strength," Deut 6:5; "as yourself," Lev 19:18).

The teacher of the law commends Jesus for his answer (Mk 12:32-33). While Jesus was not the only (or even necessarily the first) Jewish thinker to identify love for God and love for other humans as being particularly important commands,[41] he may well have been the first to make this point by designating Deuteronomy 6:4-5 and Leviticus 19:18 as the two commandments that "the Law and the Prophets hang on" (Mt 22:40).[42] Jesus tells the teacher of the law, "You are not far from the kingdom of God," and Mark concludes by noting that "from then on no one dared ask him any more questions" (Mk 12:34).

Jesus here defines the essence of holiness—the life that God commands—as loving God with everything and loving one's neighbor as oneself. But is such a life possible, or is it merely an ideal to aspire to? As John Oswalt rightly reminds us,

> A commandment assumes the possibility of compliance. Imagine that we are in a tall building and we suddenly see someone falling past an open window. So I shout out the window at the person falling, "Don't hit the sidewalk!" What would you think? At best you would think that

---

[40]France, *Mark*, 480.

[41]See Testament of Dan 5.3; Testament of Issachar 5.2; 7.6; Jubilees 36.7-8; Philo, *On the Special Laws* 2.63; *On the Decalogue* 108-10; 154; *On the Life of Abraham* 208; cited in France, *Mark*, 477.

[42]France comments that "for [Jesus'] explicit linking together of these two very familiar OT texts we have no Jewish precedent" (*Mark*, 477-78).

I had lost my mind. That person cannot help but hit the sidewalk, and it is foolish, if not cruel, to say such a thing to them.[43]

In addition, the Old Testament tells us that some individuals did keep these commandments. The author of 2 Kings notes that king Josiah kept the Shema, saying that he "turned to the LORD— with all his heart and with all his soul and with all his strength, in accordance with all the Law of Moses" (2 Kings 23:25). And the Old Testament contains numerous instances of individuals loving their neighbors (Ruth/Naomi, Boaz/Ruth, etc.). Jesus was certainly aware of such Old Testament examples of obedience, and it seems likely that he would have expected as much or more of his own followers in light of his own life, death, and resurrection and the coming of the Spirit. Therefore, while this all-encompassing love for God and neighbor that Jesus teaches is certainly not easy, it seems that Jesus does envision it as being possible by God's grace.

Jesus' High Priestly Prayer (Jn 17). Holiness and love come together again in Jesus' "High Priestly Prayer" (Jn 17). This prayer concludes the "Farewell Discourse" (Jn 13:31–17:26), where Jesus prepares his disciples for his departure. Jesus begins by praying for himself (Jn 17:1-5) and goes on to pray for his present disciples (Jn 17:6-19) and future disciples (Jn 17:20-26). These latter two sections are particularly important for our purposes, for in them Jesus describes the sort of life he desires for his followers.

Jesus' prayers for his followers focus on two closely related elements: unity and sanctification. In John 17:11, Jesus prays for his present disciples, "Holy Father, protect them by the power of your name, the name you gave me, so that they may be one as we are one." As D. A. Carson comments, "The implication seems to be that various dark forces will strive to break up this unity; and nothing

---

[43]John N. Oswalt, *Called to Be Holy: A Biblical Perspective* (Nappanee, IN: Francis Asbury, 1999), 108.

less than the power of the Father's name—that is, the revealed character of God—is adequate for the task of protection."[44] Jesus provided this protection while he was on earth, but now that he is departing, he requests that the Father protect his disciples so that they may be unified. Jesus elaborates on the nature of this unity in his prayer for his future disciples:

> I pray . . . that all of them may be one, Father, just as you are in me and I am in you. May they also be in us so that the world may believe that you have sent me. I have given them the glory that you gave me, that they may be one as we are one—I in them and you in me—so that they may be brought to complete unity. Then the world will know that you sent me and have loved them even as you have loved me. (Jn 17:20-23)

As in John 17:11, Jesus prays that believers may be one as he and the Father are one. But he also requests that believers may be united to himself and the Father "so that the world may believe that you have sent me" (Jn 17:21). The next two verses seem to explain this statement: Jesus has given believers the glory that the Father gave him; so that they may be one with him, with the Father, and with each other. Scholars dispute the precise nature of this glory, but whatever it is, it enables believers to "participate in that unity [that exists] within the Godhead."[45] Thus, believers can be one with each other because they have been drawn into the life of the triune God. Such unity apparently requires perfecting, for Jesus prays that believers "may be brought to complete unity" (Jn 17:23). The word for "complete" here is *teteleiōmenoi*, a form of the verb *teleioō*, which is related to the word *teleios* discussed above. Jesus' request for complete unity is bold, but it is more than an impossible ideal. As Raymond Brown notes, "Apparently in Johannine thought the

---

[44]D. A. Carson, *The Farewell Discourse and Final Prayer of Jesus: An Exposition of John 14–17* (Grand Rapids, MI: Baker, 1980), 189.

[45]George R. Beasley-Murray, *John*, 2nd ed., Word Biblical Commentary 36 (Waco, TX: Word, 1987), 302.

believers are to be brought to completion as one *in this life*, for this completion is to have an effect on the world."[46]

Jesus also prays that the Father will sanctify his disciples: "Sanctify them by the truth; your word is truth. As you sent me in to the world, I have sent them into the world. For them I sanctify myself, that they too may be truly sanctified" (Jn 17:17-19). The verb for "sanctify" here is *hagiazō*. It is related to the adjective *hagios* ("holy"), which Jesus uses a few verses earlier when he addresses God as "Holy Father" (Jn 17:11). Jesus is therefore asking that the Father make the disciples holy as he is holy. But this sanctification not only makes the disciples like the Father; it also makes them like Jesus. Earlier in John, Jesus describes himself as "the one whom the Father set apart [*hēgiasen*, a form of *hagiazō*] as his very own and sent into the world" (Jn 10:36). Now, Jesus prays for the disciples to be sanctified, and he sends them into the world (cf. Jn 20:21-22). The holiness that Jesus desires for his followers is therefore a consecration to mission that mirrors his own life. Yet Jesus' holy life is not only the model for the life of his disciples; it also constitutes the basis for it: "For them I sanctify myself, that they too may be truly sanctified" (Jn 17:19). "For" translates the Greek *hyper*, which is used elsewhere in John to foreshadow Jesus' sacrificial death (Jn 6:51; 10:11, 15; 11:50-52; 15:13; 18:14). Thus, when Jesus speaks of sanctifying himself, he seems to be referring to his obedient death on the cross, the ultimate act of consecration.[47] And according to Jesus, the goal of his sacrifice is not merely the disciples' initial salvation but also their sanctification.

CONCLUSION

At the beginning of this chapter, I noted that the Old Testament raises a pressing question: Can humans really be holy? The Gospels

---

[46]Raymond E. Brown, *The Gospel According to John (xiii–xxi)*, Anchor Bible 29a (New York: Doubleday, 1970), 771, emphasis original.

[47]Brown, *John (xiii–xxi)*, 766-67; D. A. Carson, *The Gospel According to John* (Grand Rapids, MI: Eerdmans, 1991), 567.

and Acts answer this question with a resounding, "Yes—through the work of Jesus and by the power of the Spirit." Luke presents Jesus as a new Adam who—in contrast to the first Adam—lives a Spirit-initiated and -empowered life that is wholly devoted to God. In Acts, Luke tells how Jesus pours out the Spirit on his disciples and thereby empowers them to live a holy, Jesus-shaped life. Jesus' own words present a similar vision of redeemed humanity. In the Sermon on the Mount, Jesus invites his disciples to live in light of God's coming kingdom—a life that requires self-sacrifice but is nonetheless possible. In Mark 12:28-34, Jesus sums up the Old Testament law (i.e., what it means to be holy) as loving God with everything (Deut 6:4-5) and loving one's neighbor as oneself (Lev 19:18). Finally, in John 17 Jesus prays that his disciples will be one with himself, the Father and each other and will be sanctified for mission like himself. Thus, according to the Gospels and Acts, humans can be holy through the work of Jesus and by the power of the Spirit. In the following two chapters, we will consider how the rest of the New Testament accords with this picture.

5

HOLINESS IN THE LETTERS OF PAUL

PAUL'S LETTERS CONTAIN a wealth of material regarding holiness. Paul uses *hagios* and related words ninety-six times (these make up more than a third of the occurrences in the entire NT),[1] and his favorite word to describe Christians is "the saints" (*hoi hagioi*), which literally means "the holy ones."[2] It is also Paul who speaks of God sanctifying believers "entirely" (1 Thess 5:23 NASB, NRSV).

For many Christians, however, Paul presents some of the most significant biblical challenges to the vision of the Christian life that we have observed in the Gospels and Acts. After all, is it not Paul who declared, "I do not do the good I want to do, but the evil I do not want to do—this I keep on doing" (Rom 7:19) and claimed *not* to be perfect (Phil 3:12 ESV)? In this chapter, I hope to show that Paul presents a view of the Christian life that is remarkably similar to what we have seen in the Gospels and Acts while also answering some of the lingering practical and pastoral questions that these foundational stories do not explicitly address.

---

[1]Paul uses *hagios* ("holy") seventy-six times, *hagiazō* ("to sanctify") nine times, *hagiasmos* ("holiness, sanctification") eight times, and *hagiōsynē* ("holiness") three times.

[2]Rom 1:7; 8:27; 12:13; 15:25-26, 31; 16:2, 15; 1 Cor 1:2; 6:1-2; 14:33; 16:1, 15; 2 Cor 1:1; 8:4; 9:1, 12; 13:13; Eph 1:1, 15, 18; 2:19; 3:8, 18; 4:12; 5:3; 6:18; Phil 1:1; 4:21-22; Col 1:2, 4, 12, 26; 1 Thess 3:13; 2 Thess 1:10; 1 Tim 5:10; Phlm 1:5, 7.

LIFE IN THE SPIRIT (GAL 5:13-26)

We begin our study of Paul with Galatians, which is likely Paul's earliest known letter.[3] From the very first verse, we can tell that something is amiss. Paul introduces himself not only as an "apostle of Christ Jesus" (his normal self-description) but emphasizes that he is "sent not from men nor by a man, but by Jesus Christ and God the Father" (Gal 1:1). And whereas Paul usually opens the body of his letters with thanksgiving,[4] here he begins with a rebuke: "I am astonished that you are so quickly deserting the one who called you to live in the grace of Christ and are turning to a different gospel" (Gal 1:6).

As we read on, it becomes evident that this "different gospel" has to do with relying on the works of the law of Moses (particularly circumcision) for salvation. Paul responds by reminding the Galatians of the true gospel. Central to the gospel is the concept of justification by faith: humans are justified (made right with God) not by works of the law but by faith in Jesus the Messiah. Yet while justification is at the heart of the gospel, it is not the sum total of it. Equally central to the gospel is the new life that justified people get to live in the present. We catch glimpses of this new life throughout the letter, but Paul focuses on it in earnest in Galatians 5:13-26. This passage constitutes one of Paul's earliest descriptions of the Christian life and therefore provides important historical context for interpreting later passages such as Romans 6–8.

Galatians 5:13-26 is familiar to many Christians because it contains the well-known fruit of the Spirit (Gal 5:22-23), which stands in contrast to the works of the flesh (Gal 5:19-21). Paul's basic point in this passage is not hard to grasp: one should avoid the works of the flesh and produce the fruit of the Spirit. But here—as with the Sermon

---

[3]In my view, Paul probably wrote Galatians after his first missionary journey and before the Jerusalem council, as opposed to after the Jerusalem Council. See F. F. Bruce, *The Epistle to the Galatians*, New International Greek Testament Commentary (Grand Rapids, MI: Eerdmans, 1982), 3-18, 43-56.

[4]See 1 Cor 1:4-9; Eph 1:15-23; Phil 1:3-11; Col 1:3-14; 1 Thess 1:2-10; 2 Thess 1:3-4; 2 Tim 1:3-7.

on the Mount in the previous chapter—the frame within which one interprets this passage is extremely important. Is Paul describing an impossible ideal, a command for the elite, or the normative Christian life?

In Galatians 5:13-14, Paul exhorts the Galatians not to use their freedom in Christ to indulge the flesh but rather to love one another, quoting Leviticus 19:18 as a summary of the entire law. But if they refuse to do so, then "watch out," he warns, "or you will be destroyed by each other" (Gal 5:15). Paul then makes a statement that has significant implications for how one interprets the rest of the passage: "But I say, walk by the Spirit, and you will certainly not carry out the desire of the flesh. For the flesh desires against the Spirit, and the Spirit against the flesh; for these are opposed to each other, so that you do not do whatever you want" (Gal 5:16-17).[5]

Paul begins by commanding the Galatians to walk by the Spirit, and he assures them that if they do, they "will certainly not carry out the desire of the flesh" (Gal 5:16). Two points here are key: first, Paul uses the emphatic negative construction in Greek ("certainly not").[6] As Daniel Wallace notes, "This is the strongest way to negate something in Greek."[7] Paul is saying that if the Galatians walk by the Spirit, there is absolutely no possibility that they will fulfill the desire of the flesh. Second, when Paul speaks of "the flesh," he is not talking about the physical body or what is essential to human nature. Rather, he is speaking of the sinful orientation that characterizes much of human existence, a power that opposes and resists God's Spirit.

Paul goes on to say that the flesh and the Spirit are diametrically opposed to each other "so that you do not do whatever you want" (Gal 5:17). But what are these desires ("whatever you want") that the

---

[5]My translation. The discussion below summarizes points that I develop further in Caleb T. Friedeman, "What the Galatians Want: A Fresh Look at ἃ ἐὰν θέλητε in Galatians 5:17," *Journal for the Study of Paul and His Letters* 10 (2020): 181-96.

[6]Greek *ou mē* + aorist subjunctive.

[7]Daniel B. Wallace, *Greek Grammar Beyond the Basics: An Exegetical Syntax of the New Testament* (Grand Rapids, MI: Zondervan, 1996), 468.

flesh-Spirit conflict prevents one from doing?[8] There are four options, each of which results in a very different understanding of this
verse, of the larger passage, and ultimately of the Christian life:

1. "so that you do not do whatever [good and evil things] you want"
2. "so that you do not do whatever [good things] you want"
3. "so that you do not do whatever [evil things] you want"
4. "so that you do not do whatever [neutral things] you want"

On the first view, the mutual opposition of the flesh and the Spirit
results in a stalemate: the believer is caught between the two powers,
unable to cooperate with either. On the second view, the flesh keeps
one from doing the good things of the Spirit. On the third, the Spirit
empowers the believer to do the good and to resist fleshly desires.
The fourth view is what we might call the non-neutrality interpretation: because the flesh and the Spirit are opposed, believers cannot
remain neutral; they must take a side.

What are we to make of all this? As the saying goes, context is king,
and in my view the context clearly supports one of these interpretations
over the others. First, we must recall that in Galatians 5:16 Paul has just
said, "Walk by the Spirit, and you will *certainly not* carry out the desire
of the flesh," and that Galatians 5:17 explains 5:16 ("For . . ."). This seems
to weigh against options 1 and 2 above, for on either of these views
Galatians 5:17 would not explain 5:16 but would contradict it by saying
that the Galatians are prevented from doing the good. Conversely, the
relationship with Galatians 5:16 weighs in favor of options 3 and 4.
Second, Paul concludes the passage by saying, "Those who belong to
Christ Jesus have crucified the flesh with its passions and desires. Since
we live by the Spirit, let us keep in step with the Spirit. Let us not become
conceited, provoking and envying each other" (Gal 5:24-26). Paul
clearly states here that believers have crucified not only the flesh but
also its passions and desires and assumes that believers *do* live by

---

[8]Interpreters also differ as to whether "so that" (*hina*) indicates purpose or result (in my view, it
is the latter). On this point, see Friedeman, "What the Galatians Want," 182-85, 193-94.

the Spirit. Again, this seems to weigh against options 1 and 2 and point us toward options 3 and 4. Third, the Greek verb for "want" in the phrase "whatever you want" is *thelō*, and Paul uses this verb twice elsewhere in Galatians to describe what the Galatians want:

> But formerly, when you did not know God, you were slaves to those that by nature are not gods. But now that you have come to know God, or rather to be known by God, how can you turn back again to the weak and worthless elementary principles, to which you want [*thelete*] to be slaves once again? (Gal 4:8-9)

> Tell me, you want [*thelontes*] to be under the law, do you not listen to the law? (Gal 4:21)[9]

Here, Paul presents the Galatians as wanting (1) to be slaves to the elementary principles that they served as pagans and (2) to be under the law. Clearly, these are not things of the Spirit but things of the flesh. The picture of the Galatians' desires that Paul gives in 4:9 and 4:21 also finds support in the rest of the letter. As noted above, Paul's whole reason for writing the letter is that he is concerned that the Galatians want to follow another gospel that is according to the flesh.

Therefore, what Paul is saying in Galatians 5:16-17 is this: If the Galatians walk by the Spirit, they will certainly not do what the flesh desires. Why? The flesh and the Spirit are opposed to each other so that when the Galatians walk by the Spirit, they do not do the fleshly things that they want. Read within this frame, Galatians 5:13-26 is a potent statement not only about what the Galatians should do but also what they can do by the power of the Spirit. The Galatians are not doomed to be continually caught in a war between the flesh and the Spirit. Rather, by the Spirit's power the Galatians can live godly lives, denying the works of the flesh (Gal 5:19-21) and producing the fruit of the Spirit (Gal 5:22-23), the foremost of which is love (cf. Gal 5:13-14). Paul does not present this new, Spirit-filled life as an optional add-on to the gospel. On the contrary, it is at the heart of the gospel. This is

---

[9]My translations.

the normative Christian life, the way the Christian life is meant to be lived.[10]

God's Will: Your Sanctification (1 Thess)

A few years after he wrote Galatians, Paul penned a very different letter to the Thessalonians. Paul visited Thessalonica during his second missionary journey but had to leave abruptly to escape persecution (Acts 17:1-9; cf. 1 Thess 2:2, 17). Undoubtedly concerned for the Thessalonian believers, Paul sent Timothy back from Athens to check on them (1 Thess 3:1-3; cf. Acts 17:16-34), and Timothy returned with a good report. Paul, probably now in Corinth (Acts 18:5), writes 1 Thessalonians to encourage these new Christians and to instruct them about what God wants to do in their lives. First Thessalonians is particularly relevant to the issue of holiness because Paul here uses *hagios* ("holy") and related words ten times, more frequently (relative to size) than in any of his other letters.[11]

In contrast to Galatians, which began with a rebuke, Paul opens 1 Thessalonians with thanksgiving and prayer for the Thessalonians' exemplary faith. He recalls how they embraced the gospel despite intense suffering (1 Thess 1:4-10; 2:14-16) and "became a model to all the believers in Macedonia and Achaia" (1 Thess 1:7). The Thessalonians have not merely survived; they have thrived, and Paul is brimming with joy because of it.

But while Paul is overjoyed at the Thessalonians' initial response to the gospel, he also wants something more for them. In 1 Thessalonians 3:10-11, he tells them, "Night and day we pray most earnestly that we may see you again and supply what is lacking in your faith. Now may our God and Father himself and our Lord Jesus clear

---

[10]Indeed, Paul states in Galatians 5:21 that those who manifest the acts of the flesh "will not inherit the kingdom of God." For a view of the Christian life that is similar to Gal 5:13-26, see 1 Cor 9:24–10:13, where Paul warns the Corinthians about the dire consequences of sin and presents the Christian life as one of godly discipline and victory over temptation.

[11]See 1 Thess 1:5-6; 3:13; 4:3-4, 7-8; 5:23, 26. *Hagi-* words occur 6.73 times per 1,000 words in 1 Thessalonians. Ephesians (6.60 times) comes in second, and Philemon (5.93 times) third.

the way for us to come to you." But what could possibly be lacking in the Thessalonians' faith? What more could God want for them? "In a word," John Oswalt rightly notes, "it is 'sanctification' or being made holy."[12]

Paul's concern for the Thessalonians' holiness is perhaps most evident in 1 Thessalonians 4:1-8. Paul reminds the believers that he and his companions instructed them about "how to live in order to please God, as in fact you are living," and urges them to do so more and more (1 Thess 4:1). "For you know what instructions we gave you through the Lord Jesus," he says, "for this is the will of God, your sanctification [*hagiasmos*]" (1 Thess 4:2-3 ESV).[13] This last statement is important on two fronts. First, Paul plainly states that sanctification is God's will for the Thessalonians. Second, it is clear in context that this teaching is no optional accessory to the gospel but is part of what Paul and his coworkers originally proclaimed. The Thessalonians have responded well to the gospel so far, living lives that are pleasing to God, but there apparently is further sanctification that God wants to accomplish in their lives. The point that Paul presses on here is sexual purity, exhorting the believers to "abstain from sexual immorality" and to control their own bodies "in holiness [*hagiasmō*] and honor" (1 Thess 4:3-4 ESV). Paul warns the Thessalonians that continuing to sin brings one under the vengeance of God, "For God did not call us for impurity, but in holiness [*en hagiasmō*]. Therefore, the one who rejects this does not reject a human being but God, who gives his Holy [*hagion*] Spirit to you" (1 Thess 4:7-8).[14]

Another area of sanctification that Paul points to is love for others. The Thessalonians are not unloving; on the contrary, Paul praises them for excelling in this area. Yet he exhorts them "to do so more and more"

---

[12]John N. Oswalt, *Called to Be Holy: A Biblical Perspective* (Nappanee, IN: Francis Asbury, 1999), 153.

[13]The NIV obscures the relationship between 4:2 and 4:3 by dropping the "For . . ." (*gar*) at the beginning of 4:3.

[14]My translation.

(1 Thess 4:10; cf. 4:1) and to live a quiet life, minding their own business and working hard as a witness to non-Christians (1 Thess 4:11-12).

Holiness also appears prominently in Paul's closing benediction: "May God himself, the God of peace, sanctify [*hagiasai*] you through and through [*holoteleis*]. May your whole spirit, soul, and body be kept blameless at the coming of our Lord Jesus Christ. The one who calls you is faithful, and he will do it" (1 Thess 5:23-24).

The Greek word here translated "through and through" is *holotelēs*, which occurs only once in the entire New Testament. It means "being totally complete, with implication of meeting a high standard,"[15] and could also be translated as "completely" or "entirely." (The phrase "entire sanctification" comes from this verse.) By using it here, Paul seems to emphasize two things: (1) the scope of sanctification—God sanctifies the whole person, "spirit, soul, and body" (1 Thess 5:24); (2) the degree of sanctification—God makes us morally complete, or "blameless" (1 Thess 5:24). Notice that here the emphasis falls on *God*. Paul certainly believes that humans must respond to grace (otherwise, why write the letter?), but sanctification is ultimately not something that the Thessalonians do for themselves. It is the work of God, the holy One who makes people holy.

When will God accomplish this entire sanctification? One might be tempted to answer, "Not until Christ returns." Paul, however, seems to expect such sanctification in the present. Two factors point in this direction. First, Paul tends to use "may . . ." sayings of this sort to express present-oriented prayers or wishes. Earlier in 1 Thessalonians, for example, he says, "Now may our God and Father himself and our Lord Jesus clear the way for us to come to you. May the Lord make your love increase and overflow for each other and for everyone else, just as ours does for you" (1 Thess 3:11-12).[16] Paul

---

[15]BDAG, 704.

[16]The verbs translated as "may . . ." here and in 1 Thess 5:23 are in the optative mood. For further examples of the optative in Pauline prayers or wishes, see Rom 15:5, 13; 2 Thess 2:16-17; 3:5, 16; 2 Tim 1:16, 18; 4:16.

here seems to voice desires for the present age, not merely for the age to come, and one would need clear contextual indicators to limit such a request to the future. One might point to Paul's mention of Christ's coming in 1 Thessalonians 5:23. Yet this leads us to the second point—namely, that Paul seems to expect God to sanctify entirely not at Christ's coming, but so that believers are ready at Christ's coming. Note that the second request (which seems to explain the first) is, "May your whole spirit, soul and body be kept blameless at the coming of our Lord Jesus Christ" (1 Thess 5:23). Paul wants the Thessalonians to be *kept* blameless, not *made* blameless, at Jesus' coming. His request, in other words, is that the Thessalonians would be made blameless now and preserved that way until Jesus' return. So when Paul says, "The one who calls you is faithful, and *he will do it*" (1 Thess 5:24, emphasis added), he seems to mean that God will sanctify the Thessalonians entirely and make them blameless in the present age.

First Thessalonians therefore presents a vision of the Christian life that is remarkably similar to what we find in Galatians, with some noteworthy accents. The Thessalonians (unlike the Galatians) are exemplary Christians, and while Paul rejoices in their faith, he also emphasizes that the Christian life is not merely about one's initial response to the gospel; God desires to sanctify believers—not just partially, but entirely. The work that God has begun in the Thessalonians, he wants to do "more and more" (1 Thess 4:1, 10), so that eventually they may be sanctified "through and through" (1 Thess 5:23). This glorious vision is encouraging, but as Oswalt notes, it is also challenging:

> There is no excuse for anyone to say, "Oh well, I just don't think I can live up to a standard like that." Of course we can't; the whole Old Testament teaches us that. But that is not the point. The point is: does God want to do this in us? Surely the answer is yes. And is he able to do it? Again the answer is yes. But now comes the frightening caveat. Yes, he is able to do what he wants if we will believe him to do it. Tragically, there are many people today who simply will not believe God to make them holy. That is what Paul was afraid might happen to the

Thessalonians, and that is why his longing was so intense to tell them about the wonderful possibilities that are already theirs in Christ.[17]

First Thessalonians thus leaves us with a pressing question: Are we willing to trust God's vision for our lives more than we trust our own?

LIFE IN THE SPIRIT, REVISITED (ROM 6–8)

Robert Louis Stevenson's *Dr. Jekyll and Mr. Hyde* tells the tragic story of Henry Jekyll, a respected scientist who becomes distraught at the war between good and evil that rages within himself. The truth, Dr. Jekyll says, is "that man is not truly one, but truly two."[18] He decides that the solution is to split the good and evil parts of himself into separate identities so that each self can pursue its desires unencumbered by the other. He creates a potion for this purpose, but instead of neatly separating his good and evil natures, the potion transforms him into the wholly evil Edward Hyde, and its antidote produces the still-conflicted Henry Jekyll. To make matters worse, Hyde gradually begins to take over, to the point that Jekyll can no longer control him. Jekyll determines that the only way out is death, and the book concludes with his confession, which turns out to be a suicide note.

Dr. Jekyll and Mr. Hyde is a classic because it captures so vividly something that everyone has felt quite viscerally: the internal struggle between good and evil. We know all too well the feeling that "there is within us a grotesque heart of darkness that we are not able to control."[19] For many of us, this inner battle is so deeply ingrained on our hearts and minds that it is difficult to imagine life—even life as a Christian—any other way. After all, doesn't Paul describe his own Christian life in this way?

---

[17]Oswalt, *Called to Be Holy*, 159.
[18]Robert Louis Stevenson, *The Strange Case of Dr. Jekyll and Mr. Hyde* (New York: Bantam, 2004), 65.
[19]Ernest O'Neill, "Dr. Jekyll and Mr. Hyde," unpublished sermon manuscript, www.worldinvisible .com/avlib/transcripts/ps098.htm.

We know that the law is spiritual; but I am unspiritual, sold as a slave to sin. I do not understand what I do. For what I want to do I do not do, but what I hate I do. And if I do what I do not want to do, I agree that the law is good. As it is, it is no longer I myself who do it, but it is sin living in me. For I know that good itself does not dwell in me, that is, in my sinful nature. For I have the desire to do what is good, but I cannot carry it out. For I do not do the good I want to do, but the evil I do not want to do—this I keep on doing. Now if I do what I do not want to do, it is no longer I who do it, but it is sin living in me that does it.

So I find this law at work: Although I want to do good, evil is right there with me. For in my inner being I delight in God's law; but I see another law at work in me, waging war against the law of my mind and making me a prisoner of the law of sin at work within me. What a wretched man I am! Who will rescue me from this body that is subject to death? Thanks be to God, who delivers me through Jesus Christ our Lord!

So then, I myself in my mind am a slave to God's law, but in my sinful nature a slave to the law of sin. (Rom 7:14-25)

Interestingly, this passage probably served as Stevenson's inspiration for *Dr. Jekyll and Mr. Hyde*.[20] Like Stevenson's novel, it strikes a chord within us, but now with a ring of scriptural authority. Paul here speaks in the first person ("I") and uses present-tense verbs to describe an inability to do the good or avoid the evil. Paul, in other words, is Jekyll and Hyde. What could be clearer? And if this was the Christian experience of the apostle Paul, what hope do you and I have to be any better? Romans 7 thus seems to constitute an insurmountable obstacle to the idea that Christians can live holy lives.

The view of Romans 7 that I have just described is very popular. Indeed, for many Christians it is simply common sense. Some readers may therefore be surprised to hear that the vast majority of

---

[20]Larry Kreitzer, "R. L. Stevenson's *Strange Case of Dr. Jekyll and Mr. Hyde* and Romans 7:14-25: Images of the Moral Duality of Human Nature," *Journal of Literature and Theology* 6 (1992): 130-33. Kreitzer notes that Stevenson (1) grew up in a Scottish Calvinist home, (2) alludes to Paul's letters several times in *Dr. Jekyll and Mr. Hyde*, and (3) mentions "the war in the members" (Rom 7:23) in connection with Jekyll in one of his letters.

early Christian interpreters did *not* read Romans 7 as a description of Paul's Christian life. As Thomas McCall points out, "Classical Christian exegesis has largely veered away from such an interpretation," noting that "Irenaeus, Origen, Tertullian, Basil, Theodoret, Chrysostom, Jerome, Ambrose, Cyril of Jerusalem, [and] Macarius, among many others, have not understood Paul to be referring to his own Christian experience."[21] Similarly, Gerald Bray acknowledges that "most of the Fathers believed that here Paul was adopting the persona of an unregenerate man, not describing his own struggles as a Christian. As far as they were concerned, becoming a Christian would deliver a person from the kind of dilemma that the apostle is outlining here."[22]

Modern New Testament scholarship has largely seconded this early Christian consensus. According to Craig Keener, "The majority of scholars today . . . contend that [Rom 7:14-25] cannot refer to the Christian life."[23] Of course, this ancient and modern consensus does not settle the matter; majority views can be wrong. But it should make us question whether it is self-evident that Paul is speaking about his Christian experience in Romans 7:14-25. It should also make us ask what these church fathers and New Testament scholars are seeing that so many of us do not.

To answer this question, we need to take a step back and view Romans 7 within its larger context. In the first five chapters of the book of Romans, Paul outlines humanity's problem (all have sinned, Rom 1:18–3:20), God's solution (justification by faith in Christ, Rom 3:21–4:25), and its implications (peace with God, new life in Christ, Rom 5:1-21). In Romans 6 Paul addresses a pressing question

---

[21]Thomas H. McCall, *Against God and Nature: The Doctrine of Sin*, Foundations of Evangelical Theology (Wheaton, IL: Crossway, 2019), 365, citing Thomas C. Oden, *Life in the Spirit*, vol. 3, *Systematic Theology* (New York: HarperCollins, 1994), 245-46.

[22]Gerald Bray, ed., *Romans*, Ancient Christian Commentary on Scripture 6 (Downers Grove, IL: IVP Academic, 1998), 189-90. I owe this reference to McCall, *Against God and Nature*, 366.

[23]Craig S. Keener, *The Mind of the Spirit: Paul's Approach to Transformed Thinking* (Grand Rapids, MI: Baker Academic, 2016), 58 (citing extensive bibliography in 58n29).

raised by the preceding chapters: "What shall we say, then? Shall we go on sinning so that grace may increase?" (Rom 6:1). Here Paul seems to imagine someone hearing what he has said about God's grace in Romans 1–5 (especially Rom 5:20-21) and saying something like this: "So since salvation is by grace through faith and God has plenty of grace to give, I can sin boldly, right?" Paul responds, "By no means!" The Greek phrase here, *mē genoito*, "has the force of abhorrence"[24] and is translated variously as "May it never be!" (NASB), "Absolutely not!" (CSB), and "God forbid" (KJV). Paul is repulsed by the thought that someone might use his gospel as license to sin.

Paul goes on to explain why it is that Christians must not keep on sinning:

> We are those who have died to sin; how can we live in it any longer? Or don't you know that all of us who were baptized into Christ Jesus were baptized into his death? We were therefore buried with him through baptism into death in order that, just as Christ was raised from the dead through the glory of the Father, we too may live a new life. For if we have been united with him in a death like his, we will certainly also be united with him in a resurrection like his. For we know that our old self was crucified with him so that the body ruled by sin might be done away with, that we should no longer be slaves to sin—because anyone who has died has been set free from sin. (Rom 6:2-7)

The theological term for this is *union with Christ*. Through baptism (a symbolic identification with Jesus' death and resurrection), believers have been united to Jesus so that what is true of Jesus is true of them. Jesus "died to sin" and "lives to God" (Rom 6:10) so believers must "count [them]selves dead to sin but alive to God in Christ Jesus" (Rom 6:11). Keener notes,

> Eleven times Paul speaks of God "reckoning" [or "counting"] righteousness to someone's account in chapter 4. In 6:11, however, he summons believers to *agree* with God's perspective; as God has

---

[24]Wallace, *Greek Grammar*, 481.

"reckoned" righteousness to them, they must reckon themselves righteous. They are righteous because they are in Christ, in whom they both died to their identity as sinners in Adam and were raised to a new master, God.[25]

In short, God has given believers a new identity in Christ, and believers must live in light of this reality. Before they knew Christ, they were "under the law" (Rom 6:14), "slaves to sin" (Rom 6:17, 20), and "free from the control of righteousness" (Rom 6:22). But now, they are "not under the law but under grace" (Rom 6:15), "set free from sin" (Rom 6:18, 22), and "slaves to righteousness/God" (Rom 6:18-19, 22). Because of their new identity in Christ, believers are both *able* not to sin and *must* not sin, for to continue sinning would be inconsistent with who they are now.

In Romans 7, Paul turns his attention to the law (i.e., the law of Moses). He begins by explaining that Christians have been freed from the law (Rom 7:1-6). Just as a married woman is bound to her husband by the law as long as he is alive but is released from that law when her husband dies, so believers have "died to the law through the body of Christ" (Rom 7:4). Before, "the sinful passions aroused by the law were at work in us" (Rom 7:5), but now believers "have been released from the law so that we might serve in the new way of the Spirit" (Rom 7:6).

But this raises a further question: "Is the law then sinful?" As in Romans 6:2, Paul responds, "Certainly not [*mē genoito*]!" (Rom 7:7). It is at this point that Paul begins using the first person:

> Nevertheless, I would not have known what sin was had it not been for the law. For I would not have known what coveting really was if the law had not said, "You shall not covet." But sin, seizing the opportunity afforded by the commandment, produced in me every kind of coveting. For apart from the law, sin was dead. Once I was alive apart from the law; but when the commandment came, sin sprang to life and I died. I found that the very commandment that was intended to bring life actually brought death. (Rom 7:7-10)

---

[25]Craig S. Keener, *Romans*, New Covenant Commentary Series 6 (Eugene, OR: Wipf & Stock, 2009), 81, emphasis original.

Paul goes on to conclude that "the law is holy, and the commandment is holy, righteous, and good" (Rom 7:12). The problem, therefore, is not the law, but sin. The law, a written record of God's will, exposes humans' sinful nature. But the law can only identify the problem, not solve it. So sin—corrupted human nature—seizes the opportunity provided by the law and disobeys God "more knowingly, rendering sin the more heinous and the sinner the more culpable."[26] In Romans 7:14-25, Paul goes on to describe the unenviable life of someone who knows the good but, due to the influence of the flesh, does not do it. We will return to this passage momentarily.

Paul brings his argument to a stunning climax in Romans 8:

> Therefore, there is now no condemnation for those who are in Christ Jesus, because through Christ Jesus the law of the Spirit who gives life has set you free from the law of sin and death. For what the law was powerless to do because it was weakened by the flesh, God did by sending his own Son in the likeness of sinful flesh to be a sin offering. And so he condemned sin in the flesh, in order that the righteous requirement of the law might be fully met in us, who do not live according to the flesh but according to the Spirit. (Rom 8:1-4)

According to Paul, Christ and the Spirit provide the answer to the dilemma of Romans 7. Through Christ's death on the cross, God condemned sin and nullified the law's claim on those who by faith are united to Christ. Believers are therefore under a new law—the law of the Spirit, who (unlike the law of Moses) gives life and empowers believers to meet the "righteous requirement of the law" (Rom 8:4). "Those who are in the realm of the flesh cannot please God," Paul says, but believers "are not in the realm of the flesh but are in the realm of the Spirit" (Rom 8:8-9).

With this context in hand, let us now return to Romans 7:14-25: Who is this Jekyll-and-Hyde character that Paul is describing? Three factors suggest that in this passage Paul does not intend to describe his

---

[26]Keener, *Romans*, 90.

(or anyone else's) Christian experience. First, in Romans 7:1-6 (which introduces Rom 7:7-25), Paul teaches that it is unbelievers, not believers, who are under the law. Romans 7:5-6 state this plainly: "For when we were in the realm of the flesh, the sinful passions aroused by the law were at work in us, so that we bore fruit for death. But now, by dying to what once bound us, we have been released from the law so that we serve in the new way of the Spirit, and not in the old way of the written code." As Keener says, Paul here "lays out the contrast that he will develop between life under the law and death in the flesh (Rom 7:7-25; as in Rom 7:5), and life in the Spirit (Rom 8:1-17; as in Rom 7:6)."[27] By introducing Romans 7:7-25 in this way, Paul provides the reader with sufficient cues to determine that the life described in this passage is that of a non-Christian.

Second, the way that Paul describes the anguished "I" in Romans 7:14-25 is precisely the opposite of how he describes believers in Romans 6 and 8.

Table 5.1. The "I" of Romans 7:14-25 compared with believers in Romans 6 and 8.[28]

"I" (Rom 7:14-25)	Believers (Rom 6 and 8)
of the flesh (7:14 ESV) nothing good dwells in me, that is, in my flesh (7:18 ESV)	not in the realm of the flesh but . . . in the realm of the Spirit (8:9)
sold as a slave to sin (7:14)	those who have died to sin (6:2) no longer . . . slaves to sin (6:6) set free from sin (6:7) sin shall no longer be your master (6:14) set free from sin . . . slaves to righteousness (6:18) set free from sin . . . slaves to God (6:22)
what I want to do I do not do, but what I hate I do (7:15) I do not do the good I want to do, but the evil I do not want to do—this I keep on doing (7:19)	[God] condemned sin in the flesh, in order that the righteous requirement of the law might be fully met in us, who do not live according to the flesh, but according to the Spirit (8:3-4)
good itself does not dwell in me (7:17) sin . . . dwells in me (7:20 ESV)	the Spirit of God dwells in you (8:9) his Spirit . . . dwells in you (8:11)
prisoner of the law of sin (7:23) in my sinful nature a slave to the law of sin (7:25)	set . . . free from the law of sin and death (8:2)

---

[27] Keener, *Romans*, 86.

[28] Adapted from Hae-Kyung Chang, "The Christian Life in a Dialectical Tension? Romans 7:7-25 Reconsidered," *Novum Testamentum* 49 (2007): 273; Keener, *Romans*, 92.

Hae-Kyung Chang rightly notes that the differences between how Paul portrays the "I" and believers are "diametrical contrasts"; they are not two ways of describing the same person.[29] Paul gives us no reason to think that one can be simultaneously "of the flesh" and "not in the realm of the flesh," "a slave to sin" and "set free from sin," and so on. The "I" of Romans 7:14-25 therefore is not, and cannot be, a Christian.

Third, to interpret Romans 7:14-25 as Christian experience would require Paul to directly contradict what he said in Galatians. As we saw above, in Galatians 5:16-17 Paul exhorts the Galatian Christians to "walk by the Spirit" and assures them that if they do, then the Spirit will empower them to deny the flesh so that they do not do whatever fleshly things they want. The "I" of Romans 7:14-25, however, wants to do the good but is not able to (Rom 7:18-19). So unless Paul in Romans is reversing the view of the Christian life that he put forth in Galatians (which seems unlikely), Romans 7:14-25 must depict a non-Christian life.

The contextual evidence therefore weighs heavily against interpreting Romans 7:14-25 as Christian experience. A few questions, however, remain: first, why does Paul use "I" if he is not talking about himself? Paul is likely speaking in character, taking on the persona of someone else in the service of his argument. This practice, sometimes called *prosopopoeia*, was a well-known device in ancient rhetoric.[30] Second, why does Paul use present-tense verbs? Paul probably does this to add vividness and intensity; "I did not do the good I wanted to do, but the evil I did not want to do—this I kept on doing" simply does not carry the same force. Indeed, Paul uses "I" with present-tense verbs elsewhere "to describe the general human condition prior to faith or in some prior situation" (Rom 3:7; Gal 2:18).[31] Third, how does the interpretation I am recommending

---

[29]Chang, "Christian Life," 273.
[30]Keener, *Mind of the Spirit*, 68-69.
[31]Oden, *Life in the Spirit*, 245.

make sense of Romans 7:24-25? "What a wretched man I am! Who will rescue me from this body that is subject to death? Thanks be to God, who delivers me through Jesus Christ our Lord! So then, I myself in my mind am a slave to God's law, but in my sinful nature a slave to the law of sin."

Paul's exclamation in Romans 7:25 should be understood as an interjection that answers the question of Romans 7:24 by anticipating the argument of Romans 8. Paul then concludes in Romans 7:25 by summing up the plight of the "I."[32]

But if Paul is not describing Christian experience in Romans 7:14-25, then who is he describing? Interpreters have proposed a variety of options, including Paul before Christ, a generic human, Adam, and Israel.[33] In my view, the most likely interpretation is that Paul is retrospectively describing his pre-Christian experience under the law.[34] The tortured existence of the "I" is what Paul sees when he looks back at his life before Christ. But this is not the life that he now lives in Christ and by the Spirit—that is the life depicted in Romans 6 and 8. Yet whichever one of these interpretations one takes, what is clear is that the life depicted in Romans 7:14-25 is not a Christian life.

I suspect that the real reason that the Christian-life interpretation of Romans 7:14-25 is so popular is that, frankly, this is how many Christians often feel. What would Paul say to this? First, as we saw in Galatians 5:13-26, there is a difference between having a sinful desire and indulging it. To be a Christian does not mean to be immune from temptation but to deny the flesh by the power of the Spirit when temptation comes. Some of us who tend toward self-condemnation may need to remind ourselves of this fact. Second,

---

[32]Ben Witherington III and Darlene Hyatt, *Paul's Letter to the Romans: A Socio-Rhetorical Commentary* (Grand Rapids, MI: Eerdmans, 2004); Keener, *Mind of the Spirit*, 60.

[33]Keener, *Mind of the Spirit*, 66-74; Douglas J. Moo, *The Letter to the Romans*, 2nd ed., New International Commentary on the New Testament (Grand Rapids, MI: Eerdmans, 2018), 449-51.

[34]It is true that Paul elsewhere describes his pre-Christian experience more positively (Gal 1:13-14; Phil 3:4-6). But as Keener notes, "Those contexts describe Paul's status or outwardly observable characteristics. Here, by contrast, if Paul addresses his pre-Christian existence at all, he is providing a retrospective view of its spiritual inadequacy" (*Mind of the Spirit*, 61; cf. Moo, *Romans*, 474).

Paul does not teach that one must exhibit flawless performance to be a Christian; otherwise, his letters to the Galatians and the Corinthians would have been much briefer: "Dearly beloved, you messed up. I regret to inform you that you are no longer Christians. Sincerely, Paul." So if we do sin, we should repent, remind ourselves of our identity in Christ, and renew our life in the Spirit. But this is much different from condoning sin as normative Christian experience.

The Jekyll-and-Hyde life, then, is not the Christian life. On the contrary, it is the life that Christ died to deliver us from. But if Stevenson's novel does not provide a blueprint for Christian existence, it does offer an important insight: the only solution to the problem of Jekyll and Hyde is death. The death that is needed, however, is not the self-destructive death of Dr. Jekyll's sort but the death of Christ for our sins and the death of our old self with him. And as Paul teaches in Romans 6, we who are united with Christ in death are also united with him in his resurrection life by the power of the Spirit.

Not Perfected Yet Perfect? (Phil 3:12-15)

Paul's letter to the Philippians sheds further light on Paul's understanding of the Christian life. Paul probably wrote this letter around AD 60–62 during his first imprisonment in Rome (Phil 1:7, 13-14, 17; 4:22; cf. Acts 28:14-31). Despite his sufferings, Paul rejoices because Christ is being proclaimed and because he trusts that things will turn out for his deliverance (Phil 1:18-19). "Whatever happens," he tells the Philippians, "conduct yourselves in a manner worthy of the gospel of Christ" (Phil 1:27). This means, among other things, that the Philippians must "stand firm in the one Spirit, striving together as one for the faith of the gospel without being frightened in any way by those who oppose you" (Phil 1:27-28).

Paul discusses these opponents in more detail in Philippians 3:1–4:1. Like the proponents of the "other gospel" in Galatians, the Philippians' adversaries seem to be requiring people to observe the law of Moses (especially circumcision for males) if they wish to be saved.

Paul, however, contends that "it is we who are the circumcision, we who serve God by his Spirit, who boast in Christ Jesus, and put no confidence in the flesh" (Phil 3:3). He rehearses his own reasons for putting confidence in the flesh but declares that he now considers these and all other things "a loss because of the surpassing worth of knowing Christ Jesus" (Phil 3:8). Paul says he does not want a righteousness that comes from the law but a righteousness that depends on faith in Jesus, "that I may know him and the power of his resurrection, and may share his sufferings, becoming like him in his death, that by any means possible I may attain the resurrection from the dead" (Phil 3:10-11). Paul goes on:

> Not that I have already obtained this or am already perfect, but I press on to make it my own, because Christ Jesus has made me his own. Brothers, I do not consider that I have made it my own. But one thing I do: forgetting what lies behind and straining forward to what lies ahead, I press on toward the goal for the prize of the upward call of God in Christ Jesus. Let those of us who are mature think this way, and if in anything you think otherwise, God will reveal that also to you. (Phil 3:12-15 ESV)

If a certain reading of Romans 7 constitutes the most common Pauline objection to the idea that Christians can be holy, a certain reading of Philippians 3:12 comes in as a close second. "I'm not perfect, just forgiven," many Christians say, citing Paul as precedent. As with Romans 7, this interpretation seems self-evident: Paul clearly states that he is not perfect. Why should we expect to do any better?

The problem with this view is that it fails to take account of the Greek in Philippians 3:12 and 3:15. The verb that Paul uses in Philippians 3:12 to say that he is not already perfect is *teleioō*, which is related to the adjective *teleios* that we met in Matthew 5:48. But a few verses later, Paul states that he and others *are* in fact *teleios*: "Let those of *us* who are *teleioi* [the plural of *teleios*] think this way" (Phil 3:15). How do we make sense of this? The ESV and many other English versions sidestep the issue by translating *teleioō* as "be perfect" and *teleios* as "mature." Yet this obscures Paul's wordplay on the *telei-* root. A far simpler solution is that "Paul is speaking about two levels of perfection."[35] Paul is not perfect in that he has not yet reached the absolute perfection that will come with the resurrection (Phil 3:11). Yet he and other Christians are perfect in that they are fully developed in a moral sense; they lack nothing in their response to the gospel.[36] However, this latter sort of perfection is not a static, glass-ceiling sort of existence where one is beyond improvement; even though Paul is *teleios*, he is still "straining forward to what lies ahead" (Phil 3:13) and exhorts those who are *teleioi* to "live up to what we have already attained" (Phil 3:16). Thus, the perfection that Paul claims for himself and others in the present is a dynamic state of moral completeness that both comes through and is sustained by constant relationship with the *teleios* One.

Paul's motto for the Christian life, therefore, is not, "I'm not perfect, just forgiven," but, "I'm not the resurrection sort of perfect, but I am the morally complete sort of perfect, and becoming more so every day." That sort of Christian life will not fit on a bumper sticker, but it will (like Paul's life) transform the world for Christ.

Holiness and Grace in Paul

Paul's vision of the Christian life is challenging. For some readers, it may sound exhausting, intimidating, or even discouraging. Holiness, after all, sounds like so much work! And isn't Paul the apostle of grace—the idea that salvation is a free gift? How, then, is holiness not just another version of salvation by works? Here I offer two points to address these concerns.

First, we need to make sure that our understanding of grace aligns with that of Paul. Grace is a way of talking about the gift of God, and

---

[35]Oswalt, *Called to Be Holy*, 142. Neither "mature" nor "complete" provides a good fit for both Philippians 3:12 and 3:15.

[36]For other passages where Paul uses *teleios* of believers, see 1 Cor 2:6; 14:20; Eph 4:13; Col 1:28; 4:12.

many of us in the modern world assume that a gift is a gift because it "escapes reciprocity," that is, it expects and receives nothing in return.[37] With this mindset, it is easy for us to think that when Paul says something like, "For it is by grace you have been saved, through faith—and this is not from yourselves, it is the gift of God—not by works, so that no one can boast" (Eph 2:8-9), he means that salvation is a gift that God gives while expecting nothing in return. However, this is almost certainly not how Paul or his original readers would have understood the statement. In Paul's Greco-Roman world, gifts were typically given to create relationships between people and expected some return (often gratitude or loyalty).[38] And more important, this does not seem to be how Paul develops his concept of grace. In his groundbreaking study *Paul and the Gift*, John Barclay demonstrates that for Paul the central feature of God's grace is not non-reciprocity, but *incongruity*: God gives without regard for the worth of the recipient.[39] So when Paul says that salvation is by grace through faith and not by works, he is not saying that no response is required but that God graciously gives us something that we neither deserve nor could earn with no regard for our worthiness (i.e., there is nothing we did or could do to merit God's favor). Good works, our grateful response to God's gift, are therefore not opposed to grace but are its intended goal. This is why Paul can go on to say in Ephesians 2:10, "For we are God's handiwork, created in Christ Jesus to do good works, which God prepared in advance for us to do." Holiness, then, is not opposed to grace but is the appropriate and expected response to it.

Second, we must not forget the Holy Spirit. For Paul, it is not as if God graciously justifies us and then in effect says, "Now you're on

---

[37]John M. G. Barclay, *Paul and the Gift* (Grand Rapids, MI: Eerdmans, 2015), 74.

[38]David A. deSilva, "Patronage," in *Dictionary of New Testament Background*, ed. Craig A. Evans and Stanley E. Porter, IVP Dictionary 5 (Downers Grove, IL: IVP Academic, 2000), 766-71; David A. deSilva, *Honor, Patronage, Kinship and Purity: Unlocking New Testament Culture* (Downers Grove, IL: IVP Academic, 2000), 121-56; Barclay, *Paul and the Gift*, 24-51, 74-75.

[39]Barclay, *Paul and the Gift*, esp. 72-73 (definition of incongruity), 562-74 (conclusions).

your own—be holy." To borrow Paul's phrase, *mē genoito*! As Paul teaches in Galatians 5:13-26 and Romans 8, those who belong to Christ have received the Holy Spirit, who works in them to produce good fruit. Of course, the Spirit does not manipulate us like puppets, forcing us to be holy against our wills. Believers have the grace-given responsibility to "walk by the Spirit" (Gal 5:16), allowing the Spirit (not the flesh) to guide their actions. And when we do so, the Spirit gives us ample power to resist the desires of the flesh (Gal 5:17).

But how does one live this Spirit-empowered life? Does one just strain or strive more? No, at least not in the usual sense of those words. Perhaps an illustration will help. When I was in high school, I was the lead singer for my church's youth band and Saturday night service. However, while I could usually hit the notes more or less on pitch, I sensed that I was working too hard at it. I would often leave rehearsals and services with my voice feeling scratchy and fatigued. So, when I went to college, I decided to take voice lessons so that I could lead worship with more ease. After one semester, I was hooked—so much so that I ended up minoring in voice. I could now sing both higher and lower than before, my voice was richer and more powerful, and although I was singing music that was far more difficult, my voice was actually less tired. What changed? In essence, I got out of the way and let the breath do what it was supposed to do. You see, the best singers do not strain; they allow the breath to flow through them, producing beautiful sound. This requires one to be intentional in controlling one's breath with the diaphragm, but good singers actually sing much more easily than bad ones, who try to control the sound with their jaw, tongue, and so on. Similarly, living by the Spirit does not mean simply straining or striving harder to be holy; it means allowing the Spirit of God to flow through us, pro-ducing holiness.[40] To be sure, this requires agency on our part, but the effort is in getting ourselves out of the way and letting go, not in

---

[40]In Scripture, both the Hebrew and Greek words for "Spirit" (*ruah* and *pneuma*, respectively) can also mean "wind" or "breath."

gritting our teeth and grasping harder. Holiness does not mean constantly straining and striving in the flesh but constantly submitting and surrendering to the Spirit.

CONCLUSION

In sum, Paul presents holiness as the normative Christian life. Of course, believers may sin and fail (as the Galatians apparently did), but this is not necessary, and it should certainly not be the norm. According to Paul, to live as a Christian means to walk by the Spirit, denying the desires of the flesh and producing the fruit of the Spirit (Gal 5:13-26). In 1 Thessalonians, Paul presents sanctification as God's will for every believer and as a work that God can do "entirely" (1 Thess 4:3; 5:23). Romans 6–8 expounds the Jesus-shaped and Spirit-empowered life of the believer in contrast to the Jekyll-and-Hyde existence of the non-Christian under the law. In Philippians, Paul presents himself and other believers as perfect, not in the sense of absolute flawlessness but in the sense of moral completeness. Therefore, for Paul as for the Gospels and Acts, the holy life is the way that the Christian life is meant to be lived, our appropriate response to God's grace as we allow the Spirit to flourish in us and flow through us.

6

HOLINESS IN THE GENERAL EPISTLES AND REVELATION

THE GENERAL EPISTLES and Revelation are often neglected within the New Testament canon. Having dealt with Jesus and Paul on a given topic, many biblical scholars and theologians are content to label the case as closed and move on to the next issue. To further complicate matters, these last nine books of the New Testament are quite diverse in style and content, and we have no idea who wrote at least one of them (Hebrews). Nevertheless, to leave these nine writings (a third of the books in the New Testament) to the side would be a mistake, for they have much to teach us, and this is particularly true when it comes to the issue of holiness. Indeed, these books present some of the strongest biblical support for the idea that Christians can live holy lives, and the varied language that their authors use to describe holiness helps to further expand our vocabulary for talking about holiness beyond *holy* and related words. To explore the theme of holiness in every one of these books would be far too much for a single chapter, so here we will focus on five of them: Hebrews, James, 1 Peter, 1 John, and Revelation.

HEBREWS: GO ON TO PERFECTION

Hebrews has been aptly described as "the book of better things."[1] The whole letter is built on a lesser-to-greater argument: the Levitical priesthood and the old covenant that it administered were good (a shadow of things to come), but Jesus (the great high priest) and the new covenant that he has established by sacrificing himself are better (the reality). The author articulates this relationship between the old and the new in the opening verses:

> In the past God spoke to our ancestors through the prophets at many times and in various ways, but in these last days he has spoken to us by his Son, whom he appointed heir of all things, and through whom also he made the universe. The Son is the radiance of God's glory and the exact representation of his being, sustaining all things by his powerful word. After he had provided purification for sins, he sat down at the right hand of the Majesty in heaven. So he became as much superior to the angels as the name he has inherited is superior to theirs. (Heb 1:1-4)

Hebrews does not denigrate the Old Testament. On the contrary, it treats the utterances of the prophets as God's own speech, and throughout the letter the author shows that the Old Testament points forward to and anticipates Jesus (sometimes in surprising ways, e.g., Heb 10:5-7). But while God spoke through the prophets "in the past . . . to our ancestors," "in these last days" he has spoken "to us by his Son." Jesus is God's climactic revelation, greater than the prophets and greater than the angels, who were thought to have mediated God's revelation at Mount Sinai (cf. Heb 2:2).[2]

With great revelation, however, comes great responsibility. After demonstrating the Son's superiority to the angels (Heb 1:5-14), the author declares,

---

[1] Karen H. Jobes, *Letters to the Church: A Survey of Hebrews and the General Epistles* (Grand Rapids, MI: Zondervan, 2011), 21, 23.
[2] Acts 7:38; Gal 3:19; Jubilees 1.27, 29; 2.1; Josephus, *Antiquities* 15.136.

We must pay the most careful attention, therefore, to what we have heard, so that we do not drift away. For since the message spoken through angels was binding, and every violation and disobedience received its just punishment, how shall we escape if we ignore so great a salvation? This salvation, which was first announced by the Lord, was confirmed to us by those who heard him. God also testified to it by signs, wonders and various miracles, and by gifts of the Holy Spirit distributed according to his will. (Heb 2:1-4)

The lesser-to-greater argument of Hebrews apparently applies not only to God's revelation but also to how one responds to it. If God expected one to obey the message he spoke through the prophets and justly punished disobedience, how much more so for the message he has spoken by his Son? The author of Hebrews is keen that we remember this heightened need for response, and it is for this reason that he includes five "warning passages" in his letter that urge readers to act on what they have heard (Heb 2:1-4; 3:7–4:13; 5:11–6:12; 10:19-39; 12:14-29).

The author of Hebrews further develops this idea of appropriate response by setting before the reader two examples, one negative and one positive. On one side stands the wilderness generation—those Israelites who came to the edge of the Promised Land, refused to enter in because of unbelief, and perished during the forty years that Israel wandered in the wilderness (Heb 3:7–4:13; cf. Ex 17:1-7; Num 14:20-38; Ps 95:7-11). On the other side stand the Old Testament saints who lived "by faith" (Heb 11). After cataloging these exemplars of faith, the author says, "Therefore, since we are surrounded by such a great cloud of witnesses, let us throw off everything that hinders and the sin that so easily entangles. And let us run with perseverance the race marked out for us, fixing our eyes on Jesus, the pioneer and perfecter of faith" (Heb 12:1-2).

Hebrews envisions the Christian as an athlete running a race, at whose finish line stands Jesus. Elsewhere, Hebrews describes obedience/ faithfulness as entering God's promised rest (Heb 3:7–4:13), drawing near to God (Heb 4:16; 7:25; 10:1, 19, 22), and reaching the heavenly Jerusalem (Heb 12:18-24). But whatever image is used, Jesus, "the pioneer and perfecter of faith," has forged the path before us and stands waiting at the culmination of the journey.

Closely related to this idea of movement toward a Jesus-shaped goal is Hebrews's use of perfection language. *Teleios* and related words occur fourteen times in Hebrews, more than any other New Testament book by far.[3] These occurrences constitute almost a third of the *telei-* language in the New Testament as a whole.[4] The high frequency of *telei-* words in Hebrews suggests both that they refer to a common concept and that this concept "was of more than average importance for the author."[5] In general, one might say that "perfection in Hebrews means the completion of God's plan of salvation."[6] However, to understand what sort of completeness God's plan of salvation entails, we need to take a closer look at how Hebrews uses perfection language.

Perhaps the most shocking thing Hebrews says about perfection is that *Jesus* was perfected. In Hebrews 2:10, the author declares, "In bringing many sons and daughters to glory, it was fitting that God, for whom and through whom everything exists, should make the pioneer of their salvation perfect through what he suffered." Clearly the "pioneer of salvation" is Jesus (cf. Heb 12:2). But what does it mean that God made Jesus perfect? Hebrews is adamant that Jesus was "tempted in every way, just as we are—yet he did not sin" (Heb 4:15; cf. Heb 7:26-27), so this cannot mean that Jesus was sinful and then became less sinful, or sinless. The author elaborates on the perfecting of Jesus in Hebrews 5:7-10:

---

[3]*Teleioō* occurs nine times (Heb 2:10; 5:9; 7:19, 28; 9:9; 10:1, 14; 11:40; 12:23), *teleios* two (Heb 5:14; 9:11), *teleiotēs* one (Heb 6:1), *teleiōsis* one (Heb 7:11), and *teleiōtēs* one (Heb 12:2). James, the book with the second highest frequency of *telei-* language in the New Testament, has six occurrences.

[4]*Telei-* words occur forty-eight times in the New Testament.

[5]Moisés Silva, "Perfection and Eschatology in Hebrews," *Westminster Theological Journal* 39 (1976): 60.

[6]Barnabas Lindars, *The Theology of the Letter to the Hebrews*, New Testament Theology (Cambridge: Cambridge University Press, 1991), 44.

During the days of Jesus' life on earth, [Jesus] offered up prayers and peti-
tions with fervent cries and tears to the one who could save him from
death, and he was heard because of his reverent submission. Son though
he was, he learned obedience from what he suffered and, once made
perfect, he became the source of eternal salvation for all who obey him
and was designated by God to be high priest in the order of Melchizedek.

Here the perfecting seems to have to do with obedience—Jesus
"learned obedience from what he suffered." As Thomas McCall notes,
"This does not mean that [Jesus] was ever *disobedient*. We should not
assume that the options here are limited to merely *obedience* and
disobedience, for someone could be *nonobedient* without being
either obedient or disobedient."[7] McCall gives the example of a
soldier, who must be either obedient or disobedient to his commanding officer once he enlists, but prior to enlisting is simply nonobedient. Jesus enlists, so to speak, in the incarnation and is perfected in obedience through suffering as a human. Indeed, as
Anthony Hoekema says, "That Christ had to go through a period of
development even in the learning of obedience will constitute a
problem only for those who have a docetic view of His person.
To be truly human means to develop."[8] But if obedience in suffering
is the way of perfection, it is not the sum total of it. Through his
obedient death on the cross, Jesus "provided purification for
sins" and "sat down at the right hand of the Majesty in heaven"
(Heb 1:3), indicating his appointment as great high priest (Heb 5:5-6;
cf. Ps 110:1, 4). Thus, "perfection for Christ implies that he has suc-
cessfully completed the human experience and appropriately been
exalted to glory in the heavenly realm" (cf. Heb 7:28).[9]

---

[7]Thomas H. McCall, "'Son Though He Was, He Learned Obedience': The Submissions of Christ
in Theological Perspective (in Dialogue with Thomas Aquinas and Karl Barth)," in *Listen, Understand, Obey: Essays on Hebrews in Honor of Gareth Lee Cockerill*, ed. Caleb T. Friedeman (Eugene, OR: Pickwick, 2017), 133, emphasis original.

[8]Anthony A. Hoekema, "The Perfection of Christ in Hebrews," *Calvin Theological Journal* 9 (1974):
36.

[9]Kenneth Schenck, *Understanding the Book of Hebrews: The Story Behind the Sermon* (Louisville,
KY: Westminster John Knox, 2003), 69.

Hebrews also speaks of the perfecting of believers. After be-ginning to speak of Jesus' high priesthood, the author declares,

> We have much to say about this, but it is hard to make it clear to you because you no longer try to understand. In fact, though by this time you ought to be teachers, you need someone to teach you the ele-mentary truths of God's word all over again. You need milk, not solid food! Anyone who lives on milk, being still an infant, is not acquainted with the teaching about righteousness. But solid food is for the mature [*teleiōn*], who by constant use have trained themselves to distinguish good from evil. (Heb 5:11-14).

The author here uses a form of *teleios* to describe Christians who, in contrast to the overgrown-infant believers, "by constant use have trained themselves to distinguish good from evil" (Heb 5:14). He goes on to say, "Therefore let us move beyond the elementary teachings about Christ and be taken forward to maturity [*teleiotēta*, from *teleiotēs*], not laying again the foundation of repentance from acts that lead to death, and of faith in God, instruction about cleansing rites, the laying on of hands, the resurrection of the dead, and eternal judgment" (Heb 6:1-2).

The NIV translates *teleios* and *teleiotēs* with "mature" and "maturity," respectively, and the contrast with infants suggests that this is cer-tainly part of what is meant. However, as noted above, *telei-* words seem to be technical terms for the author of Hebrews, so to translate as "mature"/"maturity" here and "perfect"/"perfection" elsewhere ob-scures how these words connect to other uses of *telei-* language in the letter. (In virtually all other instances, the NIV translates *telei-* language in Hebrews with "perfect" and related words.)[10] And as we read on, it becomes evident that the author means more by these words than merely maturity. In Hebrews 9:9, the author asserts that the sacrifices of the old covenant could not "perfect [*teleiōsai*] the conscience of the worshiper" (ESV). He explains more fully in Hebrews 10:

---

[10]In Heb 9:9, the NIV translates *teleioō* as "to clear."

The law is only a shadow of the good things that are coming—not the realities themselves. For this reason it can never, by the same sacrifices repeated endlessly year after year, make perfect [*teleiōsai*] those who draw near to worship. Otherwise, would they not have stopped being offered? For the worshipers would have been cleansed once for all, and would no longer have felt guilty for their sins. (Heb 10:1-2)

By contrast, Jesus through his once-for-all sacrifice "has made perfect [*teteleiōken*] forever those who are being made holy" (Heb 10:14). There is, therefore, a sense in which all believers are perfect: Jesus has purified "our consciences from acts that lead to death, so that we may serve the living God" (Heb 9:14), bringing us near to God's goal for humanity. However, there is also a perfection that the author exhorts believers to press on to (Heb 5:11–6:12), and the ultimate goal is to reach the heavenly Jerusalem and to join "the spirits of the righteous made perfect [*teteleiōmenōn*]" (Heb 12:23). Hebrews thus "asserts both that the readers have been perfected *and* that perfection is an end toward which they are to advance."[11]

The concept of holiness/sanctification is also central to Hebrews' vision of the Christian life and overlaps significantly with that of perfection. In Hebrews 2:10, the author describes Jesus as "the one who makes people holy" and believers as "those who are made holy." He goes on to explain that by his death Jesus broke "the power of him who holds the power of death" and freed "those who all their lives were held in slavery by their fear of death" (Heb 2:14-15). From one perspective, this sanctification has been accomplished in the atonement: "we have been made holy through the sacrifice of the body of Jesus Christ once for all" (Heb 10:10; cf. Heb 10:14, 29; 13:12). But it is also something that Christians continue to grow in and live out. The author says that, like a human father, "God disciplines us for our good, in order that we may share in his holiness" (Heb 12:10). This latter sort of holiness is of utmost importance, for the author exhorts his readers, "Make every

---

[11]Timothy L. Marquis, "Perfection Perfected: The Stoic 'Self-Eluding Sage' and Moral Progress in Hebrews," *Novum Testamentum* 57 (2015): 191, emphasis original.

effort to live in peace with everyone and to be holy; without holiness no one will see the Lord" (Heb 12:14).

Hebrews, therefore, like the Gospels, Acts, and Paul, envisions the Christian life as being Jesus-shaped.[12] Jesus has pioneered the path of perfection through obedient suffering, and by his once-for-all sacrifice he has opened the way for others to follow. To be a Christian means at the most basic level to live by faith—to live "as if God's promise for the future is sure and his power in the present is real."[13] In Hebrews, God's promise for the future is that Jesus' once-for-all sacrifice—and this alone—truly atones for sin, makes us holy and perfect in God's eyes, and frees us to live holy lives in the present as we, like Jesus, learn obedience through suffering. If this is so, then true faith not only means mentally assenting to this vision but also living as if God is powerful enough to accomplish it. The wilderness generation came to the edge of what God had promised and failed to enter in. We must not make the same mistake.

JAMES: PERFECTION VERSUS DOUBLE-MINDEDNESS

The book of James is clearly a letter, but it is no ordinary letter. As Karen Jobes notes, "James has a greater frequency of imperatives than any other book in the New Testament, considering its length."[14] Such features have led many scholars to see James as "a wisdom book in the tradition of Jewish wisdom literature" about how to live "wisely in God's kingdom announced by Jesus Christ."[15] Central to the Jewish wisdom tradition is the notion of the two ways—the way

---

[12]David Peterson, *Hebrews and Perfection: An Examination of the Concept of Perfection in the "Epistle to the Hebrews,"* Society for New Testament Studies Monograph Series 47 (Cambridge: Cambridge University Press, 1982), 187: "The perfecting of Christ 'through suffering' provides a pattern for Christian discipleship. Christians share to a certain extent in the same struggle or context that Christ endured and, because he pioneered the way, they have the prospect of enjoying his victory if they share his faith and manifest the same sort of perseverance in the face of hostility and suffering."

[13]Gareth L. Cockerill, *The Epistle to the Hebrews,* New International Commentary on the New Testament (Grand Rapids, MI: Eerdmans, 2012), 542.

[14]Jobes, *Letters to the Church,* 161.

[15]Jobes, *Letters to the Church,* 162.

of wisdom and the way of folly. It is therefore not surprising that James sets before his readers two contrasting ways of existing.

The first is the way of *double-mindedness*. Toward the beginning of the letter, James exhorts his readers to seek wisdom, saying,

> If any of you lacks wisdom, you should ask God, who gives generously to all without finding fault, and it will be given to you. But when you ask, you must believe and not doubt, because the one who doubts is like a wave of the sea, blown and tossed by the wind. That person should not expect to receive anything from the Lord. Such a person is double-minded [*dipsychos*] and unstable in all they do. (Jas 1:5-8)

The Greek word translated as "double-minded" (Jas 1:8) is *dipsychos*, literally two-minded (*psychē* in Greek can mean "life, soul, spirit, heart, or mind"). It is a rare word that occurs nowhere prior to James but a number of times in the apostolic fathers, perhaps drawing on James.[16] According to Eduard Schweizer, "It denotes the divided man as opposed to the 'simple' [i.e., wholehearted] man."[17] First Clement, one of the writings from the apostolic fathers, uses it to describe Lot's wife, who looked back at Sodom and Gomorrah and became a pillar of salt (1 Clem. 11.2; cf. Gen 19:26). Here, James uses it to describe someone who asks God for wisdom but doubts, failing to believe that God can provide. Such a person has succumbed to a deep dichotomy within their being (similar to Stevenson's Jekyll and Hyde) and, James says, "should not expect to receive anything from the Lord" (Jas 1:7).

James returns to this issue of double-mindedness in chapter 4:

> What causes fights and quarrels among you? Don't they come from your desires that battle within you? You desire but do not have, so you kill. You covet but you cannot get what you want, so you quarrel and fight. You do not have because you do not ask God. When you ask, you

---

[16]See 1 Clement 11.2; 23.3; 2 Clement 11.2; Shepherd of Hermas 12.3; 23.6; 34.1; 39.5-6; 41.2; 43:1-2, 4, 13; 47.2; 50.3; 73.1-2; 95:3; 98:1-3.

[17]Eduard Schweizer, "δίψυχος," *TDNT* 9:665.

do not receive, because you ask with wrong motives, that you may spend what you get on your pleasures. (Jas 4:1-3)

Here again we see the Jekyll-and-Hyde problem—people fighting with their sinful desires and losing the battle. Notice that James does not shrug his shoulders and say, "Well, that's not good, but it's about the best we can hope for." On the contrary, he exclaims,

You adulterous people, don't you know that friendship with the world means enmity against God? Therefore, anyone who chooses to be a friend of the world becomes an enemy of God. Or do you think Scripture says without reason that he jealously longs for the spirit he has caused to dwell in us? But he gives us more grace. That is why Scripture says:

"God opposes the proud

but shows favor to the humble."

Submit yourselves, then, to God. Resist the devil, and he will flee from you. Come near to God and he will come near to you. Wash your hands, you sinners, and purify your hearts, you double-minded [*dipsychoi*]. Grieve, mourn and wail. Change your laughter to mourning and your joy to gloom. Humble yourselves before the Lord, and he will lift you up. (Jas 4:4-10; cf. Prov 3:34)

Rather than condoning double mindedness as the normative Christian life, James urges the double-minded to respond to God's grace, repent, and purify themselves. All of this implies that James has a higher hope for the Christian than the Jekyll-and-Hyde life.

This leads us to James's second way: *perfection* or *completeness*. Five of the nineteen New Testament occurrences of *teleios* are found in James, making it the most frequent user of this word both relative to size and absolutely.[18] In three of these cases, *teleios* is used for things (Jas 1:4, 17, 25), but in two it is used to describe humans. In James 1:2-4, he tells his readers, "Count it all joy, my brothers, when you meet trials of various kinds, for you know that the testing of your

---

[18]Matthew and 1 Corinthians each use *teleios* three times.

faith produces steadfastness. And let steadfastness have its full [*teleion*] effect, that you may be perfect [*teleioi*] and complete [*holoklēroi*], lacking in nothing" (ESV). Like Hebrews, James speaks of Christians enduring and growing through trials. He describes the full effect of the steadfastness produced by this testing with two complementary adjectives: *teleios* and *holoklēros*. We have already met *teleios* in the two preceding chapters and our study of Hebrews. *Holoklēros* occurs only here in the New Testament. A leading Greek dictionary defines it as pertaining "to being complete and meeting all expectations, *with integrity, whole, complete, undamaged, intact, blameless.*"[19] Here in James 1:4, to be *teleios* and *holoklēros* means to be morally complete ("lacking in nothing"), to be whole and pure in the sense that Søren Kierkegaard spoke of when he said, "Purity of heart is to will one thing."[20] This sort of life contrasts markedly with the double-mindedness of James 1:8 and 4:8. Indeed, it is its opposite.[21]

James discusses the *teleios* person again in chapter 3: "Not many of you should become teachers, my fellow believers, because you know that we who teach will be judged more strictly. We all stumble [*ptaiomen*] in many ways. Anyone who is never at fault in what they say is perfect [*teleios*], able to keep their whole body in check" (Jas 3:1-2). The verb James uses for "stumble" is *ptaiō*, which "is applied figuratively to spiritual failure both in Judaism and the New Testament."[22] Here it almost certainly refers to sins, not merely mistakes. At first glance, James's admission that "we all stumble in many ways" might seem to suggest that sin is inevitable, and that becoming a *teleios* person is an impossible ideal. Indeed, James goes on to detail the power and wickedness of the tongue, concluding that "no human being can tame the tongue" (Jas 3:8). However, as we have seen

---

[19]BDAG, 703.
[20]Søren Kierkegaard, *Purity of Heart Is to Will One Thing: Spiritual Preparation for the Office of Confession*, trans. Douglas V. Steere (New York: Harper & Row, 1956).
[21]Ralph P. Martin, *James*, Word Biblical Commentary 48 (Waco, TX: Word, 1988), lxxix.
[22]Douglas J. Moo, *James*, Tyndale New Testament Commentaries (Grand Rapids, MI: Eerdmans, 1985), 120.

already, James seems to present being *teleios* as a real possibility in James 1:4. Further, as we read on, it becomes evident that the unbridled tongue is not a necessity in the Christian life.

> With the tongue we praise our Lord and Father, and with it we curse human beings, who have been made in God's likeness. Out of the same mouth come praise and cursing. My brothers and sisters, this should not be. Can both fresh water and salt water flow from the same spring? My brothers and sisters, can a fig tree bear olives, or a grapevine bear figs? Neither can a salt spring produce fresh water. (Jas 3:9-12)

The double-minded here becomes the two-tongued, someone who both praises God and curses humans with the same organ. James recognizes that such people exist, but he is clear that "this should not be" (Jas 3:10). He explains using the metaphor of a spring and Jesus' own image of a tree and its fruit (Mt 7:15-20; Mk 12:33-35; Lk 6:43-45). In the same way that fresh springs produce fresh water and trees bear fruit in accordance with their kind, Christians should produce good works, not evil ones. The double-minded and two-tongued life is therefore neither the necessary nor the normative Christian life. To be a Christian means to become *teleios*.

In 1916, Robert Frost penned these iconic lines:

> Two roads diverged in a yellow wood,
> And sorry I could not travel both
> And be one traveler, long I stood
> And looked down one as far as I could
> To where it bent in the undergrowth . . .
> I shall be telling this with a sigh
> Somewhere ages and ages hence:
> Two roads diverged in a wood, and I—
> I took the one less traveled by,
> And that has made all the difference.[23]

---

[23]Robert Frost, "The Road Not Taken" (1916), www.poetryfoundation.org/poems/44272/the-road-not-taken.

James, too, writes of two diverging ways and warns us that we cannot "travel both / And be one traveler." The fragmented existence of the double-minded is a path that many follow, but for James it is not the Christian life. The way of wisdom—the way of the Messiah— is certainly less traveled, for it leads through trials. However, according to James, a faithful response to these trials develops steadfastness and, best of all, leads to perfection.

First Peter: Called to Be Holy

Holiness plays a key role in 1 Peter. The body of the letter can be divided into two major sections. In the first, Peter describes the new identity that Jesus has given to believers (1 Pet 1:3-2:10); in the second, he explains how they should live out this identity in their culture (1 Pet 2:11–5:11). Central to this identity is the reality of holiness. We first hear of holiness in the introduction, where Peter greets his readers as "God's elect, exiles scattered throughout the provinces of Pontus, Galatia, Cappadocia, Asia and Bithynia, who have been chosen according to the foreknowledge of God the Father, through the sanctifying work of the Spirit [*en hagiasmō pneumatos*], to be obedient to Jesus Christ and sprinkled with his blood" (1 Pet 1:1-3).

The fact that Peter writes to Christians in a number of provinces in Asia Minor, as opposed to a single city, suggests that he probably has in mind a mixed audience of both Jewish and Gentile backgrounds.[24] But whatever his readers were before, what really matters is that they have been brought together by the work of the triune God: the foreknowledge of the Father, the sanctification of the Spirit, and obedience to Jesus and sprinkling with his blood. Thus, from the outset we find that sanctification by the Spirit and obedience to Jesus are central to Christian identity.

---

[24]Such an audience is also suggested by Peter's frequent use of the Old Testament in both quotations and allusions (which would be most understandable to Jewish Christians) and his mention of the Gentile lives that at least some of his readers formerly lived (4:3).

Peter opens the body of his letter with an outpouring of praise to God the Father for what he has done in Jesus (1 Pet 1:3-12). Through Jesus' resurrection, God has granted believers "new birth into a living hope" (1 Pet 1:3). They can "greatly rejoice" in this salvation, even if they are suffering "grief in all kinds of trials" (1 Pet 1:6). Peter further emphasizes the lavishness of God's gift by noting that the prophets eagerly anticipated it (though they did not live to see it in person) and that "even angels long to look into these things" (1 Pet 1:12).

Peter, like Hebrews, stresses that so great a salvation merits an appropriate response: "Therefore, with minds that are alert and fully sober, set your hope on the grace to be brought to you when Jesus Christ is revealed at his coming. As obedient children, do not conform to the evil desires you had when you lived in ignorance. But just as he who called you is holy, so be holy in all you do; for it is written: 'Be holy, because I am holy'" (1 Pet 1:13-16; cf. Lev 19:2).

Believers must not go back to the evil way that they lived before they knew Christ. On the contrary, Peter commands them to be holy as God is holy, just as YHWH himself commanded in Leviticus. Oswalt summarizes what Peter teaches about holiness in this passage as follows: "(1) Holiness first of all defines a way of behaving; (2) It is a way of behaving which is determined by the character of God; (3) It is a way of behaving which all Christians are supposed to manifest; and (4) It is a way of behaving which is markedly different from that of unbelievers."[25]

But perhaps someone will protest, "But that is impossible— humans can't actually be holy!" However, as Oswalt reminded us above, "a commandment assumes the possibility of compliance."[26] When God commands us to be something, he also gives us the grace to fulfill this command. A commandment of God is, therefore, "A picture of who God is and a promise of what we can become."[27] So

---

[25]John N. Oswalt, *Called to Be Holy: A Biblical Perspective* (Nappanee, IN: Francis Asbury, 1999), 2.
[26]Oswalt, *Called to Be Holy*, 108. See also page 117 of this book.
[27]Matt Friedeman and Ray Easley, *Hidden in the Heart: A Christian Catechism* (Jackson, MS: Teleios, 2013), 8. Cf. Wesley, "Upon Our Lord's Sermon on the Mount," *WJW* 5:314.

when God commands us, "Be holy, because I am holy," we must not dismiss his words as a nice but impossible thought, but instead pray with Saint Augustine, "Give what you command, and then command whatever you will."[28]

Holiness also plays a significant role in 1 Peter 2:4-10. Peter portrays Jesus as "the living Stone," and believers as "living stones" who "are being built into a spiritual house to be a holy priesthood, offering spiritual sacrifices acceptable to God through Jesus Christ" (1 Pet 2:4-5). For unbelievers, however, Jesus the cornerstone becomes a stumbling block (1 Pet 2:8). By contrast, Peter declares, his readers are

> a chosen people,
>> a royal priesthood,
> a holy nation,
>> God's special possession,
> that you may declare the praises
>> of him who called you out of darkness
>>> into his wonderful light.
> Once you were not a people,
>> but now you are the people of God;
> once you had not received mercy,
>> but now you have received mercy. (1 Pet 2:9-10)[29]

Virtually the whole passage is composed of Old Testament titles for Israel (Ex 19:6; Is 43:20-21; Hos 2:23; cf. Hos 1:6-9). Peter is telling these believers who hail from Jewish and Gentile backgrounds that they have been molded into one people of God—called, chosen, and holy.

And with that, Peter turns to what it means to live as holy people in an unholy world. "Dear friends, I urge you, as foreigners and exiles, to abstain from sinful desires, which wage war against your

---

[28] Augustine, *Confessions* 10.29, 40 in *The Works of Saint Augustine: A Translation for the 21st Century*, vol. 1, ed. John E. Rotelle, trans. Maria Boulding (Hyde Park, NY: New City, 1997), 263.

[29] NIV text arranged according to the rhetorical analysis in Caleb T. Friedeman, "The Rhetorical Design of 1 Peter 2,9-10," *Biblica* 101 (2020): 124-31.

soul. Live such good lives among the pagans that, though they accuse you of doing wrong, they may see your good deeds and glorify God on the day he visits us" (1 Pet 2:11-12).

To be God's holy people apparently means not doing certain things ("abstain from sinful desires") and doing others ("live good lives"). But the holy life is not merely a list of "dos" and "don'ts"; as Peter has shown us in the first part of the letter, it flows from the new identity that God has given believers in Jesus. So when Christians do things like submitting to authority (1 Pet 2:13–3:7), suffering for what is right (1 Pet 3:8-22), and the like, they are not simply trying to "be good people" on their own steam; they are living as who they really are in Christ by the power of the Spirit.

A consistent theme that runs throughout Peter's discussion of the Christian life is that of suffering. Although first-century Christians certainly experienced persecution from Roman officials, the sorts of trials that Peter has in mind seem to be less official and centralized: Christian slaves being unjustly beaten by harsh masters (1 Pet 2:18-20), believers being slandered and shunned by unbelievers for refusing to participate in the dominant pagan lifestyle (1 Pet 2:12; 3:16; 4:4), and so on. Peter urges his readers not to repay evil with evil but to do good, even if that means suffering for it. Why? "Because Christ suffered for you, leaving you an example, that you should follow in his steps" (1 Pet 3:21).

In 1 Peter 4:1-3, Peter makes an important statement:

> Therefore, since Christ suffered in his body, arm yourselves also with the same attitude, because whoever suffers in the body is done with sin. As a result, they do not live the rest of their earthly lives for evil human desires, but rather for the will of God. For you have spent enough time in the past doing what pagans choose to do—living in debauchery, lust, drunkenness, orgies, carousing and detestable idolatry.

What does Peter mean by "whoever suffers in the body is done with sin" (1 Pet 4:1)? He is presumably not talking about physical suffering in general, for many people undergo physical pain and continue to sin. Rather, as the first part of the verse makes clear, he is speaking about suffering with the mind of Christ—suffering for righteousness. Wayne Grudem helpfully paraphrases: "Whoever has suffered for doing right, and has still gone on obeying God in spite of the suffering it involved, has made a clear break with sin."[30] Peter emphasizes that this break with sin is not only in principle but also in practice, for those who have suffered for righteousness "do not live the rest of their earthly lives for evil human desires, but rather for the will of God" (1 Pet 4:2), renouncing the pagan lifestyle of the surrounding culture. Theologically, what is important here is that Peter clearly thinks that it is possible for Christians not to sin, not just now and again but as a way of life.[31] Thus, when believers today say things like, "I sin every day in word, thought, and deed," they are either operating with a very different definition of sin than Peter is (i.e., one that encompasses things like unintentional errors) or are considerably out of step with Peter's vision of the Christian life. Peter presents the holy life as the way the Christian life is meant to be lived and (however much it may surprise us) assumes that it is possible for at least some Christians not to sin.

First John: The Children of God and Sin

First John, like many of the New Testament documents, was written in the midst of intense conflict. A group of heretics had recently arisen within the church and exited from it (1 Jn 2:18-23), and much of what John says seems to be aimed at helping the believers to navigate this situation. John never gives a systematic description of his opponents, but the controversy seems to have centered around two issues: Christology and ethics. The heretics deny that Jesus is the Messiah (1 Jn 2:22) and has come in the flesh (1 Jn 4:3). In addition, they

---

[30]Wayne Grudem, *1 Peter*, Tyndale New Testament Commentaries (Grand Rapids, MI: Eerdmans, 1988), 167.

[31]*Pace* Grudem, *1 Peter*, 167.

apparently claim to be without sin (1 Jn 1:8, 10) and to know God while blatantly disobeying him (1 Jn 1:6; 2:4, 9, 11; 4:20).[32] John's response to the heretics' aberrant ethics provides some of the most important New Testament material for understanding how Christians relate to sin.

John begins with a message that he claims to have heard from Jesus: "God is light; in him there is no darkness at all. If we claim to have fellowship with him and yet walk in the darkness, we lie and do not live out the truth. But if we walk in the light, as he is in the light, we have fellowship with one another, and the blood of Jesus, his Son, purifies us from all sin" (1 Jn 1:5-7). God is utterly holy (light), and so it is not possible to say that one knows him while simultaneously living in sin (darkness). John continues:

> If we claim to be without sin, we deceive ourselves and the truth is not in us. If we confess our sins, he is faithful and just and will forgive us our sins and purify us from all unrighteousness. If we claim we have not sinned, we make him out to be a liar and his word is not in us. My dear children, I write this to you so that you will not sin. But if anybody does sin, we have an advocate with the Father—Jesus Christ, the Righteous One. (1 Jn 1:8–2:2)

Some understand 1 John 1:8 to mean that everyone sins continuously, so anyone who says that they haven't sinned (in the last hour, day, etc.) is deceiving themselves. And if one defines sin as anything that humans do that does not measure up to God's ultimate intentions for his creation, this is probably true. However, by that definition no one could know God because everyone would be walking in darkness continually (cf. 1 Jn 1:6-7)! John therefore seems to be defining sin more narrowly (see further below). It seems better to interpret 1 John 1:8 in light of the parallel statement in 1 John 1:10:[33]

---

[32]Gary M. Burge, Lynn H. Cohick, and Gene L. Green, *The New Testament in Antiquity: A Survey of the New Testament Within Its Cultural Contexts* (Grand Rapids, MI: Zondervan, 2009), 415-17.
[33]Wesley, "Christian Perfection," *WJW* 6:14-15.

If we claim to be without sin, we deceive ourselves and the truth is not in us. (1 Jn 1:8)

If we claim we have not sinned, we make him out to be a liar and his word is not in us. (1 Jn 1:10)

John is saying, in other words, that everyone has sinned; no one can claim to be guiltless before God on their own merits (cf. Rom 3:23). What he does not say is that everyone sins all the time or that sin is a necessary part of the Christian life. John does, however, think that it is possible for Christians to sin, for he teaches that Christians who do sin should confess what they have done and receive forgiveness from Jesus (1 Jn 1:9; 2:1). We may sum up John's teaching thus far in two points:

1. Everyone has sinned (1 Jn 1:8, 10).
2. It is possible for Christians to sin; if they do, they should repent and receive forgiveness from Jesus (1 Jn 1:9; 2:1).

John discusses believers' relationship to sin in more detail in 1 John 2:28–3:10. He begins by exhorting his readers, "So now, little children, remain in him so that when he appears we may have confidence and not be ashamed before him at his coming. If you know that he is righteous, you know this as well: Everyone who does what is right has been born of him" (1 Jn 2:28-29 CSB). The mention of believers as being born of God launches John into an extended meditation on what it means to be children of God. Throughout the entire passage, John emphasizes that God's children are known by the fact that they imitate the righteousness of their Father.

Everyone who commits sin practices lawlessness; and sin is lawlessness. You know that he was revealed so that he might take away sins, and there is no sin in him. *Everyone who remains in him does not sin*; everyone who sins has not seen him or known him.

Little children, let no one deceive you. The one who does what is right is righteous, just as he is righteous. The one who commits sin is of the devil, for the devil has sinned from the beginning. The Son of God was revealed for this purpose: to destroy the devil's works. *Everyone who has been born of God does not sin, because his seed remains in him; he is not able to sin, because he has been born of God.* This is how God's children and the devil's children become obvious. Whoever does not do what is right is not of God, especially the one who does not love his brother or sister. (1 Jn 3:4-10 CSB, emphasis added)

The italicized statements in 1 John 3:6, 9 have understandably provoked much discussion. What does John mean that "everyone who remains in him does not sin" and that "everyone who has been born of God does not sin" and even "is not able to sin"? And how do these statements square with John's earlier admission that it is possible for Christians to sin? One popular solution is to interpret the present-tense verbs as referring to habitual sin. The NIV takes this route:

No one who lives in him *keeps on sinning*. (1 Jn 3:6)
No one who is born of God *will continue to sin*. (1 Jn 3:9)

The ESV is similar:

No one who abides in him *keeps on sinning*. (1 Jn 3:6)
No one born of God *makes a practice of sinning*. (1 Jn 3:9)

To be fair, the present tense in Greek can sometimes indicate continuous or habitual action. However, the presence of this usage is determined based on the character of the verb (e.g., "I [customarily] *fast* twice a week and *give a tenth* of all I get"; Lk 18:12) and/or the immediate context ("For *whenever* you *eat* this bread and *drink* this cup, you *proclaim* the Lord's death until he comes"; 1 Cor 11:26),[34] and both indicators are lacking here. Many commentators therefore regard this interpretation as less than satisfactory.[35]

---

[34]Daniel B. Wallace, *Greek Grammar Beyond the Basics: An Exegetical Syntax of the New Testament* (Grand Rapids, MI: Zondervan, 1996), 521-22; Constantine R. Campbell, *Basics of Verbal Aspect in Biblical Greek* (Grand Rapids, MI: Zondervan, 2008), 65.

[35]E.g., Stephen S. Smalley, *1, 2, 3 John*, Word Biblical Commentary 51 (Waco, TX: Word, 1984), 151-52; Robert W. Yarbrough, *1-3 John*, Baker Exegetical Commentary on the New Testament (Grand Rapids, MI: Baker Academic, 2008), 183; Karen H. Jobes, *1, 2, and 3 John*, Zondervan

Another solution is to understand 1 Jn 3:6, 9 as merely descriptions of an ideal: children of God *should* not sin, even if they inevitably do. However, as Stephen Smalley notes, this interpretation "does not account fully for the apparently absolute form of John's statements in 3:6, 9 and 5:18. Not only *should* Christians be without sin; they *are* sinless."[36]

A better interpretation may be found by considering two issues. First, what sort of sin is John referring to? It is helpful to recall at this point that John is not writing in the abstract but is responding to the "antichrists" who have recently left the church (1 Jn 2:18-27). What sort of sin have they committed? They have apparently denied that Jesus is the Messiah who came in the flesh, claimed to be without sin, and blatantly disobeyed God while claiming to know him. These are clearly willful sins against what God has revealed, not unintentional errors. Indeed, this may be why John says, "Everyone who commits sin practices lawlessness; and sin is lawlessness" (1 Jn 3:4 CSB).[37] It therefore seems likely that in 1 John 3:6, 9 John is referring to willful sins.

Second, what sort of statements are 1 John 3:6 and 3:9? As noted above, the habitual use of the present tense does not seem likely here. There is, however, a use of the present tense that would fit well in this context—namely, the gnomic present. This use of the present makes "a statement of a general, timeless fact" and "typically takes a generic subject or object," as in 1 John 3:6 and 3:9 ("Everyone who . . .").[38] Gnomic presents make proverb-like pronouncements about the way things usually are (tacitly acknowledging that there may be exceptions).[39]

Exegetical Commentary on the New Testament (Grand Rapids, MI: Zondervan, 2014), 147. It is also worth noting that (1) if John wanted to communicate that believers do not sin, one would expect him to use present-tense indicatives and (2) if John simply meant to say that the children of God don't sin "regularly" or "frequently," he could have easily added an adverb to make this clear.

[36]Smalley, *1, 2, 3 John*, 161, emphasis original.

[37]Cf. Colin G. Kruse, "Sin and Perfection in 1 John," *Australian Biblical Review* 51 (2003): 60-70; Yarbrough, *1-3 John*, 181-84; Jobes, *1, 2, and 3 John*, 147-48.

[38]Wallace, *Greek Grammar*, 523.

[39]I recall one of my undergraduate professors repeatedly emphasizing that "proverbs are not promises or guarantees" but "wise generalizations."

We find many examples of such statements in everyday life. For example, when I was growing up my parents would tell my siblings and me things like, "Friedemans are leaders," and "Friedemans don't lie." Of course, we did not always behave as leaders or tell the truth. However, the point was not to describe our current behavior but rather to remind us how we could and should live because of who we were. And over time such statements shaped us to be people who fulfilled them.

What John is saying, then, is this: as a general rule, *God's children do not commit willful sin.* Of course, it is possible for them to sin, and if they do, they should confess their sin and receive forgiveness from Jesus. But the normative Christian life—the way that believers both should and can live—is one of righteousness: keeping God's Word (1 Jn 2:3; 3:22; 5:3), being perfected in love (1 Jn 2:5; 4:12, 17-18), and abstaining from willful sin (1 Jn 3:6, 9; 5:18).

Yet just as important as John's assertions that the children of God do not sin are his reasons why this is possible:

- The seed of the *Father* abides in them (1 Jn 3:9).
- They abide in the *Son*—the sinless one (1 Jn 3:5-6).
- They have received the *Spirit*, the confirmation that the Son abides in them (1 Jn 3:24; 4:13).

John's vision of the Christian life is, therefore, an optimism of grace. He believes that Christians can be holy not because he is confident in humans but because he is confident in the power and desire of the triune God to deliver humans from the penalty, power, and presence of sin.

REVELATION: HOLY GOD, HOLY PEOPLE

Revelation is an enigmatic book, so much so that one scholar has described it as "the paradise of fanatics and sectarians."[40] Yet if there

---

[40]G. B. Caird, *A Commentary on the Revelation of St. John the Divine*, Black's New Testament Commentaries (London: A. & C. Black, 1966), 2.

is much in Revelation that is difficult to understand, one thing at least is unambiguous: God is holy, and his people, too, must be holy. In Revelation 4–5, John receives a vision of God's heavenly throne room. God sits enthroned, surrounded by twenty-four elders on twenty-four other thrones. Around the throne are four living creatures, each with six wings and covered with eyes all around. "Day and night," John observes, "they never stop saying, 'Holy, holy, holy is the Lord God Almighty, who was, and is, and is to come'" (Rev 4:8).

If this sounds familiar, it is because the four creatures are quoting Isaiah 6:3, where Isaiah sees YHWH and hears the seraphim declaring these same words. The phrase "who was, and is, and is to come" is based on Exodus 3:14 ("I am who I am") and descriptions of YHWH that echo this passage in Deuteronomy and Isaiah (Deut 32:39; Is 41:4; 43:10; 44:6; 48:12).[41] It communicates God's "infinity and sovereignty over history."[42] For John, as for Moses and Isaiah before him, YHWH is the holy One, and his holy character is the foundation of all reality.

In Revelation, things associated with God (i.e., holy things) are frequently depicted with the color white. Jesus has white hair (Rev 1:14) and rides on a white horse (Rev 19:11), and God sits on a great white throne (Rev 20:11). Interestingly, "white" is used most frequently in Revelation to describe the clothing of the saints (literally, "the holy ones").[43] As we will see, this imagery provides significant insight into John's vision of the Christian life.[44]

In Revelation 3, Jesus says to the church in Sardis,

> I know your deeds; you have a reputation of being alive, but you are dead. Wake up! Strengthen what remains and is about to die, for I have

---

[41]G. K. Beale, *The Book of Revelation: A Commentary on the Greek Text*, New International Greek Testament Commentary (Grand Rapids, MI: Eerdmans, 1999), 187-88, 332.

[42]Beale, *Revelation*, 332.

[43]*Leukos* ("white") occurs sixteen times in Revelation (Rev 1:14; 2:17; 3:4-5, 18; 4:4; 6:2, 11; 7:9, 13; 14:14; 19:11, 14; 20:11). *Leukainō* ("to make white") appears once (Rev 7:14). At least seven of these occurrences refer to the garments of the saints (Rev 3:4-5, 18; 4:4; 6:11; 7:9, 13; possibly Rev 19:14 as well).

[44]I am grateful to Stephen Smith for suggesting this imagery as a way into the issue of holiness in Revelation.

found your deeds unfinished in the sight of my God. . . . Yet you have a few people in Sardis who have not soiled their clothes. They will walk with me, *dressed in white*, for they are worthy. The one who is victorious will, like them, be *dressed in white*. I will never blot out the name of that person from the book of life, but will acknowledge that name before my Father and his angels. (Rev 3:1b-2, 4-5; emphasis added)

One might be tempted to take the white clothing as merely a reference to forgiveness, indicating the cleansing of sins. Yet it is clear in context that Jesus is writing to believers, all of whom have received initial forgiveness. However, some of them have soiled their clothes (= lived unholy lives), and others have not (= lived holy lives). As G. K. Beale notes, the believers who will walk in white "are 'worthy' (ἄξιος) in that they are willing to follow the model of Jesus, who was considered 'worthy' (ἄξιος) because he endured suffering on account of his faithful testimony (cf. Rev 5:9, 12)."[45] White, then, "represents not mere purity but a faithful, noncompromising spirit, which stands in contrast to those who have 'stained their garments,' that is, have compromised."[46] Jesus stresses to the Christians in Smyrna that such wholehearted devotion is what he expects of those who bear his name.

John develops this connection between the saints' white garments and holiness throughout Revelation. In Revelation 7, John sees a great multitude wearing white robes and worshiping God. One of the elders tells John that these are people "who have come out of the great tribulation; they have washed their robes and made them white in the blood of the Lamb" (Rev 7:14). Beale rightly comments that the image of white robes here "connotes a purity that has been demonstrated by persevering faith in Christ's redemptive death (= 'blood'), that faith tested by a purifying fire."[47] Conceptually parallel to the language of white garments is that of clean linen. In chapter 19, John hears what sounds like a great multitude shouting,

---

[45]Beale, *Revelation*, 276.
[46]Beale, *Revelation*, 278.
[47]Beale, *Revelation*, 437.

Hallelujah!
    For our Lord God Almighty reigns.
Let us rejoice and be glad
    and give him glory!
For the wedding of the Lamb has come,
    and his bride has made herself ready.
Fine linen, bright and clean,
    was given her to wear. (Rev 19:6b-8a)

Just in case we missed the point, John explains: "Fine linen stands for the righteous acts of God's holy people" (Rev 19:8b). According to John, the church—Jesus' bride—is holy, characterized not only by the status of "righteous" that God grants to all who have faith in Jesus (initial justification) but also but also by the righteous acts that are the fruit of true faith and union with the Messiah.

The book of Revelation climaxes with John's vision of the new creation:

> Then I saw "a new heaven and a new earth," for the first heaven and the first earth had passed away, and there was no longer any sea. I saw the Holy City, the new Jerusalem, coming down out of heaven from God, prepared as a bride beautifully dressed for her husband. And I heard a loud voice from the throne saying, "Look! God's dwelling place is now among the people, and he will dwell with them. They will be his people, and God himself will be with them and be their God. 'He will wipe every tear from their eyes. There will be no more death' or mourning or crying or pain, for the old order of things has passed away." (Rev 21:1-4; cf. Isa 65:17; 66:22)

In the new creation we find echoes of Eden, God's original intent, including a river (Rev 22:1-2; cf. Gen 2:10-14) and the tree of life (Rev 22:2; cf. Gen 2:9). But everything is expanded and developed. The tree of life, once a single tree in the midst of the garden, now lines both sides of the river. And the garden has now become a city. In short, what we find here is "the *people* of God in the *place* of God dwelling in the *presence* of God."[48] God's plan of redemption has been fully accomplished.

But who are the people of God who enjoy unlimited access to God's presence in this new creation? Even at this point in the book, John is not content to let us revel in this glorious vision of the future; he wants to make sure that we are part of it. Throughout his description of the new creation, he also reminds us who will—and who will not—enter into it. "Those who are victorious will inherit all this, and I will be their God and they will be my children. But the cowardly, the unbelieving, the vile, the murderers, the sexually immoral, those who practice magic arts, the idolaters and all liars— they will be consigned to the fiery lake of burning sulfur. This is the second death" (Rev 21:7-8).

"Those who are victorious" (or "who conquer") is language that Revelation repeatedly uses to describe following Jesus faithfully despite temptations and trials.[49] It is these victors who will inherit the new creation and enjoy its benefits. But for those who persist in rebellion against God, only the lake of fire remains. John similarly says regarding the new Jerusalem, "Nothing impure will ever enter it, nor will anyone who does what is shameful or deceitful, but only those whose names are written in the Lamb's book of life" (Rev 21:27). And if we think that having one's name written in the Lamb's book of life simply means saying a sinner's prayer and then living however one wishes afterward, we should remember Jesus' words to the church in Sardis: "Yet you have a few people in Sardis who have not soiled their clothes. . . . The one who is victorious will, like them, be dressed in white. I will never blot out the name of that person from the book of life" (Rev 3:4-5).

The implication, of course, is that those who continue to soil their clothes (= rebel) will have their names blotted out of the book of life.

---

[48]Richter, *Epic of Eden*, 104, emphasis original; cf. 129.

[49]*Nikaō*, the Greek verb used here, occurs seventeen times in Revelation (Rev 2:7, 11, 17, 26; 3:5, 12, 21; 5:5; 6:2; 11:7; 12:11; 13:7; 15:2; 17:14; 21:7).

In the epilogue to Revelation, Jesus declares,

> Look, I am coming soon! My reward is with me, and I will give to each person according to what they have done. . . . Blessed are those who wash their robes, that they may have the right to the tree of life and may go through the gates into the city. Outside are the dogs, those who practice magic arts, the sexually immoral, the murderers, the idolaters and everyone who loves and practices falsehood. (Rev 22:12-15)

At first glance, it might seem like John has marred what should be a happy ending with sober warnings about who will and will not participate in God's new creation. But we must recall that John has not written a fairy tale, but a revelation—a book that unveils how things really are.[50] And as is true so often in Revelation, the reality is both more sobering than we had realized and more glorious than we could have hoped. God is holy, holy, holy, and humans have rebelled against him. The cancer of sin runs deep in creation, and so the cure must also cut deep. But God has paid the price of redemption himself in the person of Jesus and offers eternal life to all freely: "The Spirit and the bride say, 'Come!' . . . Let the one who is thirsty come; and let the one who wishes take the free gift of the water of life" (Rev 22:17). And, best of all, the resurrection life of God's new age will not wait for the future but permeates the present, as the holy God creates for himself a holy people in the here and now.

CONCLUSION

The General Epistles and Revelation are a diverse group of writings. However, this diversity and the unity that we find within it allow these books to make an important contribution to our study of holiness. Hebrews, James, 1 Peter, 1 John, and Revelation each speak of the holy life in their own idiom. Hebrews uses the language of

---

[50]The Greek word for "revelation" (*apokalypsis*) can also mean "uncovering" or "unveiling." One of the literary genres that Revelation draws on is apocalypse, a type of literature where someone receives a heavily symbolic vision of reality from a heavenly perspective, often guided by a heavenly being. For examples of this genre, see Daniel 7–12, 1 Enoch, 4 Ezra, and 2 Baruch.

perfection and holiness, James contrasts the ways of perfection and double-mindedness, 1 Peter calls believers to holiness against the dominant pagan lifestyle, 1 John depicts not sinning as the norm for the children of God, and Revelation presents the saints as clothed in the white garments of righteous deeds. Yet for all this diversity of language, these books declare with one voice that Christians not only *should* be holy but also that they *can* be holy by God's grace.

The unity-in-diversity that we observe in the General Epistles also holds true for the New Testament as a whole. From Matthew to Revelation, the New Testament authors attest that the holy life is the normative Christian life—the way the Christian life is meant to be lived—using a rich diversity of words, phrases, and imagery. The doctrine of holiness, therefore, is not based on a small group of passages that use *holy* and related words. It is, rather, based on a vision of the Christian life that spans the entire New Testament.

Part Three

"LET THOSE OF US WHO ARE PERFECT THINK THIS WAY"

Holiness in Christian History

7

EARLY FOUNDATIONS FOR HOLINESS

THE HISTORY OF CHRISTIANITY is replete with biblical and theological language that addresses holiness in personal life: sanctification, deification, transformation, restoration, renewal, imparted righteousness, godliness, maturity, and piety, to name a few. For the purpose of our exploration, we must choose a word or phrase that helps us see the extent to which holiness appears throughout church history and organically connects to a Wesleyan understanding of holiness.

With this in mind, we have selected "perfect" or "perfection" as the lens through which to study the historical witness to holiness.[1] The Wesleyan tradition is known for its doctrine of Christian perfection, which forms the dominant rubric through which personal holiness is understood. Wesleyans, however, are hardly the first to do this. Teaching on perfection pervades theological

---

[1]A survey of historical teaching on Christian perfection in three chapters requires clear parameters. These chapters will therefore focus on pastors, teachers, and theologians who explicitly address or discuss Christian perfection in present life. Furthermore, the language of "perfection" surveyed is limited to the term found in Matthew 5:48 and 19:21 and related words. Finally, outside of patristic writers, focus is placed on the Western theological tradition. Therefore, other terms related to holiness and sanctification are not included in the survey, and the Eastern tradition is not addressed. Scripture quotations in discussions of primary sources are those of the writer in view unless otherwise noted.

discussions of holiness, especially as the church has reflected on Christ's command "to be perfect" (Mt 5:48; 19:21). While there are obviously limitations to our approach, such as overlooking theologians and ecclesial movements that may omit such vocabulary, it provides an accessible overview of holiness essential to the development of Wesleyan teaching and a foundation to our "neo-holiness" model.

The Apostolic Fathers

The Christian witness to Christ's teaching on perfection outside the New Testament begins with the apostolic fathers, a group of writers from the late first to the mid-second century, whose corpus of literature is considered by many to be "a fairly immediate echo of the preaching of the Apostles."[2] Their importance is derived primarily from their close personal contact with the apostles or their association with the apostles' disciples. They wrote from many different regions of the Roman Empire to address pastoral and theological issues arising in the infant church. Their literature is punctuated with references to, statements about, and occasional elaborations on Christian perfection.

What Christian perfection entails. The apostolic fathers define Christian perfection in two related ways. First, they describe it as a perfection of love in believers, explicitly and implicitly summarized in the two great commandments—the love of God and the love of neighbor.[3] Christian love is the dominant rubric by which perfection is understood. Every aspect of the Fathers' doctrine is a logical development of love or application of love. Perfect love entails a singularity of devotion and obedience to God and a sacrificial love of friends, strangers, and enemies.

---

[2] Johannes Quasten, *Patrology,* vol. 1 (Westminster, MD: Christian Classics, 1950), 40.

[3] 1 Clement 49.5–50.3; Ignatius, *To the Ephesians* 14.1-3; Didache 1.4; 6.2; 10.5; Polycarp, *To the Philippians* 3.1-3; 12.1-3; Shepherd of Hermas 2.9.1; 3.5.1-3. Unless specified otherwise, English translations of the apostolic fathers are taken from Kirsopp Lake, *The Apostolic Fathers,* vols. 1 and 2, Loeb Classical Library (New York: MacMillan, 1914).

Specifically, perfect love is described in different ways by the apostolic fathers, depending on the pastoral context in which they wrote. For example, Clement connects perfect love of God to the Corinthian church's submission to divinely appointed elders.[4] Ignatius of Antioch ties it to the call for "perfect faith."[5] The Didache, an anonymous treatise from the patristic era, describes it as "walking in the way of life."[6] Barnabas links it to the call to be a "perfect temple."[7] And the Shepherd of Hermas relates it to serving the Lord with a pure heart.[8]

The perfect love of neighbor is Clement's exhortation to suffer willingly in service of others.[9] Ignatius appeals to it in his instruction on the treatment of schismatics.[10] The Didache cites it in the need to "turn the other cheek."[11] It undergirds Barnabas' expectation for the church to be "a light to the nations."[12] And Polycarp uses it to encourage Christians to pray for their enemies.[13]

Second, the apostolic fathers teach that Christian perfection entails freedom from sin. Negatively, this means that Christians are free from deliberate or willful sin. Positively, they live lives of complete obedience to the commandments of God.[14] While the Fathers primarily focus freedom from sin on outward actions, they relate Christian perfection to inward attitudes and intentions as well. Clement equates perfection to an attitude of selflessness.[15] Ignatius attaches it to deliverance from "evil desires."[16] Barnabas sees it as the

---

[4]1 Clement 1.2.
[5]Ignatius, *To the Ephesians* 14.1.
[6]Didache 6.2.
[7]Barnabas 4.12-14.
[8]Shepherd of Hermas 3.5.1-2.
[9]1 Clement 51.2.
[10]Ignatius, *To the Philadelphians* 1.3.
[11]Didache 1.7.
[12]Barnabas 14.5.
[13]Polycarp, *To the Philippians* 12.3.
[14]1 Clement 1.2, 9.2-12:8; 50.5-6; Ignatius, *To the Ephesians* 14.2-3; Didache 1.4 -6.2; Barnabas 4.7-14, 6.10-19, 14.5-9; Polycarp, *To the Philippians* 3.1-3; Shepherd of Hermas 2.9.1; 3.5.1-3.
[15]1 Clement 49.6.
[16]Ignatius, *To the Ephesians* 8.1.

law of God written on human hearts.[17] The Didache portrays it as deliverance from pride and jealously.[18] Polycarp connects it to purity of intention toward enemies.[19] And the Shepherd of Hermas even asserts that it brings freedom from temptations.[20]

The possibility of Christian perfection in the present life. The apostolic fathers point to the attainability of Christian perfection in life. Each of the Fathers teaches that Christians can be perfected in love, be freed from deliberate sin, and have pure hearts. While they do not provide detailed discussions of how perfection occurs, they acknowledge Christians in this life who have experienced it, while also recognizing Christians who have not. For those yet to be perfected, there is exhortation and offers of hope.[21]

Clement gives no exact details about when "perfecting in love" takes place, but he speaks of present Christians already perfected and implores the Corinthians to pray for their personal perfection with the expectation that God will do it.[22] Ignatius describes a Philadelphian bishop with a "perfect mind" yet recognizes that not all Christians are perfect, though they "may be" in the future as they are filled with the Holy Spirit.[23] The Didache assumes there are Christians who are walking entirely in the way of life, and as such are perfect, while encouraging those unable to do so to do what they can.[24] Likewise, Barnabas exhorts believers, "If, therefore, this does not exist at present, yet still he has promised it to us."[25] Finally, the Shepherd of Hermas portrays perfection with an expectation that every believer is walking in it.[26]

---

[17]Barnabas 4.7-11.
[18]Didache 5.2.
[19]Polycarp, *To the Philippians* 3.1-3; 12.1-3.
[20]Shepherd of Hermas 2.9.1.
[21]1 Clement 50.1-3; Ignatius, *To the Ephesians* 14.1-3; 15.1-3; Ignatius, *To Polycarp* 1.3-3.2; Ignatius, *To the Philadelphians* 1.1-3, 3; Didache 6.2, 10.5; Polycarp, *To the Philippians* 12.1-3; Shepherd of Hermas 2.9.1; 3.5.1-3.
[22]1 Clement 50.2-3.
[23]Ignatius, *To the Philadelphians* 1.1-2; Ignatius, *To the Ephesians* 8.1-2.
[24]Didache 6.2.
[25]Barnabas 6.19.
[26]Shepherd of Hermas 3.5.1-2.

The means of Christian perfection. The apostolic fathers clearly teach that Christian perfection is the work of God, made possible through the redemptive life of Christ and the sanctifying presence of the Holy Spirit. Specifically, Clement teaches that perfection is made possible through the redemptive exchange of Christ's life for human lives, whereby he "gave his blood for us, his flesh for our flesh, and his soul for our souls."[27] Ignatius states that it happens through the filling of the Holy Spirit.[28] The Didache identifies the means as divine deliverance from the way of death.[29] Barnabas teaches that perfection comes through Christ's earthly life and humanity's "second fashioning" by the Holy Spirit into the image of God.[30] Finally, the Shepherd of Hermas implies that one receives perfection through the exercise of divinely given faith.[31]

While the apostolic fathers recognize Christian dependency on God for perfection, they do not absolve believers of all responsibility. They expect Christians to make decisions, take appropriate actions, and exercise discipline over their minds and bodies for the realization of perfection. While Clement acknowledges that the Corinthians have fallen from perfection, he also teaches that they play a part in regaining it through repentance, a return to compassion, and obedience to their leaders.[32] Ignatius implies that the Philadelphians must cooperate with the Holy Spirit to be perfect.[33] The Didache encourages Christians to walk in the way of life as much as possible, to be as perfect as they are able.[34] Finally, Polycarp and the Shepherd of Hermas assume Christians can choose to walk in the way of perfection or not to do so.[35]

---

[27]1 Clement 49.6.
[28]Ignatius, *To the Ephesians* 8.1-2.
[29]Didache 1.4; 6.2.
[30]Barnabas 6.10-19.
[31]Shepherd of Hermas 2.9.1-3.
[32]1 Clement 1.2; 9.2–12.8.
[33]Ignatius, *To the Philadelphians* 1.1-2; 3.
[34]Didache 6.2.
[35]Polycarp, *To the Philippians* 3.1-3; 12.1-3; Shepherd of Hermas 3.5.1-3.

Later Greek fathers in the second and third centuries. While the language of Christian perfection is found repeatedly in the literature of the apostolic fathers, the first theologian to give it a clear, comprehensive treatment is Irenaeus in *Against Heresies*. Book one of his treatise provides a detailed description of Gnostic systems of Christian perfection, and the last four books give the church's teaching in multiple discussions.[36] Clement of Alexandria at the end of the second century pens two treatises with a focus on Christian perfection: *The Instructor* and *Stromata*.[37] Origen follows in the first half of the third century by writing extensively on the subject in Alexandria and Caesarea.[38] Like Irenaeus, Clement and Origen seek to distinguish Gnostic forms of perfection from the church's understanding.

The apostolic fathers' doctrine of Christian perfection plays a significant role in these later Fathers by forming a foundation for understanding Christian perfection and establishing the parameters and trajectory for future work on the doctrine. Their common understanding of Christian perfection forms the interpretive foundation on which these later ante-Nicene theologians build and apply their doctrines of Christian perfection, as well as evaluate other competing views of perfection. Irenaeus, Clement of Alexandria, and Origen extensively address, develop, and apply the doctrine of Christian perfection found in the apostolic fathers.[39]

---

[36]The Gnostics were a heretical movement in the second century church who believed the world was created and ruled by a lesser deity, the Demiurge. They did not believe in the goodness of the material world and linked salvation to esoteric knowledge. The key passages on Christian perfection in Irenaeus, *Against Heresies* book one are 1.6.1–1.8.4; 1.11.5; 1.13.1,6; 1.21.1-4; 1.29.3; 1.31.2. The rest of his teaching can be found in 2 pref.; 2.26.1; 2.28.1-2, 9; 2.30.7; 3.1.1; 3.2.1; 3.3.1; 3.12.5, 13; 4.9.2-3; 4.11.2-5; 4.20.12; 4.27.1; 4.37.7–4.39.4; 5.1.1-3; 5.6.1-2: 5.8.1–5.9.3; 5.21.2; 5.36.3. Unless specified otherwise, English translations of the ante-Nicene, Nicene, and post-Nicene fathers in this chapter are taken from *ANF*, *NPNF*[1], and *NPNF*[2].

[37]For Clement of Alexandria's central discussions of Christian perfection, see *The Instructor* 1.1; 1.6; *Stromata* 2.19, 22; 4.1, 17-26; 5.1,10; 6.1, 8-9, 12; 7.3, 10-14.

[38]Origen's best and most complete teaching on Christian perfection is his *Commentary and Homilies on the Canticle of Canticles*.

[39]While there are differences between the apostolic fathers' doctrine of Christian perfection and the later ante-Nicene fathers, their differences are minor in comparison to the "common ground" they share.

The indebtedness of these later writers to the apostolic fathers is established by their own admissions. Irenaeus, who in his youth was influenced by the preaching of Polycarp, confesses in *Against Heresies* that he develops his doctrine of Christian perfection as an articulation of the "rule of faith," the clear teaching of the church passed down to him and to which he is obliged to be faithful.[40] Similarly, Clement of Alexandria appeals to the "rule of faith," the tradition of the church with which he has been entrusted, in his teaching on Christian perfection. He explicitly connects his doctrine to Clement of Rome's "perfect and well-grounded knowledge" and "perfect ministry," as well as the Shepherd of Hermas's "perfect fast."[41] In the same way, Origen in his *First Principles* takes great care to articulate and distinguish the "unmistakable rule of faith," the consensual tradition of the church operative in his time, in his articulation of Christian perfection. While Origen is known for his speculative work, he is careful to distinguish his imaginative theology from the "rule of faith's" doctrine of Christian perfection.[42]

The connection between the apostolic fathers and the later Greek writers of the ante-Nicene period is seen most clearly in one observation. When Irenaeus, Clement of Alexandria, and Origen articulate the "rule of faith's" teaching on Christian perfection, it is essentially the same as the apostolic fathers, although developed more extensively. Specifically, they connect Christian perfection with love in believers. Irenaeus teaches that perfection is a love marked by the fulfillment of the two greatest commandments—to love God and neighbor—which are the "precepts of an absolutely perfect life."[43] Clement of Alexandria summarizes perfection as a love that leads Christians to freely and willingly lay down their lives for God and

---

[40]See *Against Heresies* 2 pref.; 2.26.1; 2.28.1-2, 9; 2.30.7.
[41]Clement of Alexandria, *Stromata* 4:17-18. For Clement of Alexandria's key passages on Christian perfection, see *The Instructor* 1.1; 1.16; *Stromata* 2.19, 22; 4.1, 17-26; 5.1, 10; 6.1, 8-9, 12; 7.3, 10-14.
[42]Origen, *First Principles*, pref.
[43]Irenaeus, *Against Heresies* 5.8.4; 5.9.2; 5.11.1.

others.[44] Origen also testifies to perfection as a dynamic love for God and neighbor, ever increasing, ever deepening.[45]

Like the apostolic fathers, these writers also tie Christian perfection to freedom from sin in outward action and inward character. Irenaeus states that in perfection the Holy Spirit works to render believers into "a greater likeness to God" by purifying them from all sin and adorning them with the fruit of the Spirit.[46] Clement of Alexandria exhorts that perfection cures Christians of the "disease of sin" and rids Christians of "habitual sinful inclinations."[47] Origen also teaches that initial perfection involves obeying the commandments of God and doing away with the "reek of sin."[48]

Finally, the connection between the apostolic fathers and these later Fathers can be seen in the development of the "image or likeness of God" as a description for Christian perfection. By the late second and early third century, this phrase becomes synonymous in the Fathers with Christian perfection. It is used to express in perfected Christians the reflection of God's character, particularly love and holiness. It is also linked to the fullness of the Holy Spirit or the abiding presence of the Spirit in the lives of believers. The Spirit's presence makes Christians into the likeness of God through the work of sanctification and empowerment for Christian living.[49]

TERTULLIAN

As we have seen so far, Greek patristic literature from the second and third centuries is replete with the language of Christian perfection and expresses highly developed doctrines of it. Perfection appears as common soteriological language in early Christianity. We now

---

[44]Clement of Alexandria, *The Instructor* 1.2; 2.1-13.

[45]Origen, *Commentary on the Canticle of Canticles* I, 1:4c-f.

[46]Irenaeus, *Against Heresies* 5.8.4; 5.9.2; 5.11.1.

[47]Clement of Alexandria, *The Instructor* 1.2; 2.1-13.

[48]Origen, *First Homily on the Canticle of Canticles* 1.2a and the *Second Homily on the Canticle of Canticles* 1.12-13.

[49]Irenaeus, *Against Heresies* 5.8.4; 5.9.2; 5.11.1; Clement of Alexandria, *Stromata* 7.11-14; Origen, *First Principles* 3.1.1-22.

turn our attention to Christian perfection as it is expressed and develops among the emerging Latin Christian writers of the late
second and early third centuries, specifically Tertullian. Since Tertullian is the first prominent Latin theologian, conversant with and
dependent on the work of Irenaeus, the Greek apologists, and apostolic fathers, one expects the language of Christian perfection.[50]

While Tertullian does not devote a treatise to Christian perfection
(like his contemporary to the east, Clement of Alexandria) or offer
any developed teaching on perfection (like Irenaeus), he does use
the language. Tertullian's overarching concept of perfection can be
seen in his discussions of four topics: Gnosticism; God; creation,
redemption and consummation; and knowledge.

Perfection and the Gnostics. Like Irenaeus, Tertullian recognizes
the language of human perfection as common to Gnostic teaching.
Gnostics call their initiates "perfect" because they trace their seed of
"perfection" back to the aeon Sophia and its germination through
the reception of "perfect" knowledge.[51] More specifically, Tertullian
states that the Valentinian Gnostics believe there is a "perfect" unbegotten, invisible aeon named Bythos. With his consort Sige, he
fathered other aeons, who in turn begat others, until there were a
total of thirty aeons, forming the Pleroma.[52] Through inappropriate
desire for knowledge of Bythos, Sophia, one of the lowest aeons,
brought forth a material being named Achamoth, who exists outside
the Pleroma. Achamoth in turn birthed the Demiurge, who has
three substances: the material and animal, which arose from Sophia's impropriety, and the spiritual, which came from Sophia's
nature as member of the Pleroma.[53] The Demiurge then fashioned

---

[50]For a discussion of Tertullian as the first major Latin theologian and his dependence on earlier
Greek fathers and apologists, see Eric Osborn, *Tertullian: First Theologian of the West* (Cambridge: Cambridge University Press, 1997), 1-26.

[51]An aeon is an emanation (from the Latin "to flow from") of God. Tertullian, *On the Prescription
of Heretics* 41.4; *Against the Valentinians* 25.2.

[52]Tertullian, *Against the Valentinians* 7-8.

[53]Tertullian, *Against the Valentinians* 9, 13, 17.

the visible world and formed Adam in his image and likeness, with "image" referring to his material existence and "likeness" to his "animal." He also unknowingly imparted to Adam a spiritual nature. Adam's trifold nature then divides among his three sons: Cain, Abel, and Seth.[54]

According to Tertullian, the Gnostics teach that all human beings descend from one of these three lineages or natures: from Cain the material, from Abel the animal, and from Seth the spiritual. Humans who are material are destined for destruction.[55] Those who are animal have the possibility of ascent to the level of the Demiurge, while the spiritual are destined for the Pleroma. Only the spiritual, "perfected" by knowledge of their true spiritual state, are the "perfect" in this life.[56]

Perfection and God. Again like Irenaeus, Tertullian uses the language of perfection to describe Christians. He states that before Christ's passion on the cross, no human being was "perfect"; he calls a person who has been baptized a "perfected servant of God," and he refers to people who have been brought to the wisdom of God in Christ as the "perfect."[57] A proper treatment of Tertullian's conception of Christian perfection, however, must begin with his understanding of God's "perfect" goodness.

When Tertullian talks about divine perfection, he ties it almost exclusively to God's goodness.[58] In *Against Marcion*, Tertullian contrasts God's "perfect" goodness with Marcion's "imperfect" deity. Because the Marcionite deity determines to redeem only some people, but not others; because he saves only the human soul, not the body; and because salvation is not "perfectly" wrought in the present but reserved for the future, he is shown to be "imperfect." In contrast—and by implication—God's "perfection" requires that all

---

[54]Tertullian, *Against the Valentinians* 20, 29.
[55]Tertullian, *Against the Valentinians* 32.
[56]Tertullian, *Against the Valentinians* 25.2-3.
[57]Tertullian, *On Modesty* 11.3; *On Repentance* 6.1, 15; *Against Marcion* 5.6.2.
[58]See Tertullian, *Apology* 45.2; *Against Marcion* 1.24-25, 2.13; *On the Resurrection of the Flesh* 14, 15.

people have the possibility of salvation, that the entirety of human nature is redeemed, and that there is in some sense a "perfect" deliverance from the soul's enemies in present life.[59]

Tertullian moreover argues that God's perfect goodness is the standard for Christian virtue and is "more perfect" than ordinary human views. Human moral understanding is deficient on two levels: it has a limited understanding of virtue, and it offers little empowerment for its realization. God, however, as a "perfect master," provides "perfect knowledge" of goodness, showing the necessity for outward and inward conformity to revealed divine law, and empowers Christians to "faithfully do his will." Christians alone, therefore, try to realize a truly blameless life.[60] God's goodness requires the obedient Christian to love God as a "perfect father" with dutiful affection.[61]

Perfection in creation, redemption, and consummation. While Tertullian does not use the language of perfection to describe humanity's original state in creation, he does teach that God made humanity in the divine image and likeness for a particular end: "perfect sinlessness."[62] Like Irenaeus and earlier Greek fathers, Tertullian distinguishes between the divine image and likeness in humanity, with *image* referring to Adam's substance as body and soul, with a focus on the human soul, and *likeness* representing the Holy Spirit's presence and moral conformity to divine goodness.

More specifically, Tertullian connects the divine image to the soul's creation as the breath of the Holy Spirit. The human soul is an actual substance created by the Spirit endowed with rationality, emotions, and will. While the soul is a corporeal substance capable of existing apart from the body, it requires the body for the "perfection" of its actions.[63] Body and soul function as a distinct but

---

[59]Tertullian, *Against Marcion* 1.24-25.
[60]Tertullian, *Apology* 45.1-7.
[61]Tertullian, *Against Marcion* 2.13.5.
[62]Tertullian, *On the Spectacles* 2.10-12.
[63]Tertullian, *On the Resurrection of the Flesh* 17.6-8.

harmonious unitary whole. As the image of God, the soul receives and conveys the likeness of God to humanity. This likeness establishes human communion with God. While the image of God can exist in humanity without the divine likeness, it is incomplete.

According to Tertullian, humanity mirrored God's perfect goodness through the divine image and likeness as created in the garden. However, in contrast to divine goodness, which is part of God's immutable nature, Adam's goodness only existed through the grace of creation. It was therefore subject to change: either growth and development or corruption and brokenness. God gave humanity's first parents the gift of free will, through which they could follow the divine commandments given to them or not. This choice was bestowed by God to enable every human being to "justly possess" the goodness already inherent in them and thereby grow in holiness. Adam was under no necessity to sin and had the ability to walk with God in "perfect sinlessness."[64]

Therefore, for Tertullian, sin is accidental to humanity's created nature and is volitional. Because of Adam's willful disobedience in the garden, humanity lost God's likeness while still retaining the divine image. Since the fall, every human being undergoes physical death, experiences deprivation of the Holy Spirit, suffers from irrationality, and bears a corrupted soul. Tertullian states, "Every soul, then, by reason of its birth, has its nature in Adam until it is born again in Christ; moreover, it is unclean all the while it remains without this generation; and because unclean, it is actively sinful, and suffuses even the flesh, by reason of their conjunction, with its own shame."[65]

Redemption comes through Christ's recapitulation of Adam. By the incarnate Son's life of perfect obedience to the Father; by overcoming every temptation and modeling the life of holiness intended for all humanity; by the voluntary sacrifice of his perfect humanity

---

[64]Tertullian, *On the Resurrection of the Flesh* 17.8.
[65]Tertullian, *Apology* 40.

on the cross as the penalty for sin; and by triumphing over death through his bodily resurrection, Christ reverses the sin of Adam. Tertullian consequently calls Christ "the more perfect Adam."[66] Through Christ's incarnate life, he states, "God held converse with man that man may learn to act as God. God dealt on equal terms with man that man might be able to deal on equal terms with God. God was found little, that man might become very great."[67]

What Christ accomplishes objectively for human life, the Holy Spirit applies subjectively. Tertullian uses the language of perfection to describe this application in four parts. First is true repentance. Repentance demands all acts of known sin be renounced and put away, making the person a catechumen: a candidate for the remission and cleansing from sin through baptism. Speaking of repentance in relation to baptism, Tertullian states, "We are not washed in order that we may cease sinning, but because we have ceased, since in the heart we have been bathed already."[68] This repentance is connected to John's baptism of repentance in the Gospels, which prepares but does not "perfect" a person.[69]

Second is water baptism in the name of the triune God, followed by an anointing with oil and the imposition of hands. Because human nature is a unitary whole of two substances (body and soul), and because both substances participate in human sin (although in different ways), God uses physical elements—water and oil—to bring about a spiritual effect in the human soul.[70] Through the waters of Christian baptism, the guilt and penalty of sin are absolved, preparing the way for the Holy Spirit. Through anointing with oil and the laying on of hands, the newly baptized receive the Spirit, restoring

---

[66]Tertullian, *On Marriage and Remarriage* 5.6.
[67]Tertullian, *Against Marcion* 2.27.
[68]Tertullian, *On Repentance* 6.
[69]Tertullian, *On Baptism* 10.6.
[70]Tertullian, *On Baptism* 5-7.

the divine "likeness" lost in the fall and establishing them in holiness.[71] While Tertullian does not use the language often, he refers to baptized believers as the "perfect" and "perfected servants of God."[72]

Third is the process of sanctification, bringing the Christian into greater conformity to the moral example of Christ. The perfection experienced in baptism is dynamic and not static. As Christians learn more about Christ and as the Holy Spirit leads the church to the "perfection" of teaching how to live in its culture, the Spirit enables Christians to experience more fully the will of God "on earth as it is in heaven."[73]

Sanctification requires not only outward alignment to God's will but also inward conformity. Tertullian asks, "What is more perfect, to forbid adultery or to restrain from even a single lustful look?"[74] He illustrates this point in *On the Apparel of Women*: "You must know that perfect modesty, that is, Christian modesty, requires not only that you never desire to be an object of desire on the part of others, but that you even hate to be one."[75]

Sanctification entails the love of God and neighbor. Tertullian teaches that God is a "perfect father" who must be loved with dutiful affection.[76] Love of God produces obedience to God. Ultimately, "perfect love" for God casts out fears of suffering and enables a believer to die for Christ.[77] Humanity is to be loved as well. He states, "For our religion commands us to love even our enemies, and to pray for those who persecute us, aiming at a perfection all its own, and seeking in its disciples something of a higher type than the commonplace goodness of the world. For all love those who love them; it is peculiar to Christians alone to love those who hate them."[78]

---

[71]Tertullian, *On Baptism* 6–8.
[72]Tertullian, *On Repentance* 6; *Against Marcion* 5.6; *On Modesty* 11.
[73]Tertullian, *On the Veiling of Virgins* 1; *Apology* 45; *On Prayer* 4.
[74]Tertullian, *Apology* 45.3.
[75]Tertullian, *On the Apparel of Women* 2.2.1.
[76]Tertullian, *Against Marcion* 2.13.5.
[77]Tertullian, *Antidote for the Scorpion's Sting* 12.4–5; *On the Running Away from Persecution* 9.3.
[78]Tertullian, *To Scapula* 1.3.

The sanctifying work of the Holy Spirit is a process by which the soul is increasingly renewed, advancing in faith and holiness daily. As the mind is formed in virtue, it "perfects" the flesh. As patience, the supreme mark of holiness as seen in Christ, grows in the "inward man," the body lives out that patience, imitating Christ in deeper and fuller ways.[79]

As already implied, this sanctifying work leads to the highest imitation of Christ in life for Tertullian: chastity and martyrdom. First, it calls Christians to renounce the lusts of the flesh and either never marry (as Christ did) or never remarry. However, if this "perfection" is too high, then Christians must practice faithful monogamy, as Christ does in his faithful relationship as a husband to the church.[80] Second, the work of the Holy Spirit enables Christians, when necessary, to express the highest form of perfection in present life, the ultimate act of Christ imitation—physical suffering and death by martyrdom, which alone ushers the soul into the intermediate state of paradise.[81]

Finally, ultimate perfection is brought in bodily resurrection at final judgment.[82] After death, the souls of Christians await resurrection with the saints in Hades, experiencing a foretaste of the judgment to come.[83] In bodily resurrection, all souls receive back "the self-same bodies in which they died," although transformed to fit life in eternity.[84] Only body and soul incorruptibly whole in perfect union with each other make Christians truly human.[85] This resurrection is made possible by the bodily resurrection of Christ. It is his resurrected humanity that is the pattern for Christian resurrection. Human beings in God's consummated kingdom have now

---

[79]Tertullian, *On Patience* 13.5-7.

[80]Tertullian, *On Marriage and Remarriage* 5.1-4.

[81]Tertullian, *Antidote for the Scorpion's Sting* 8.7; 12.4-5, 9-11; *On the Running Away from Persecution* 14.2-3.

[82]Tertullian, *On the Resurrection of the Flesh* 17.6-8; 40.6-10; 58.1-10.

[83]Tertullian, *On the Soul* 46, 48.

[84]Tertullian, *On the Soul* 46.

[85]Tertullian, *On the Resurrection of the Flesh* 45.17.

reached full development and perfection; they are now incorruptibly sinless, perfect like God.

Perfection and knowledge. Significant for Tertullian is the role of knowledge in Christian perfection. He repeatedly connects the language of perfection to revealed wisdom and knowledge. In his treatise *To the Nations*, Tertullian argues that the person who has true knowledge of God, leading to proper "fear of the Lord," possesses "full and perfect" wisdom, even if ignorant of all else.[86] Because humanity is unable to fully grasp divine truth in one moment, the Holy Spirit superintended the unveiling of God and the gospel gradually over time, allowing them to be brought to "perfection."[87] Divine wisdom and truth existed latently under "figures, allegories, and enigmatical types" in the Old Testament but are revealed fully in Christ.[88]

Divine knowledge and wisdom are necessary for the "perfection" of faith. People are unable to exercise faith "perfectly" in a God not yet fully revealed to them.[89] This is one of the reasons Tertullian encourages delay in baptism until people are duly prepared. Even when Scripture appears to advocate immediate baptism, like the Ethiopian eunuch with Philip, there was careful reading and instruction in God's Word before the eunuch experienced the "perfect" work of salvation through baptism.[90] Knowledge of the gospel is an indispensable means of God's grace that "renews all things from carnal to spiritual" and empowers a life of obedient conformity to the "perfect knowledge" of God's goodness.[91]

Later Latin Fathers in the third and fourth centuries. Among the Latin fathers of the third century, Tertullian's articulation of the doctrine of Christian perfection is the clearest. This does not mean,

---

[86]Tertullian, *To the Nations* 2.2.4.
[87]Tertullian, *On the Veiling of Virgins* 1.4.
[88]Tertullian, *Against Marcion* 5.6.2.
[89]Tertullian, *Against Marcion* 4.29.3.
[90]Tertullian, *On Baptism* 18.2.
[91]Tertullian, *On Prayer* 1.2; *Apology* 45.1.

however, that other Latin writers of the era neglect it. Like Tertullian, their theology is embedded in discussions of particular problems arising in the church and must be extracted from these discussions. Cyprian, the most significant of these fathers, reflects the central ideas of Christian perfection found in Tertullian: the love of God and neighbor, restoration of the *imago Dei*, and freedom from sin.

Cyprian's most extensive comments on Christian perfection are found in *On the Advantage of Patience*, a treatise with obvious literary dependence on Tertullian's work on the same subject. Specifically, in his discussion of the patience exhibited by Jesus Christ, Cyprian states,

> And that we may more fully understand, beloved brethren, that patience is a thing of God, and that whoever is gentle, and patient, and meek, is an imitator of God the Father; when the Lord . . . was instructing his disciples to perfection, he laid it down and said, "You shall love your neighbor and hate your enemy. But I say unto you, love your enemies, and pray for them which persecute you that you may be the children of your Father which is in heaven. . . . Be you therefore perfect, even as your Father in heaven is perfect." He said the children of God would thus be perfect.[92]

Like Tertullian, Cyprian ties perfection to Jesus' command to love God and neighbor. In *On the Advantage of Patience*, Cyprian connects the love of neighbor to the practice of patience with enemy, which imitates and reflects God's longsuffering love for humanity. He describes it here as the distinguishing mark of Christian perfection.[93] Elsewhere, in *On the Lapsed*, Cyprian makes clear that Christians can only "be perfect" when their "heart and mind" are focused on the love of God, unshackled by the love of possessions, enabling them to "cleave to Christ with undivided ties."[94] As with

---

[92]Cyprian, *On the Advantage of Patience* 5.
[93]Cyprian, *On the Advantage of Patience* 5. Cyprian mentions perfection in relationship to humanity in a short treatise *On the Benefits of Good Works and Mercy*.
[94]Cyprian, *On the Lapsed* 11.

Tertullian, this perfect love of God empowers Christians to offer their lives freely without worldly constraint in the perfect imitation of Christ: martyrdom.[95]

Cyprian also links Christian perfection to the restoration of the divine likeness in humanity, again following Tertullian's lead. In *On the Lapsed*, he states that perfection occurs through new birth when the divine likeness lost by Adam is restored and manifests itself through the Christian practice of patience.[96] Cyprian connects the *imago Dei* in humanity to God's moral goodness, manifested supremely in Christ's submission to the Father in the incarnation; his life of humble service to humanity; his benevolence to sinful humanity; his death on behalf of enemies; and his empowering resurrection. Furthermore, Christ's "full and perfect" patience makes possible the restoration of divine likeness in humanity.[97] Because Christ lived a life of patience, Christians, through the Holy Spirit, can do the same.

For Cyprian, the restoration of humanity's divine likeness, with patience as its distinguishing mark, necessitates freedom from sin. Cyprian concurs with Tertullian: Adam's sinful disobedience rooted in impatience led to the loss of divine likeness. For Christians to be "perfected," to have the likeness of God restored, they must live in obedience to God, free from willful sin (that which caused Adam and others to lose God's likeness in the first place), and have the *imago Dei* "shine" in all their actions.[98]

As already intimated, Cyprian believes in the possibility of Christian perfection in this life. He speaks of the apostles as ones who "were perfected." Their perfection involved actively loving their enemies, having the divine image restored in their lives, and becoming like God in all their virtues.[99]

---

[95]Cyprian, *On the Lapsed* 11.
[96]Cyprian, *On the Lapsed* 5.
[97]Cyprian, *On the Lapsed* 5.
[98]Cyprian, *On the Lapsed* 5-6.
[99]Cyprian, *On the Lapsed* 5.

The Latin tradition of perfection continues into the fourth century through Ambrose of Milan. Working with Jesus' teaching on perfection in Matthew 5:20-48 and 19:16-26, Ambrose recognizes that Christian perfection entails not just outward conformity to the law of God, which he terms "ordinary duty," but heart alignment as well, which is "perfect duty."[100] Perfection is found in the alignment of action and intention.[101] It is the love of God and neighbor in heart and life. Outwardly, its supreme manifestation is found in mercy to the poor and to one's enemies because mercy embodies God's love and Christ's command, "Be perfect as your Father in heaven is perfect."[102]

Ambrose teaches, more specifically, that there are two levels of perfection: one in present life and one in the kingdom of God to come. The first is relative perfection, and the second absolute perfection. The first was experienced by David in the Old Testament and Paul in the New. Both were able to bless and forgive their enemies. In their mercy, the love of God and neighbor was demonstrated in their lives.[103] Their perfection of love consisted in their human passion being controlled by reason, which furnished them with the cardinal virtues: prudence, justice, fortitude, and temperance.[104]

While relative perfection can be experienced in the present life, absolute perfection comes in the next, when humanity is made incorruptibly holy and is fully like God.[105] Ambrose finds this distinction illustrated in Philippians 3. Paul testifies to not yet being perfect: "Not as though I had already attained, either were already perfect; but I follow after, if that I may apprehend it" (Phil 3:12). The context here is Paul's discussion of humanity's perfection in the resurrected state. Paul has not obtained that perfection. Yet in the same

---

[100] Ambrose, *On the Duties of the Clergy* 1.11.36-38.
[101] Ambrose, *On the Duties of the Clergy* 1.30.151.
[102] Ambrose, *On the Duties of the Clergy* 1.11.38.
[103] Ambrose, *On the Duties of the Clergy* 1.48.244-47.
[104] Ambrose, *On the Duties of the Clergy* 1.25.114-15.
[105] Ambrose, *On the Duties of the Clergy* 1.48.248.

passage he states, "We, then, that are perfect" (3:15).[106] This is the relative perfection in life that Paul knows.

GREGORY OF NYSSA

Gregory of Nyssa, one of the Cappadocian fathers from the middle and late fourth century, follows the Greek patristic tradition in his significant discussion of Christian perfection. He incorporates many of the themes found in earlier theologians. His most sustained treatments of the subject are three treatises: *Life of Moses*, *On Virginity*, and *On Perfection*.

Gregory's general understanding of perfection. Gregory's teaching on Christian perfection begins with God. The very nature of God is goodness. Because the divine nature is infinite, God's goodness is without limits, unsurpassable in every virtue. There is no evil in God to constrain or circumscribe goodness in any way. God's infinite nature, God's moral character, makes God perfect.

To be clear, Gregory believes perfection in goodness is only limited when its contrary is present. Since the divine nature excludes anything contrary to its goodness, it is without any boundaries.[107] He states, "Since, then, it has not been demonstrated that there is any limit to virtue except evil, and since the divine does not admit of any opposite, we hold the divine nature to be unlimited and infinite . . . perfect."[108]

No human being, therefore, can experience perfection, the perfection only God has. Christians, through their knowledge of God, desire the highest good, which is God. They long to share in God's unlimited goodness without qualification. They cannot, however, ever arrive since there is no boundary or marker to that which is infinite. Gregory states, "It is, therefore, undoubtedly impossible to

---

[106]Ambrose, *On the Duties of the Clergy* 3.2.11.
[107]Gregory of Nyssa, *Life of Moses*, trans. Abraham Malherbe and Everett Ferguson (New York: Paulist, 1978) 1.7.
[108]Gregory of Nyssa, *Life of Moses* 1.7.

attain perfection, since, as I have said, perfection is not marked by limits . . . How then would one arrive at the sought-for boundary when he can find no boundary?"[109] As finite creatures, humans can never be divine.

Gregory, nevertheless, acknowledges the weight of Jesus' command, "Be perfect as your Father in heaven is perfect." While Christians may never realize divine perfection, they can participate in God and share in divine goodness. Through this participation, Christians can experience infinite growth in the divine. Human perfection, therefore, "lies precisely in this—constant growth in the good," the experience of continual growth in God though union with the divine.[110] God's perfection admits no development or corruption. It is immutable. Human perfection, in contrast, is dynamic, defined by continual growth.

Because humanity is created, Gregory believes they are mutable by nature. They are defined by change. Through the exercise of free will, humanity moves toward good or evil. Because of the fall of humanity's first parents, humanity has a propensity for evil. They, however, are not defined by it. Christians are called and empowered to grow toward the good, becoming ever more like God. He states,

> No one should lament his mutable nature, rather, by always being changed to what is better and by being transformed from glory to glory, let him so be changed. By daily growth he always becomes better and is always being perfected, yet never attains perfection's goal. [Christian] perfection consists in never stopping our growth towards the good nor in circumscribing perfection.[111]

Christian perfection for Gregory, in the end, is continual growth "from glory to glory" in the moral goodness that is God. Through

---

[109]Gregory of Nyssa, *Life of Moses* 1.7.

[110]Gregory of Nyssa, *Life of Moses* 1.9.

[111]Gregory of Nyssa, *On Perfection*, in *Saint Gregory of Nyssa: Ascetical Works*, trans. Virginia W. Callahan, Fathers of the Church 58 (Washington, DC: The Catholic University of America Press, 1967).

participation in the divine through Christ, believers experience "rest" and "movement."[112] Christ, through his incarnate life, addresses and overcomes all impediments to human participation in the good. The movement of the human soul has true stability because it remains "firm and unchanging in the good," "furnishing the heart with wings for the upward journey through firmness of the good."[113] Through this positive mutability, Christians increasingly grow into the image of God, freed from alteration to evil. This liberates believers to experience increasing degrees of perfection in present life that continues into the next.

Gregory's specific understanding of Christian perfection. According to Gregory, human beings were created by God in the beginning with an immaterial, immortal soul, which is the image of God, and a material body made like the animals. These two, intimately related to each other, form human nature. As made in the divine image, humanity possesses the gifts of freedom, independence, and self-determination, through which they decide to remain in the virtue ordained by God in creation or not. Humanity's first parents were seduced by the adversary in the garden, turned away from goodness, and became subject to evil. The consequences were devastating: the divine image in humanity experienced corruption, inclining them to sin, and the physical body became mortal, subjecting humanity to death.

The human soul, more specifically, is composed of "the rational, the spirited and the appetitive."[114] As originally created, reason directed the soul's will and passions in the love of God and neighbor. The spirited and appetitive parts supported and gave drive to the rational while following the guidance of reason. A radical shift took place, however, after Adam and Eve's disobedience. Reason was

---

[112]Gregory of Nyssa, *Life of Moses* 2.252-53.
[113]Gregory of Nyssa, *Life of Moses* 2.252-53.
[114]Gregory of Nyssa, *Life of Moses* 2.96, 123.

displaced, and the soul became ensnarled with "earthly desire," no longer focused on the love of God.[115]

God in divine goodness could not allow humanity to remain in their corruption. Neither could God bring human redemption through divine fiat. Human nature could only be saved through the incarnation of the eternal Son: he assumed full human nature, a rational soul and physical body, in order to restore the divine image from corruption and impart immortality to the body. Through the assumption of human nature and overcoming all temptation in life, he made possible the restoration of the divine image in present life and the resurrection of the body in the life to come. The Son's human soul makes possible the restoration of reason as the leader of human will and passion; his human body redeems our bodies from death.

The Son's incarnate life paves the way for human imitation. Following the teaching of the apostle Paul, Gregory teaches more specifically that Jesus Christ is the image of the invisible God, and Christians are called to be conformed to his image. Gregory states, "If we are to become the invisible God's image, we must model the form of our life upon the pattern given us . . . What is that model? . . . That prototype is the image of the invisible God; having become man through the Virgin, he was tempted in all things according to the likeness of human nature yet did not experience sin."[116]

In his treatise *On Perfection*, Gregory teaches that human perfection is found in becoming like Christ, embodying exactly everything the name "Christian" implies. Believers learn the full meaning of that name and then conform to it. The Son's incarnation makes it possible for evil and sin to be utterly removed and "the adversary annihilated" in human life.[117]

Christian life must manifest all the qualities of Christ. Because the incarnate Son exists in two natures, divine and human, he has

---

[115]Gregory of Nyssa, *Life of Moses* 2.60.
[116]Gregory of Nyssa, *On Perfection* 95.
[117]Gregory of Nyssa, *On Perfection* 95-96.

two sets of attributes. Both must radiate from the life of a Christian. Christ's human qualities must be imitated, while his incommunicable divine attributes are worshiped in love and reverence.[118]

Gregory examines the meaning of the "Christian" name by reflecting on the apostle Paul's description of Christ. For example, Paul calls Christ the "wisdom and power of God." Therefore, those who have Christ's name have wisdom in choosing the good and power to be victorious over sin. Christians exhibit Christ as "peace" through the destruction of the enemy, through the elimination of the "civil war" within humanity. Believers live out Christ as "redemption" when they no longer live for themselves, but for him who gave his life for humanity. Christians imitate the Passover lamb, offering themselves as a "propitiatory sacrifice by purifying" their "souls through the mortification of their limbs." Therefore, they live in the flesh but not according to the flesh.[119]

Although Gregory focuses his treatise on Christian perfection on the imitation of Christ, he makes clear that it is grounded in participation in Christ. Gregory recognizes that Christ, through his incarnation, becomes human for humans to become united with God. Through his humanity, Christians participate in his divinity.[120] He states that Jesus "became the image of the invisible God out of love so that in his own form which he assumed," Christians "might be conformed through him to the stamp of the archetypal beauty."[121] These ever-increasing levels of perfection through participation begin in baptism, which applies to the believer the purification of human nature found in Christ's death and resurrection.

Gregory concludes by teaching that Christians are defined by their thoughts, words, and deeds. Reason must guide human thoughts; then speech, which expresses human thoughts; and finally

---

[118]Gregory of Nyssa, *On Perfection* 95.
[119]Gregory of Nyssa, *On Perfection* 95-110.
[120]Gregory of Nyssa, *On Perfection* 110-15.
[121]Gregory of Nyssa, *On Perfection* 116.

action, which brings into being our thoughts and words. Each of these must reflect the names of Christ, which can only come from Christ.[122] In comparing Christ to a pure fountain of water, Gregory states, "He who draws to himself thoughts as from a pure, incorruptible fountain will resemble the prototype as a water drawn into a jar resembles water gushing from a fountain. Christ possesses one pure nature which is the same for anyone who participates in it."[123]

AUGUSTINE

We conclude this chapter with the younger contemporary of Gregory of Nyssa, Augustine of Hippo. He represents the climax of the Latin church in the first five centuries of Christianity. While his doctrine of Christian perfection is not as high or robust as many of the Fathers who precede or come after him, his teaching nevertheless stands in a long historical line of testimony about a Christian's victory over willful sin and a life defined by the love of God and neighbor.

Augustine's perspective on perfection is best viewed through his *ordo salutis* ("order of salvation"). In AD 394 he identifies four basic stages in salvation, which he would utilize throughout his ministry as priest and bishop: a life "prior to the law," "under the law," "under grace," and "in peace."[124] He acknowledges, however, that some Christians may not pass through all stages. For example, in the case of infant baptism, a child moves from a life "prior to the law" to one "in grace," bypassing the stage of "under the law."[125]

Prior to the law. Because of original sin inherited from our first parents, Augustine believes every human being is born into life "prior to the law." They live in ignorance of sin and follow their carnal desires without the restraint of conscience or established

---

[122]Gregory of Nyssa, *On Perfection* 118-22.
[123]Gregory of Nyssa, *On Perfection* 121.
[124]Augustine, *Propositions from the Epistle to the Romans*, trans. Paula Fredriksen Landes (Atlanta, GA: Society of Biblical Literature, 1982) 13.1–18.4.
[125]Augustine, *Enchiridion* 119.

prohibitions.[126] He interprets the apostle Paul's statement, "And I was alive once without the law" (Rom 7:9), as describing Paul's early childhood before he could reason, or an age of accountability.[127]

Under the law. The second stage is a life "under the law." Here, people recognize their sinfulness through an awakened conscience and the revelation of God's law. Knowledge of the law produces anxiety over their guilt and prepares them for the grace of salvation. They learn how sinful they really are. They are aware of the condemnation of God on their lives and want to some extent to live in accordance with the law but are unable to do so. They are slaves to sin and the fear of God.[128] They want to change, but the power of carnal desire is too strong, and they find greater pleasure in committing sin.[129] Sin deceives them continually "with its false sweetness."[130]

Augustine believes a person is defeated at this stage because he does not yet love righteousness for the sake of God and for the sake of righteousness itself. "And so when he sees righteousness on the one hand and temporal comfort on the other, he is drawn to the weight of temporal longing and thus abandons righteousness, which he was trying to hold on to only in order to have the comfort he now sees he will lose if he holds on to righteousness."[131]

People "under the law" may conform to the law, but only if it is beneficial to them. The desires of the flesh may lead to obedience, but only for selfish reasons. When keeping the law is no longer beneficial, a person discards it.

---

[126] Augustine, *Propositions for the Epistle to the Romans* 13.1–18.4; *Enchiridion* 118.

[127] Augustine, *Against Two Letters of the Pelagians* 1.14, 16.

[128] Augustine, *Propositions from the Epistle to the Romans* 13.1–18.4; *Enchiridion* 118; *To Simplician on Various Questions*, in *Earlier Writings*, trans. John H. S. Burleigh, The Library of Christian Classics 6 (Philadelphia: Westminster, 1953) 1.2.

[129] Augustine's experience with the pears, recounted in his *Confessions* 2.9-14, is a classic Christian example of this.

[130] Augustine, *To Simplician* 1.5.

[131] Augustine, *Augustine's Commentary on Galatians: Introduction, Text, Translation, and Notes*, ed. and trans. Eric Plummer, Oxford Early Christian Studies (Oxford: Oxford University Press, 2006), 46.

Under grace. The only way humanity's sinful desires can be defeated is through a true love of God and love of the commanded good. In the absence of real love, carnal desire always triumphs. In the third stage of salvation "under grace," Augustine teaches that God gives the love of God to the human heart through the infusion of the Holy Spirit, empowering the Christian to "delight" in the law of God and walk in accordance to love. While Christians still have desires of the flesh, and the flesh conflicts with the Spirit, the love of God triumphs over these desires so that believers do not obey them.[132]

At this point, it may be helpful to catalog chronologically some of Augustine's key statements on life "under grace" to demonstrate his consistent belief in a Christian's victory over willful sin. Augustine in his description of the third stage clearly states in AD 395, "When this happens, even though certain fleshly desires fight against our spirit while we are in this life, to lead us into sin, nonetheless our spirit resists them because it is fixed in the grace and love of God, and ceases to sin. For we sin not by having this perverse desire but by consenting to it."[133] In AD 398 he writes to his friend Simplicius, "When grace forgives sin and infuses a spirit of charity, righteousness ceases to be hard and becomes even pleasant."[134] Speaking about the perfection of righteousness possible in the present life and experienced "under grace," he teaches in AD 415, "But whensoever [the believer] suffers not sin to reign in his mortal body to obey it in the lusts thereof, and yields not his members as instruments of unrighteousness unto sin . . . it does not reign, because its desires are not obeyed."[135] Augustine affirms in AD 422 that the apostles did not consent to the lusts of the flesh and lived "under grace." He declares, "I do say that although they were free from consent to depraved lusts, they nevertheless groaned concerning

---

[132] Augustine, *Enchiridion* 118.
[133] Augustine, *Propositions from the Epistle to the Romans* 13.1–18.10.
[134] Augustine, *To Simplician* 1.7.
[135] Augustine, *Concerning Man's Perfection in Righteousness* 9.28.

the concupiscence of the flesh, which they bridled by restraint with such humility and piety, that they desired rather not to have it than to subdue it."[136] Then, in the *Enchiridion*, the most systematic account of his mature theology (AD 422), Augustine describes the Christian in the third stage of salvation:

> But if God has regard to him, and inspires him with faith in God's help, and the Spirit of God begins to work in him, then the mightier power of love strives against the power of the flesh, and although there is still in man's own nature a power that fights against him (for his disease is not completely cured), yet he lives the life of the just by faith, and lives in righteousness so far as he does not yield to evil lust, but conquers it by the love of holiness.[137]

While Augustine remains consistent in his teaching that a Christian "under grace" is empowered to walk in love and not consent to sinful desires, he does nuance some of the finer points of his teaching, particularly his conception of sin and his understanding of the intensity of sinful desires. First, Augustine develops his definition of sin. In AD 395, Augustine acknowledges that a Christian still experiences the lusts of the flesh but does not sin. At this point in his theology, he defines sin as the consent of the will—to obey, or to act according to sinful desire. Simply having sinful desires is not sin.[138] Elsewhere, he writes that God's condemnation does not rest on the one "engaged in battle, but on the one defeated in battle."[139]

However, by the opening decades of the fifth century, Augustine's hamartiology expands. He begins to see sinful desire itself as personal sin and in need of the absolution brought about through the Lord's Prayer ("Forgive our debts, as we forgive our debtors") and through almsgiving. While he only sees it as venial sin and not

---

[136]Concupiscence is an inordinate, often sensual, desire. Augustine, *Against Two Letters of the Pelagians* 1.24.

[137]Augustine, *Enchiridion* 118.

[138]Augustine, *Propositions to the Romans* 13.1–18.10.

[139]Augustine, *Commentary on Galatians*, 46.

mortal, it is still sin a Christian must bear until the resurrection of the body.[140]

Augustine comes to see sinful desire as sin because it falls short of the perfect love of God and neighbor, which is the ultimate end of the law. A Christian operates out of the love of God; the love of God enables a person's obedience, but because of the desires of the flesh, love is not perfect.[141] Augustine states:

> It is not the mere "doing" of a good thing that is not present to him, but the "perfecting" of it. For in this, that he yields no consent (to the desires of the flesh), he does good; he does good again, in this, that he hates his own lust . . . But how to perfect the good is not present to him; it will be, however, in that final state, when the concupiscence which dwells in his members shall exist no more.[142]

Second, Augustine sees the intensity of sinful desire in Christian life more clearly. Early in his theological thought, Augustine recognizes or acknowledges concupiscence in the third stage, but does not give significance to it. However, while writing *Confessions,* he begins to address the psychological dynamics and intensity of fleshly desires in detail. These command Augustine's attention in ways not seen in his earlier work.[143]

Nevertheless, while Augustine paints concupiscence in the third stage with greater intensity, he persistently maintains a Christian's victory over it. Christians can overcome their sinful desires because of the love of God shed abroad in their hearts. Because Christians "under grace" have true love, love subdues all other desires, enabling

---

[140]According to Roman Catholic theology, a venial sin is a lesser sin that injures a person's relationship with God, but does not break it. A mortal sin is grave, leading to damnation if left unrepented. See James Wetzel, "Sin," in *Augustine Through the Ages: An Encyclopedia,* ed. Allan D. Fitzgerald (Grand Rapids, MI: Eerdmans, 1999), 800-802.

[141]Augustine, *On Man's Perfection in Righteousness* 8.19; *Enchiridion* 121.

[142]Augustine, *On Man's Perfection in Righteousness* 11.28.

[143]Compare Augustine's treatment of concupiscence or fleshly desires in his earlier theological work in *Propositions from the Epistle to the Romans* 13-18 and *Commentary on Galatians* 46 with his mature theological treatments in *Against Two Letters of the Pelagians* 1.13-27 and *Against Julian* 2.2.5; 6.23.70-73.

the Christian to walk in love. This provides Christians a relative perfection in the present life.[144]

In peace. In the fourth and final stage of salvation, a life is "in peace." This will occur when Christians are bodily resurrected in the age to come. Then, there will be nothing in humanity that resists the love of God, but every part will work harmoniously together. There will be the perfection of love in which people will love God with all heart, soul, and mind. All human action will embody the perfect love of God and neighbor. Sin and sinful desires will be impossible to humanity since they will be like God, having true freedom—to do only what is in accordance with love.[145] Here, Christians experience absolute human perfection.

Conclusion

While Christian perfection is nuanced in different ways among prominent patristic writers of the first five centuries, central themes emerge. Perfection consists in the experience of the supremacy of the love of God in human life, manifested in freedom from the power of sin, liberating a believer for a life of obedience to Christ and love of neighbor. While some among them believe complete purity in love happens in perfection, others argue for vestiges of inward sin remaining until death. There are, therefore, higher and lower views of perfection, particularly regarding the developing question of original sin. Perfection, nevertheless, comes from the Spirit's fullness and restoration of the image or likeness of God in human lives, modeled supremely in the incarnate Son, Jesus Christ. The experience of Christian perfection, by and large, remains an expectation or possibility for every believer.

---

[144] Augustine, *On Man's Perfection in Righteousness* 11.28.

[145] Augustine, *Propositions to the Romans* 13.1–18.4; *Commentary on Galatians,* 46; *Eighty-Three Different Questions,* trans. David L. Mosher, Fathers of the Church 70 (Washington, DC: Catholic University of America Press, 1977) 66.3; *Concerning Man's Perfection in Righteousness* 3.8; 8.19; *Against Two Letters of the Pelagians* 1.24; *Enchiridion* 118.

8

HOLINESS IN THE MIDDLE AGES

THE DOCTRINE OF CHRISTIAN perfection is significantly present in the writings of the ante-Nicene and Nicene fathers. When the Roman Empire legalized and embraced Christianity, movements arose within the church that were dedicated to the attainment of perfection. Martyrdom, seen as the ultimate expression of Christian perfection when the church existed at the peripheries of Roman society, subsided with Christianity's new status. Asceticism came to the fore in its place and found expression in monasticism. While asceticism was always a part of Christianity individually and corporately, Christians began to retreat from cities to seek God in the wilderness and isolated communities in response to encroaching secularism.

JOHN CASSIAN (AD 360–435)

At the dawn of the Middle Ages, the search for Christian perfection moved from the church's mainstream into monasticism. Two expressions arose. The first and oldest is anchoritism (from the Latin and Greek "to withdraw") or eremitism (from the Latin and Greek "living in the desert"), which followed the examples of Moses, Elijah, and Elisha, who retreated to the desert, pursuing God in solitary isolation. It began with the hermit Antony, who was seized as a young man by Christ's call to perfection: "If you want to be perfect, go, sell your possessions and give to the poor, and you will have treasure in heaven. Then come, follow me" (Mt 19:21).[1] In response, he immediately gave up his riches and retreated to the deserts of Egypt, where he devoted himself to prayer and spiritual warfare. As martyrdom waned in early Christianity, Antony became the ideal example of perfection.

The second form of monasticism is cenobitism (from the Latin and Greek "community life" or "common life"), which modeled itself on the example of the earliest New Testament church in Acts. These communities shared common resources, devoting themselves to spiritual life with other pilgrims, seeking Christian perfection. In the fourth and early fifth centuries, monastic rules, ascetical treatises, collections of spiritual statements, and hagiographic stories were developed in the cenobitic tradition. John Cassian's *Conferences* represent the maturity of this movement and the spirituality governing it. In them, Cassian traces the pilgrimage of human life, identifying the challenges and means by which perfection is realized in life.

Cassian was trained in the monastic tradition of Egypt, where he experienced both of its primary forms. However, he came to believe that the cenobitic approach to asceticism was the only true way to perfection. After spending time in Constantinople and Rome, he traveled to Marseilles in Gaul, where he established two monasteries, one for men and the other for women. Cassian states his purpose in writing *Conferences*, a collection of spiritual wisdom gleaned from conversations with monastic leaders: "purity of heart," which is "evangelical perfection."[2]

The ordo of perfection in John Cassian. Cassian's most significant overview of Christian perfection appears in conference eleven, "On

---

[1]Scripture quotations in discussions of primary sources are those of the writer in view unless otherwise noted.

[2]John Cassian, *The Conferences*, trans. Boniface Ramsey (New York: Paulist Press, 1985) 1.4.3.

Perfection." Specifically, he identifies three ascending stages of the spiritual life leading to ultimate perfection: fear, hope, and love, also identified as the slave, the hired hand, and the son.

The first stage: The fear of a slave. Christian life begins with the fear of hell, the ultimate consequence of sin. Virtue is embraced and vice rejected because impending judgment threatens. Cassian compares this stage of a believer's life to an enslaved person motivated by the threat of a master's discipline. Obedience is obtained by dread rather than love.[3] Spiritual stability at this stage, however, is tenuous. Because a Christian is motivated by fear and not the love of God, there is a return to what is truly loved when fear is removed or subsides.[4] Sin is once again embraced because it still rules the human heart.

While recognizing problems with this first stage, Cassian sees a "measure" of perfection in it. He quotes Psalm 128:1, "Blessed are all they that fear the Lord," and teaches that God's kingdom begins in human life here.[5]

The second stage: The hope of a hired hand. "Hope" is the second stage in the spiritual journey toward perfection. Cassian compares "hope" to a hired hand who no longer fears punishment like a slave but is motivated by the expectation of compensation. Self-denial, ascetic practices, and imitation of Christ come with the expectation of earthly and heavenly reward. Christians shun sin and embrace virtue for personal profit.[6]

This stage is deficient because it ultimately focuses on the benefits of virtue, the advantages of a holy life, and the privileges of being a citizen in God's kingdom rather than the good of God alone. If fear of punishment and the promise of reward are removed, then a Christian easily returns to the life of sin.[7] The believer has yet to

---

[3]Cassian, *The Conferences* 2.11.6.
[4]Cassian, *The Conferences* 2.11.8.
[5]Cassian, *The Conferences* 2.11.12.
[6]Cassian, *The Conferences* 2.11.6-8.
[7]Cassian, *The Conferences* 2.11.8.

realize "purity of heart." Their relationship with God is bound by fear or hope rather than truly being voluntary.[8]

Even with its limitations, Cassian teaches there is a "kind" of perfection in hope expressed as a hired hand. He cites Isaiah 49:6, "It is a great thing for you to be called my servant."[9]

The third stage: The love of a son. According to Cassian, the path to ultimate Christian perfection moves from fear to hope and from hope to love. The final stage of spiritual life is "evangelical perfection" or "purity of heart," when believers love God and love virtue for the sake of goodness itself and for God's own self.[10] Cassian's key points here are crucial.

Christian perfection in love, to begin with, reflects the nature of God's own love. God does the good not out of fear of punishment or the hope of reward but simply for the love of goodness. Cassian states, "For under cover of his own goodness, he bestows all the fullness of good things on the worthy and unworthy because he cannot be wearied by wrongs, nor be moved by passions at the sins of humanity, as he ever remains perfect goodness and unchangeable in nature."[11]

Perfection in love, therefore, is what gives shape to the image of God in believers. Like God, they "delight in goodness for the pleasure of goodness itself."[12] Like God, they do not "admit into their heart anything that is opposed [to virtue] . . . but ultimately hate it with the utmost horror."[13] And like God, they love their enemies and do good to those that hate them (Mt 5:44), fulfilling the "evangelic command of perfection" (Mt 5:48).[14] Cassian teaches, "For how can a weak and fragile human be like him, except in always showing a

---

[8]Cassian, *The Conferences* 2.11.8.
[9]Cassian, *The Conferences* 2.11.12.
[10]Cassian, *The Conferences* 2.11.6, 12.
[11]Cassian, *The Conferences* 2.11.9.
[12]Cassian, *The Conferences* 2.11.9.
[13]Cassian, *The Conferences* 2.11.8.
[14]Cassian, *The Conferences* 2.11.9.

calm love towards the good and evil, just and unjust, an imitation of God . . . by doing good for the love of goodness itself."[15]

Cassian describes this highest stage in spiritual life as the love of a son who trusts in the Father's generosity with the knowledge that all the Father has is his as well. Christians operate in such love because they know God loves them, rather than from any need within God or as a reward for their actions.[16] They, in turn, love God for no other reason than God's own self, leading them to "strive to be worthy of receiving the image and likeness of the Father" and "to proclaim in imitation of the true Son: 'All that the Father has is mine.'"[17]

The perfect filial love of God expresses fear, but one quite different from a slave. It is the same fear said of Jesus Christ, "and there shall rest upon him the Spirit of fear" (Is 11:3). Fear here is expressed in an "earnest affection" to avoid offending God, to refrain from any "offence against love."[18] The perfect love of a son establishes the Christian in virtue and goodness, thereby strengthening the bond of perseverance through life. It provides the surest foundation for motivation in virtue.

Cassian emphasizes that the ascent to Christian perfection is one of divine grace in cooperation with human will. Through the habitual practice of monastic disciplines like "fastings, vigils, withdrawal from the world, and meditation on Scripture," Christians experience divine grace empowering the ascent in the stages of perfection. He warns, however, that monastic spiritual disciplines are never an end in themselves but a means of divine grace by which "purity of heart" comes. Christians seek God's perfecting grace in these recognized means.[19] Because they are best practiced within the context of a monastery, monks are the Christians most likely to experience such perfection in this life.

---

[15]Cassian, *The Conferences* 2.11.9.
[16]Cassian, *The Conferences* 2.11.12.
[17]Cassian, *The Conferences* 2.11.7.
[18]Cassian, *The Conferences* 2.11.13.
[19]Cassian, *The Conferences* 1.1.7.

No sinless perfection in the present life. Cassian lived during the fourth-century Augustinian-Pelagian debates. The Pelagians denied original sin and argued for humanity's capacity to live free from all sin. They believed any person could live a sinless life. Cassian strongly rejected such teaching.[20]

Cassian's understanding is grounded in the apostle John's first letter. John declares, "Everyone born of God does not sin, for His seed is in him, and he cannot sin, because he is born of God" (1 Jn 3:9), and "We know that everyone who is born of God does not sin, but his birth of God preserves him, and the wicked one does not touch him" (1 Jn 5:18). Cassian teaches explicitly that "sin" here refers to "mortal sin," and not to every kind of sin. As John indicates in the same epistle, there is sin that leads to spiritual death and sin that does not (1 Jn 5:16). Christians must be free from mortal sin, like murder, sexual immorality, and pride, because spiritual death is the consequence.[21]

Cassian continues his reflection on John's letter, highlighting his statements, "If we say we have no sin, we deceive ourselves and the truth is not in us" (1 Jn 1:8) and "If we say that we have not sinned, we make Him a liar, and His word is not in us" (1 Jn 1:10). Cassian interprets "sin" here to mean "trivial faults" committed by "word, and thought, ignorance, and forgetfulness . . . and surprise."[22] These sins arise from the physical infirmities and requirements of the mortal body. While these faults are not spiritually threatening to the Christian, they still require "those who serve Christ most faithfully" to pray regularly, "Forgive us our trespasses."

Christian perfection in later cenobitic teaching: Benedict (AD 480–547) and Gregory (AD 540–604). Commitment to the

---

[20]Cassian is the transitional figure between the last chapter and this one. While Augustine and Cassian are contemporaries, Cassian lived longer than Augustine. Cassian also became the central theological writer of the early cenobitic tradition, which is a focus of the present chapter.

[21]Cassian, *The Conferences* 2.11.9.

[22]Cassian, *The Conferences* 2.11.9.

experience of Christian perfection through monasticism, as seen in John Cassian, follows the cenobitic tradition into the sixth century through Benedict of Nursia. In founding monasteries, Benedict developed a *Rule* to guide his followers. Its purpose is to provide a spiritual guide to the true love of God through obedience.

Through the theme of humility, Benedict describes twelve steps in the human soul's ascent to Christian perfection. The first is to keep the fear of God continually at the fore of life and remember all God's commands. The second step is self-denial, having the attitude of Christ, who confessed, "I have not come to do my own will, but the will of Him who sent me" (Jn 6:38). Third is obedience to one's superiors, submitting to God's care through them. The fourth step is endurance in suffering, persevering in obedience regardless of circumstances or personal costs. Fifth is confession of sin, especially sinful thoughts and secret transgressions. The sixth step is contentment with lowliness, accepting whatever is demanded or required in one's position. Seventh is recognition and embrace of one's inferiority, identifying with the psalmist's statement, "I am truly a worm, not a man, a shame of men and an outcast of people" (Ps 22:6). The eighth step is adherence to the rule of the monastery. Ninth is silence, refraining from speech through mastery of the tongue. Tenth is the avoidance of excessive laughter. The eleventh is speech marked by modesty and patience. Last is inward humility of heart, manifested outwardly in thought, word, and action.[23]

Benedict writes that when a monk has ascended the steps of humility, cleansed from sin, "he will presently arrive at that love of God which, being perfect, puts fear outside." The person who is perfected in love will then "begin to keep without any difficulty" all that God asks, "no longer through fear of hell, but for love of Christ . . . and delight in virtue."[24] As seen in Cassian and Benedict, the spiritual

---

[23]Benedict of Nursia, *The Rule of St. Benedict*, trans. W. K. Lowther Clarke (London: SPCK, 1931) 7.
[24]Benedict of Nursia, *The Rule of St. Benedict* 7.

journey among the monastics begins with fear of God but leads to perfect love of God.

Gregory the Great, a lay monk who was later ordained and eventually elected pope, followed the teachings of Cassian and Benedict. In his teaching on the spiritual ascent to Christian perfection, he appropriates the seven gifts of the Holy Spirit found in Isaiah 11:2-3 to describe the path.[25]

Before the climb can begin, a Christian must stand on the "porch" of humility and faith. The Holy Spirit, who alone makes possible perfection, rests on the humble, and faith in God leads to the virtues of perfection. Once on the porch, the ascent begins.[26] The first step is fear of God, arising from the experience of God's holiness and inner awareness of future judgment. Second is godliness, marked by physical compassion for the poor. To godliness, knowledge is added, equipping the Christian to know what basic actions are required in relationship to God and neighbor. Next is fortitude, empowering one to do the good acquired through knowledge. The fifth step is counsel, enabling "foresight to protect everything" that is done through "fortitude." To counsel, understanding is added, making possible growth in maturity through what the Spirit has already imparted.[27] Finally, wisdom is bestowed, enabling mature Christians to recognize the reality of present life. While they have experienced some level of perfection in love and empowerment to walk in the love of God and neighbor, there is still greater need of God's perfecting grace. Whatever level of perfection in love is attained in life, there is always more. Vestiges of sin remain and come into even greater clarity as one draws closer in union with God. Ultimate perfection only takes place in the life to come.[28]

---

[25]Gregory the Great, *The Homilies of Saint Gregory the Great on the Book of the Prophet Ezekiel*, trans. Theodosia Gray (Etna, CA: Center for Traditionalist Orthodox Studies, 1990) 2.7.7-20.

[26]Gregory reverses the order of gifts found in Is 11:2-3. Isaiah begins with wisdom and then finishes with fear. Gregory, however, believes Isaiah begins with the highest step and traces backward spiritual progress.

[27]Gregory the Great, *Ezekiel* 2.7.7-8.

[28]Gregory the Great, *Ezekiel* 2.7.11-12.

In the end, Gregory's understanding of Christian perfection is like Augustine's. While Christians may truly love God and neighbor, having the love of God subjugate all contrary desires, sinful impulses from the fall remain. Gregory also solidifies the direction of Christian perfection in the Middle Ages: only those dedicated to the monastic life can reach it. Solitary focus in life is required to attain it. Ordinary life, with its responsibilities, has too many distractions.

BERNARD OF CLAIRVAUX (AD 1090–1153)

At the end of the eleventh century, a new monastic order formed in the eastern French town of Cîteaux: the Cistercians (from the Latin name of Cîteaux). They arose from the Benedictine tradition, seeking to follow the *Rule of St. Benedict* more closely. The most famous of their early leaders was Bernard, founder and abbot of the monastery in Clairvaux, who wrote extensively on the perfection of love in humanity.

In his most famous work, *On Loving God*, Bernard begins with the question: Why should God be loved? Answer: because of God's gracious work on behalf of humanity and for all the benefits given by God's love to humanity, God should be loved for no other reason than himself. No one is loved more justly than God.[29] Bernard then inquires how humanity can truly love God. Answer: because God is the initiator and end of human love; because he incites and empowers love; because he directs humanity in the way of love; because he liberates from all that inhibits love; humanity can truly love God.[30] This perfection in love is supremely a divine work, and Bernard describes it.

Bernard's* ordo *of perfection. After answering the two initial questions of his work, Bernard describes the grace-initiated

---

[29]Bernard of Clairvaux, *On Loving God*, in *Bernard of Clairvaux: Selected Works*, trans. G. R. Evans, Classics of Western Spirituality (New York: Paulist Press, 1987) 1-2.
[30]Bernard of Clairvaux, *On Loving God* 7.

process by which humanity moves from the lowest degree of love to the highest: (1) love of self for self's sake, (2) love of God for self's sake, (3) love of God for God's sake, and (4) love of self for God's sake.

First degree: Love of self for self's sake. Bernard teaches that love is a natural human affection that comes from God and, ultimately, is directed to God. However, because of humanity's weakness as physical creatures, people "are compelled" to love and serve themselves first. "The spiritual does not come first. The natural comes first and is followed by the spiritual" (1 Cor 15:46).[31] Because love of self is necessary in this world, God implants it in humanity. The temptation of self-love is to become excessive, discarding its divinely ordained constraints. Self-love as given by God, therefore, becomes the occasion for lust, an excessive love of pleasure.[32]

According to Bernard, closely connected to the love of self for self's sake is the love of neighbor. He believes the love of another is an extension of the love of self, since self and neighbor share the same human nature. He states, "So our selfish love grows truly social, when it includes our neighbor in its circle."[33] This love for other functions as a natural curb to human lust. When humanity works to meet the needs, and even the pleasures, of neighbors, self-denial is required. Love of others then leads to temperance and righteousness. It begins to move the inward direction of human love outward.[34]

Second degree: Love of God for self's sake. Bernard teaches that God, as the source of everything good in life, leads humanity to love God. The necessities of life drive humanity to love God for self's sake. This is a continuation of love's direction outward. For example, God blesses humanity with protection. When a trouble-free life is experienced, people in pride may conclude they are the

---

[31]Bernard of Clairvaux, *On Loving God* 8.
[32]Bernard of Clairvaux, *On Loving God* 8.
[33]Bernard of Clairvaux, *On Loving God* 8.
[34]Bernard of Clairvaux, *On Loving God* 8.

ultimate cause of their security. When threats arise and safety becomes tenuous, however, they turn to God. This movement of the soul initiates a love of God for self's sake.[35] Bernard, speaking of a person who has experienced this second degree of love, states, "He perceives that he cannot exist by himself, and so begins by faith to seek after God, and to love him as something necessary to his own welfare."[36]

Third degree: Love of God for God's sake. The second degree of love leads naturally to the third. Bernard teaches about such a person, "When he has learned to worship God and to seek him, meditating on God, reading God's word, praying and obeying his commandments, he comes gradually to know what God is, and finds him altogether lovely."[37]

As humanity relies on God through the challenges and tribulations of life, and sees God's repeated provision, they start to love God. They love God not merely for their own sake but for God's. Through these experiences the "grace of God is tasted, and by frequent tasting it is proved . . . how sweet the Lord is" (Ps 34:8).[38] Humanity begins to love God unselfishly, which leads them to "praise God for his essential goodness."[39]

Once they experience love of God for God's sake, the love of neighbor becomes second nature, "for whosoever loves God rightly, loves all God's creatures."[40] Fulfillment of divine commands is no longer a burden. Love now is described by Bernard as "pure" since it is manifested in inward intentions and outward actions. Love is not motivated any longer by selfish desires. In this sense, it is "disinterested." It reflects Christ's love in that it seeks the good for others. It seeks what is right and appropriate in all affairs, which is the same

---

[35]Bernard of Clairvaux, *On Loving God* 9.
[36]Bernard of Clairvaux, *On Loving God* 15.
[37]Bernard of Clairvaux, *On Loving God* 15.
[38]Bernard of Clairvaux, *On Loving God* 15.
[39]Bernard of Clairvaux, *On Loving God* 15.
[40]Bernard of Clairvaux, *On Loving God* 15.

love received from God. "Whosoever loves in this fashion, loves even as he is loved."[41]

Fourth degree: Love of self for God's sake. Bernard sees the love of God for God's sake as the perfection in love presently possible. Christians, through the Holy Spirit, can be sustained presently in such love. It is not ultimate perfection, however. The highest love happens when there is love of self for God's sake.

The fourth degree of love occurs when humanity experiences ecstatic union with God, when the compulsion to think of self and to address the present needs of the human body is removed.[42] It is a "rapturous" experience of union in mind and will with God. All hindrances to the love of God in heart, soul, mind, and strength are removed. It is a "godlike" existence. Bernard states,

> As a drop of water poured into wine loses itself, and takes the color and flavor of wine; or as the bar of iron, heated red-hot, becomes like fire itself, forgetting its own nature; or as the air, radiant with sun beams, seems not so much to be illuminated as to be light itself; so in the saints all human affections melt away by some unspeakable transmutation into the will of God.[43]

Humanity continues to exist, but in "another beauty, a higher power, a greater glory."[44]

Bernard believes there are some Christians in present life who experience fourth degree love, but it is unsustainable. Humanity's present bodies are too "fragile," too "sickly" for it.[45] Only glorified, resurrected bodies have the capacity for such love. The human soul, therefore, in the intermediate state of death cannot attain full consummation with God. The highest love requires the perfected body with the glorified soul for its realization.[46]

---

[41]Bernard of Clairvaux, *On Loving God* 15.
[42]Bernard of Clairvaux, *On Loving God* 11.
[43]Bernard of Clairvaux, *On Loving God* 10.
[44]Bernard of Clairvaux, *On Loving God* 10.
[45]Bernard of Clairvaux, *On Loving God* 10.
[46]Bernard of Clairvaux, *On Loving God* 11.

Bernard's **Sermons on the Song of Songs.** While the role of the Holy Spirit is implied in *On Loving God,* Bernard makes it explicit in his *Sermons on the Song of Songs.* Drawing on the greatest commandment to love God with all one's "heart, soul, and mind" (Mt 22:37; Mk 12:30), he identifies three ways that Christians rise to the highest love of God.

First is "carnal," which is to love God with all one's "heart." God is loved for selfish reasons. While not the higher degrees of love, a believer only arrives at "carnal" love as a gift of the Holy Spirit.[47] Second is rational or intellectual love of God, which is to love God will all one's "soul." The Holy Spirit imparts this love as Christians focus on Christ's humanity, his life and ministry. As they grow in their knowledge of Christ, the Spirit imparts greater love for Christ, leading them to have a mind like Christ, one that seeks to do not their "will, but the will of the Father."[48] Finally, there is "spiritual" love, which loves God with all one's "strength." This love is only empowered by "the fullness of the Spirit." Bernard describes it as an "energy so great and an aide so powerful . . . neither vexations, nor sufferings, nor even the fear of death, can ever bring about defection from righteousness."[49]

While Bernard believes ultimate perfection in love occurs in resurrection, he recognizes a level of perfection in the present life that brings purity, righteousness, and a reflection of Christlikeness through the Holy Spirit's infusing power. Christians can walk with purity of love, resulting in the love of God for God's sake and the love of neighbor. They can also have a foretaste of ultimate perfection in fleeting moments, when "God will be all in all."

---

[47]Bernard of Clairvaux, *Sermons on the Song of Songs,* trans. Hugh Martin (London: SCM, 1959), 20.1, 9.

[48]Bernard of Clairvaux, *Sermons on the Song of Songs* 20.8.

[49]Bernard of Clairvaux, *Sermons on the Song of Songs* 20.9.

THOMAS AQUINAS (AD 1225–1274)

One of the greatest mendicant (from the Latin "to beg") orders to arise in the thirteenth century is the Dominicans. Established to preach the gospel and fight heresy, they quickly became the focus of the Middle Ages' intellectual activity. Dominicans combined con-templative life in monasteries and active engagement with the world around them. Their greatest scholar was Thomas Aquinas, the leading theologian in the medieval church.

The concept of perfection is central to Thomas's theology. He ad-dresses his understanding most concisely in his *Summa Theologica* and the treatise *The Perfection of the Spiritual Life*. Thomas's teaching forms the foundation of contemporary Roman Catholic teaching on perfection today.

The levels of perfection in love of God. Thomas begins with the assertion, "The perfection of Christian life consists in love."[50] Love is perfection because it brings about the proper end of humanity, union with God. He then proceeds to identify three levels of per-fection in love, from the highest to the lowest.[51]

First is divine perfection. Here, God is loved to the degree to which God is worthy of love. The lover gives to the beloved all that the beloved deserves without equivocation. This "absolute" per-fection is impossible for humanity. As finite creatures, humanity in this life, and even in the life to come, will never be able to love God to the infinite extent he is worthy of love. Such perfection only exists in God. Only God can love God in this way.[52]

Second is unqualified human perfection. Here, God is always loved to the full extent of human capability. There is no deviation or diminishment of human capacity in love of God. Every thought, word, and affection is directed wholly to God. One's focus is fixed

---

[50]Thomas Aquinas, *Summa Theologica*, trans. Fathers of the English Dominican Province (New York: Benzinger Brothers, 1922), 2a-2ae, Q. 184. Art. 1.

[51]Aquinas, *Summa Theologica*, 2a-2ae, Q. 184. Art. 2.

[52]Aquinas, *Summa Theologica*, 2a-2ae, Q. 184. Art. 2.

on God, "beholding him, seeing all things through him, and judging all according to his truth."[53] Thomas describes this state as "an absolute totality on the part of the lover, so that the affective faculty always tends to God as much as it possibly can." Such perfection is humanly impossible in the present life but will be enjoyed in glory when humanity is brought into incorruptible union with God.[54]

Finally, there is Christian perfection. Here, God is loved not in the totality seen in the first two levels, but the believer experiences the removal of all "obstacles to the movement of love toward God." Everything contrary to the love of God is excised from life. Nothing is left hindering the direction of human affections toward God. Christians renounce all mortal sin, all that is contrary to the love of God, and leave behind whatever else that "hinders" love from "tending wholly to God." Through the removal of these obstacles, human life naturally bends or leans continually toward the love of God.

Thomas recognizes two levels at which all obstacles to love are removed as biblical "precepts" and "counsels." The commands of Christ ("precepts") are binding on every Christian. Believers are to be free from mortal sin, therefore, enjoying some level of perfection. "Counsels," on the other hand, are exhortations, not binding on Christians but necessary for the attainment of the highest perfection of love in life.[55]

Christ's counsels focus on the renunciation of earthly possessions, so they no longer have any hold on human affections (Mt 19:21); the renunciation of earthly ties and family (Lk 14:26; 1 Cor 7:32); and the practice of self-denial, the abnegation of human will.[56] This higher level of perfection is at the center of all vows undertaken in holy orders. While the first level of Christian perfection in the love

---

[53] Aquinas, *The Perfection of the Spiritual Life* 4.
[54] Aquinas, *Summa Theologica*, 2a-2ae, Q. 184. Art. 2.
[55] Aquinas, *The Perfection of the Spiritual Life* 5-6, 13-14; cf. *Summa Theologica*, 2a-2ae, Q. 184. Art. 3.
[56] Aquinas, *The Perfection of the Spiritual Life* 7-10.

of God is expected of all Christians, the highest perfection, while possible in life, will not be attained by all.[57]

Perfection in the love of neighbor. While Thomas focuses on the love of God in his discussion of human perfection, he does not neglect the necessity of the love of others. He recognizes that the perfection of spiritual life comes through fulfillment of Jesus' two greatest commandments: the love of God with heart, soul, mind, and strength and the love of neighbor (Mt 22:37), supremely manifested in the love of enemy (Mt 5:44).[58]

As with the twofold nature of perfection in love of God, the elimination of mortal sin, and all hindrances to love, there are two levels at which perfection operates in love of neighbor. First is to love neighbor as oneself. According to Thomas, this is a "precept" or "command" of Christ and is required for all persons. Every believer must live out this experience of perfection. It is necessary for personal salvation. To love a neighbor as oneself means that it is sincere. People are loved not because of what they provide but from a genuine desire to see them flourish, reflective of the love of self. It is also rightly ordered, whereby the care of a neighbor's soul is sought above all else, even more than their physical well-being. Furthermore, it is holy, directed by and empowered by love of God. Finally, it is practical. Love of neighbor leads to actions befitting such love, seeking their prosperity and guarding them from adversity.[59]

The second level exceeds the previous "common perfection." According to Thomas, this is "counsel," not binding on Christians as a command but as an exhortation. It is comprehensive, extending beyond human friendship and acquaintances to strangers and enemies. For the sake of others, it endures physical hardships, sacrifices personal resources, and lays down physical life if necessary.

---

[57] Aquinas, *Summa Theologica*, 2a-2ae, Q. 184. Art. 2.
[58] Aquinas, *The Perfection of the Spiritual Life* 8.
[59] Aquinas, *The Perfection of the Spiritual Life* 8.

Believers work in love to bestow on their neighbor "such spiritual benefits as are supernatural and exceed human reason."[60]

Like love of God, this highest perfection in love for neighbor is at the heart of all vows taken in holy orders. While the first level of Christian perfection is expected for all Christians, the highest perfection, while possible in life, will not be attained by all.[61]

The work of sanctification in the perfection of love. Thomas has a dynamic understanding of perfection, admitting different levels in Christians. Through the grace of the Holy Spirit, it begins with empowerment to walk in obedience to Christ's commands (precepts), where all impediments to the love of God and neighbor are removed. Every Christian for Thomas is perfected theoretically through the sacraments of baptism and confirmation, where the Spirit is imparted in fullness.[62] It develops, though, as a believer matures by eliminating all that is incompatible with the love of God and neighbor through the counsels (exhortations) of Christ. These impediments are not contrary to love, just not conducive to it, as exemplified by the threat of wealth, family loyalties, and self-will. As Christians follow the councils of Christ, they become more perfect, leading to the fullest expression of Christian love.

BONAVENTURE (AD 1221–1274)

The Franciscans, another mendicant order, arose in the thirteenth century through the initiative of Francis of Assisi. Franciscans required their members to take vows of poverty and rely on strangers for their basic needs as they traveled to preach. They sought to emulate the life and ministry of Christ. Through the leadership of Giovanni di Fidanza, later named Bonaventure (Latin for "Good Luck"), the Franciscans became the most influential order at the time in the Roman Catholic Church.

---

[60] Aquinas, *The Perfection of the Spiritual Life* 14.
[61] Aquinas, *Summa Theologica*, 2a-2ae, Q. 184. Art. 2.
[62] Aquinas, *Summa Theologica*, 2a-2ae, Q. 72, Art. 7

Bonaventure believed that Christ is the "one true master" who offers knowledge that begins in faith, develops through reason, and is perfected through mystical union with God.[63] His most developed treatise on this subject is *On the Perfection of Life for Sisters*.[64]

True self-knowledge: The beginning of the ascent to perfection. Bonaventure believes the rise to perfection begins with a descent into one's conscience through a thorough personal examination. A Christian must consider all their past and present "defects," "loves," "actions," and "sins," lamenting over any "bitterness of heart." Perfection in self-knowledge is essential. How is it possible to explore what is greater than self without examining oneself?[65]

To aid self-reflection, Bonaventure teaches that human sin arises from three sources: carelessness, concupiscence, and wickedness. Through carelessness, humanity fails to guard their hearts, use their time wisely, and work in Christ-honoring ways. Through concupiscence, believers allow desire for pleasure and vanity to flourish in their lives. And through wickedness, Christians permit indignation and bitterness against neighbor to grow in their heart; they envy their neighbor's prosperity, rejoice in their adversities, and become indifferent to them. Time must be spent in self-reflection in these areas, and remorse and amendment of life must be experienced.[66]

True humility: The natural consequence of self-knowledge. According to Bonaventure, knowledge of oneself naturally leads to humility. He quotes Bernard, "Humility is the virtue by which man, in authentic self-knowledge deems himself worthless."[67] True humility is necessary for the ascent to perfection. If pride is the

---

[63]Tim Noon and R. E. Houser, "Saint Bonaventure," *Stanford Encyclopedia of Philosophy*, ed. Edward N. Zalta (Winter 2020), https://plato.stanford.edu/archives/win2020/entries /bonaventure/.

[64]Bonaventure, *On the Perfection of Life for Sisters*, trans. Paul Hanbridge (Leichhardt: Capuchin Friars of Australia, 2012).

[65]Bonaventure, *On the Perfection of Life for Sisters* 1.1.

[66]Bonaventure, *On the Perfection of Life for Sisters* 1.2-6.

[67]Bonaventure, *On the Perfection of Life for Sisters* 2.1.

beginning of every sin, then humility is the source of every virtue. Christians, however, must beware of false humility.[68]

If a believer is to experience "perfect humility," then three actions are necessary: contemplation of God, remembrance of Christ, and personal "watchfulness." Through active contemplation, Christians recognize more clearly divine authorship of their good works, both their source and empowerment. No person can take credit for any good work performed. Through disciplined reflection on Christ's life, believers have his example of humility as a model and repudiation of pride. Bonaventure states, "Given the greatest has become the least and the immeasurable the smallest, what should be more deplored . . . than the one, who, though rotten and a worm, proceeds to magnify himself."[69] Finally, through ongoing examination of personal life, recognizing "you are dust and to dust you will return," believers see more clearly their sins, the transitory nature of life, and their impotence to control it.[70]

True poverty: Necessary for perfection according to Christ. Bonaventure identifies poverty as the next virtue in perfection's path. This is clearly taught by Christ: "If you wish to be perfect, go and sell everything you have and give to the poor" (Mt 19:21). "Perfect poverty," however, is accomplished not just by disposal of worldly blessings, but when it is embraced with love.[71]

From where does love of poverty arise? Bonaventure identifies two sources: the example of Christ and God's promise to the poor. Jesus was "poor at his birth, poor in his way of life, poor in his death."[72] How can Christians seek wealth when their Lord, "the God of gods, the Lord of the world, the King of heaven," embraced the way of poverty? Only through imitation of Christ can all spiritual goods of Christ be made available to the believer. Jesus also promises

---

[68]Bonaventure, *On the Perfection of Life for Sisters* 2.1.
[69]Bonaventure, *On the Perfection of Life for Sisters* 2.4.
[70]Bonaventure, *On the Perfection of Life for Sisters* 2.5.
[71]Bonaventure, *On the Perfection of Life for Sisters* 3.2.
[72]Bonaventure, *On the Perfection of Life for Sisters* 3.2.

to those who embrace poverty, "Blessed are the poor in spirit, for theirs is the kingdom of heaven" (Mt 5:3). This kingdom, according to Bonaventure, is none other than Christ himself.[73]

True silence: An indispensable aid in perfection. An indispensable aid in the path of perfection is silence. Bonaventure believes, "Just as sin is not absent from too much talk" (Prov 10:19), so brevity of speech protects against evil.[74] More specifically, the practice of silence helps Christians maintain tranquility in their lives. Unless they are diligent in "guarding their mouths" (Ps 38:2), their "tongues" become a "fire, a universe of iniquity."[75]

One benefit of silence is compunction; it leads to godly regret. When Christians are silent, opportunities to reflect on life open. Silence yields recognition of personal flaws and delays in spiritual development. Another advantage is that silence helps minimize focus on worldly concerns, directing the heart to more eternal matters. Finally, it leads to a solitary life, where dialogue with God defines a Christian's conversation.[76]

True dedication to prayer: Another necessary action for perfection. Perfection is impossible without commitment to prayer, according to Bonaventure. Only through prayer are worldly temptations, lies of the devil, and spiritual impediments overcome. Believers tepid in prayer present to God a "dead soul in a living body."[77] A Christian "gains more than all the world is worth in one hour of prayer because with a modicum of devout prayer a man acquires the kingdom of heaven."[78]

Bonaventure describes the nature of perfecting prayer. First, with the "body upright and heart elevated, with all the senses shut off and without clamor . . . with a contrite heart," Christians reflect on

---

[73]Bonaventure, *On the Perfection of Life for Sisters* 3.3-10.
[74]Bonaventure, *On the Perfection of Life for Sisters* 4.1.
[75]Bonaventure, *On the Perfection of Life for Sisters* 4.1.
[76]Bonaventure, *On the Perfection of Life for Sisters* 4.3-5.
[77]Bonaventure, *On the Perfection of Life for Sisters* 5.1.
[78]Bonaventure, *On the Perfection of Life for Sisters* 5.1.

their wretchedness, past, present, and future.[79] Regarding their past and present, they confess all sins committed, recall the goodness of God ignored, and identify any divine grace lost. Regarding the future, they remember the day of judgment and the threat of hell, keeping it as a check on their lives. Second, believers express thanksgiving to God for all his benefits that they have received or will receive. Gratitude fills their hearts and overflows in appreciation for their creation, for their new birth as Christians, for the forgiveness of sins, for the life of Christ and the gift of the Holy Spirit. Finally, prayer is offered with singularity of heart, with one desire to be pleasing to God.[80]

True remembrance of Christ's passion: Nourishment for the path to perfection. Disciplined reflection on the Passion of Christ fuels devotion and attentiveness in Christian life. It leads, most importantly, to self-crucifixion. As a believer ponders Christ's death on the cross, Bonaventure states, "through the door of his pierced side, he enters the heart of Jesus himself. Transformed there into Christ by the most ardent love of the Crucified, fixed by the nails of divine fear, pierced to the heart by the lance of love, pierced through by the sword of interior compassion," he then seeks "nothing else but to die on the cross with Christ."[81]

True perfection in love: Love of God and neighbor for God's sake. Bonaventure makes clear that every point made in his discussion leads to Christian perfection: the love of God and love of neighbor for the sake of God. Without this love all virtues are vain; with it all virtues are present. Such love melts vice like wax before a flame. Perfection in love comes from the Holy Spirit's work in the believer's life.[82] As a fulfillment of Christ's command in Matthew 22:37 (cf. Mk 12:30; Lk 10:27), to love God with all one's heart is to be inclined to

---

[79]Bonaventure, *On the Perfection of Life for Sisters* 5.2.
[80]Bonaventure, *On the Perfection of Life for Sisters* 5.2-10.
[81]Bonaventure, *On the Perfection of Life for Sisters* 6.2.
[82]Bonaventure, *On the Perfection of Life for Sisters* 7.1.

love nothing other than God, to take "no delight in any kind of splendor than in God." To love God with all one's soul is to love with an undivided will, to bring personal will in full alignment with the divine. To love God with all one's mind is to love with remembrance, never forgetting the immeasurable grace of God manifested throughout life.[83]

This perfection in love is dynamic in nature, ever increasing in measure throughout life, and culminating in the next. Bonaventure states, "The more someone loves God here, the more he rejoices in God there. Therefore, love God very much here, so that you may rejoice there very much. May the love of God increase in you here, so that there you may be completely possessed by the joy of God."[84]

True perseverance: The realization of ultimate perfection. Christian perfection in love, according to Bonaventure, does not prevent the possibility of regression or the loss of what has been gained. Corruptibility remains in life. Sin, therefore, is always a possibility for believers until mortal life is transformed after death. While perfection in love and the fullness of virtue guard against sin, the threat of temptation exists. True perseverance, therefore, is necessary for all Christians. The good that began in present life must be brought to completion and not derailed.[85] Bonaventure states, "Though all the virtues may run together, indeed only perseverance receives the prize, since it is not the one who begins, but the one who perseveres who will be saved."[86]

CATHERINE OF SIENA (AD 1347–1380)

Catherine of Siena closes our examination of Christian perfection in the Middle Ages. Her life and theology had many influences, including Gregory the Great and Thomas Aquinas. Catherine's

---

[83]Bonaventure, *On the Perfection of Life for Sisters* 7.
[84]Bonaventure, *On the Perfection of Life for Sisters* 8.8.
[85]Bonaventure, *On the Perfection of Life for Sisters* 7.1-8.
[86]Bonaventure, *On the Perfection of Life for Sisters* 7.1.

developed doctrine of Christian perfection combines the monastic and mystical traditions. She uses many images to describe what perfection is and how it is attained.

The bridge. Catherine's most famous image of Christian perfection is a bridge.[87] Because of humanity's fall in the garden, union with God has been severed. Sin defines human existence. Catherine pictures this problem as a dangerous river, with humanity on one side of the bank and God on the other. The incarnation of God's Son establishes a single bridge through which the river is crossed, and union with the Father restored. Humanity must cross over Christ, the bridge, through three steps that correspond to the stages of spiritual life.[88]

The first takes a Christian pilgrim to the "wounded feet of Christ," where God is loved out of fear rather than love. God is sought for the sake of self. The second step leads to the "wounded heart" of Jesus, where genuine love for God arises but is tainted by selfishness. Through meditation on Christ's love for humanity, a Christian experiences fulfillment of God's promise in Ezekiel 36:26, "A new heart also will I give you, and a new spirit will I put within you: and I will take away the stony heart out of your flesh, and I will give you a heart of flesh." This transformation ushers the Christian into a new level of existence, the third step—Christian perfection. The believer now loves God for God's sake and walks in joyful obedience to God. Catherine describes it as the "mouth of Christ," whereby Jesus speaks to the believer and claims "his bride with a nuptial kiss." Union with the Father through Christ is restored.[89]

Light. Catherine also describes Christian perfection and its path through the imagery of light. The first light is "ordinary," whereby a person acquires initial knowledge of self and God. Self-knowledge

[87]Catherine of Siena, *Dialogue*, trans. Algar Thorold (New York: Cosomo, 1907), 21-22, 25-30.
[88]Catherine of Siena, *Dialogue* 21-22.
[89]Catherine of Siena, *Dialogue* 25-30.

reveals disordered love, sin, irresponsibility, and a heart of rebellion. The fleeting nature of worldly goods is grasped and desire for virtue arises.[90]

Through deeper knowledge of self and God, the believer is illuminated by a second light, leading to genuine godly humility. This humility guards a person from distortion of truth arising from self-love of others, freeing them from the judgments of others. Here, holy desires are strengthened, and human will empowered.[91]

In the third "perfect" light, the Christian is "clothed" in God's will. This light discloses to human "memory, understanding and will" the significance of Jesus' self-sacrificial love on the cross. Such knowledge elicits a desire to be like Christ in his death. The believer "is clothed in perfect light" and loves God "sincerely without any other concern than the glory and praise" of God. Love of God and neighbor become the sole motivation of action.[92]

In this final light, a Christian has become "perfect" in the practice of humility, patience, and obedience. Humility is born from a thorough realization that any good obtained or performed by a person comes from God. God alone is the source of all good in them and through them. Obedience is established through the surrender of disordered will, and one receives spiritual release to pursue all perceived good. Patience becomes the "marrow of charity," which alone enables the love of neighbor. Without patience, no perseverance can be maintained in the face of adversity or personal cost to self.[93]

Tears. Another way Catherine describes Christian perfection is by five states of emotion or "tears." The first addresses the tears of those who live in rebellion against God. Their love is disordered. "Their guilt and grief are more or less heavy, according to the measure of their disordinate love." They shed tears of death, the recompense

---

[90]Catherine of Siena, *Dialogue* 98-101.
[91]Catherine of Siena, *Dialogue* 102-5.
[92]Catherine of Siena, *Dialogue* 106-9.
[93]Catherine of Siena, *Dialogue* 109.

of their sin. This is the state of humanity as a result of the fall and personal sin.[94]

The second state expresses the beginning of spiritual life. It commences with divine conviction of personal sin and a turn to God for mercy. Eyes weep "in order to satisfy the grief of the heart." Repentance arises, however, not from true love of God, but from fear of final judgment. Selfishness defines Christian life.[95]

Through growth in knowledge of self and God, in which the soul's vices are discovered and the goodness of God is perceived, the believer experiences a third state of tears. Genuine love of God takes root in the human soul, increasingly liberating it from selfishness. Because God's love in Jesus Christ is experienced, "tears issue from the very fountain of the heart."[96]

The love of God "shed abroad" in the human heart empowers the fourth state in human life: the love of neighbor for Christ's sake. Christians who shed these tears love their neighbor without the reciprocation of love and without thought of personal gain. They love "solely for the praise and glory" of God.[97]

Finally, there are tears of "perfect peace" produced by union with God. Perfection in love of God and neighbor is not static but ever increasing. Catherine states, "For the soul is never so perfect in this life that she cannot attain to a higher perfection in love." Perfection here is marked by deep spiritual longing, "tears of fire," rather than bodily tears.[98]

Perfection in love. In the end, Catherine understands Christian perfection supremely as the love of God and neighbor. Christians have full power of their soul, directing desires and will to one end: the divine good. Such perfection only occurs when the three "daughters" of love—patience, courage, and perseverance—are

---

[94]Catherine of Siena, *Dialogue* 86-88.
[95]Catherine of Siena, *Dialogue* 89-91.
[96]Catherine of Siena, *Dialogue* 92-93.
[97]Catherine of Siena, *Dialogue* 94-95.
[98]Catherine of Siena, *Dialogue* 96-97.

rooted in a person's life.[99] When Christians experience perfection, they surrender to God in all things[100]

CONCLUSION

The ante-Nicene and Nicene periods of Christianity believed Christian perfection was possible for every Christian. As Christianity became the established religion of the Roman Empire and the church transitioned into the Middle Ages, the experience of Christian perfection was principally relegated to monastics and mystics. Theologians of the Middle Ages differed in their description of Christian perfection and the path to it, but great common ground existed among them. Like the early church fathers, they believed it to be the perfect love of God and neighbor, a perfection in love for the sake of God and others. They believed that divine grace communicated perfection to Christians through ascetic discipline and spiritual practices of monasticism. Because of the demands of ordinary life, many thought normal Christians could not attain perfection.

As we will see in the next chapter, with the initiation of the Protestant Reformation, the doctrine, message, and experience of Christian perfection was not lost. Its experience, however, moved from the cloisters of the monastery and the spiritually elite back to the ordinary Christian. Indeed, as we will see, the first Protestant statement of faith, the Lutheran Augsburg Confession, makes this point clear.[101] We now turn our attention to the rise of Protestantism and its witnesses to Christian perfection.

---

[99]Catherine of Siena, *Dialogue* 50-55.
[100]Catherine of Siena, *Dialogue* 50-55.
[101]"The Augsburg Confession," in *Creeds and Confessions of the Reformation Era*, vol. 2, *Creeds and Confessions of Faith in the Christian Tradition*, ed. Jaroslav Pelikan and Valerie Hotchkiss (London: Yale University Press, 2003), 135.

9

HOLINESS IN THE PREMODERN
AND MODERN ERA

With the dawn of the Protestant Reformation in the sixteenth century, the possibility of Christian perfection moved from the cloisters of religious orders to ordinary Christians. The desire to restore the church and correct the abuses of Rome through a return to Scripture led to a rediscovery of Christian perfection for laity. The first formal Protestant statement of faith, the Augsburg Confession (AD 1530) makes this clear: "Christian perfection is this, to fear God sincerely, and again to conceive great faith . . . to ask, and with certainty to look for help from God in all our affairs, according to our calling . . . to do good works diligently . . . in these things doth consist true perfection . . . *it does not consist in celibacy, or mendicancy, or in vile apparel.*"[1]

Early Protestant Perfectionists

Early Protestant teaching on Christian perfection found expression in different branches of the Reformation. What united these

---

[1]The Augsburg Confession, Article 27, emphasis added. Scripture quotations in discussions of primary sources are those of the writer in view unless otherwise noted.

expressions was an optimism about the work of Jesus Christ and the impartation of the Holy Spirit to restore fallen humanity. Christians are empowered to walk in obedience to Christ and live sinless lives in conformity to Jesus' teaching.

Melchior Hoffman (AD 1495–1543). Perhaps the earliest Protestant advocate for Christian perfection was Melchior Hoffman, a leader in the Anabaptist branch of the Reformation. Hoffman divided human history into three ages: (1) the Old Testament under the law, (2) the New Testament under Christ (who established a higher spiritual law and restored human freedom), and (3) present time under the Holy Spirit, who fills believers' hearts, imparting Christ's spiritual law.[2]

Hoffman's teaching on perfection was grounded in Christology. Jesus is the eternal, uncreated, divine, omnipresent Son of God whose redemptive work is received by a believer directly through faith in his sinless life, death, and resurrection—not through any mediating means, such as sacraments or priests. This salvation, an embodiment of the holiness of the Father, consists of reconciliation to God and rebirth into an obedient life, empowered by love.[3] Hoffman believed, more specifically, in the restoration of humanity's original condition through Christ as the new Adam, whereby the divine law is written on human hearts, constituting a new and "perfect" human being ready to stand before God in future judgment. The reborn believer sees reality through the light of Christ and is enabled by the Holy Spirit to reflect that light in the world around. The grace of the Father through the Son in the Spirit is none other than the "re-creating love" of God in human life. This love enables believers to rediscover humanity's purpose—perfection in

---

[2]It should be noted that Hoffman as an Anabaptist would have been at odds with the mainstream Protestant Reformers. Gary K. Waite, "David Joris' Thought in the Context of the Early Melchiorite and Munsterite Movements in the Low Countries, 1534–1536," *The Mennonite Quarterly Review* 62 (1988): 306.

[3]Sjouke Voolstra, "The Word Has Become Flesh: The Melchiorite-Mennonite Teaching on the Incarnation," *The Mennonite Quarterly Review* 57 (1984): 155-60.

obedience and love. Hoffman taught Christian perfection as the right of every believer by virtue of Jesus' redemptive life.[4]

Sebastian Castellio (AD 1515–1563). Another early Protestant proponent of Christian perfection came from the Reformed tradition: Sebastian Castellio, a French preacher, professor, and theologian. While primarily known for his advocacy of religious freedom, Castellio had one of the most optimistic views of divine grace in early Protestantism. While he and John Calvin held much in common, he disputed Calvin's understanding of predestination and Christian perfection.[5]

According to Castellio, every human being has the possibility of perfection in this life because God created humanity in the divine image. Calvin, from Castellio's perspective, attributed too much power to sin and not enough to Christ's redeeming work. Humanity can refrain from sin and walk in all of God's commandments because of the sufficiency of Christ's human life. He states, "Christ alone can heal the malady of sin, but he can heal it." Elsewhere he writes the ability to be free from sin is made possible through a "participation in Christ," making the human will "persistent" in obedience.[6] Through appropriation of the patristic teaching that "the unassumed is unhealed," Castellio taught that Christ can heal thoroughly humanity's desire and will, enabling perfection in obedience and love.[7]

Dirk Volckertsz Coornhert (AD 1522–1590). Another voice proclaiming Christian perfection at the Reformation's launch was

---

[4]Voolstra, "The Word Has Become Flesh," 155-60.

[5]John Calvin in a treatise from 1545 thoroughly scorns the perfectionism of his day. See Jean Calvin, *Contre la secte phantastique et furieuse des Libertins qui se nomment spirituelz*, ed. G. Baum, E. Cunitz, and E. Reuss, *Ioannis Calvini opera quae supersunt omnia*, 22 vols. (Brunsvigae, 1863–1900), 7:177, 181, 205.

[6]Sebastiani Castellionis, *Dialogi IV: De, fide* (Goudae: Typis Caspari Tournaei, 1613), 2.212. English translation taken from Rufus M. Jones, *Spiritual Reformers of the 16th and 17th Centuries* (London: Macmillan, 1914), 100.

[7]See Ferdinand Buisson, *Sebastien Castellion, sa vie et son oeuvre* (1515-1563), in *Etude sur les origines du protestantisme liberal francais*, 2 vols. (Nieuwkoop, NL: Brill, 1964), 2:166-215. Castellio's understanding of perfection is found in all four sections of Sebastiani Castellionis, *Dialogi IV: De praedestinaatione, electione, libero arbitrio, fide* (Goudae : Typis Caspari Tournaei, 1613).

Dutch theologian Dirk Volckertsz Coornhert. He objected to the Heidelberg Catechism's fifth question, regarding obedience to God's commandments: "Canst thou keep all this perfectly? No; for I am by nature prone to hate God and my neighbor."[8] The catechism, he taught, contradicted the apostle John's clear declaration, "Everyone who has been born of God does not sin" (1 Jn 3:9 CSB). Coornhert believed Christian perfection empowered people to live in a "state of sinlessness."

Coornhert wrote extensively on "perfectionism." His most sustained treatment was *Jacob's Ladder*.[9] Following similar *ordines salutis* ("orders of salvation") from the ancient and medieval church, he describes the rise to perfection in ascending steps within three classes of humanity. First are the godless, who blissfully participate in sin with no sense of guilt. They are outwardly focused on the physical world with no knowledge of their true spiritual condition or God's goodness in Christ.[10] All humanity begins here at the base of the spiritual ladder.[11]

The key to salvation and progress toward perfection, according to Coornhert, is knowledge of self and God. Self-knowledge consists principally in realization of one's sinfulness and the harm it brings; it leads to damnation. Knowledge of God leads to an awareness of God's moral perfection and humanity's reflection of it through the *imago Dei*. The spiritual climb advances in increasing growth through experiential knowledge. Coornhert believed that every person who seeks God will share in the divine nature and arrive at perfect obedience.[12]

---

[8]*The Heidelberg Catechism*, ed. Phillip Schaff, *The Creeds of Christendom with a History of Critical Notes*, 3 vols., 4th ed. (Grand Rapids, MI: Baker, 1966), 3:309.

[9]Dirk Volckertsz Coornhert, *Ladder Jacobs, of Trapp der Deughden*, 1584, *Wrecken*, I, 165r-76v. Discussion here is based on Mirjam G. K. van Veen, "'No One Born of God Commits Sin': Coornhert's Perfectionism," in *Dutch Review of Church History* 84 (2004): 338-57.

[10]Van Veen, "'No One Born of God Commits Sin,'" 344-45.

[11]Coornhert rejects the idea of original sin. Humanity follows the example of Adam. They are misled into sin and are ignorant of this until divine grace illuminates this reality.

[12]Van Veen, "'No One Born of God Commits Sin,'" 345-46.

The second group are sinners, composed of "servants" and "mercenaries" who, through conscience and God's Word, recognize their sinfulness before a holy God. Spiritual ascent begins at the first rung with the "servant" who feels remorse over their sin, seeking to walk in obedience to God from fear of punishment. At the second rung, the "mercenary" lives a repentant life, not out of fear, but with the expectation of reward. Both servant and mercenary have some success in obedience, operating from different motives, but still experience failure. They remain sinners because of their self-preoccupation.[13]

Finally, there are children of God, consisting of "weak children," "adults," and "wise fathers." The next rung in the ascent to perfection is from mercenary to "weak children." All children of God are born again with the power to be victorious over sin. Weak children have become participants in the divine nature. They are motivated by genuine love for God but are still hindered by bad habits acquired over life. As children grow, they discard their sinful behavior, taking the ladder's next step, becoming "adults." Finally, they ascend the final rung to "wise fathers," who are united with God and are living images of Christ. "Fathers" experience fully Paul's declaration, "It is no longer I who live, but it is Christ who lives in me" (Gal 2:20) and are freed to pursue all godly virtue.[14] They are perfect in a Christian, but not in an absolute, sense.

Coornhert believes Christians arrive at this state through a dynamic synergism (i.e., God and humanity cooperate in this work). A person is "neither capable of working out one's own salvation, nor is one completely passive."[15] Perfection in love of God brings "resignation" or "sabbath" in life, where Christians lose all self-interest and pray only for God's will. With such rest in God perfected, Christians no longer worry about personal life or worldly affairs.[16]

---

[13]Van Veen, "'No One Born of God Commits Sin,'" 344, 348.

[14]Van Veen, "'No One Born of God Commits Sin,'" 344-45.

[15]Van Veen, "'No One Born of God Commits Sin,'" 348.

[16]Van Veen, "'No One Born of God Commits Sin,'" 349-50.

Peace, therefore, characterizes them, because the need to control or dictate life's circumstances no longer exists.

PERFECTION IN THE EARLY LUTHERAN
AND REFORMED TRADITIONS

Christian perfection was a subject of discussion and debate in the early Lutheran and Reformed movements. Sebastian Castellio represents the first proponents of the Reformed tradition. The Augsburg Confession points to initial Lutheran thought on the doctrine. It is a subject of considerable reflection by Lutheran scholastic Philip Melanchthon, who states, "All men, in whatever vocation they are, ought to seek perfection, i.e., to increase in the fear of God, in faith, in brotherly love, and similar spiritual virtues."[17]

Philip Melanchthon (AD 1497–1560): Lutheran teaching on perfection. Martin Luther believed sanctification in this present Christian life is a process of being healed from sin where "perfect health" is never attained. He rejected any idea of sinlessness in the church. He pictured the church as an infirmary for the sick, who are in need "of being made well." Heaven, in contrast, is the place of health and complete righteousness. He states, "Righteousness does not yet dwell here, but it is preparing a dwelling place for itself here in the meantime by healing sin. All the saints have had this understanding of sin. . . . And thus they all have confessed that they were sinners."[18]

While remaining true to the general thrust of Luther's teaching, Melanchthon goes further in his theology of sanctification. Melanchthon's teaching is grounded in 1 Timothy 1:5, "The goal of the command is love, which comes from a pure heart and a good conscience and a sincere faith." He does not believe a Christian in

---

[17]Philip Melanchthon, *Apology of the Augsburg Confession*, trans. F. Bente and W. H. T. Dau (Sunnyvale, CA: Loki, 2017), 171-82.

[18]Martin Luther, "Lectures on Romans," in *Luther's Works*, vol. 25, ed. Hilton C. Oswald (St. Louis, MO: Concordia, 1972), 262-63.

the present life is ever free from the "great infirmity, that is to say, a darkness in the mind regarding God, and in the will and heart a corrupt inclination, and many wicked desires."[19] Christians carry original sin throughout life. They also commit "sins of ignorance and omission" because of the body's frailties, but not voluntary acts or acts of the will.[20] Melanchthon cites 1 John 1:8: "If we say that we do not have sin, we are liars." Here, John is speaking of the Adamic weakness and the involuntary sins of the regenerate, but not actual intentional transgressions of the known law of God.[21]

The "righteousness of a good conscience" is when Christians, in the power of the Holy Spirit, fight against their inward sin, the desires of the flesh. In this struggle, they do not "knowingly or willingly" give way or "indulge" them. Through leaning into the godly desires of the Spirit's fruit, Christians are victorious over temptation and walk in outward conformity to the law, even if complete inward alignment is lacking.[22]

Melanchthon picks up the apostle Paul's point in Romans 6:14, "Sin shall not have dominion over you." He connects Paul's statement to the divine warning given to Cain before he murdered Abel, "If you do well, you will be received, and if you do evil, sin lies at the door until it is revealed, waiting to attack you, but you must rule over it" (Gen 4:7). When Christians allow the desires of the flesh to reign in their lives, manifesting in outward sin, "they are torn away from God and later driven into all kinds of crimes, and encounter punishment both in this life and hereafter."[23] These are "mortal sins" and are spiritually dangerous to the Christian. More specifically, they manifest an "evil conscience, that is, the intention of committing

---

[19]Philip Melanchthon, *The Chief Theological Topics: Loci Praecipui Theologici 1559*, trans. J. A. O. Preus (Saint Louis, MO: Concordia, 2011), 230.

[20]Melanchthon, *Chief Theological Topics*, 231.

[21]Melanchthon, *Chief Theological Topics*, 231.

[22]Melanchthon, *Chief Theological Topics*, 232.

[23]Melanchthon, *Chief Theological Topics*, 236.

sin."[24] They lead to spiritual death. While Christians may fall into them, they must not rule in them.

In the end, Melanchthon believes that a Christian's "pure heart, good conscience, and sincere faith" are "far from the perfection of the law, and yet in the case of the those who have been reconciled," they are "pleasing to God for the sake of His Son the Mediator who presents our prayers and our worship before the Father and overlooks our weaknesses."[25]

John Calvin (AD 1509–1564): Reformed teaching on perfection. John Calvin is typically not considered a proponent of Christian perfection. He does, nevertheless, use the language of "perfection" to describe Christian life.[26] According to Calvin, sanctification in life has two movements: mortification of the flesh and resurrection to life. Calvin taught that believers participate in Christ's death and resurrection, instituting new life. He describes it as a "circumcision of the heart" and eradication of impiety and a "double heart."[27]

Calvin believed a Christian's participation in these two movements is never completed in this present life. Like Augustine, Luther, and Melanchthon, he taught that "concupiscence" remains throughout life, and even if it never leads to acts of sin, it remains sin. Believers, therefore, are never free from sin, although spiritual progress is made as they practice self-denial, mortifying the sinful desires of twisted self-love.[28] Essential to sanctification is the surrender of life as a "living sacrifice" (Rom 12:1), whereby the practice of self-denial is combined with sober, righteous godliness, leading to an "indissoluble chain," constituting "complete perfection."[29]

---

[24]Melanchthon, *Chief Theological Topics*, 235.
[25]Melanchthon, *Chief Theological Topics*, 181.
[26]See Ronald S. Wallace, *Calvin's Doctrine of Christian Life* (Edinburgh: Oliver and Boyd, 1959), 321–26; Thomas A. Noble, *Holy Trinity: Holy People: The Theology of Christian Perfecting* (Eugene, OR: Cascade, 2013), 68–70.
[27]John Calvin, *Institutes of the Christian Religion*, trans. Henry Beveridge (Peabody, MA: Hendrickson, 2008), 3.3.3.
[28]Calvin, *Institutes*, 3.3.1–2, 7.
[29]Calvin, *Institutes*, 3.3.3.

Ronald Wallace argues that Calvin sees Christian perfection as a wholehearted life of self-denial. In Calvin's reflection on "perfect Job," he describes Job's perfection as "the dedication of the whole heart and mind to God with one single aim, without any doubleness or hypocrisy or holding back in any part."[30] Wallace believes that while Calvin maintained such perfection is impossible in present life, there is, nevertheless, "a victory over sin and wholehearted surrender which by the grace of God may be called 'perfection.'"[31] Thomas Noble summarizes Calvin's position: "There is a level of perfection possible in this life and a level of perfection that is not."[32]

ROMAN CATHOLICS ON PERFECTION

One of the significant impacts that the Protestant Reformation had on Roman Catholicism was to move Christian perfection into everyday life, making it accessible to anyone baptized. Laity, once again, were exhorted to realize Christ's command to "be perfect" (Mt 5:48).

Francis de Sales (AD 1567–1622). Francis de Sales begins his *Introduction to a Devout Life* with the recognition that it is "an error, nay more, a very heresy, to seek to banish the devout life from the soldier's guardroom, the mechanic's workshop, the prince's court, or the domestic hearth."[33] He teaches this devotion is rooted in the love of God, which shines in the human soul as grace, making humanity acceptable to God; it strengthens in life, empowering obedience in "charity"; and it attains perfection when it leads the Christian to "act carefully, diligently, and promptly."[34] Simply put, perfection is realized when divine love works in human hearts, causing a person

---

[30]Wallace, *Calvin's Doctrine of Christian Life*, 326.
[31]Wallace, *Calvin's Doctrine of Christian Life*, 326.
[32]Noble, *Holy Trinity: Holy People*, 70.
[33]Francis de Sales, *Introduction to the Devout Life*, trans. John K. Ryan, Image Classics (New York: Image, 1966) 1.3.
[34]De Sales, *Introduction to the Devout Life* 1.1.

not only to practice all God's commands but to do so "readily and diligently."[35]

The accessibility of perfection to people from every station of life is verified by the testimony of the Old and New Testaments, as well as church history. De Sales furnishes the examples of Abraham, Isaac, David, Job, Tobias, Sarah, Rebecca, and Judith from the Old Testament and the Apocrypha; Joseph, Lydia, Martha, Aquila, and Priscilla from the New Testament; and Constantine, Helena, and Gregory from church history. Each of these examples of secular vocation participated in the "path of perfection."[36]

According to de Sales, Christian perfection begins with the purification of the soul, the forsaking of sin. While this cleansing of sin can happen instantaneously, more often it occurs gradually, by "slow degrees, step by step."[37] Purification occurs throughout life, beginning with the elimination of mortal sins, which can destroy spiritual life, and continues with the elimination of venial sins, until the end of present life. The normative life in the path of perfection consists of being aware of our imperfections but not "consenting to them."[38]

More specifically, purification is not only the abandonment of outward sin, mortal sin, but of its affections as well. Too often Christians resolve to sin no more, but it "goes sorely against them to abstain from the pleasures of sin."[39] De Sales compares it to a sick person "who abstains from eating melon when the doctor says it will kill him, but who longs for it, talks about it, bargains when he may have it . . . and thinks those who are free to eat of it very fortunate."[40] To realize Christian perfection, the heart must be cleansed from all affections pertaining to sin.

---

[35]De Sales, *Introduction to the Devout Life* 1.1.
[36]De Sales, *Introduction to the Devout Life* 1.3.
[37]De Sales, *Introduction to the Devout Life* 1.4.
[38]De Sales, *Introduction to the Devout Life* 1.5.
[39]De Sales, *Introduction to the Devout Life* 1.7.
[40]De Sales, *Introduction to the Devout Life* 1.7.

The work of sanctification must go deeper still. It must address all tendencies toward venial sin. While Christians are freed from mortal sin, complete liberation from venial sin is not possible in life. Venial sins are addressed progressively in life. Christian perfection, however, brings freedom for any desire for venial sin. De Sales states, "It is altogether one thing to have said something unimportant, not strictly true, out of carelessness or liveliness, and quite a different matter to take pleasure in it."[41] If venial sins are permitted "to linger in the heart, or, worse still if we take pleasure in them, then the sweetness of divine love in life will soon be spoilt."[42]

François Fenelon (AD 1651–1715). At the center of François Fenelon's doctrine of Christian perfection is love, the fulfillment of the greatest commandment: the love of God with all heart, soul, and strength (Deut 6:5). This love is defined by an "interior destruction of egotistical, self-centered desires that resist our abandoning ourselves by an act of pure love to God's will."[43] Obedience to God, motivated by pure love, free from self-interest, characterizes Christian perfection.[44] This experience is realized by the grace of God in human life, leading a Christian to come to a place of complete abandonment to God.[45]

Fenelon, more specifically, believes there are five levels of "disinterested" love. First is the love of a servant, which loves the good for the benefits conferred by the good. Second is the love of God for salvation brought to a person. The third and fourth are varying degrees of self-interest and true love of God. Finally, there is disinterested love of God, which is motivated by neither the fear of

---

[41]De Sales, *Introduction to the Devout Life* 1.22.

[42]De Sales, *Introduction to the Devout Life* 1.22.

[43]François Fenelon, *Fenelon: Selected Writings*, ed. and trans. Chad Helms, Classics of Western Spirituality (New York: Paulist, 2006), 68.

[44]Fenelon, *Fenelon: Selected Writings*, 103-4.

[45]François Fenelon, *Maxims of the Saints*, trans. Watkin W. Williams (Oxford: A. R. Mowbray, 1909), articles 8-9.

punishment nor the hope of reward.[46] Here, God is loved so purely by Christians that they are willing to forsake their own happiness with God out of love for God. Personal happiness is subordinated to God's.[47] Such love was manifested by Moses in his intercession on behalf of Israel (Ex 32:32), by the apostle Paul in his love for Israel (Rom 9:3), and in the lives of saints from church history.

Fenelon distinguishes self-love in Christian perfection from selfishness. Personal desire for happiness, properly ordered in God, is appropriate and natural to being human. When self-love, however, "passes its appropriate limit, it becomes selfishness . . . selfishness was the sin of the first angel" whose love of self "rested in himself" instead of God.[48]

Fenelon teaches all virtue is included in perfect love. He states, "He who is in the state of pure or perfect love, has all the moral and Christian virtues in himself."[49] The virtues of temperance, forbearance, chastity, truth, kindness, forgiveness, and justice have their "foundation, source, or principle" in disinterested love of God.[50] Christian virtues arising from perfection in love empower a Christian to fulfill the commands of God.[51]

Madam Guyon (AD 1648–1717). Madame Jeanne-Marie Guyon reflects the optimism of this distinct body of Roman Catholic teaching on perfection for the ordinary believer. She testifies, "Far from being incapable of this perfection, the simple are more fit for it." The uneducated, she contends, are more humble, ready to receive the truth of the riches in Jesus Christ, because their intellect does not burden them.[52]

---

[46]Patrick Riley, "Review of *Fenelon Philosophe* by Henri Gouhier," *The Philosophical Review* 90 (1981): 288.

[47]Fenelon, *Maxims of the Saints*, article 2.3.

[48]Fenelon, *Maxims of the Saints*, article 16.

[49]Fenelon, *Maxims of the Saints*, article 16.

[50]Fenelon, *Maxims of the Saints*, article 4.

[51]Fenelon, *Maxims of the Saints*, article 11.

[52]Madam Guyon, *A Short and Very Easy Method of Prayer*, ed. J. W. Metcalf (New York: M. W. Dodd, 1853), 3.

Like Fenelon, Guyon focused her teaching on the experience of disinterested love, abandonment to God, and the role of contemplation. She taught that in perfect love the human will, with memory and understanding, is subsumed by the divine will. All impediments to divine grace's activity in the human soul are removed. Far from making the human soul a passive receptor of God's work, perfect love energizes human life. It does not make a Christian incapable of sin in life or falling from grace; rather it empowers a believer to subordinate all self-will to the will of God.[53]

PERFECTION IN PIETISM

Pietism arose in the seventeenth century in response to the spiritual aridity of Lutheran scholasticism. It sought to bring genuine Christianity into the life of the church and individual believers. With the Anabaptist tradition, Pietism generally emphasized the pursuit of perfection while teaching its ultimate unattainability in life.[54] Nevertheless, witnesses to a relative perfection, a Christian perfection, existed among their greatest teachers.

Johann Arndt (AD 1555–1621). The heart of Arndt's teaching on Christian perfection is in the third book of his seminal work, *True Christianity*.[55] Arndt teaches that there is a place for divine activity in every human soul. The *imago Dei* in humanity establishes an internal space for any action of God in people. More important, God intends to dwell here more than any other part of creation. It is where union between God and humanity takes place.[56]

Arndt describes the threefold spiritual movement leading to divine union, following human stages of development. First is "childhood," marked by repentance through self-denial, a turning

---

[53]Madam Guyon, *A Short and Very Easy Method of Prayer*, 5.
[54]Paul M. Bassett and William Greathouse, *The Historical Development*, vol. 2, *Exploring Christian Holiness* (Kansas City, MO: Beacon Hill, 1985), 187.
[55]Johann Arndt, *True Christianity*, trans. Anthony W. Boehm and Charles H. Schaeffer (Philadelphia: Lutheran, 1868).
[56]Arndt, *True Christianity*, 2.29.

away from the world toward Christ. Second is "manhood," a greater spiritual illumination "through the contemplation of divine things, through prayer, through cross bearing, through all of which the gifts of God are increased." Finally, there is "old age," which brings complete union with God through love, which is "the perfect age in Christ" and makes "a perfect man in Christ."[57] Here, a Christian "gives God his heart completely and fully, rests alone in God, gives himself over to him, holds to him alone . . . participates in all that is God and Christ, becomes one spirit with God, receives new powers, new life . . . righteousness and holiness.[58]

More specifically, this perfection still admits "indwelling sin," but that sin does not reign.[59] The more Christ rules in the human heart, the more believers become aware of their remaining imperfection. Without Christ's rule, they would be ignorant of their true state before God.[60] Crucial for Arndt is recognizing that perfection is not the end but a result of seeking union with God through Christ.

Philip Jakob Spener (AD 1635–1705). Spener's most significant contribution to the doctrine of Christian perfection is *Pia Desideria*.[61] Spener embraces Luther's teaching on justification, seeing imputed righteousness as positional perfection in Christ. He cautions, at the same time, against any tendency to excuse sin within such teaching. Christians are called to actual perfection. The unmistakable fruit of regeneration is holiness. Growth in sanctification, however, leads believers to see more clearly their imperfection. While absolute perfection is impossible, Spener believes, "we are nevertheless under obligation to achieve some degree of perfection" in the present life.[62]

This Christian perfection, which admits continual growth in life, is described by Spener in different ways. It entails a life without

---

[57] Arndt, *True Christianity*, 2.30.
[58] Arndt, *True Christianity*, 1.22.
[59] Arndt, *True Christianity*, 1.16.
[60] Arndt, *True Christianity*, 2.4-6.
[61] Philip Jacob Spener, *Pia Desideria*, trans. Theodore Tappert (Philadelphia: Fortress, 1964).
[62] Spener, *Pia Desideria*, 80.

"hypocrisy," "free of manifest offences," and "filled with many fruits of faith."[63] Supremely, it is perfection in love that flows from God to the believer and aspires to greater perfection, fortifying human intention to do the will of God.[64] In this life, however, Christians never realize ultimate perfection, which brings sinlessness and no longer admits any growth.[65]

August Hermann Franke (AD 1663-1727). August Franke's theological reflection and teaching embrace Arndt and Spener's focus on freedom from outward sin in perfection. Significant for the Pietist tradition is his interpretation of Paul's teaching in Romans 7. In contrast to Lutheran and Reformed scholastics, Franke taught that Paul's description of the person who desires to do the good but is unable to do so (Rom 7:14-25) is a Christian who is not yet fully converted. Franke believed that by divine grace through the Holy Spirit, believers experience a "significant breakthrough" in which the dilemma of Romans 7 is overcome. It is a clear and definite transition from existence under sin to one under grace.[66]

Like Arndt and Spener, Franke did not believe that Christian perfection in life entailed freedom from all sin. Perfection begins with an awakening in human life, whereby a person recognizes their sin and threat of divine judgment. Perfection develops in them, leading them to Christ, who alone can deliver them from their sinful desires. This process positions the Christian, finally, for the liberation of their will as they persevere before God in prayer until breakthrough comes, freeing the believer from the predicament of Romans 7:14-25.[67]

---

[63]Spener, *Pia Desideria*, 80-81.

[64]Spener, *Pia Desideria*, 96.

[65]Spener, *Pia Desideria*, 80.

[66]August Francke, "Von der Verpflichtung auf die Bekenntnisschriften," in Adolf Sellschopp, ed., *Neue Quellen zur Geschichte August Hermann Franckes* (Halle, DE: Niemeyer, 1913), 142-48.

[67]Markus Matthias, "August Hermann Francke (1663-1727)," in *The Pietist Theologians: An Introduction to Theology in the Seventeenth and Eighteenth Centuries*, ed. Carter Lindberg (Oxford: Blackwell, 2005), 107-8.

THE QUAKER TRADITION

The Religious Society of Friends began with the religious awakening of George Fox (AD 1624–1691) in 1646 and his understanding of the "Inner Light" of Jesus Christ. Central to Fox's teaching is a Christian's emancipation from sin, both within and without. He testified to an experience whereby God restored him to a state of Adamic perfection.[68] He believed that through Christ's atoning work a believer is brought into "the righteousness, holiness, and image of God," where "the unrighteousness, unholiness, and image of Satan" is put to death.[69]

William Penn (AD 1644–1718), the founder of what became the state of Pennsylvania, also advocated for the Quaker belief of "perfect freedom from sin and a thorough sanctification in body, soul, and spirit, whilst on this side of the grave, by the operation of the holy and perfect Spirit."[70] He clarifies that while this perfection is salvation from the "nature and defilement of sin," it is not absolute, still admitting human "infirmities."[71]

Quaker theology reached its mature expression in the work of Robert Barclay (AD 1648–1690). His theology was imbued with the early church fathers, medieval scholastics, and Protestant reformers. Two of his works are critical in his teaching on Christian perfection: *An Apology for the True Christian Divinity* and *Catechism and Confession of Faith.*[72] Following Augustinian thought appropriated by John Calvin and Martin Luther, Barclay recognized the problem of humanity's total depravity because of Adam's fall. The scriptural centerpiece of his doctrine is Genesis 6:5, "The LORD saw how great the wickedness of the human race had become on the earth, and that every inclination of the thoughts of the human heart was only evil

---

[68]George Fox, *Journal*, ed. Thomas Ellwood, 8th ed., 2 vols. (London: Friends' Tract Association), 1:28.

[69]Fox, *Journal*, 1:345.

[70]William Penn, *A Testimony to the Truth of God*, ed. Abram R. Barclay (Manchester: W. Irwin, 1874), xi.

[71]Penn, *Testimony*, xi.

[72]Robert Barclay, *An Apology for the True Christian Divinity* (New York: Samuel Wood and Sons, 1827); *A Catechism and Confession of Faith* (London: A. Soule, 1690).

all the time."[73] However, no matter how depraved, every human has "divine light" infused into the soul. While the soul has no spiritual capacity, this inner light makes salvation possible.[74]

According to Barclay, humanity's ultimate purpose is true knowledge of God, which is realized through the work of Christ and the Holy Spirit. The Father can only be known through the Son, and the Son through the Holy Spirit. This knowledge of God is imparted directly to the soul, bypassing its natural rational capacities.[75] Divine light in conjunction with the Scriptures seeks to bring spiritual birth to humanity, whereby "the body of death and sin comes to be crucified and removed, and their hearts united and subjected to the truth; so as not to obey any suggestions or temptations of the evil one, but to be free from actual sinning and transgressing the law of God, and in this sense perfect."[76]

Barclay grounds his understanding in the apostle Paul's teaching from Romans 6:14, "For sin shall not have dominion over you." In the larger context of the chapter, Paul exhorts Christians not to continue in sin (Rom 6:1-2, 15) because they have died to sin through the grace of God in Christ. If a Christian continues in sin, then there is only one consequence: death (Rom 6:23). More specifically, Barclay teaches that Christ's command to "be perfect, as the Father is perfect" (Mt 5:48) defines every true Christian because God's commands "are not grievous" (1 Jn 5:3). He sees examples of perfection in the Old Testament figures of Noah, who is said to be "perfect in his generations" (Gen 6:9), and Job, who was a "perfect and upright man" (Job 1:8). The New Testament describes Zechariah and Elizabeth, the parents of John the Baptist, as "blameless" in God's eyes (Lk 1:5-6). And the saints in heaven were "just men made perfect" in this life (Heb 12:22-23).[77]

---

[73]Barclay, *Apology*, prop. 4.2.
[74]Barclay, *Apology*, prop. 5.6.15-16.
[75]Barclay, *Apology*, prop. 5.6.14.
[76]Barclay, *Apology*, prop. 8.
[77]Robert Barclay, *A Catechism and Confession of Faith*, chap. 7.

Perfection realized through spiritual birth is not absolute but grows and matures. While Christians exist in the present life, they retain the possibility of sin.[78] Barclay states that those who have experienced Christian perfection "may, by disobedience, fall from it . . . make shipwreck of faith, and having tasted the heavenly gift, and been made partakers of the Holy Ghost, again fall away."[79] Nevertheless, growth in perfection brings greater stability, protecting Christian life from threat of "total apostasy."[80]

THE ANGLICAN TRADITION

William Law (AD 1686–1761) represents the clarion call to Christian perfection in the Anglican tradition. He devoted his life to reflection, teaching, and exhortation to perfection. In his early life, Law wrote his most detailed work on the subject: *A Treatise upon Christian Perfection*.[81]

Law recognizes the problem with the language of perfection—how it is subject to misunderstanding. He defines it simply as "the right and full performance of those duties which are necessary for all Christians, and common to all states of life."[82] Far from any Pelagian understandings, Law argues that the foundation for all discharge of duty is spiritual regeneration. God's grace is the only means by which "we are disposed toward that which is good, and made able to perform it."[83] To participate in transforming and empowering grace, people must "deny themselves" all unholy "tempers," "ways," "enjoyments," and "indulgences" in life, which make them "less disposed" to embrace grace as it is communicated to them. This embrace means taking up the cross of Jesus Christ, which opposes the values and practices of the fallen world. The rejection of

---

[78]Barclay, *Apology*, prop. 8.
[79]Barclay, *Apology*, prop. 9.
[80]Barclay, *Apology*, prop. 9.
[81]William Law, *A Treatise on Christian Perfection*, ed. Erwin Paul Rudolph (Carol Stream, IL: Creation, 1975).
[82]Law, *Christian Perfection*, 5.
[83]Law, *Christian Perfection*, 134.

wealth, the acceptance of suffering, and the practice of humility are essential here.[84]

Law emphasizes that Christ's command to be perfect is for every believer, not just for cloister communities, not simply tied to a particular station in life. Regardless of position or work, Christians can offer their lives as a sacrifice to God. They can have their hearts and minds turned continually toward God because of the divine image in every person and the character of God. In another treatise, *A Serious Call*, Law writes, "All orders of people are, to the utmost of their power, to make their life agreeable to that one Spirit for which they are all to pray."[85]

For Law, perfection is no less than a life "wholly devoted to God." In his exposition of 1 John 3:9, Law writes that this is not "an absolute state of perfection, and incapable afterward of falling into anything sinful" but defines a believer who "is possessed of a temper and principle that makes him utterly hate and labor to avoid sin; he is therefore said not to commit sin."[86] Law teaches further that perfection is Christlikeness, walking in devotion to God according to one's station in life as Jesus did, where humility, receptiveness, and adoration define life.[87]

Law carries many of the themes of his early works into his later writings. Although this body did not attain the popularity of his earlier treatises, they are significant and display a mystical turn in life. Law believed in the original perfection of humanity's first parents, which was the life of the triune God who had breathed into humanity the "self-existent, self-moving qualities of his own being." Because of the fall, humanity lost not only moral perfection but also mental and rational acuity. Adam "died to all the influences and operations of the Kingdom of God on him," and this fallen world

---

[84]William Law, *Christian Perfection*, 122-28.

[85]William Law, *A Serious Call to a Devout and Holy Life* (London: W. Innys, 1750), 110.

[86]William Law, *A Practical Treatise on Christian Perfection*, in *The Works of Rev. William Law*, 9 vols. (London: G. Moreton, 1893), 3:27.

[87]Law, *Practical Treatise*, 3:27.

"became opened in him."[88] The present condition of humanity is a type of hell.

Salvation, then, is a restoration of humanity's original condition of perfection. It is the reinvigoration of the life that was lost. It begins with the Word of life being spoken into each person, a divine light, "which lighteth every man" (Jn 1:9) coming into existence. This light or "seed" operates as hope in humanity, seeking completion in Christ's glorified humanity and the Holy Spirit's impartation. It is by Christ living in humanity through the Holy Spirit that believers experience victory over their sinful condition and righteousness becomes the natural state. Divine love fills the human heart, introducing a "new world," putting an end to the former way of living. This opens "new senses in you, and makes you see high to be low, and low to be high; wisdom to be foolishness and foolishness to be wisdom."[89] This love empowers human love in the fulfillment of the law and every Christian duty.

How then do people enter Christian perfection? It is by having the nature of God "rekindled" in them. In the moment when a person recognizes their sinfulness and cries out in need to Christ, the "mercy of God and the misery of man are met together."[90] It is the simple exercise of faith in Christ that saves and imparts God's kingdom of God. Christ is near, ready to save and to restore humanity to original perfection.[91]

THE WESLEYAN TRADITION

John Wesley (AD 1703–1791), in mature reflection on his years of leadership overseeing the eighteenth-century Methodist revival, wrote a letter to Robert Carr Brackenbury asserting that Christian perfection "is the grand depositum which God has lodged with the

---

[88]R. Newton Flew, *The Idea of Christian Perfection in Christian Theology: An Historical Study of the Christian Ideal for the Present Life* (London: Oxford University Press, 1934), 306.

[89]William Law, *The Spirit of Love*, in *The Works of Rev. William Law*, 8:109.

[90]Law, *The Spirit of Love*, 8:109.

[91]Law, *The Spirit of Love*, 8:109.

people called Methodists; and for the sake of propagating this chiefly He appeared to have raised us up."[92] Since the dawn of Methodism within Anglicanism, the doctrine, message, and experience of Christian perfection have been central to the Wesleyan tradition.

John Wesley's doctrine of Christian perfection. In early 1729, several influences converged in John Wesley's life, convincing him "not only to read, but to study, the Bible, as the one, the only standard of truth, and the only model of pure religion." In the same year, Wesley established clearly in his mind the goal of Christianity: holiness of heart and life, holiness capable of changing the world. As the years progressed, Wesley's doctrine of Christian perfection came into focus and characterized his message of salvation.

Wesley's definition of Christian perfection. On the most basic level, John Wesley defined Christian perfection (also named "entire sanctification" by Wesley), as a work of God's grace whereby Christians are cleansed from the internal being of sin (original sin) and set free to love God with everything and to love others as themselves.[93] They are delivered from the internal principle of selfishness and sin that persists stubbornly in them because of the fall of humanity's first parents. Wesley believed that believers are set free from outward sin, or the power of sin, in new birth.[94] In entire sanctification they are set free from inward sin, being released to serve God and others with their undivided heart, fulfilling the two great commandments.[95]

Wesley also described Christian perfection as the complete renewal of the moral image of God in humanity. Prior to the fall, the moral image, mediated by the Holy Spirit, enabled humanity to

---

[92]Wesley, "Letter to Robert Carr Brackenbury (September 15, 1790)," *WJW* 13:9.

[93]Wesley, "A Plain Account of Christian Perfection," *WJW* 11:366-67. Christian perfection and entire sanctification are synonyms in the Wesleyan tradition. "Christian perfection" is language found in historic Christianity, while entire sanctification is located primarily in the Wesleyan tradition.

[94]Wesley, "The Great Privilege of Those That Are Born of God," *WJW* 5:223-33.

[95]Wesley, "The Scripture Way of Salvation," *WJW* 6:43-54.

enjoy true righteousness, holiness, and love of God in the immediacy of a relationship with God. The moral image formed the guiding principle of humanity's disposition, thoughts, words, and deeds. While the moral image was destroyed in the fall, the image is partially restored in the new birth, experiences ongoing restoration through progressive sanctification, and is renewed completely through entire sanctification. As such, the fully renewed moral image in Christian perfection forms the trajectory of all human actions in thought, word, and deed.[96]

Because of the problematic nature of the language "entire" and "perfection," Wesley endeavored to be clear in his many discussions about what it does and does not entail. For Wesley, entire sanctification, or Christian perfection, does not include the perfection of knowledge, freedom from mistakes, freedom from infirmities, or exemption from temptation. As such, Christian perfection is not Adamic or divine perfection. While Christians may be renewed completely in the moral image, the natural and political images are still marred, resulting in sins of infirmity from clouded reasoning and mistakes in judgment.[97] This is one reason why Wesley was reluctant to call it a "sinless perfection."[98] Furthermore, it is not divine perfection because it is subject to change, positively or negatively. Perfection can intensify or grow throughout life or be subject to loss through deliberate sin.[99]

---

[96]Wesley, "The End of Christ's Coming," *WJW* 6:267-77.

[97]Wesley, "Christian Perfection," *WJW* 6:1-22. In historic Christian thought, only divine perfection is static. Human perfection, in contrast, is dynamic. We can make a distinction between absolute human perfection that the righteous will have in heaven; Adamic perfection that our first parents had in the garden before the fall; and Christian perfection that is possible in the present life. Wesley believed even in heaven, absolute human perfection will continue to grow and intensify.

The Wesleyan language of entire sanctification is "entire" in the sense that it addresses every harmful problem of personal sin in relationship to God: guilt, power, and condition. It does not overcome all sin, such as sins of infirmity. Sins of infirmity, however, do not harm our relationship with God.

[98]Wesley, "Principles of a Methodist," *WJW* 8:363-65.

[99]Wesley, "On Perfection," *WJW* 6:411-24.

The means of Christian perfection. As the Spirit transforms Christians progressively from new birth in their attitudes, interests, and actions, he convicts the believer of vestiges of selfishness and sin. While believers live in obedience to Christ, their hearts are divided. Pride and selfishness manifest themselves below the surface. Believers see more clearly an internal principle that is contrary to Christ, causing them to stumble into "sins of surprise," making them "prone to wander" from the God they love as the hymn "Come Thou Fount of Every Blessing" acknowledges. As they begin to struggle against their internal sin and its outward manifestation, they realize there is little they can do to decisively squelch it. If they are to be delivered from this "state," only Christ can do it.

Wesley taught that just as believers experience new birth through faith, they are entirely sanctified by faith.[100] Like saving faith, sanctifying faith is a divine gift, not human work. Only when divine grace comes to create sanctifying faith, often mediated through the means of grace, can they have sanctifying faith to exercise. Christians, as such, cannot be entirely sanctified at any given moment but only in those times and places in which divine grace imparts sanctifying faith. Wesley taught believers must actively seek entire sanctification, therefore, in the appointed means of grace, waiting for the Holy Spirit to create this faith.[101]

John Wesley describes well the nature of sanctifying faith. First, he says that "it is a divine evidence and conviction" that God promises in the Scriptures. Only the Holy Spirit gives believers eyes to see the promise of perfection in sanctifying faith. Faith at this point, however, is only an intellectual apprehension and not enough to sanctify. Second, Wesley teaches, "it is a divine evidence and conviction" that God "is able to do" what he has promised. Faith is taken to a deeper level. The Holy Spirit convinces believers that Christ indeed sanctifies people. Third, Wesley adds that the

---

[100]Wesley, "The Scripture Way of Salvation," *WJW* 6:52-53.
[101]Wesley, "The Scripture Way of Salvation," *WJW* 6:52-53.

Spirit must convince seekers that Christ "is able to do it now." Finally, Wesley states this "divine evidence and conviction" has one last element: Christ does it now in the Christian. Only the Holy Spirit imparting this truth directly to our hearts can empower a Christian to believe a seeming impossibility—a life defined by holy love.[102]

Later Methodists: Francis Asbury (1745–1816), Thomas Ralston (AD 1806–1891), and William B. Pope (AD 1822–1903). Francis Asbury led the first generation of Methodists in the newly formed United States of America. He testified to the experience of entire sanctification a year after he was "graciously justified."[103] As a leader in the early American Methodist revival, he observed people as they were "convicted, converted, and sanctified."[104] Like John Wesley, he believed a Christian was set free from the power of sin through justifying grace and from the state of sin at entire sanctification.[105] Entire sanctification, like the new birth, was by faith and expected as a "present salvation."[106] Although Asbury taught it as a realizable experience, he believed it could be lost and warned those who profess Christian perfection not to place "too much confidence in past experience."[107]

After John Wesley and Francis Asbury died, more scholarly attention was given to the formal articulation of Methodist beliefs. The first systematic theology in the Wesleyan tradition was British theologian Richard Watson's *Theological Institutes*, published in 1831. American Methodist scholar Thomas Ralston followed in 1847 with his *Elements of Divinity*.[108] Ralston largely affirmed John Wesley's teaching on the deliverance from the guilt and power of

---

[102]Wesley, "The Scripture Way of Salvation," *WJW* 6:52-53.

[103]Francis Asbury, *The Journal and Letters of Francis Asbury*, ed. Elmer T. Clark, 3 vols. (Nashville: Abingdon, 1958), 1:88.

[104]Asbury, *The Journal and Letters of Francis Asbury*, 2:47.

[105]Asbury, *The Journal and Letters of Francis Asbury*, 3:323.

[106]Asbury, *The Journal and Letters of Francis Asbury*, 1:339.

[107]Asbury, *The Journal and Letters of Francis Asbury*, 1:235.

[108]Thomas N. Ralston, *Elements of Divinity* (Nashville: Abingdon-Cokesbury, 1924).

sin in conversion and inbred sin in entire sanctification. He also contributed strong arguments for a perfection of love in the present life.

Ralston believed "the general tenor of Scripture" teaches that Christian perfection is "within the reach of the 'least of the saints'" and "is attainable in this life" when believers meet the conditions for its attainment.[109] To deny its realization until death is to give "the last enemy" of humanity, death, more "efficiency" than the "blood of Christ" and "influence of the Holy Spirit."[110] Furthermore, he taught the apostle John's witness to perfection in love and cleansing from all sin applied to every believer and not just to those at death's door. John's promises in 1 John 1:7 and 3:3 address living Christians and take place in this life.[111]

If Christian perfection is for every believer, Ralston answers, "It matters but little whether this eminent state of holiness is gained by a bold, energetic, and determined exercise of faith and prayer, or by a more gradual process. . . . The great matter is . . . that we lose no time, but arise at once, and 'press toward the mark for the prize of the high calling of God in Christ Jesus.'"[112]

British Methodist William Burt Pope published his systematic theology in 1875.[113] Like Methodists before him, Pope affirmed that entire sanctification is the aim of Christ's work. Pope addressed the role of personal consecration in the experience of perfection. Consecration is the work of the Holy Spirit whereby the Spirit dedicates to God's possession and service all that a person surrenders. Like Wesley, Pope taught that sanctifying faith is a gift of grace, but he also believed full consecration to God is as well.[114] Consecration by

---

[109]Ralston, *Elements of Divinity*, 466-67.
[110]Ralston, *Elements of Divinity*, 469.
[111]Ralston, *Elements of Divinity*, 470.
[112]Ralston, *Elements of Divinity*, 470.
[113]William Burt Pope, *A Compendium of Christian Theology*, 3 vols., 2nd ed. (New York: Hunt and Eaton, 1899).
[114]Pope, *Compendium*, 3:23.

the Spirit produces in Christians the character of Christ, making them partakers of the Savior's consecration."[115]

Pope also emphasized the progressive nature of sanctification leading to Christian perfection. He believed the Holy Spirit is given to believers in new birth without measure, yet love of God and neighbor given by the Spirit "abounds more and more."[116] Like Ralston, Pope argued that entire sanctification is "the perfection of the regenerate state." He states, "The Spirit of entire sanctification is only the Spirit of the beginning of grace exerting an ampler power. Never do we read of a higher life that is other than the intensification of the lower; never of the second blessing that is more than the unrestrained outpouring of the same Spirit who gave the first."[117]

Nineteenth-century holiness movement: Phoebe Palmer (AD 1807–1874) and J. A. Wood (AD 1828–1905). By the end of the first quarter of the nineteenth century, the doctrine and message of Christian perfection faced difficult days in the United States. The fires of early Methodism's teaching on holiness were waning. A new generation of leaders arose, stretching across a vast array of Protestant traditions. As a result, Wesley's teaching on Christian perfection experienced certain modifications and emphases.

In contrast to Wesley, nineteenth-century holiness teaching, by and large, linked baptism with the Holy Spirit to Christian perfection rather than to new birth. It emphasized the human ability to meet the conditions of consecration and faith to attain perfection and therefore focused on an instantaneous experience rather than a process. At times, this teaching could downplay deliverance from the power of sin at conversion, relegating it along with freedom from the inward condition of sin to entire sanctification. Finally, it distinguished entire sanctification from Christian maturity. Perfection

---

[115]Pope, *Compendium*, 3:53.
[116]Pope, *Compendium*, 3:37-38.
[117]Pope, *Compendium*, 3:97.

in love was viewed as a normative Christian experience that makes possible maturity, rather the being synonymous with it.

Many scholars identify Phoebe Palmer as the mother of the holiness movement. Her most important work, *The Way of Holiness*, established many of the distinguishing characteristics of this particular expression of Wesleyan teaching.[118] For ease of communication and to assist seekers, Palmer sought to simplify Wesleyan teaching. Most significant was her three-step approach to the appropriation of sanctification: consecration, faith, and testimony. First is consecration, surrendering everything to God. The image here is the placement of life in its entirety on an altar to God. The second is faith. A seeker must believe that Christ can and wants to sanctify the believer. There must be confidence in God to sanctify everything placed on the altar. Finally, the Christian must testify to the experience of entire sanctification as an act of faith. Christians demonstrate their confidence in Christ by publicly confessing their sanctification experience.[119]

Methodist Episcopal minister J. A. Wood followed in Palmer's footsteps. Wood became one of the founders of the National Camp Meeting Association for the Promotion of Holiness. In his work *Perfect Love*, Wood offers practical advice for perfection's realization.[120] First, seekers must have a clear understanding of what is sought: "the extermination of sin in the soul," "the renewal of the image of God, so that the fountain of thought, affection, desire, and impulse is pure."[121] Second, they must make a "firm and decided resolution to seek" until they "obtain the victory—a pure heart."[122] Third, they must make every effort to "feel the need" for entire sanctification. Hunger and thirst for perfection through "prayer, searching the Scriptures, meditation, and self-examination" must

---

[118]Phoebe Palmer, *The Way of Holiness* (New York, 1854), 210.

[119]Palmer, *Way of Holiness*, 106-221.

[120]John A. Wood, *Perfect Love* (Philadelphia: National Publishing Association, 1877).

[121]Wood, *Perfect Love*, 78.

[122]Wood, *Perfect Love*, 78.

be fostered.[123] Finally, entire consecration of life to God must happen. Wood exhorts, "Search and surrender, and re-search and surrender again, until you get every vestige of self upon the altar of consecration."[124]

PENTECOSTALISM

Pentecostalism has significant roots in the American Wesleyan-holiness teaching of the nineteenth century. The earliest Pentecostal denomination, formed in 1897, was the Church of God in Christ, established by Baptist preachers Charles H. Mason and Charles P. Jones, who experienced entire sanctification in Jackson, Mississippi. They formed a church in Lexington, Mississippi, in 1896 and began to preach the Wesleyan message of Christian perfection as "a second definite work of grace" experience. In 1906, Mason and leaders in the church traveled to Azusa, California, to hear William J. Seymour preach. As they listened, they experienced "baptism in the Holy Ghost" with the evidence of speaking in tongues. The Church of God in Christ in 1907 became the first "full-fledged" Pentecostal denomination, adding an article on Spirit baptism as a third work of grace after justification and entire sanctification.[125]

William J. Seymour (AD 1870–1922). William J. Seymour became the most significant leader in early Pentecostalism through his leadership of the Azusa Street revival, which began in 1906 and lasted until 1915. Though raised in the Roman Catholic Church, he experienced new birth and entire sanctification under Wesleyan-holiness teaching in Indianapolis, Indiana. After spending time at God's Bible School and College in Cincinnati, Ohio, he traveled to Houston, Texas, where he sat under the teaching of Charles Parham, who described another significant divine work subsequent to entire

---

[123]Wood, *Perfect Love*, 78-79.
[124]Wood, *Perfect Love*, 79.
[125]Vinson Synan, *The Twentieth-Century Pentecostal Explosion* (Altamonte Springs, FL: Creation House, 1987), 75-80.

sanctification. Seymour soon experienced his "personal Pentecost" and spoke in tongues.

At the heart of the Azusa Street revival, Seymour's teaching had a threefold understanding of the gospel, which became the foundation of all Pentecostal holiness denominations. First is justification, whereby a person's sins are forgiven through Christ's atoning work. Second is entire sanctification, otherwise known as Christian perfection. Seymour's belief here was grounded in 1 Thessalonians 4:3, "It is God's will that you should be sanctified." The sanctified life happens through the crucifixion of the "old man." Unless the old self is put to death completely, it remains a constant irritant in life. Through Christ Jesus, however, the Christian is liberated from the "breed of sin, the love of sin, and carnality." Seymour believed this deliverance included freedom from the power and condition of original sin, making the believer "pure in heart" (Mt 5:8), bestowing perfect love.[126] Finally, there is baptism with the Holy Spirit, which empowers the believer for service and gifts of the Holy Spirit. The evidence of Spirit baptism is speaking in tongues.[127]

William Durham (AD 1873–1912). Seymour's theology established the foundation for early Pentecostal teaching on perfection. As Pentecostalism grew, the "finished work" of Christ theology in William Durham gained traction among groups outside of the Wesleyan-holiness tradition. Durham, who once preached entire sanctification as a second definite work of grace, began to teach that a believer is sanctified at conversion and not as a second blessing.

Durham testifies, "I began to write against the doctrine that it takes two works of grace to save and cleanse a man. I denied and still deny that God does not deal with the nature of sin at conversion. I

---

[126]William J. Seymour, "Sanctified on the Cross," in *William J. Seymour and His Azusa Street Sermons*, ed. Douglas Harrolf (Norwalk, CT: HJ Publishing, 2016), 57-58.

[127]William J. Seymour, "The Baptism of the Holy Ghost," in *William J. Seymour and His Azusa Street Sermons*, ed. Douglas Harrolf (Norwalk, CT: HJ Publishing, 2016), 59-64.

deny that a man who is converted or born again is outwardly washed and cleansed but that his heart is left unclean with enmity against God in it. . . . This would not be salvation."[128] Christians remain in a state of sanctification if they abide in Christ. If sin arises, then the believer must look to the finished work of Christ on the cross for victory. According to Durham, the danger in Wesleyan-holiness teaching is to look to an experience of entire sanctification and not to Christ for sanctification.[129]

A modified expression of Durham's theology is found in the Assemblies of God's article on "Entire Sanctification" in their 1917 *Statement of Fundamental Truths*: "The Scriptures teach a life of holiness without which no man shall see the Lord. By the power of the Holy Ghost we can obey the command, 'be holy, for I am holy.' Entire sanctification is the will of God for all believers and should be pursued by walking in obedience to God's word."[130] Here, entire sanctification is not expressed as a second definite work of grace, but a reality arising from the conduct of daily life by all Christians.

THE WESLEYAN TRADITION IN THE TWENTIETH CENTURY

Teaching on Christian perfection, particularly in the Wesleyan tradition, continued in the twentieth century. Three representative figures stand out: E. Stanley Jones, Mildred Bangs Wynkoop, and Thomas C. Oden.

E. Stanley Jones (1884–1973). Eli Stanley Jones was a Methodist missionary to India. In 1938, *Time* magazine recognized him as the greatest missionary of his time. In his spiritual autobiography, *A Song of Ascents*, Jones testified to an experience of entire sanctification while a student at Asbury University in Wilmore, Kentucky.[131]

---

[128]William Durham, "The Pentecostal Testimony," June 1911, 18.

[129]Durham, "Pentecostal Testimony," 72.

[130]"The Assemblies of God, A Statement of Fundamental Truths, 1916," in *Modern Christianity*, vol. 3, *Creeds and Confessions of Faith in the Christian Tradition*, ed. Jaroslav Pelikan and Valerie Hotchkiss (New Haven, CT: Yale University Press, 2003), 428.

[131]E. Stanley Jones, *A Song of Ascents* (Nashville: Abingdon, 1968), chap. 3.

As Jones reflected on Christian perfection, he developed two clarifying ideas to the doctrine, which were essential to his understanding of "heart purity." First, he tied entire sanctification to the "conversion of the subconscious," where the drives of "sex, self, and the herd" are cleansed. They are not eliminated since they are integral to the human person. The drive for sex is no longer an end in itself, but directed to creation and creativity. The human self ceases to try to be God, but seeks God's glory in all things. The herd mentality breaks from any allegiance to larger society and is "fastened on the fruitfulness of the Kingdom of God."[132]

Second, Jones believed that Christian perfection delivered the "conscious and subconscious minds" from all sin and "evil bent." In this sense, sin is "eradicated." The driving urges of subconscious humanity remain, however, and must be "suppressed." These natural urges for Jones often become the source of temptation as they "try to climb back in the saddle and become dominant again."[133]

Jones equated Christian perfection with the experience of baptism with the Holy Spirit. In addition to the purifying work of the Spirit in the "conscious and subconscious," he connected it with the power for believers to be effective witnesses for Christ. He encouraged them to diligently hunger and thirst for this gift until the Father gives it.[134] In contrast to many of the Methodist leaders of his day, Jones expected Christian perfection to be a normative Christian experience.

Mildred Bangs Wynkoop (1905–1997). Church of the Nazarene theologian Mildred Bangs Wynkoop was the most constructive Wesleyan theologian of the twentieth century. She synthesized the theology of John Wesley, the American holiness tradition, and her work as a biblical scholar to provide other ways of understanding Christian perfection.

---

[132]E. Stanley Jones, *A Song of Ascents*, chap. 3.
[133]E. Stanley Jones, *A Song of Ascents*, chap. 3.
[134]E. Stanley Jones, *A Song of Ascents*, chap. 3.

Wynkoop was critical of the holiness movement's emphasis on two definite works of grace: justification and entire sanctification. In her view, this led Wesleyans to see them as separate, unconnected experiences and to be overconfident in their ability to solve the root problems of humanity. She also rejected what she perceived to be the Wesleyan tradition's dependence on Greek philosophy. Instead, she turned to a Hebraic, relational perspective of humanity. She saw salvation, and more particularly Christian perfection, as thoroughly moral.[135]

More specifically, Wynkoop argued that the image of God in humanity does not reside in human nature but encompasses "all that is essential to human beings dynamically involved in moral relationships."[136] Humanity was created to have loving relationships. As such, she rejected the idea that the divine image was lost in fall. People do not cease being relational because of our first parents' disobedience.[137] They continue to interact with God and each other relationally. Sin for Wynkoop is perverted love, "love locked into a false center," rather than a corruption or privation within humanity as earlier Wesleyans taught.[138] Sin is fundamentally anti-relationship. Divine grace, therefore, engages the whole person at the point of moral responsibility in relationships, seeking to have human love "locked" into Christ.

At the point of justification, Wynkoop believed God gives himself completely to the Christian. There are, therefore, no "higher or lower levels of grace."[139] Sufficient grace is given in new birth for a Christian to walk in the perfection of love. A second experience was not necessary. Most Christians, however, fail to fully appropriate what God makes available in conversion, leading to a subsequent moment in which they become "locked" into Christ.[140]

---

[135]Mildred Wynkoop, *A Theology of Love: The Dynamic of Wesleyanism* (Kansas City, MO: Beacon Hill, 1972), 47.
[136]Mildred Wynkoop, *A Theology of Love*, 146.
[137]Mildred Wynkoop, *A Theology of Love*, 146-47.
[138]Mildred Wynkoop, *A Theology of Love*, 158.
[139]Mildred Wynkoop, *A Theology of Love*, 332, 334.
[140]Mildred Wynkoop, *A Theology of Love*, 334, 347.

Christian perfection for Wynkoop refers to the moral integrity of personal love, one centered in Christ. It is single-minded devotion of the whole person to God. It is a moral union with Christ in which a believer's commitment of "the self to God" is so complete "there is no contrary purpose in the heart."[141] Perfection is "right relationship" or integrity in relationships "relative to the believer's moral capacity," which can "wax and wane" through life. This led Wynkoop to believe that the expression of Christian perfection varied from believer to believer.[142]

Thomas C. Oden (1931-2016). It is fitting to conclude our historical sketch of the doctrine of Christian perfection with United Methodist theologian Thomas C. Oden. In the third volume of his systematic theology, *Life in the Spirit*, Oden taught that Christian perfection, which he also calls "full salvation" and "perfect love," is a real possibility in the present life. He argued further that the historical doctrine of Christian perfection is "arguably closer to consensual reception than its exegetical alternatives." It is a "majority protoconsensual view awaiting fuller refinement."[143] As such, it does not exist at the peripheries of historic teaching about salvation but is central to it.

With the support of a plethora of historic theologians, doctrinal statements from different traditions in the church, and scriptural exegesis, Oden presented this perfection as a "full responsiveness" or a "maximal cooperation" with sanctifying grace. It leads to a life continually deepened and enriched by spiritual virtues, to a mortification of the sinful state, to a will surrendered totally to God, to obedience to God, and to the love of God with a blameless heart.

As such, it is a life free from habitual and willful sin. This freedom, however, is qualified by Oden. Christian perfection still experiences

---

[141]Mildred Wynkoop, *A Theology of Love*, 319.

[142]Mildred Wynkoop, *A Theology of Love*, 277.

[143]Thomas C. Oden, *Life in the Spirit*, vol. 3, *Systematic Theology* (New York: HarperCollins, 1992), 226.

the realities of human infirmities in body and mind, leading believers to fall short of absolute human perfection. It, therefore, is not sinless. Oden also taught that no state of perfection in this life frees a person from temptation and the possibility of intentional sin. Christians will only realize incorruptibility after death. In the end, Christian perfection is an expression of the maturation of "full responsiveness to "perfecting grace."[144]

CONCLUSION

As we conclude this survey of Christian perfection in church history, we arrive at the beginning of the twentieth century. The purpose of our overview has been to accentuate the breadth and depth of Protestant teaching on the subject, as well as to note Roman Catholic contributions. The doctrine, message, and experience of Christian perfection have had a vital place in the Western church.

Christian perfection did not die in the twentieth century but remains central to the theologies of Anabaptist, Pietist, Quaker, Wesleyan, Anglican, Pentecostal, and Roman Catholic traditions. It also continues to arise sporadically in Lutheran and Reformed circles, as well as in the Restorationist tradition (Churches of Christ, Independent Christian Churches, and Disciples of Christ). These expressions of Christian perfection have roots in church history.

We now turn our attention to a focused discussion of Christian perfection in the Wesleyan tradition. In the following chapters, we seek to give a more detailed account of the doctrine and experience of holiness found in churches and denominations claiming to be spiritual heirs of John and Charles Wesley.

---

[144]Thomas C. Oden, *Life in the Spirit*, 227-35.

Part Four

"MAY THE GOD OF PEACE SANCTIFY YOU ENTIRELY"

A Theology of Holiness

10

HOLINESS AND HUMAN SIN

CHRISTIAN PERFECTION has been our designated lens through which to see the doctrine of holiness in church history. It also provides a familiar framework for articulating a comprehensive Wesleyan account of holiness. In the systematic treatment that follows, we travel a path established by earlier theologians like Irenaeus, Tertullian, Thomas Aquinas, Catherine of Siena, and John Wesley. We use perfection as a way of talking about the doctrines of God, creation, fall, redemption, and consummation in the discussion of holiness.

More specifically, in this chapter we begin by describing God's immutable perfection, the glory and yet necessary incompleteness of Adamic perfection, the problem of the fall, and human sinfulness. In the next chapter, we explore the experience of Christian perfection after original sin and absolute human perfection in final consummation with God. In the third and final chapter of this section, we seek to offer a constructive Wesleyan model for the experience of Christian perfection, of personal holiness in heart and life. At the heart of Wesleyan theology is the desire for a genuine experience of the perfect love of God and neighbor. We conclude, therefore, with a description of what we call a neo-holiness "middle way" theology as a guide for the experience of holiness.

Divine Perfection in Holiness and Love

Two attributes of God's perfection are central to our biblical and historical discussion of human perfection: holiness and love. God is holy. To make this statement theologically is to recognize that God is "wholly other" than us or any part of the created order. While God fully inhabits creation, he must not be confused with it. He is independent of creation and transcends it, and he is not circumscribed by it in any way. Every part of our universe depends on God for its beginning and continued existence, but God has no need of it. To attribute holiness to God in this sense is to recognize the absolute ontological distinction between creator and creation.

God's holiness, though, also applies to his character. Holiness inheres in the divine nature. God is morally good, righteous, and just, which applies to his values, his actions, and his requirements of us. God is ethically pure, incapable of sin. He is the standard of every moral excellence. God does not will the good because it is good, nor is it good because he wills it; God's will is the expression of his holiness. Positively, God strengthens and empowers the good, while negatively, he opposes and judges all unrighteousness and evil.

Humanity is called to be holy as God is holy, not ontologically but ethically. Whatever else it means for humanity to bear the image of God, holiness is at its core. Our lives must align with God's character and will. Without actual holiness, we cannot experience that ultimate perfection with God, which is the essence of heaven.

While divine holiness can be distinguished from God's love, it cannot be separated. God is also love. Biblically and theologically, love comprises two inseparable parts: the desire for union or fellowship with another and the decisions or actions to bring it about. Love is demonstrated supremely in the triune life of God between Father, Son, and Holy Spirit. To say that "God is love" recognizes

God as a divine community of persons who give themselves in self-giving union to each other. To say God loves the world is to recognize his desire for fellowship with us and the alignment of his will with it.[1]

We can see holiness more clearly now. When Wesleyan theology speaks of God's absolute moral purity, it expresses what love demands for true union in relationship. Holiness is what makes life-giving fellowship with the other possible. Humanity has been created to love God, love one another, and love the created order. Holiness is what enables the full expression of love for which we have been created. It makes possible true human flourishing and creation's perfection.

These two attributes of divine perfection are foundational to a Wesleyan theology of human perfection. To begin to understand God's call for us to be holy and its challenges in human life, we must examine two closely related areas in Christian teaching: anthropology (the doctrine of humanity) and hamartiology (the doctrine of sin). The first sets the context of Christian perfection by exploring humanity's creation, purpose, and fall, while the second gives an account of humanity's most pressing obstacle to the life of perfection for which we are made.

ANTHROPOLOGY: HUMANITY'S ORIGINAL PERFECTION AND FALL

Blaise Pascal argues that Christian anthropology must address humanity's grandeur and misery.[2] The Scriptures make clear the greatness: humanity is created to be like God (Gen 1:26-27). The psalmist teaches that God has "crowned" us with "glory and honor" and placed all creation under our stewardship (Ps 8:5-6). Jesus affirms that as human beings we are "gods, sons of the Most High"

---

[1]See Thomas C. Oden, *The Living God*, vol. 1, *Systematic Theology* (Peabody, MA: Prince, 2001), 118-23.
[2]Blaise Pascal, *Pensées*, trans. W. F. Trotter (New York: E. P. Dutton, 1958), 14-52.

(Jn 10:35). Peter declares that we are "partakers of the divine nature" through Christ (2 Pet 1:4). Humanity, as such, is made to participate in God's glory by being like God. This is the perfection for which we have been created.

At the same time, the Old and New Testaments paint a picture of our wretchedness. The apostle Paul in Romans 3:23 declares that "all have sinned and fallen short of the glory of God." Many Protestant theologians, unfortunately, have interpreted "the glory of God" here to mean a moral standard that Jews and Gentiles have failed to maintain. More likely, however, Paul has in mind Psalm 8, which references humanity's creation in Genesis. God created humanity to be like God and have "glory and honor." God's intentions, nevertheless, were tragically discarded through human sin. Humanity's first parents rebelled against God, and since then sin has defined human existence. Humans have not realized the glory God intended for them. We fail to be like God, with devastating consequences.

Adamic perfection/original perfection: Humanity created in the image of God. The Old Testament begins with a striking testimony to humanity's grandeur and original perfection. Genesis describes humanity as the climax of creation. Human beings are the last act of God before rest on the seventh day. Humanity is formed from the "dust of the ground" and given the "breath of life," becoming a "living soul" (Gen 2:7). As embodied souls, humans are also made in the "image and likeness of God." This sets us apart as unique in the world, and we command a dignity and glory unlike any other creature. God places his stamp of approval "very good" on our nature as embodied souls and our place in the world as his image-bearers (Gen 1:27).

Historic Christian views of the imago Dei. As human beings we are embodied creatures, but we are more than our bodies. What does it mean, however, to be created in the "image and likeness" of God? How are we to understand humanity's original perfection? Historically, the *imago Dei* has been interpreted in three different ways. The first and oldest theory teaches that the divine image encompasses our rational and creative abilities as well as our moral and affective capacities. As human beings, we have the power to understand the world around us, make sound judgments about it, and act accordingly. Like God, who is defined by holiness and love, we are made to reflect God's absolute moral purity by walking in righteousness and reflecting divine love in perfectly ordered affections directed to the love of God, neighbor, and the world around us. As created in the garden, the divine image in Adam and Eve enabled them to act with sound perception and reason, infused by holy love. Here the *imago Dei* exists as rational, spiritual, and moral capacities in the individual.[3]

A second view, in contrast, proposes that the image of God is found principally in our social relationships, not in our individual moral and rational nature. As Christians, we do not believe God is a solitary person but a communion of infinite love between persons: Father, Son, and Holy Spirit. From this perspective, the divine image is not found in the human self, but in human relationships of self-giving love, mirroring what is expressed between Father, Son, and Holy Spirit. Humanity is a communal being, not a private self. So, when God creates humanity in his image, he creates them "male and female" in a network of relationships. Adam and Eve, together in their relationship with God and each other, mirror the social communion who is God.[4] Their perfection is found in the beauty of these relationships.

The final perspective takes note of how Genesis connects humanity's creation as the *imago Dei* to the exercise of "dominion" in the world. Immediately after "male and female" are created in the divine "image and likeness," God gives them charge of the garden. They are

---

[3]Charles Hodge, *Systematic Theology*, 3 vols. (Grand Rapids, MI: Eerdmans, 1952), 2:96-97; H. Orton Wiley, *Christian Theology*, 3 vols. (Kansas City, MO: Beacon Hill, 1943), 2:31-32.

[4]Emil Brunner, *The Christian Doctrine of Creation and Redemption* (London: Lutterworth, 1952), 55-60, 105-6; Karl Barth, *Church Dogmatics* (Edinburgh: T&T Clark, 1958), III/1, 184, 197-98; Stanley Grenz, *Theology for the Community of God* (Nashville: Broadman & Holman, 1994), 225-33.

stewards of creation. The divine image here is not so much specific capacities in the individual or found in human social relationships; rather, it exists in what humanity does in the world. As we exercise responsible care for the world, we reflect God's stewardship of the entire created order. In wisely cultivating, nourishing, and developing creation, Adam and Eve perfectly embody the divine image. They are "little gods" in relationship to the world.[5]

John Wesley's teaching on the imago Dei. These three theological understandings of the *imago Dei*, while different, are not incompatible. John Wesley brings aspects of these three views together in his teaching on Adam and Eve. As intended by God in the garden, John Wesley understands the divine image in humanity to comprise three parts: (1) the moral, (2) the natural, and (3) the political. The moral image enables humanity to enjoy the presence of God, holiness, and righteousness.[6] The natural image renders rationality, understanding, free will, and perfectly ordered emotions or affections. Humanity can see the world clearly and understand intuitively how best to respond to it.[7] The political image furnishes humanity with the power of leadership and management, whereby humanity exercises dominion over the created order and walks perfectly in relationship with the world.[8]

As created in the garden before the fall, human beings desire, know, will, and perfectly perform God's intentions for humanity. Holiness, righteousness, and love inform humanity's reasoning, understanding, will, and emotions, all of which result in the wise exercise of stewardship in the created order, rightly ordered relationships with fellow humanity, and perfect love and obedience to God. Wesley, in his sermon "The End of Christ's Coming," summarizes Adamic perfection accordingly:

---

[5]Norman Snaith, "The Image of God," *Expository Times* 86, no. 1 (1974): 24; Leonard Verduin, *Somewhat Less Than God: The Biblical View of Man* (Grand Rapids, MI: Eerdmans, 1970), 27.
[6]Wesley, "The New Birth," *WJW* 6:66.
[7]Wesley, "The End of Christ's Coming," *WJW* 6:269-71.
[8]Wesley, "The General Deliverance," *WJW* 6:242-45.

God created man . . . "in knowledge," but also in righteousness and true holiness. As his understanding was without blemish, perfect in its kind; so were all his affections. They were all set right, and duly exercised on their proper objects. And as a free agent, he steadily chose whatever was good, according to the direction of his understanding. In so doing, he was unspeakably happy; dwelling in God, and God in him; having an uninterrupted fellowship with the Father and the Son, through the eternal Spirit; and the continual testimony of his conscience, that all his ways were good and acceptable to God.[9]

Human persons as the imago Dei. The three historic theories of the *imago Dei* and John Wesley's trifold understanding of the image make one thing clear: the first humans were created by God as *persons*. To be the image of God is to be a person whose identity is formed in relationships. God is a divine community where each person is constituted by a distinctive relationship with the other persons.

God is Father, Son, and Holy Spirit. This is the very identity of God. The Father is the person of the Father because he has eternally begotten a Son. The Son is the person of the Son because he has a Father from eternity. The Holy Spirit is the person of the Holy Spirit because he is eternally "breathed" (*spirated*) by the Father and the Son. The Father is not the Son, and the Son is not the Holy Spirit. Each of the divine persons is "who" that person is because of the distinctive relationships with the others.[10] While the divine persons share the same attributes of nature, they each have distinctive personal attributes not shared by the others: the Father alone is eternally "unbegotten," the Son alone is eternally "begotten," and the Spirit alone is eternally "spirated."

As created in the image of God, Adam and Eve are constituted as persons. Through their creation as persons with rational, creative,

---

[9]Wesley, "The End of Christ's Coming," *WJW* 6:270-71.
[10]See Thomas Aquinas, *Summa Theologica*, 5 vols., trans. Fathers of the English Dominican Province (Notre Dame, IN: Christian Classics, 1981), 1a, Qs. 29, 32-43.

and moral capacities forged in the crucible of relationships with God, with each other, and in the exercise of stewardship in creation, they image God, who is a comm-*union* or comm-*unity* of persons.[11] They are formed as distinctive persons through their social relationships and decisions made within them. Each aspect of Wesley's trifold image enables them to mirror what takes place in the divine life.[12] Through the moral, natural, and political image, they can walk as persons in a communion of holy love with God, with humanity, and with the created order. It is these relationships and the decisions made within them that form our first parents as distinct but not independent people. This is humanity's original perfection.

Issues in Adamic perfection: Potentiality and corruptibility of humanity in the garden. While made in the image of God in the garden, Adam and Eve are not ultimately where God wants humanity to be. While created perfect, they are not ultimately perfect. God's goal for us has never been Genesis 1–2, but Revelation 21–22. God's plan "before the foundation of the world" is to bring all of creation in union with himself. This union is described beautifully in the language of marriage and consummation in the New Testament's final chapters. Christ's saving work, as such, is not about returning us to life in the garden before the fall but about taking us far beyond it.

From potentiality to actuality. Even before sin enters humanity's story, God must address two issues in Adam and Eve if humans are to experience absolute human perfection in glory with God: potentiality and corruptibility. Both arise from the mutability of created nature. The first is potentiality. While made in the image of God, we are not fully formed as persons at creation. Our personhood can only be forged through the relationships and experiences we have in life, as well as the decisions and choices we make in response to

---

[11]Michael Horton, *The Christian Faith: A Systematic Theology for Pilgrims on the Way* (Grand Rapids, MI: Zondervan, 2011), 387-96.

[12]Wesley, "The End of Christ's Coming," *WJW* 6:269-71.

them. Adam and Eve are "blank slates" in the garden and can only develop as persons through their interactive relationships with God, each other, and the world around them. They must grow and mature as people through the exercise of free will and habituating their holy affections through practice.[13] Only then, as mature persons, can they receive all God has for them in final union in heaven.

Therefore, while Adam and Eve bear God's image in the garden, they are not yet fully like God. Theologically, we acknowledge that God is "pure act."[14] This means God is fully actualized as persons in Father, Son, and Holy Spirit. There is no unrealized potential in God. The divine persons do not grow or develop in any way: mentally, emotionally, intellectually, or personally. In contrast, we continue to grow and develop as persons. Because we will be more actualized as persons in heaven, we will be more like God than Adam and Eve before the fall. The created order functions as the means by which we are actualized as persons.

From corruptibility to incorruptibility. The second issue God must address is corruptibility. While made in the divine image, we are unlike God in that we are capable of sin. While God is incorruptibly good, God created Adam and Eve with every benefit or advantage to realize his will for them. Through the *imago Dei* the love of God and neighbor came naturally to them, and they were able to relate to the world wisely. Their heart, mind, and will were properly ordered. Because they were creatures, however, and not the incorruptible creator, they were subject to change, both positive (in the form of personal growth) and negative (in the experience of corruption and sin). God must deal with the latter. God must bring humanity to a place where they are made incorruptibly holy, no longer subject to sin, evil, and death. God does this in the end by bringing humanity into full union with himself in heaven, the new creation. Because humanity is always

---

[13]Kenneth J. Collins, "John Wesley's Topography of the Heart: Dispositions, Tempers, and Affections," *Methodist History* 36, no. 3 (1998): 162-75.

[14]Aquinas, *Summa Theologica*, 1a, Q. 9.

a creature and never God, incorruptibility is only possible through the grace of full participation in the divine nature.

Adam and Eve are not yet fully like God in the garden. God is incorruptibly holy. He never does what is contrary to his character. God's freedom is not what we associate normally with free will. Our natural tendency is to see Adam and Eve's will in the garden as true free will: to have good and evil as real options before us. Our first parents, however, only had partial freedom. True freedom is to do only what is in accordance with holy love as God does. No human being in this life, save one, is fully like God. We will only reflect God's freedom fully in the kingdom to come. Therefore, Christian theology affirms free will in heaven, while denying the possibility of sin. Our freedom will fully be like God's, defined by holiness.

The purpose of humanity. One of the most famous questions in Protestant theology comes from the Westminster Shorter Catechism: "What is the chief end of humanity?" The answer: "To glorify God and enjoy Him forever." Our discussion has already established a foundation on which to provide an answer that leads to God's glory and enables humanity to share in the joy of that glory.

We are created for relationships—we are persons of love. As human persons, reflecting the *imago Dei*, Adam and Eve are created for relationships. They are formed by God to give and receive love. Jesus helps us to see our purpose when he summarizes "all the law and prophets" with these two commands: "Love the Lord your God with all your heart and with all your soul and with all your mind" and "Love your neighbor as yourself" (Lk 22:37-38). Genesis narrates a description of our first parents' intimate friendship with God and each other. As human persons created in God's image, we see that Adam and Eve do not have their completion in their solitary selves, but first in God and then each other. They are whole only as they are bound in these fellowships of self-giving love.

They also are created to love the created order. In contrast to the ancient religious texts on how the world came into being, Genesis teaches that God directly created the physical universe with purpose and declared it "very good" (Gen 1:31). Creation is an expression of divine love. There is nothing inherently evil or sinful about the physical world. As a part of the created order, God made humanity as embodied souls in the divine image (Gen 2:7) with the expressed purpose of exercising stewardship over it (Gen 1:27). Humanity is made for union with the world.

Humans, therefore, are creatures of love. As people, we are defined by what and who we love. As we have seen, everything God has created is good, and God has formed us to be social beings in a web of relationships. Through these relationships personhood is forged. Only when we love God supremely can all other loves or relationships be "rightly ordered." Our love for God properly directs all other "loves" in creation so that we appropriately desire relationships with God, other people, and creation, and then act to make it so. The divine image in humanity makes it possible for us to have "rightly ordered" love, which leads not only to humanity's happiness but also to the flourishing of creation.

We are created to become fully like God. Adam and Eve are created as "embodied souls." This is what we are as human beings. Our fundamental distinction as humans comes not from "what" we are but in "who" we are. We are different persons. There is a different subject expressed in each human nature. A person is the "I" or subject of each "embodied soul." While a distinction between human nature and person can be made, they are inseparably one and influence one another. Hence, bodily resurrection is central to our personal redemption and eternal life.

Our formation as persons is mediated through our human nature as "embodied souls" on two levels. First, who we are as persons is formed through every relationship and experience. When we are asked to describe "who" we are, we share the story of our lives including when and where we were born, family relationships and friendships, education and work experiences, and what we enjoy doing for leisure. We recognize how collectively these aspects of our lives shape the person we are.

On this level we are more passive in personal formation; our relationships and experiences come to us and shape who we are. On the next level, however, we play an active part in our own development through our responses to relationships and experiences. Part of who we are is a result of both deliberate and unconscious decisions made in life including our interaction with parents, friends, teachers, mentors, spouses, and children and the choices we make. Because we are rational beings who exercise our will, we have a say in who we are and who we become.

How human beings come to be persons is a dynamic process, both passive and active, mediated through our nature as "embodied souls." Human nature is the medium through which we receive in life and through which we direct our lives. Who we are as persons is forged in the crucible of life, and our "embodied soul" is the medium.

Adam and Eve are placed in the Garden of Eden where they can develop as persons. The garden is about formation. Humanity has the opportunity to embrace the foundation of perfection given in creation and move to absolute human perfection. God desired our first parents to become fully like him, to be holy as he is holy. While humans are created in the divine image, the garden provides the means through which they have a say in their formation. They can embrace the holiness of heart and life given to them by God in their creation and mature to become fully like God, or they can rebel against this call. They can be defined by their love of God or by another love. They can share in the blessedness of God's glory or the misery of their self-glory. Regardless, they must make choices that will define who they are.

The fall of humanity: The origin and condition of sin. Now we are at a better place to address the origin and condition of sin. Adam and Eve were created in glory, with the opportunity for the *imago Dei* to be developed more fully in their formation as persons. Their sin led to death and devastation for all humanity. They were created perfect and were intended for an even greater perfection, but sin threatened to disrupt God's work.

How sin is possible. How does sin in all forms come about in a world created by God as good and holy? Christian theology has offered a threefold response. First, while every part of creation is good, it is mutable. The very fact the universe came into being out of nothing (*creatio ex nihilo*) means it is mutable. It is marked by change. At one time it did not exist, and now it does. It has moved from nothing to something. It has "change" written all over it. To be created is to be mutable. Any created substance, therefore, is intrinsically mutable because it has already experienced change and continues to alter through time. If the created order is mutable by nature, it can change either for better or worse. Sin and all forms of corruption are an inevitable possibility (but not necessity) of creation.

Second, God made human beings as rational and loving creatures. Like the rest of creation, they are good and holy, but mutable in their *desires* and *wills*. Because their desire and free will are created, they are subject to change for better or worse as well. Humanity never ceases being creatures of love and defined by that love, but what they love can alter. They can habituate their holiest desires and align their will with God or depart from the love for which they are created. Sin enters the world when mutable desires and wills deviate from the love of God, when love is no longer ordered rightly in them.

Finally, we recognize that evil is a broken or corrupted good. It is the privation of the good. All God has created is good, a declaration made repeatedly by God. As such, evil has no independent existence; it does not exist apart from an intrinsic good. Evil is the expression of creation's corruption. Evil occurs when the good of creation is changed for the worse. Behind all evil, therefore, is something good. More specifically, sin is the corrupted expression of human desire and will. As creatures of love, we were created to desire and will union with God, each other, and creation. All sin is a corrupted expression of rightly ordered love.[15]

Concrete examples of sin as a corrupted good. This is clearer when we look at three concrete examples. First, God has created us with the need to eat food to fuel our bodies. He has made us to enjoy food as well. When the desire for food becomes corrupted in us, however, it leads to gluttony and all types of eating disorders. Next, God has created sex as a means of procreation and as a pleasurable expression of the most intimate love between husband and wife. When our desire for sex, however, becomes broken in us, it causes all kinds of sexual immorality. Finally, God has made us to love ourselves. We are commanded to "love our neighbor as we love ourselves." But when self-love becomes disordered in us, all forms of pride and selfishness arise.

In each of these instances, we see sin as a corrupt expression of good desires and exercise of will. The love of food, sex, and self is good, but when corrupted in us, our love of them becomes disordered. We do not rightly love the good of creation.

Consequences of the fall. While Adam and Eve were created in the image of God, they were corruptible. Through their disobedience in the garden, the image of God in humanity was marred. Their original perfection lay in ruins. Genesis paints a devastating picture of its impact. It reverses the original conditions of human life. Morally, humanity was left completely dead to God, self-focused and helpless to change. Naturally human reason, understanding, and free will were marred, and human affections became inordinate and undisciplined. Politically, humanity's relationship to the created order and

---

[15]For a more developed treatment of these points, see Augustine, *Enchiridion* (*NPNF*[1] 3:237–76); Thomas Aquinas, *Disputed Questions on Evil*, trans. John A. Oesterle and Jean T. Oesterle (Notre Dame, IN: University of Notre Dame Press, 1995) question 1, articles 1-3; Boethius, *Consolation of Philosophy*, trans. Victor Watts (London: Penguin, 1999), book 4; Dionysius the Areopagite, *The Divine Names and the Mystical Theology*, trans. C. E. Rolt (London: Macmillan, 1920), 4.

ability to organize socially were seriously damaged. Only vestiges of the divine image remained, replaced by "the image of the Devil."[16] Humanity became defined by pride and self-will. Because of humanity's unique relationship within the created order as "little gods," creation descended into chaos, mirroring its stewards.

To be fully human is to be holy; to be human is to be like God. All sin is a corruption of human nature and the *imago Dei*. It is the marring of human personhood. The idea "to sin is human" does not understand what true humanity is. We sin not because we are human, but because we are less than human. Sin is the expression of our diminished humanity.

HAMARTIOLOGY: THE PROBLEM OF SIN

Sin is the great enemy of humanity. God's love for us compels him to save us. When the angel Gabriel appeared to Joseph to explain Mary's miraculous pregnancy, he instructed Joseph to name the baby "Jesus" because he would "save his people from their sins" (Mt 1:21). The apostle John reiterates Gabriel's declaration: Jesus came to "destroy the devil's work" (1 Jn 3:8), "sin and all its fruits."[17] This is the purpose of the Son of God's incarnation.

In the previous section, we defined sin as a corrupted good. At this point, we want to ask more specifically, What is sin? In answering the question, we want to look at sin holistically. To begin, we will look at sin through its major biblical descriptions and follow with an extended discussion of its theological categories.

The biblical language of sin. The Scriptures use a wide array of terms, images, and metaphors for sin. Much of this language can be divided into three distinct groups: (1) legal, (2) relational, and (3) cultic. These together provide a fuller picture of sin's problem.[18]

---

[16]Wesley, "The End of Christ's Coming," *WJW* 6:272.
[17]Wesley, "The End of Christ's Coming," *WJW* 5:268.
[18]William B. Pope, *Compendium of Christian Theology*, 3 vols. (New York: Phillips and Hunt, 1887), 1:352. Pope refers to these as the court, family, and temple metaphors.

Legal language. Perhaps the most well-known biblical portrait of sin is legal. Sin is the violation of God's law. God makes clear what he expects from us. He draws a clear line in the sand and warns us of the penalty if we cross it. God told Adam and Eve they could eat from any tree in the Garden of Eden, but they must refrain from eating fruit from the tree of knowledge of good and evil, or death would be the consequence (Gen 2:16-17). The apostle Paul teaches that God gave the Gentiles a clear internal code of conscience and the Jews a written law to follow; both are guilty of deliberate disobedience and stand under divine condemnation as a result (Rom 1:18–3:20).[19]

God gives each of us some measure of light regarding what he requires of us, yet we do not walk accordingly. Our disobedience leaves us under God's condemnation. We stand guilty in God's court of law under the threat of eternal death as judgment.

Relational or familial language. A second way the Bible describes sin is in social terms. Sin is what harms relationships. Genesis reveals that humans are communal beings. Adam and Eve walk in intimacy with God, love one another, and exercise wise stewardship of creation. Jesus summarizes the Old Testament's teaching on humanity's chief end as a call to love God with all heart, soul, mind, and strength, and to love one's neighbor as oneself. Relationships define human existence. Sin, therefore, is described as injury to the social bonds of humanity. Sin is more than broken law; it undermines relationships, which, if left unchecked, irreparably severs them. Sin's consequences, therefore, are described not only in terms of guilt, but of alienation, separation, hostility, unfaithfulness, and idolatry.[20]

Through our sinful thoughts, words, and deeds, we undermine the very relationships through which we gain ultimate meaning. We

---

[19]See Wiley's discussion of the New Testament language of *hamartia* and *parabasis* in *Christian Theology*, 2:82-83.

[20]See Wiley's discussion of the New Testament language of *parapiptein* and *adikia* in *Christian Theology*, 2:83-84.

experience estrangement from God, each other, and the created order. Sin is what destroys the bonds of love for which we are created.

Cultic or worship language. A final set of language about sin is taken from the Jewish temple and ceremonial law. Sin is defilement or uncleanness. Instruments used in worship are required to be "clean," set apart wholly for the purposes of God. They must not be desecrated intentionally or unintentionally. Any type of contamination renders them unfit for use before a holy God. The children of Israel are called in the Old Testament to be a "holy nation," set apart from the sinfulness of the world for God's holy purposes. This call extends to the church in the New Testament. The problem of sin, therefore, goes beyond the issues of guilt and alienation and strikes at the very essence of humanity.

Sin is a defilement that pollutes us and makes us unholy. We are created in the image of God to be holy as God is holy. Sin is a soiling of the divine image in us, making us unsuitable for God. Our desires are corrupted by it, and our will is left impotent to align with God's. We are slaves to our defilement.[21] While legal and relational understandings of sin are primarily external to us, cultic language points to its internal damage.

Theological categories of sin. To begin to understand salvation from sin—which is at the heart of Jesus Christ's life, death, resurrection, and exaltation—we must see it fully. One way to do so is to look at it biblically as we have done. Legally, our sins must be forgiven, and our guilt absolved. Christ addresses God's judgment of sin through justification. Relationally, our union with God, with each other, and with creation must be restored. Christ works to overcome estrangement and alienation in our relationships through reconciliation. Finally, we must be cleansed of sin's defilement, the corruption of the *imago Dei* that forms us as persons. Christ brings this to our lives through sanctification.

---

[21]See Wiley's discussion of the New Testament language of *anomia* and *asebeia* in *Christian Theology*, 2:85-86.

Another way to think holistically about the problem of sin is to think about it in theological categories. Sin, as such, can be described or understood as a state, as an act, and as an infirmity.

Sin as a state—original sin. The term *original sin* has a twofold meaning. It can refer to Adam and Eve's transgression in the garden (i.e., humanity's first sin), or it can describe the concrete consequences of their sin for us—slavery to sin. For our discussion, *original sin* refers to the latter, the state of sin in which all humans come into existence since the fall. It is the source of our sinfulness. We sin because we are sinners. Theologians also call it inherited depravity, the condition of sin, or the state of sin in humanity.[22] It is defined in at least these three phenomenological and ontological ways.

1. A phenomenological definition of original sin. The most common way to talk about original sin is through its manifestation in human life. We experience a "bent" or "propensity" toward rebellion, disobedience, selfishness, and sin in life.[23] We balk at the love of God and neighbor. Instead of being good stewards of the created order, we "naturally" exploit it for selfish gain. Living a virtuous life, doing what we know to be right, comes with great struggle. When push comes to shove, when our best intentions meet the realities of life, our sinful tendencies rise to the surface no matter how hard we try to suppress them.

One way to glimpse the sinful orientation of our hearts is to observe what we think, say, or do when we believe no one is watching. We see it in the thoughts we never share with others; the offensive words we speak "off record" because we want to keep them from the public. We strive to suppress our corrupted impulses when we are "in the light," but when the cover of "darkness" comes, the propensity of our heart is revealed.

We see the power sin exerts in human life. While it might first appear that we have some control over sin in life, upon closer

---

[22]J. Kenneth Grider, *A Wesleyan-Holiness Theology* (Kansas City, MO: Beacon Hill, 1994), 277-78.
[23]See Millard J. Erickson, *Christian Theology* (Grand Rapids, MI: Baker Academic, 2013), 528; Article 7 of the United Methodist Church's "Articles of Religion."

inspection we see we are enslaved to it. The apostle Paul teaches that even when we know the good to be done, and when we want to walk in obedience to God, too often we do not have the power to follow through with our good intentions (Rom 7:7-25). If we search our hearts, we find sin as the default position in our desires and will. A godly life of virtue, the love of God and the love of neighbor, does not come easily to us. Something inside us resists what God requires of us. Knowledge of God's law is met with great internal rebellion; our heart rises and declares "I won't," or if we have some desire to obey, the will cries out "I can't."

2. An ontological definition of original sin. The phenomenological definition of original sin describes well how the condition of sin manifests itself in human life, but it does not identify what causes our sinful propensity. It does not tell us exactly what original sin is.

Theologians throughout church history have offered several proposals. Some argue that it is an actual nature that attaches to our embodied souls, either a physical substance in our bodies, like a "sin" gene, or a spiritual nature that inheres in our souls, like the presence of demons.[24] Others teach it as the absence or deprivation of the Holy Spirit's reign in human life. Only the Spirit ruling in human life can rightly direct human desires and will. Without the Spirit's fullness, our love becomes disordered.[25] Some propose that it is habituated attitudes and behavior communicated to a person from early age through larger society. Still others believe it is corruption or privation of the *imago Dei* in us, more specifically the moral image.[26]

While these theories are not mutually exclusive and are often combined in multiple ways, two are central: (1) privation of the moral image of God and (2) absence of the Spirit's reign. In contrast to Gnosticism, which separates the body and soul, treating the soul

---

[24]Michael J. Boivin, "Finding God in Prozac or Finding Prozac in God," *Christian Scholar's Review* 32, no. 2 (2003): 169-75.

[25]Augustine, *Concerning Man's Perfection in Righteousness*, 11.28.

[26]Wesley, "The End of Christ's Coming," *WJW* 6:271-72; "On Original Sin," *WJW* 6:60; "On the Fall of Man, *WJW* 6:223-24.

as good and the body as evil, historic Christianity portrays human nature and human personhood as a unified whole that is created in the moral, natural, and political image of God. Through the disobedience of our first parents, however, the divine image in humanity is corrupted; our nature and personhood are injured.

This harm is described by Christian theology in ways including corruption, brokenness, diminishment, or privation. Corruption, to be clear, is not a "thing" added to us, like a contagion, infection, or substance; it is loss of full expression of the *imago Dei* in our nature and personhood. Brokenness conveys the damage sustained to the divine image. Diminishment communicates its deterioration. Privation speaks of its loss.[27]

A winter coat is a helpful illustration. To say the coat is corrupted, as we use it in theology, does not mean it has gotten dirty from playing outside. Dry mud does not keep it from being a coat or interfere with its intended purpose, which is to keep warm and protect from the weather. If the coat, however, is broken in two, torn in half, its purpose is threatened unless repaired. If the coat wears away gradually through use, its material becomes thin, eventually becoming too diminished to protect against the elements. The same is true if the coat develops holes through rough play and becomes increasingly a privation of the cloth that makes it a coat. In each instance, nothing is added detrimentally to the coat; it only experiences different forms of deterioration.

The human problem is corruption, brokenness, diminishment, or privation of our nature and personhood.[28] This particularly applies to the moral image of God in us that is lost through the absence of the rule of the Holy Spirit in human life. The New Testament calls the corrupted divine image in us "the flesh," and it expresses human nature and personhood under the reign of sin (Rom 8:4-9; Gal 5:17).

---

[27]See Thomas H. McCall, *Against God and Nature: The Doctrine of Sin*, Foundations of Evangelical Theology (Wheaton, IL: Crossway, 2019), 218-33.

[28]McCall, *Against God and Nature*, 218-33.

In other passages, Paul refers to it as "the old self" (Rom 6:6; Eph 4:22; Col 3:9) and our "worldly" condition (1 Cor 3:1). Our human bodies, souls, minds, and wills are corrupted. The Holy Spirit of God no longer directs our desires and will. Our love is disordered. This is our condition as a result of the fall.

3. The ontology and phenomena of original sin. Because of the utter devastation of the moral image of God in us through the fall, humanity is left spiritually bankrupt, self-focused, and helpless to change.[29] The desire for divine union and holiness required for it have shifted. As human beings we have not quit longing for union, but the object of our union has shifted. We have exchanged the supreme love of God and the love of neighbor for the love of ourselves and creation. We love creation more than the creator (Rom 1:22).

The corruption of the moral image has been described by many Christian theologians as disordered love.[30] As we have seen, everything God has created is good, and God has formed us to be social beings in a web of personhood is forged through these relationships. Only when we love God supremely can all other loves or relationships be "rightly ordered." Our love for God properly directs all other "loves" in creation, so that we appropriately desire relationships with people and creation. With the moral image corrupted in us, however, our loves become disordered and inordinate. Without the supreme love of God directing our lives, chaos reigns in our relationships.[31]

Early church father John Chrysostom describes our problem well in his teaching on humanity's first parents. After Eve was formed and brought to Adam, the Scriptures state they were "naked, and they felt no shame" (Gen 2:25). After they ate the forbidden fruit,

---

[29]John Calvin, *Institutes of the Christian Religion* 2.1.4-5, 8-9; Wesley, "Original Sin," *WJW* 6:54-65; "The End of Christ's Coming," *WJW* 6:267-77; "The Spirit of Bondage and Adoption," *WJW* 5:98-111.

[30]Augustine articulated the direction of this theological understanding in *City of God* 15.22-23 and *On Christian Doctrine*, 1.27-28.

[31]Wesley, "On the Deceitfulness of the Human Heart," *WJW* 7:335-36.

however, they became ashamed. Chrysostom asks, "What caused their change in attitude toward nakedness?" Before their disobedience, he answers, Adam and Eve were so focused on the "other," they did not take notice of themselves.[32] With the moral image of God in them, they loved God supremely and gave themselves in full love to their spouse and to creation. Even their self-love was formed by the love they received from God and their spouse. After the moral image was corrupted by the fall, their attention turned inward. They became self-focused and realized their nakedness for the first time. Without the supreme love of God properly directing all other loves, Adam and Eve's love became disordered, focused in unhealthy ways on themselves and other parts of creation.

Sin as an act—intentional, habitual, and surprise. At what point did temptation transition into sin? When did our first parents' transgression take place? Our natural response is to believe when they ate the forbidden fruit. This outward act of disobedience, however, arose from an internal fall already conceived in their hearts.[33] The holy, God-given desires in them became corrupted and led to the outward act of sin.

As their heirs, we are brought into existence in a state of sin, with the image of God broken in us. The sinful condition in us, original sin, leads to all manner of sinful acts. What are acts of sin? Like our first parents' sin, they are transgressions of a known law of God. Adam and Eve knew they were disobeying God. Unlike sins of infirmity (to be discussed later) where ignorance is the driving cause, we know these to be wrong.

Knowledge of God's law comes to us from several sources: the clear teaching of Scripture; the light of conscience through general revelation; personal conviction given to a Christian by the Holy Spirit; or a church's corporate conviction. We commit acts of sin

---

[32]John Chrysostom, *Homilies on Genesis 1–17*, trans. Robert C. Hill, Fathers of the Church 74 (Washington, DC: Catholic University of America Press, 1986), 207-22.

[33]Wesley, "The End of Christ's Coming," *WJW* 6:271-72.

when we knowingly violate God's will. These sins can be intentional, habitual, or surprises in our lives.

1. Intentional sins. Intentional sins are deliberate and willful transgressions of the known will and law of God. We choose not to walk in obedience to the light God has given us. We want our will over God's. The power to obey God is in us; we simply choose otherwise.[34]

This is the clear operating definition of sin that Paul uses in Romans. The apostle begins the book by addressing the Gentiles. He says they have been given a law to follow: the law of conscience. They have chosen, however, not to follow this internal law and God has handed them over to judgment as a result (Rom 1:18-32). Paul then turns to the Jews (Rom 2:17-3:23). They have been given a written law. Still, they have intentionally broken the written law. His teaching culminates with Romans 3:23, "For all have sinned . . ." Both Gentile and Jew have been given a law and they have deliberately disobeyed it. When Paul states, "For the wages of sin is death" (Rom 6:23), his point is to warn Christians of the dangers of willful transgression of the known law of God, not sins committed unintentionally or in ignorance. James echoes Paul when he states, "If anyone, then, knows the good they ought to do and does not do it, it is sin for them" (Jas 4:17).

2. Habitual sins. Habitual sin or strongholds of sin are compulsive behaviors over which we have little or no control in life and regularly commit. We know they are wrong, but when we sense their seductive pull and feel their power grow in us, we fall helplessly into their clutches. Even if we recognize their destructive consequences and even come to a place where we want freedom from them, we have little strength to resist. They control our lives.[35]

---

[34]Diane Leclerc, *Discovering Christian Holiness: The Heart of Wesleyan-Holiness Theology* (Kansas City, MO: Beacon Hill, 2010), 160-62.

[35]Thomas McCall, *Against God and Nature*, 300-301.

Habitual sin arises in our lives from two sources: inherited and acquired depravity. Inherited depravity or the state of sin in which we are born often manifests itself concretely in different ways. While we share the same propensity to sin, the way it is expressed in our desires will differ from person to person. Some people are drawn to particular sins more than others. Original sin manifests itself uniquely in people's lives so that some are prone to certain strongholds of sin from birth, while others are not.

Acquired depravity, in contrast, arises from intentional choices we make in life or ones that are inflicted on us that habituate certain sinful attitudes and behaviors. Augustine defines a habit as "that thing which is added to someone in such a way that he could just as well not have it." Often, it begins with an intentional sin, over which we have some control, but as we indulge in it more, it fortifies our desire and codifies our will, so that the sin gains ultimate control and defines our lives. A pattern of sinful attitudes and behavior becomes ingrained in us.[36]

Most often, strongholds of sin reflect a combination of inherited and acquired depravity. For example, human sexuality and sexual orientation are not spared from the corrosive influence of sin. Human sexual predisposition and drive for the opposite sex, originally created good and holy by God, have been corrupted by original sin. This corruption is manifested in different ways, including homosexual inclinations, which, when combined with life in a fallen order and the consequences of habituated decisions, lead to different types of sexual strongholds.

3. *Sins of surprise.* Finally, there are "sins of surprise." They are not willful like intentional sin; they are not habitual behaviors and often give no obvious clues or trigger warnings of their approach in life. Rather, they "seize" us in the moment before we have a chance to think about them. They are not planned and are not really chosen.

---

[36]Grider, *A Wesleyan-Holiness Theology*, 411-16.

We commit them without thinking. As with any act of sin, we know it to be sin.[37]

For example, in the heat of the moment we may utter a curse word under our breath without thinking. We rarely if ever curse. We did not plan or want to say it, but we spoke the words before we even realized it. Also, we may go through a period in life with great anxiety, caused by too many commitments and responsibilities, coupled with problems in our most important relationships. When a coworker then speaks a word of criticism to us, we explode in ungodly anger. We normally do not struggle with such anger, and we did not see it coming. Nevertheless, it happened without thinking. These are sins that surprise us and express our sinful state. In some ways, they are unintentional sins because we did not intend or want them to happen.

Sin as infirmity—sins from lack of wisdom, knowledge, or health. If the moral image establishes our desire for God and neighbor, then the natural image empowers us to know what love requires for real union and to align our will with it. The natural image of God in Adam and Eve enabled them to know what holy love requires in all relationships and to walk accordingly. They could look at the world and know intuitively what was needed in every instance. They were then able to do it through the exercise of will.

After the corruption of the natural image in the fall, vestiges of human rationality remain, but our understanding and judgment are clouded. We no longer see clearly the world in which we live. Confusion reigns. Humans lack the knowledge, wisdom, and understanding to walk fully in the supreme love of God and neighbor. We look at the world around us and recognize that our perceptions and judgments about it are limited at best and mistaken at worst. Even if the human heart is properly oriented and the mind has complete power of will, restrictions in understanding and judgment lead to mistakes in every area of human relationships. We may have a desire

---

[37]Wesley, "The First-Fruits of the Spirit," *WJW* 8:93-94. .

to do what is right and have the will to do it, but we do not always have clarity about what needs to be done. Our problem is that we see "through a glass darkly" (1 Cor 13:12).

Because of the moral image's corruption, humanity lost the immediacy of a relationship with God. Apart from God's grace, we have no knowledge of God or his requirements for us. Even when divine revelation is given by the Holy Spirit to human conscience or through the Scriptures, we wrestle in discerning what it means and how exactly to apply it in life.

We struggle also in knowing what is best in our relationships with the people we love most. Husbands may love their wives and want to honor them but struggle in knowing how to respond appropriately when problems arise in marriage. Parents make poor decisions raising their children, even though they are acting in what they believe is their best interest. Friends give poor advice to one another, even though they want to offer wise counsel. The human heart and will are not the problem in these cases; human understanding and judgment are.

Our problem here extends beyond our human rationality. We also experience the limitations of our physical bodies and feebleness of mind. We bear the consequences of the fall in our bodies. We make commitments to people and "forget" to carry them out. We make promises, with the intention and ability to fulfill them, but then fail to do so because of poor memory. We commit to meet with a friend for breakfast and then overlook another appointment scheduled at the same time. We also experience physical and mental problems as well, over which we have little or no control. Alzheimer's disease may cause an otherwise kind person to speak and act in hurtful ways. Clinical depression may lead even the most positive Christian to fall into despair.

Our diminished rationality and bodies lead to errors in judgment and actions in all human relationships. We call these mistakes "sins of infirmity" because they are unintentional and arise from limitations in human reasoning and body. They are sin because they keep us from fulfilling the perfect will of God in relationships with him, others, and the created order. They are sin because they cause harm to varying degrees in our social relationships.[38]

John Wesley's theological summary of the problem of sin. Because John Wesley was an evangelist and sought to communicate Christian teaching to the masses, he developed a simple systematic overview of sin that focused on sin's fundamental problems: guilt, power, and being.[39]

The guilt of sin. Guilt is a legal term. God is a judge who holds us responsible for our lives. Guilt means we are culpable or responsible for our sin and liable for its consequences: death. Wesley believed as human beings corrupted by the fall of our first parents, we bear guilt on two levels: original sin and personal sin.

Historically, theologians and church traditions are divided on whether we have any responsibility for original sin, the state of sin in which we are born. One position argues that while we inherit the consequences of original sin, a sinful condition and death, there is no guilt. God does not hold us liable because of Adam's personal sin and the sinful condition into which we are born. We only incur guilt when we intentionally break God's law like our first parents.[40] While this view is primarily found in the Eastern Orthodox tradition, many Protestants are advocates of it as well, including Jacob Arminius.[41]

The other view teaches that Adam and Eve were either the federal head or natural head of humanity, so their sin is legally and effectively our sin. In the federal view, our first parents represented all

---

[38]For more significant discussion of infirmity, see Grider, *A Wesleyan-Holiness Theology*, 292-93; Thomas C. Oden, *Christ and Salvation*, vol. 2, *John Wesley's Teachings* (Grand Rapids, MI: Zondervan, 2012), 249-50.

[39]Randy Maddox calls these the penalty, plague, and presence of sin in *Responsible Grace: John Wesley's Practical Theology* (Nashville: Kingswood, 1994), 143. Kenneth Collins identifies them as the guilt, power, and being of sin in *The Theology of John Wesley: Holy Love and the Shape of Grace* (Nashville: Abingdon, 2007), 301.

[40]J. N. D. Kelly, *Early Christian Doctrines* (New York: HarperCollins, 1978), 347.

[41]Keith D. Stanglin and Thomas H. McCall, *Jacob Arminius: Theologian of Grace* (Oxford: Oxford University Press, 2012), 149-50.

humanity through covenant with God, and because of their sin, all are treated as if they committed the offense. Here guilt for their disobedience is imputed or reckoned to us.[42] Another variation is the natural headship theory, which teaches we are in some "real" sense in Adam and Eve, and we committed their act of disobedience with them. Here, original sin is not imputed, but imparted to us.[43] In the end, both views believe humanity stands under the judgment of God before any personal sin is committed.

John Wesley, more specifically, holds a federalist view.[44] So, if humanity is to be redeemed, there must be absolution for original sin. He also believes we bear guilt for all forms of personal sin, either intentional or unintentional, known, or unknown. We need atonement not only for the state of sin but also for all acts of sin and all sins of infirmity. We are responsible for it all.

The power of sin. Sin is a power exerted over human will. Because of the fall, humanity has a problem with the exercise of will. Our will balks at the demands of the supreme love of God and neighbor. When God's desires become known to us, they meet resistance at the level of will. In *Confessions,* Augustine observes the problem our will encounters when confronted with God's command:

> The mind gives an order to the body and is at once obeyed, but when it gives an order to itself, it is resisted. What causes it? The mind commands the hand to move and is so readily obeyed that the order can scarcely be distinguished from its execution. Yet the mind is mind and the hand is part of the body. But when the mind commands the mind to make an act of the will (e.g., to forgive enemy), these two are one and the same and yet the order is not obeyed. . . . The mind orders itself to make an act of the will, and it would not give this order unless it willed to do so; yet it does not carry out its own command.[45]

---

[42] Michael Horton, *The Christian Faith,* 415.
[43] Augustine, *The City of God,* 13.14.2.
[44] Wesley, "The Doctrine of Original Sin," *WJW* 9:262, 332-34.
[45] Augustine, *Confessions,* 8.9.

The human will balks at the demands of holy love through defiance and weakness. Our will cries in rebellion "I won't" to the will of God. We may know what God wants from us; we may have insight about what needs to be done in love, but our will refuses to submit to God's commands. It asserts itself in opposition to the good. It is hostile to holy love.

If the human will surrenders its rebellion, it then succumbs to weakness: our will cries out in defeat, "I can't" to God's directions. Even when there is desire to do the will of God, the will is weak. It cannot follow through. Paul describes our problem in Romans 7:22-23: "For in my inner being I delight in God's law; but I see another law at work in me, waging war against the law of my mind and making me a prisoner of the law of sin at work within me."

John Wesley calls our will's stubbornness and weakness "the power of sin" in human life. We recognize the good we are called to do and the sin we need to avoid, but we are incapable of aligning our will with God's. No matter how hard we try, sin has dominion over our will.[46]

The being of sin. John Wesley in his theology of sin recognizes the phenomenological and ontological condition of sin. Regarding its manifestation, he describes it as "any sinful temper, passion, or affection; such as pride, self-will, love of the world, in any kind of degree; such as lust, anger, peevishness; any disposition contrary to the mind which was in Christ."[47]

The source of such dispositions is found in the "deprivation" of the presence of God in human life, which is the core of the moral image of God. Wesley sees "the moral image as neither a capacity within humanity nor a function that can be employed independently of the creator, because it consists in a relationship in which the creature receives continuously from the creator and mediates further

---

[46]Wesley, "On Sin in Believers," *WJW* 5:146.
[47]Wesley, "Sin in Believers," *WJW* 5:137.

what is received."[48] Without the fullness of the Holy Spirit's presence in human life, we can neither receive nor mediate divine love and holiness.

Compounding this deprivation is the debilitation of the natural image. The natural image of God is not lost, but it is corrupted, directed toward different ends than originally created. Human understanding, reason, and will are employed to "rationalize our self-seeking goals, defend ourselves against our self-induced securities, and idealize our bondage."[49]

More specifically, as human beings we are creatures of love. The deprivation and debilitation of the *image Dei* does not destroy this fundamental reality. Instead, it redirects the focus of our love, what we ultimately desire and what we align our will with. As a result, we experience inordinate love of ourselves, other people, and creation. Our sinful state is defined by idolatry. We do not seek our happiness in God but in the world. Even in the state of sin, we can love others, love creation, and love our work with an "unutterable" affection with "strength and tenderness," but not without it being idolatrous. For Wesley, it is this idolatrous (disordered, inordinate) love that plagues our lives and manifests itself in all acts of sin.[50]

Some sins are worse than others. Now that we have looked at the different categories of sin biblically and theologically, we need to ask the question, Are some sins worse than others? The idea of all sin being the same before God is commonly accepted in the church. It pervades contemporary Christianity. Through sermons, Sunday school classes, Bible studies, or friendly conversations with other Christians, we pick up the idea quickly. To question it is to invite immediate suspicion and disbelief.

---

[48]Theodore Runyon, *John Wesley's Theology Today* (Nashville: Abingdon, 1998), 18.
[49]Runyon, *John Wesley's Theology Today*, 18.
[50]Wesley, "Spiritual Idolatry," *WJW* 6:435-44.

The rationale for such teaching varies. To exalt the holiness of God, some Christians try to show how even the smallest infraction of divine law is as bad as the greatest before God's absolute moral purity. Others argue if every sin has the same punishment, death, as certain biblical passages seem to suggest, then every transgression is practically the same to God. Similarly, Christians claim that because all sin separates us from God and requires the sacrificial death of Christ to forgive, it must be equal to God. Perhaps the most popular motivation is to protect Christians from pride. If we think certain sins are worse than others before God, then we will be tempted to think our personal sin is not as bad as other people's.

No major Christian theologian or historic Christian tradition has ever taught the equality of sin. It exists only as "folk theology," a belief uncritically held by laity and preachers. Unfortunately, such teaching has serious consequences.

One of the most famous examples of Christian instruction on degrees of sin is the Roman Catholic distinction between mortal and venial sins. Mortal sins are so serious they lead to a Christian's spiritual death if they continue without amendment of life. Venial sins, in contrast, are "light"; they do not harm irreparably a believer's relationship with God. Mortal sins are to be avoided at all costs and venial sins are to be worked on through sanctification.[51]

Unfortunately, the idea of some sins being worse than others is dismissed too quickly as "Catholic teaching." Every major historical expression of Christianity, however, has recognized that there are degrees of sin before God. Classic Christian understanding is captured well in the Presbyterian tradition's *Westminster Larger Catechism*:

> Q. 150. Are all transgressions of the law of God equally heinous in themselves, and in the sight of God?

---

[51]*Catechism of the Catholic Church*, 2nd ed. (Washington, DC: United States Catholic Conference, 2011), §1855-63.

A. All transgressions of the law are not equally heinous; but some sins in themselves, and by reason of several aggravations, are more heinous in the sight of God than others.[52]

The Eastern Orthodox tradition of Christianity makes similar distinctions. How many times and in what manner a sin is done are taken into consideration in the evaluation of a sin's severity.[53]

Historic Christian teaching here is grounded in the way the Scriptures make a distinction between intentional and unintentional sin; between sins done with a "high hand" and those that are not; between knowledge or ignorance of God's law; and between minor details of God's laws and major matters. It is also seen in the way discipline is exercised among members of the believing community. Not all sins require disciplinary measures, while others require more serious responses. Jesus indicates further that the experience of hell's severity by the unrighteous is determined by their sinfulness (Lk 10:12-14). Hell is not equally experienced. Finally, the Scriptures portray sin as having relational and purity concerns, and not just legal ones. Sin must be seen in light of its impact on people's relationships with God, each other, and creation, as well as the degree to which it defiles and corrupts them and others.

Historic teaching is fortified by theological reflection as well. Sin can be evaluated by the degree to which it is a corrupted good. Everything God has created is good. The more sin is privated of its original goodness, the worse it is. Because God is the creator of the good, he is fully aware of the degree to which it has been corrupted. God knows the extent to which the good is diminished.

---

[52]See the "Westminster Larger Catechism," in *Creeds and Confessions of the Reformation Era*, vol. 2, *Creeds and Confessions of Faith in the Christian Tradition*, ed. Jaroslav Pelikan and Valerie R. Hotchkiss (London: Yale University Press, 2003), 619-20.

[53]George Dokos, *A Manual of Confessions by Our Righteous God-bearing Father Nikodemos the Hagiorite* (Thessalonica: Uncut Mountain, 2006), 83.

CONCLUSION

In summary, God is immutably perfect in holiness and love. By creating humanity in his image, God desired to move humanity from original perfection in the garden, from personal potentiality and corruptibility, to absolute human perfection, to full actuality in incorruptible union with himself. God wanted to make us fully like him through full consummation with him. However, human sin arose through unbelief, pride, and disobedience. Sin as a state, as an act, and as an infirmity plagues human life. In the language of John Wesley, we live under the guilt, power, and being of sin. We now turn our attention to God's work of salvation, leading to Christian perfection in this life and absolute human perfection in the next.

11

HOLINESS AND REDEMPTION

GOD CREATED HUMANITY to share in his glory, to bear his image in creation, and to become fully like him in consummation. When humanity fell in the garden and became slaves to sin, God's purposes were not ultimately thwarted. In holy love, God moved to redeem us. Through the Father's sending of the Son in the incarnation and the Son's giving of the Holy Spirit at Pentecost, God manifested his love: his desire to be in fellowship with us and his action to overcome every obstacle to it. God demonstrated his holiness by dealing thoroughly with the problem of sin. He manifested his holy love by not settling for anything less than true union with humanity. Through the work of the triune God, we can be made holy in the present life through Christian perfection and be made incorruptibly perfect in the world to come through full participation in the life of God. We turn our attention now to God's redemptive work that makes possible the experience of Christian perfection in this life and absolute perfection in the life to come.

CHRISTIAN PERFECTION MADE POSSIBLE BY THE
FATHER, THROUGH THE SON, IN THE HOLY SPIRIT

The Father saves us from the devastation of sin by sending his eternal Son in the incarnation. At an appointed time in creation, the Son of God assumed a human body, soul, mind, and will, uniting in his person divine and human natures, without diminishment or change of either one. He became fully human without ceasing to be entirely God. We can be redeemed only through one who is both God and human.

As the theandric (literally "God-man") one, the eternal Son is given the name "Jesus" and the title "Christ." The name speaks of his identity as the Lord (Jesus means "the Lord saves") and of his mission ("he will save his people from their sins"). His title points to his office as the Messiah, who ushers in "the last days of the Spirit . . . poured out on all flesh," thereby restoring the fortunes of humanity, lost by our first parents.

Why the Son must be fully God. To redeem humanity, Jesus Christ must be fully divine for three reasons. As God, he has authority to forgive sin. When Jesus speaks forgiveness over our sin, it is not the expression of a kind sentiment, but the authoritative declaration of God. If he is not God, his absolution carries no more power than another human being. Because he is divine, however, his forgiveness has final and absolute vindication over all guilt incurred by our lives. We can be certain of our exoneration before God.[1]

As God, Jesus also has the power to refashion humanity. Only God can create; therefore, only God can recreate. Our redemption requires both spiritual and physical resurrection, a reconstitution of humanity so powerful that it is equal to the act of creation itself. If Jesus is not God, then he is unable to make us fully alive again. He must revive and restore the image of God in humanity and raise our mortal bodies from death to incorruptibility, overcoming every consequence of sin. No human being or creature, no matter how good,

---

[1]Thomas F. Torrance, *The Mediation of Christ* (Colorado Springs, CO: Helmers & Howard, 1992), 58.

resourceful, or gifted, has such power. Because Jesus is God, we can be confident of his power to transform us in nature and person.[2]

Finally, as God, Jesus makes his atoning sacrifice on the cross efficacious for all. Without his divine nature to energize atonement, the gift of his sinless humanity on the cross has limited, if any, benefit. His humanity alone is not able to expiate for all sin or atone for every sinner. Because the one who is crucified is the eternal, divine Son of God, the sacrifice made on the cross is efficacious for all. We can be assured of the full benefits of Christ's atoning work, regardless of who we are or what we have done.[3]

Why the Son must be fully human. Jesus Christ must also be fully human for two reasons. First, through full assumption of human nature, he makes possible the restoration and healing of our embodied souls. The apostle Paul teaches that the ultimate redemption of our physical bodies occurs through Christ taking his human body through death and resurrection (1 Cor 15:12-24, 42-49). His physical body rescues our bodies from death. We will be bodily resurrected because Jesus is bodily resurrected.

Our greatest problem, however, is not our bodies, but our souls: our desires, mind, and will. These must be healed of their corruption. Christ also assumed a human soul in order to redeem every aspect of humanity. Through assumption of a human soul, Christ makes possible the salvation of human hearts and will. Through his humanity, Christ is the divine image intended for us. He restores the image of God in us and enables us to experience rightly ordered love for God, neighbor, and creation. Our human souls are healed through his human soul. Because he grew and developed in his human soul, we can as well, becoming actualized as human persons, reflecting the *imago Dei*.[4]

---

[2] Athanasius, *On the Incarnation of the Word*, 8.4-9.3.
[3] Anselm, *Cur Deus Homo*, trans. Sidney N. Deane (Pantianos Classics, 2016), 1.5, 25; 2.6-7; Millard J. Erickson, *Christian Theology* (Grand Rapids, MI: Baker Academic, 2013), 642.
[4] Thomas C. Oden, *Classic Christianity: A Systematic Theology* (New York: HarperOne, 2009), 272-74.

Second, being fully human, Jesus is the second Adam who lived a life of perfect obedience and submission to the Father, succeeding where the first Adam failed. Christ lived a life of perfect faith and confidence in God as he grew and developed as a human being, culminating in the surrender of his life in crucifixion. The entirety of his life is salvific, not just his work in death and resurrection. The human life he lives paves the way for us to live like him. He shows us what it is to be fully human.[5]

Because of the fall of humanity's first parents, we are born into Adam with its deleterious consequences. We come into life with a bent or propensity to rebellion, disobedience, and sin. Through regeneration, the hold of the first Adam is broken, and we are united with the second Adam, Jesus Christ, with his salvific benefits. We can become fully human again. We can walk in obedience to God and live a life defined by the love of God and neighbor. We can be united with Christ in his humanity. We can walk in loving, obedient faith and confidence in God as Jesus did.

Why the Son must die on the cross. While the Son's saving work encompasses the entirety of his earthly life, it culminates in his death, resurrection, and exaltation to the right hand of the Father. No single view of the atonement can capture fully what Jesus Christ accomplishes on the cross. While there are many perspectives here, two are most relevant. First, through his sacrifice on the cross, Jesus pays the penalty of sin for humanity. He absolves us from the guilt of breaking God's law and offending God's character. God has created a moral order that humanity has broken, and there are consequences for it. Christ's death bears the penalty for having broken the divine law and pardons us from the just punishment for sin.[6]

More than law, however, has been violated; God is personally offended by our sin. Our sin is an insult and affront to God's character. To resolve this conflict between God's holiness and our guilt, Christ

---

[5]Irenaeus, *Against Heresies*, 3.18.1; 4.6.2; 5.21.1.
[6]Oden, *Classic Christianity*, 418, 431-32.

dies on the cross and perfectly satisfies the personal demands of God's holiness.[7] Atonement here is what makes possible the experience of justification and reconciliation, which is the foundation for salvation's work in our lives.

Second, because of the fall in the garden, we are enslaved to Satan. As John Wesley says, we now bear "the image of the Devil."[8] With this servitude, we live in bondage to sin and death. Through Christ's death on the cross and bodily resurrection, the power of Satan is broken, the chains of sin are unshackled, and death no longer has dominion over our mortal bodies.[9] Martin Luther describes Jesus' work in death as "Christ invading the territory of the evil powers and principalities and conquering them," freeing humanity from their domination.[10] Because Christ conquered the grave, through him we will do the same. Christ's work through the cross and resurrection frees humanity from all that keeps us from sharing in God's glory as image-bearers in this life. Sin and the devil no longer have dominion over us.

Why we need Pentecost. The Holy Spirit is called the "Spirit of the Son" (Gal 4:6). Jesus' work as the Messiah culminates with his exaltation to the "right hand of God," where he exercises his royal office as King and sends the Holy Spirit to his people.[11] The Father redeems us by sending the Holy Spirit through the Son at Pentecost. What the Son objectively accomplished through his incarnation, life, death, and resurrection, the Holy Spirit subjectively applies to human life. The Holy Spirit liberates us from the deleterious hold of Adam's fall and unites us with the victorious life of Christ. The Spirit brings us in union with Jesus' humanity, so that we participate in his human soul, mind, and will.[12]

---

[7]Oden, *Classic Christianity*, 432-33.

[8]Wesley, "The New Birth," *WJW* 6:68.

[9]Oden, *Classic Christianity*, 433-34.

[10]Roger E. Olson, *The Mosaic of Christian Belief* (Downers Grove, IL: IVP Academic, 2016), 274.

[11]John N. Oswalt, *Called to Be Holy: A Biblical Perspective* (Nappanee, IN: Francis Asbury, 1999), 89-96.

[12]Irenaeus, *Against Heresies*, 5.1.1; 5.6.1; 5.12.4.

The Spirit reigns in our lives as he does in Christ's, rightly ordering our love and thereby restoring the image of God in us. We are freed once again to live out the purposes of God for our lives: to love God with our entire being, to love our neighbor as ourselves, and to steward creation in love. We can reflect divine holiness in life, to be holy as God is holy. We are able to share in God's glory presently and more fully in consummation. We can experience Christian perfection in present life and ultimate human perfection in the life to come.

The place of Christian community is the church. During his earthly ministry, Christ was the primary means of God's grace in the world. While God's grace was at work in other areas of the world at this time, God was primarily working through Christ in the world. Through his obedient life, sacrificial death, triumphal resurrection, and exaltation, Christ objectively accomplished the work of salvation and made God's saving, sustaining, and sanctifying grace available to the world. The church, made manifest in local communities, is now the body of Christ through which God is primarily working in the world, through which Christ channels his saving, sustaining, and sanctifying grace in the Holy Spirit.

The church is the instrument through which Christ's work is applied to human lives by the Holy Spirit. This is why a Christian must be a part of a local congregation. To not be a part of a local church is to risk cutting oneself off from God's sustaining and sanctifying grace. This is why the early church fathers, beginning with Cyprian, said, "He can no longer have God for his Father, who has not the Church for his mother."[13] The Christian community is the "womb" through which we are born and realize the fullness of Christ's salvation.

John Wesley, more specifically, made clear to his immediate followers and theological heirs that the experience of holiness happens within community. Wesley developed "The Nature, Design, and

---

[13]Cyprian, "On the Unity of the Church," *ANF* 5:423.

General Rules of the United Societies" as a communal discipline for Methodists seeking regenerating and sanctifying grace. It required all Methodists to meet regularly in a small group called a class meeting, where members collected money "for the relief of the poor," gave an account of the state of their relationship with God, and held each other accountable for their agreed upon way of life.[14]

This common life consisted of three "General Rules." The first identified particular sins to be avoided like drunkenness and profanity. The second addressed concrete ways to do good like feeding the hungry and visiting those in prison. The final rule described spiritual disciplines expected to be consistently practiced as a means of grace: worship, prayer, Scripture reading, and receiving the Lord's prayer. The class meeting, along with larger Methodist societies, established a spiritual environment in which members experienced God's grace working in them.[15]

The following discussion of the theology and experience of salvation presupposes the work of the Father, through the Son, in the Holy Spirit as the foundation for its theology. It assumes the church and Christian community as the context for its experience.

THE THEOLOGY AND EXPERIENCE OF SALVATION

At this point, we want to explore how the redemptive work by the Father through the Son in the Holy Spirit occurs in human life. How do we experience God's salvation? We also want to examine more specifically the ways in which God sets us free from the problem of sin, restores the image of God in us, reorients our love, empowers us for holy living, and forms us into the persons God intends. We also want to explore Wesleyan teaching on Christian perfection, which is the heart of soteriology (the study of salvation).

In Christianity, few doctrines are more important than salvation. John Wesley famously declares, "I only want to know one thing . . .

---

[14]Wesley, "The Nature, Design, and General Rules of the United Societies," *WJW* 9:69-73.
[15]Wesley, "The Nature, Design, and General Rules of the United Societies," *WJW* 9:69-73.

the way to heaven."[16] He expresses the sentiment of many Christians and God-seekers. Of course, by "heaven" Wesley did not mean simply the life we have after death, but present experience as well: the realization of God's rule in human hearts.

The study of Christian salvation raises two intimately related questions: (1) what is salvation, and (2) how are people saved? The content of salvation entails several related ideas: forgiveness of sin; adoption as children of God; reconciliation with God and humanity; deliverance from the power and state of sin; renewal in the image of God; perfect love; bodily resurrection; final justification; and "life everlasting." These ideas express concretely the biblical and theological categories of justification, adoption, regeneration, sanctification, and glorification found in most basic Christian teachings. The means of salvation, in comparison, address spiritual awakening, repentance, faith, and perseverance, which are crucial throughout salvation's experience. This is how we are made holy in heart and life.

An ordo salutis. To answer questions about the content and means of salvation, theologians and Christian traditions develop an *ordo salutis* ("order of salvation"). An *ordo* reflects our biblical, historical, and theological reflection on redemption, combined with our personal and corporate experience.

An *ordo salutis*, more specifically, is a rational, linear, theologically coherent account of salvation. Many churches and denominations articulate them to varying degrees in their official doctrinal statements. Theologians describe them in detailed discussions of soteriology. These *ordines* (plural of *ordo*) paint a picture of divine redemption in human life, enabling us to see each aspect of salvation in relationship to the whole. Some are very basic in their accounts, while others are deep and complex. Pastorally, an *ordo* functions as a map to guide us from the moment we are regenerated, through the experience of sanctification in present life, to glorification after

---

[16]Wesley, "Preface," *Sermons on Several Occasions*, 2 vols. (London: J. Kershaw, 1825), 1:vii.

death. As a theological framework, we use it most often to inform the spiritual counsel we give people as they navigate the experience of salvation.

A via salutis. The problem with an *ordo salutis* is that the actual experience of salvation is usually far messier than described. To use Augustine's *ordo*, as seen in an earlier chapter, people often waver between "prior to the law" and "under the law," and between "under the law" and "under grace," or they bypass stages altogether, moving from "prior to the law" to "under grace." The disorderliness of experience requires some qualifications of an *ordo*. We do this by acknowledging a *via salutis* ("way of salvation").

If an *ordo salutis* is the theological conception of salvation, a *via salutis* is the actual experience of it. An *ordo* expresses doctrinal understanding; a *via* recognizes lived reality. To read an *ordo* is to see a clear and orderly presentation of Christian redemption; to live a *via* is to know its messiness. The *via salutis* acknowledges that personal experience of salvation rarely follows our precise description of it. Generally, there are discrepancies between the two.

For example, the New Testament presents a clear order of salvation: repent, believe, be baptized, and receive the Spirit. Yet, when we read concrete experiences of salvation in the book of Acts, we see that this order is not always operative. When Philip preaches the gospel to the Samaritans, they genuinely believe his message and are baptized, but they do not immediately receive the Spirit. Rather, the Spirit comes later to them when Peter and John visit Samaria (Acts 8:4-17). The apostle Paul repents after meeting Christ on the Damascus Road, but he does not receive the Spirit until days later in the city after speaking with Ananias, and all of this occurs before his baptism (Acts 9:9-17). Likewise, Cornelius receives the Spirit before baptism (Acts 10:44-48). While all elements of the New Testament *ordo* exist in each of these testimonies, they are experienced differently, rather than in a fixed order.

Paul presents a clear *ordo salutis* in Romans. As we saw in an earlier chapter, Paul expects the power of sin to be broken in conversion. The dilemma he paints in Romans 7:14-25 is of a person who desires the good but is unable to do it. He describes an individual without the Spirit (i.e., someone not yet regenerated). As Paul works with people pastorally, however, he calls members of the Corinthian church "Christian" who are controlled by sin. Paul's *ordo* in Romans, however, indicates that this should not be and need not be. So, he challenges them by God's grace to move beyond living as "mere humans" (1 Cor 3:3).

A theological *ordo*, therefore, better serves as a guide rather than a rule in Christian experience. It helps us see what is lacking in personal experience. It serves as exhortation to seek Christ for what is missing in Christian life, and it supports us as we pursue genuine experience in Christ. When an *ordo* becomes a rigid standard to which all experience must conform, legalism, judgmentalism, and discouragement soon follow.

A WESLEYAN-HOLINESS *ORDO SALUTIS* OF CHRISTIAN PERFECTION

We are now ready to explore how God works to restore the divine image in humanity and bring us to his ultimate purposes, how we experience Christian perfection in this life and absolute perfection in the life to come. As stated earlier, we must not understand this construct as a neat and orderly process; the realization of personal salvation in life is rarely as linear and clear as an *ordo* appears. The *ordo* operates only as a general conceptual framework to guide the church in its proclamation, instruction, and discipleship. Personal experience will look differently from Christian to Christian, and yet a general conformity to the ultimate end of salvation exists.

Divine initiative is fundamental to a Wesleyan-holiness soteriology. God's grace initiates, undergirds, and makes possible growth in the restoration of the *imago Dei* and our development as persons. At this point, we must ask, "What is grace?" If we are not careful, theology can make grace appear to be a commodity, a substance that God distributes. Divine "grace," however, is nothing more than the unmerited work of God in us, for us, and through us.[17] It is simply God working on our behalf. More specifically in salvation, grace is the work of the Holy Spirit, communicating to us all the benefits of the Father through the Son's incarnate life, death, resurrection, and exaltation.

Prevenient grace. Because of Adam and Eve's disobedience in the garden, the moral image of God (holiness, righteousness, love, and relationship to God) is destroyed in humanity, while the natural and political image are extensively impaired. Consequently, all human beings apart from divine grace are spiritually dead to God, thoroughly sinful, under divine condemnation, helpless to change, ignorant of their predicament, and incapable of grasping it. Because of our disordered love of creation and servitude to sin, our formation as persons bears the image of the devil.[18]

If we are going to be saved, God must take initiative. We have no resources to offer. Wesleyans believe that God makes the first move by giving everyone prevenient (from the Latin *praevenio*, meaning "to come before") grace. This grace has twofold power: (1) it makes possible reception of further grace and (2) enables our response to it. As God's grace comes at different times and places in life, prevenient grace enables us to receive what the Spirit is doing and then to embrace or resist it. In any positive human action in redemption, there is first God's grace seeking to create necessary change in us, followed by our reception and cooperation with it through prevenient grace.[19]

---

[17]Wesley, *Instructions for Children* (London: M. Cooper, 1745), lesson 8, question 1. Here Wesley defines grace as "the power of the Holy Spirit, enabling us to behave, love and serve God."

[18]Wesley, "On the Doctrine of Original Sin—Part II," *WJW* 9:261-88.

[19]Kenneth J. Collins accurately and fully describes John Wesley's doctrine of prevenient grace in *The Theology of John Wesley: Holy Love and the Shape of Grace* (Nashville: Abingdon, 2007), 14-15, 73-82. See also Wesley, "Predestination Calmly Considered," *WJW* 10:229; "A Dialogue Between a Predestinarian and a Friend," *WJW* 10:392.

As such, we cannot recognize our fallen state unless *the Spirit brings* illumination. We cannot repent of our sins unless *the Spirit empowers* it. We cannot turn toward God unless *the Spirit enables* us. And we cannot exercise faith to believe when we hear the gospel unless *the Spirit generates* it. Prevenient grace does not grant us the ability to do what is often attributed as our responsibility in salvation: understanding, repentance, and faith. It only creates "space" where the Holy Spirit can bring them into our life with our consent.

Prevenient grace, therefore, is the foundation of a Wesleyan-holiness soteriology. Through its preparatory work, every person is a candidate for salvation. The *imago Dei* can be renewed in us and final incorruptible union with God realized again. On one hand, it makes possible the experience of every act of grace in salvation. On the other hand, it is powerless to do anything. Unless the Holy Spirit moves in other ways, prevenient grace does nothing.

Growth in grace. If we are completely dependent on God's grace for every aspect of salvation, a question arises: How does God give saving grace to people? How does God work to create spiritual awakening, repentance, and saving faith in human lives? Wesleyans believe that the Spirit does this through general and special revelation.

First, God actively reveals himself in the world. Creation testifies to his existence. The Holy Spirit works through the world's beauty and order to illuminate the truth of a creator. The Spirit also labors to write God's character on our conscience, forming an internal law by which we experience remorse when violated. The Spirit, therefore, seeks to establish basic knowledge of God and a sense of moral rectitude through general revelation. As grace comes in the form of general revelation, prevenient grace enables us to receive the Spirit's work and, as we embrace it, to experience initial spiritual growth.[20]

Second, God reveals himself more particularly through the history of Israel and ultimately in the incarnation of the eternal Son,

---

[20]Collins, *The Theology of John Wesley*, 39, 123.

Jesus Christ. Knowledge of God's special revelation is contained in the Old and New Testaments. Scripture, therefore, is the primary means by which we know God (and ourselves). God reveals himself, our sin, and Christ's salvation through it. As we are exposed to the Bible, and particularly the gospel of Jesus Christ, the Holy Spirit seeks to create in us the reality described and promised in them. Prevenient grace provides the context within us where the Spirit's work in general revelation is furthered through special revelation.[21]

How quickly we grow in grace is determined primarily by the Spirit and only secondarily by us. Because grace is solely the work of God, we cannot determine it. We cannot control what God does, when he does it, or through which means he accomplishes it. Wesleyans further believe that God seeks to redeem every person, to make us holy through union with Christ, but that God in his wisdom works in us differently, sometimes bringing salvation more quickly, other times more slowly. We can only choose to embrace or resist divine grace as it comes to us.

Spiritual awakening. What the Holy Spirit begins in human life through general revelation he seeks to complete through special revelation. The Holy Spirit works to awaken us to our true spiritual state. By divine grace, we see increasingly the enormity of sin's problem in our lives. We can no longer ignore or excuse it. We recognize sin as an expression of who we are as persons. We sin because we are sinners. We grasp with increased understanding that we are capable of any evil under the right conditions in life. The idea of humanity's basic goodness is exposed as a lie.

The Spirit exposes further our impotence to change. We know through moral conscience and the teaching of Scripture what righteousness requires, yet we find a force within us that balks at it, compelling us to think and act in ways we know are wrong. The state of sin in us leads to all manner of sinful acts. This realization often

---

[21]Thomas C. Oden, *God and Providence*, vol. 1, *John Wesley's Teachings* (Grand Rapids, MI: Zondervan, 2012), 70-71.

develops over time. We think we have freedom to do whatever we will, but when we seek to do what is right, our resolve falters. The power of sin has an intractable grip on us. While there are moments when we keep the moral law, fooling us into thinking we are in control, sin's power asserts itself whenever it wishes. We find that even when we do what is right, our motivation is rooted in the corrupt, fallen conditions of the heart. Disordered love controls our desires, and our will lives enslaved to it.

Spiritual awakening begins as God pricks our human conscience, but it is clarified and roused further through the truth of the gospel. As we are exposed to scriptural teaching, God communicates grace to us, bringing conviction of our utter sinfulness before him and knowledge of our moral destitution. If we do not resist, God's holy love exposes our unrighteousness, disordered desires, and moral impotence. It holds up a mirror by which we see our corruption as persons. This awakening drives us to seek change if we embrace it, and through the gospel it leads us to Jesus Christ.[22]

Evangelical repentance. Evangelical repentance is closely joined with spiritual awakening. Awakening enables people to see the problem of sin, their malformation, while repentance leads them to turn from it. Awakening leads to illumination, while repentance directs us to change. The Holy Spirit works through conscience and the gospel to convict people of sin, to create guilt and shame over sin, and finally to elicit genuine remorse. Repentance marks the initial forays of the Spirit in heart transformation. A desire for God's holiness is ignited in humanity. A rupture arises in the first Adam's hold on us.

Evangelical repentance is not self-generated. It arises out of an inner conviction of the Holy Spirit that accepts the consequences of our actions, begs forgiveness, seeks change, and habituates repentance when sin is committed. We do not seek relief from sin's guilt

---

[22]See Christopher T. Bounds, "How Are People Saved? The Major Views of Salvation with a Focus on Wesleyan Perspectives and Their Implications," *Wesley and Methodist Studies* 3 (2011): 31-54.

simply to be free of its discomfort, but also because we desire to be free from sin itself. With the Spirit's illumination through the gospel, we desire to love God and neighbor above all else, which is the fulfillment of divine law. A longing to be renewed in God's image and experience incorruptible union with God is rekindled.[23]

While repentance marks transformation in desire, it does not yet fully empower our will. The power of sin still rules. We continue to commit all manner of sinful acts, transgressions of the known law of God. Before spiritual awakening and repentance, we enjoyed and had satisfaction in sin, but now we abhor it. We live in frustration because of the disparity between the holiest desires of our heart and the sinful reality of our experience.[24] Regrettably, we are still slaves to disordered love and to the devil because we are unable to align our will with new desires.

For John Wesley, evangelical repentance leads to "fruit worthy of repentance" manifested in an active seeking of God in the means of grace.[25] We eagerly look for Christ in the places we are most likely to encounter him in his saving power. Wesley classified these "channels" into two categories: piety and mercy. The former includes traditional spiritual disciplines: prayer, reading the Scriptures, holy Communion, fasting, and Christian small groups. The latter consists of good works: visiting the sick and those in prison, feeding the hungry, and giving generously to the needs of others.[26] Through repentance and its fruit, Wesley believes that at some point the Spirit will impart saving faith to us that, when exercised, leads to new birth.[27]

Saving faith. As people respond positively to the Spirit's work of repentance, they open themselves to further work, namely, the

---

[23]Collins, *The Theology of John Wesley*, 156-58.

[24]Wesley, "The Spirit of Bondage and of Adoption," *WJW* 5:98-111.

[25]Wesley, *Explanatory Notes on the New Testament*, 2 vols. (Grand Rapids, MI: Baker, 1986), on Mt 3:8.

[26]Wesley, "Minutes of Several Conversations," *WJW* 8:322-24.

[27]Wesley, "Letter to Isaac Andrews, January 4, 1784," in *Letters of John Wesley*, ed. John Telford, 8 vols. (London: Epworth, 1931), 7:202.

creation of saving faith. Such faith transcends a simple intellectual assent of belief in Christ and the redemption he offers. It is, instead, a "sure confidence" in the human heart that Christ did it "for me."[28] It is not merely affirming propositional truths about the gospel; it is a personal experience of that truth. While it is one work of the Holy Spirit to persuade us that Christ came to save us from our sins, it is another work to convince the heart that he did it "for me."[29]

Pivotal to understanding Wesleyan-holiness teaching here is that saving faith is a gift of God, wrought by the Holy Spirit in human minds and hearts. It is not produced by us. A cursory look at John Wesley's Aldersgate experience illustrates this truth. Wesley describes his experience on May 24, 1738, as one in which his heart was "strangely warmed." Consequently, he testifies, "I felt I did trust Christ, Christ alone for salvation; and an assurance was given me that He had taken away my sins. He had taken away my sins, even mine, and saved me from the law of sin and death."[30] Wesley's "faith" in this moment is not so much an action he takes, but an event happening within him, a divine work creating heart conviction of Christ's personal love and redemption of himself. Wesley's heart is acted on by a power within him creating personal faith in Christ. It is the Holy Spirit.

This understanding of Wesley's experience is substantiated further by his journals. Months prior to Aldersgate, he was convinced by Peter Bohler that salvation is "by grace through faith," and he began to preach it fervently.[31] Wesley grasped this truth intellectually by grace but struggled with personal faith. Wesley believed in "his head" but struggled in "his soul." Persistent doubt kept Wesley from believing in Christ for his salvation. Wesley's experience at Aldersgate, however, led him to see that saving faith is "a

---

[28]Wesley, "Salvation by Faith," *WJW* 5:7-16.
[29]Wesley, "Salvation by Faith," *WJW* 5:7-16; "The Scripture Way of Salvation," *WJW* 6:43-54; "On Faith," *WJW* 7:195-202.
[30]Wesley, "Journals," *WJW* 1:103.
[31]Wesley, "Journals," *WJW* 1:101-3.

divine evidence and conviction . . . a sure trust in the mercy of God in Christ . . . the conviction that the Son of God loves me and has given himself for me."[32]

Because saving faith is a gift of divine grace, we cannot exercise it at any moment we decide, but only after the Spirit has imparted it to us. We, therefore, cannot determine when we experience new birth, but only in those appointed "windows" when saving faith is communicated to us, we embrace its creation and exercise it.[33] These opportunities may come when we have no concern or care for God, bursting into our hearts suddenly and powerfully, compelling us to believe in Christ, or it may happen after seeking the Lord for an extended period, or we may be unable to recognize exactly when it happened. The experience of saving faith is neither a legal nor an intellectual transaction, but a deeply personal encounter with Christ. Because of its intimate nature, it will be different for each of us.

For the spiritually awakened who do not immediately experience saving faith but desire it, they must trust Christ with what faith they have. The Holy Spirit works in his wisdom and timing. We must embrace when and how he works and not resist it. In the meantime, we must persist in the means of grace, seeking Christ, until saving faith comes. Wesley states accordingly, "Faith is the work of God; and yet it is the duty of man to believe. And every man may believe if he will, though not when he will. If he seeks faith in the appointed ways, sooner or later the power of the Lord will be present, whereby (1) God works, and by his power (2) man believes."[34]

New birth. In the moment people receive and exercise saving faith in Christ, they experience new birth. They are no longer in the

---

[32]Wesley, "Salvation by Faith," *WJW* 5:7-16; "The Scripture Way of Salvation," *WJW* 6:43-54; "On Faith," *WJW* 7:195-202.

[33]Steve DeNeff states this explicitly in *Whatever Became of Holiness?* (Indianapolis: Wesleyan, 1995), 53-63. By "moments," I do not mean any specific duration of time. These moments can last for minutes, days, weeks, or months. I only mean a period of time in which God is at work bringing a person to salvation.

[34]Wesley, "Letter to Isaac Andrews, January 4, 1784," in *Letters of John Wesley*, 7:202.

first Adam, but the second. They are brought into union with Christ and begin to participate in his humanity. The objective work of Christ's life begins to be applied to our lives by the Holy Spirit. New birth has three concomitants (from the Latin *concomitor*, "to companion together"): justification, adoption, and regeneration.

Justification. First, we are justified. God pardons our sin and receives us into divine favor. The guilt incurred by sin, through act and infirmity, is absolved through Christ's atonement and his righteousness is imputed to us (Rom 4:5). We have a new standing before God, where our lack of conformity to the divine law is not held against us. Christ's righteousness, instead, is reckoned to us. His righteousness counts as ours, acquitting us of sin.[35]

Logically, justification forms the foundation for the rest of salvation. Christ's subsequent work through the Holy Spirit flows from justification and not the other way. We are not justified because we are God's children and regenerated; we are adopted and renewed through justification. What God does *for* us precedes what he does *in* us. Imputation of Christ's righteousness is the foundation for its impartation. In John Wesley's analogy of salvation as a house, prevenient grace serves as the porch, while justification is the door through which we enter the rooms of sanctification.[36] We cannot live in holiness without passing through the entrance of justification.

Adoption. Second, we are adopted as daughters and sons of God (Jn 1:12-13). If justification addresses the legal problem of sin, adoption treats its relational issues. Because of sin, humanity lives in alienation from God. While made to be God's children, we bear the devil's image. Accordingly, as Augustine teaches, we find our identity as members of the "city of man" rather than the "city of God." We are defined by our love of the fallen world, a "city" that lives in active opposition to God, rather than Christ's rule, the "city" that

---

[35]Wesley, "Justification by Faith," *WJW* 5:53-64.
[36]Wesley, "Principles of a Methodist Farther Explained," *WJW* 8:415.

reflects his holiness. Through new birth, not only are we reconciled to God, and become citizens of his kingdom, we become something even greater—the children of God.

As adopted children, we are made members of the family of God. Families give us our most fundamental sense of identity. They tell us who and whose we are. Without reconciliation to God through Jesus Christ, other identities and relationships define us, keeping us from becoming the person God desires. In new birth, though, we receive a new identity and a new family, forming us into the person God desires.

As daughters and sons of God, we enjoy all the rights and privileges that come with being children. Even though we are adopted children, we share the relationship with the Father that Jesus has as the Son by nature. We are seated with Christ at the Father's right hand, sharing in Christ's present rule (Eph 2:6); we are heirs with him to the coming kingdom. As children we have confident access to the throne of God with Christ.[37]

Regeneration. Third, we are regenerated, which is the climax of new birth. Regeneration at its heart has the initial restoration of the moral image of God (Jn 3:1-9). Here, the Holy Spirit works in believers, raising them from death in sin to life in Christ, and imparting righteousness to them (Col 2:13). To the transformation of desire experienced in repentance, God now brings empowerment of will. The power of sin is broken in us, and the sinful condition is dealt a serious blow. We are now able to walk in obedience to God's revealed will, even if we still experience selfish desires. While the state of sin continues, it is greatly diminished. We experience the first fruit of being in the second Adam. Because the moral image of God is partially restored in regeneration, it is called initial sanctification.[38]

---

[37]Thomas C. Oden, *Christ and Salvation*, vol. 2, *John Wesley's Teachings* (Grand Rapids, MI: Zondervan, 2012), 218-19.
[38]Wesley, "The New Birth," *WJW* 6:65-77.

Protestant theology traditionally sees justification and adoption as objective works of God, what Christ does *for* us, and regeneration as a subjective work, what Christ does through the Holy Spirit *in* us. While helpful, this fails to grasp the power of justification and adoption when united with regeneration. When we are gripped by the depths of our depravity and the enormity of our guilt in repentance, then seized by the truth of justification in our hearts, liberating freedom takes hold of us and transforms us. Furthermore, when we know in our soul, not just in our minds, that we are God's children, this new identity liberates us from the lies spoken over us through other names and identities. Justification and adoption, as such, contribute to initial sanctification.

Assurance of salvation. Essential to a Wesleyan-holiness view of redemption is assurance of salvation. We can know we are redeemed children of God through the witness of the Holy Spirit. Christian assurance is grounded in Paul's declaration in Romans 8:16, "For the Spirit bears witness with our spirit that we are the children of God." Paul teaches there are two active participants working together here: God's Spirit and our spirit.

First, God's Spirit is a subjective witness, an "inward impression upon the soul" testifying to the heart that we are God's children, that we are in right relationship with God. We sense all divine condemnation is lifted. The frustration experienced in evangelical repentance is lifted by a profound sense of freedom. This "impression" often brings feelings of joy and abiding peace. It is a gift the Holy Spirit gives, imparting to us humble confidence of our adoption as daughters and sons of the Father.

Second, our spirit joins as an objective witness. In an examination of our heart and lives under the direction of Scripture, we search for evidence of new birth. Most significant is personal victory over the power of sin. While sin may remain "in fragmented forms," its "primal vitality is broken." We will still experience the consequences and effects of sin in life, but it no longer controls us.

We can align our will with the desire to walk supremely in love of God and neighbor.[39]

Another way to describe Christian assurance: it is an inward experience with external qualities, where we work in collaboration with the Holy Spirit. The objective witness helps ensure we do not fall into presumption, mistaking feelings for reality, while the inward witness guards against a "works" oriented righteousness in which we earn our salvation. Neither the external life of a Christian nor internal feelings are the basis of our salvation; they are only a sign of it.

John Wesley's teaching on the subject is helpful. He asserts that the "witness of the Spirit" is the privilege of every believer. All Christians can know they are God's children. Not every believer, however, will have this assurance. It, therefore, is not essential to salvation. He states, "But that, as to the transports of joy that usually attend the beginning of" salvation, "especially in those who have mourned deeply," the Spirit "sometimes giveth, sometimes withholdeth them, according to the counsels of his own will."[40]

In contrast to the Reformed tradition, assurance of salvation in Wesleyan-holiness theology is only a witness to present salvation. Because ultimate salvation in bodily resurrection and final judgment is contingent on continued faith in Christ, certainty about final salvation is unknowable to us. Since saving faith is a gift of grace, grace must sustain and grow it. Through prevenient grace, we can experience increasing sanctification in life by cooperating with divine grace; likewise, we can regress by resisting the Spirit's work. If we develop a posture of defiance to the Spirit's work in our lives, saving faith may diminish to the point of loss and we cease to be partakers in Christ's salvation.

Progressive sanctification beyond new birth. Expressed in the most general terms, sanctification addresses the entire work of

---

[39]Wesley, "The Witness of the Spirit, I," *WJW* 5:111-23; "The Witness of the Spirit, II," *WJW* 5:123-34.

[40]Wesley, "Journals," *WJW* 1:101-3.

transformation by the Holy Spirit in human lives from the moment we are regenerated until we are given glorification in death and bodily resurrection. The ultimate end of the Spirit's work is to restore the full image of God in humanity, making humans like Christ in our formation as persons. When the Spirit takes residence in our lives in new birth, he begins the process of transforming our attitudes, interests, and actions, bringing us into greater union with Christ as the second Adam. This process of inward transformation and outward conformity to Christ's humanity is progressive sanctification.

More specifically, through regeneration, we are set free from the power of sin. We are empowered by the Spirit to walk in obedience to God. Intentional sin and habituated sin are broken.[41] We must be freed from their hold because they pose great spiritual danger. Paul teaches in Romans 6:23 that the consequence of such sin is "death." While many use the apostle's statement here to argue for the equality of sin, that all sin is the same in God's eyes because it has the same punishment, the letter's context reveals otherwise. We see that Paul is speaking to believers. He first encourages them with the truth; they need not sin (Rom 6:1, 15). Then, he speaks more forcefully; they must not sin, because sin leads to death (Rom 6:23). Paul, however, is not talking about sin in general, but a specific type if sin: a deliberate transgression of the known law of God. Intentional sin, therefore, must be addressed early in Christian life. It must be a part of initial sanctification because, if unchecked, it will destroy what the Spirit has birthed in us.

Other types of sin remain in new Christians. They are addressed by the Holy Spirit through progressive sanctification. First, sins of infirmity persist.[42] While they need the atoning work of Christ to absolve, they do not impact our relationship with God because they are not willful. They arise from ignorance, misunderstanding of God's will, and mental limitations. Christians grow as they become

---

[41]Wesley, "The First-Fruits of the Spirit," *WJW* 5:87-97.
[42]Wesley, "The First-Fruits of the Spirit," *WJW* 5:92-97.

more knowledgeable of God's will, grow in wisdom, and bring their lives into greater conformity with Christ's life as they are enabled.

Second, new believers struggle with "sins of surprise," which impact their relationship with God to the degree to which their wills cooperate with them. They are not premeditated or intentional; rather, they arise from a prior decision over which we had some control, such as ungodly anger coming from lack of sleep; from a sudden, unexpected assault from the devil; and from the state of sin that remains, such as selfish defensiveness toward a spouse when confronted with marital problems.[43] While will often plays some role, these sins tend to be spontaneous reactions within Christians. We grow as the Spirit empowers us to habituate behavior that promotes holiness, to become more spiritually sensitive to the schemes of the devil, and to confront involuntary actions rooted in the sinful condition.

In progressive sanctification, the Spirit continues to restore the moral image of God, along with the natural and political image.[44] Together with growth in knowledge of God, ourselves, and the fallen world, we are empowered with better understanding and judgment. The end of the Spirit's work is to free us for formation as persons who truly image the character of Christ in heart and life. This formation turns us outward from ourselves and compels us to give ourselves in love of others. We increasingly take the same posture in the world as Christ—that of a servant.

Repentance of believers. As the Spirit transforms Christians progressively in their attitudes, interests, and actions, he begins confronting us with an internal principle of selfishness and sin, persisting stubbornly in us. Sometimes in powerful conversion experiences, Christians may not initially sense it. The momentum and power of new birth can lead them to believe they are free from inward sin. They sense no rival to the Spirit's reign in them. They

---

[43]Wesley, "The First-Fruits of the Spirit," *WJW* 5:87-92.
[44]Wesley, "The New Birth," *WJW* 6:65-77.

love God with all their "heart, soul, mind and strength" and their neighbor as themselves.[45]

As time passes and their experience subsides, however, sin, once dormant in them, rises to the fore. While they live in obedience to Christ, their heart is divided. Pride and selfishness manifest themselves below the surface. They see more clearly an internal principle contrary to Christ, causing them to stumble into "sins of surprise," making them to leave the God they love. As they begin to struggle against their internal sin, and its outward manifestation, they realize there is little they can do to decisively squelch it. If they are to be delivered from this "state," only Christ can do it.[46]

Frustration builds as Christians experience a disparity between the holiest desires of their heart and what they find their lives to be. They long to love God and neighbor without reservation, yet they recognize within themselves a nature that works to subvert Christ's lordship in them. While they walk in outward conformity in discipleship, they know that complete alignment is lacking within them. They have a divided heart. The greater part desires Christ's kingdom above all else in their lives, while the other part works subversively to assert its selfish rule once again. They turn to Christ to be delivered from the last major stronghold of resistance, clinging to the human heart and will.[47]

Sanctifying faith. As we respond positively to the Holy Spirit's illumination and conviction through repentance, we open ourselves up to grace capable of creating sanctifying faith. The Holy Spirit helps us to see and believe that Christ can liberate us not only from the guilt and power of sin, but from its very condition as well.

Just as we experience new birth through faith, we are entirely sanctified by faith. Like saving faith, sanctifying faith is a divine gift, not a human work. Only when grace comes to create sanctifying

---

[45]Wesley, "The Scripture Way of Salvation," 6:43-54.
[46]Wesley, "The Repentance of Believers," *WJW* 5:156-70.
[47]Wesley, "The Repentance of Believers," *WJW* 5:156-70; "The Scripture Way of Salvation," 6:43-54.

faith, often mediated through the means of grace, can we exercise sanctifying faith. A Christian, as such, cannot be entirely sanctified at any given moment, but only in those times and places in which divine grace imparts sanctifying faith. We must therefore actively seek entire sanctification, to be set free from the condition of sin, in the appointed means of grace, waiting for the Holy Spirit to create this faith in us.

John Wesley describes well the nature of sanctifying faith. First, he says, "it is a divine evidence and conviction" that God promises it in the Scriptures.[48] Not all Christians read the Bible and see the possibility of full salvation in this life. Many believers, even scholars, study the Scriptures and arrive at different conclusions. Only the Holy Spirit can give us eyes to see the promise of heart holiness in it. Faith at this point, however, is only an intellectual apprehension and not enough to sanctify us.

Second, Wesley teaches, "it is a divine evidence and conviction" that God "is able to do" what he has promised.[49] Our faith is taken to a deeper level. The Holy Spirit convinces us that Christ indeed sanctifies people. It is not a work done only in Scripture, only in the past, but it is what Christ does now in Christians. Still, such faith is not yet personal; it only entails a deeper understanding of the truth.

Third, to this belief Wesley adds that the Spirit must convince us that Christ "is able to do it now" in us.[50] We know it is easier to believe that God sanctifies others than to believe he can do it in us. At best, we can believe he perfects us in love over a long process of time, but not in a moment. Sanctifying faith must become deeply personal at this point. The Spirit must speak directly to us, divine person to human, creating faith to believe in Christ to work decisively and swiftly in us.

---

[48]Wesley, "The Scripture Way of Salvation," *WJW* 6:52.
[49]Wesley, "The Scripture Way of Salvation," *WJW* 6:52.
[50]Wesley, "The Scripture Way of Salvation," *WJW* 6:53.

Finally, Wesley states that this "divine evidence and conviction" has one last element: Christ does it now in us.[51] Only the Holy Spirit imparting this truth directly to our heart can empower us to believe a seeming impossibility—a life defined by holy love. Sanctifying faith at the deepest level intuitively recognizes and acknowledges the Holy Spirit's sanctifying work in the moment. At this point, we thankfully embrace sanctifying grace without resistance.

Christian perfection/entire sanctification. Entire sanctification or Christian perfection is when divine grace by faith sets us free *from* the state of sin and sets us free *to* love God with all our being and to love others as ourselves. We are delivered from the internal principle of selfishness and sin, persisting stubbornly in us. In new birth we are set free from sin's guilt and power, but in entire sanctification we are liberated from its condition, releasing us to serve God and others without reservation, fulfilling the two great commandments. We no longer experience division in desire or will. Both operate in harmony, making perfection in love possible. The fruit of the Spirit given in new birth now flourishes in fullness.[52]

Entire sanctification happens in us through the Spirit's complete restoration of the moral image of God. As created in the garden, the moral image enabled us to enjoy true righteousness, holiness, and love in the immediacy of the Spirit's rule within us. It formed the guiding principle of our disposition, thoughts, words, and deeds. Through new birth it is regenerated; through progressive sanctification it develops; and through entire sanctification it exists in wholeness once again. The Spirit reigns supremely through us, rightly ordering our love.[53]

Because of confusion over the language of "entire" and "perfection," Wesleyan-holiness teaching is often misunderstood. To clarify, entire sanctification is not divine perfection. God alone is

---

[51]Wesley, "The Scripture Way of Salvation," *WJW* 6:53.
[52]Collins, *The Theology of John Wesley*, 293-97, 300-302.
[53]Collins, *The Theology of John Wesley*, 293-97, 300-302.

immutable in nature and character. Christian perfection, in contrast, is subject to fluctuation or change, either positive or negative. It can intensify or grow throughout our lives or be corrupted and lost through intentional sin and spiritual neglect. Because grace is necessary to sustain and nourish this perfection, sin's being and power can return if one does not continually depend on and cooperate with the Holy Spirit.

Entire sanctification is also not Adamic or a "sinless" perfection. It is not a perfection of knowledge or wisdom. It is not freedom from mistakes caused by cognitive limitations, nor is it an exemption from temptation or the possibility of intentional sin. Even with the moral image's restoration, the natural and political image remains marred. Clouded reasoning and mistakes in judgment continue, causing sins of infirmity. It is "entire," however, because it fully addresses the most problematic aspects of sin: guilt, power, and condition. We are liberated from every impediment to a relationship with Christ and a life of rightly ordered love.[54]

Assurance of entire sanctification. Christians can know they are genuinely sanctified, perfected in love. Like assurance of new birth, we can know we have been sanctified entirely by the partnership of an objective and subjective witness. The objective testimony of genuine experience, the "witness of our spirit" involves a personal examination of our hearts and actions. Wesleyan theologian and pastor Steve DeNeff's questions here are helpful: Is my conscience clear? Is my religion an obsession or a hobby? Do my closest friends and family see holiness of heart and life in me? Am I able to walk in obedience to God solely out of the love of God and neighbor? Do I love God without reservation? If we cannot answer these questions affirmatively, most likely entire sanctification has not happened.[55]

To the objective witness, the subjective witness of the Holy Spirit is added. In this "inward impression upon the soul," the Holy Spirit

---

[54]Wesley, "Christian Perfection," *WJW* 6:1-22; "On Perfection," *WJW* 5:411-25
[55]Steve DeNeff, *Whatever Became of Holiness?*, 141-50.

testifies to the believer's heart that entire sanctification has happened. So, we may ask, Do I have the witness of the Holy Spirit that entire sanctification is accomplished in my life? Just as we can have "an inward impression upon the soul" that we are a child of God, it is possible to have a similar witness in the experience of entire sanctification.[56]

Ultimately, assurance here is a subjective experience with discernible qualities, where we work in cooperation with the Holy Spirit. The objective witness helps insure we do not fall into presumption, mistaking feelings for reality, while the inward witness guards against a legalistic righteousness, where sanctification is reduced to outward conformity to the law of God. In the end, however, it is possible for Christians to be perfected in love and not have the Spirit's internal witness. Because assurance is personal and not empirically verifiable, its experience is not uniform.

Progressive sanctification beyond Christian perfection is Christian maturity. One of the distinctives of Wesleyan-holiness theology that sets it apart from the larger Wesleyan theological tradition is the belief that entire sanctification is the means to Christian maturity, not the realization of it. We believe perfection in love should happen early in Christian life, not late, as the larger Methodist tradition teaches. It is the normative Christian life, rather than the exception among ordinary believers.

Christian maturity consists of two elements: (1) power with purity and (2) knowledge, wisdom, and understanding. It is possible for a person to be set free from inward and outward sin and perfected in love but not have the wisdom, experience, and knowledge necessary for Christian maturity. At the same time, we cannot become fully mature without the experience of entire sanctification. We can know what to do in each situation but not have the power or rightly ordered love to execute it in a way fitting for spiritual maturity.

---

[56]Keith Drury, *Holiness for Ordinary People* (Indianapolis: Wesleyan, 1983), 89-95.

This maturation process is dependent on divine grace. The sanctified life and its development only happen through continual empowerment by the Holy Spirit. John Wesley compared it to a vine connected to a branch. If the vine is joined with the branch, nourishing sap flows to the vine. It lives and grows. If the vine is severed from the branch, the vine withers and dies. In the same way, we must be connected continually to Christ, continually dependent on Christ for the grace necessary to walk in inward and outward holiness.

The sanctified life is ultimately a dynamic reality intensifying and growing after entire sanctification, leading us to Christian maturity and beyond. More specifically, it involves growth in knowledge of God through study of Scripture, Christian teaching, and spiritual disciplines. This knowledge is not just increase in cognitive understanding about God, but a deeper personal relationship with him. False conceptions and misunderstandings about God formed in our mind and heart through sin increasingly dissipate. We see God more clearly, leading to greater love for him. We also learn more of his will, not just for humanity, but more specifically for us individually. We recognize more fully what holy love entails for us in relationship to God, to others, and to the created order. With the moral image restored in us, we are empowered by the Spirit to bring our will in greater alignment with God's desires as we acquire knowledge.

Transformative self-understanding takes place as well. Through the Holy Spirit's illumination, we identify spiritual, mental, and emotional wounds in our lives, inflicted on us by the sin of others, which cause "sins of infirmity" that impair our relationships. Healing takes place as they are brought into light and forgiveness bestowed. We also become more attuned to the world's distorted messages that play a role in our personal formation. The Holy Spirit makes us aware of the lies we have believed and enables us to reflect the divine image more fully in our own individuated, deeply personal way.

Practical and godly wisdom is learned through experience of trial and error. Our judgment improves. In progressive sanctification, love of God and neighbor intensifies throughout life. Because the natural and political image, however, is never restored fully until death, we inadvertently cause harm. Injury comes from lack of wisdom and understanding, not love. Through the Holy Spirit's work, we learn from our mistakes, seeing more clearly what is needed in each situation. As we mature, we have better clarity in life and greater insight on how to act in love, to bring about true fellowship with others.

Finally, the Holy Spirit gives us gifts and graces with which to serve others and perfect the church. As we grow in maturity, they are sharpened and honed. We are sanctified in order to be liberated from the reign of human self and to be turned outward in love and service to the church and world. Perfection in love propels us to go into the world to share the gospel of Jesus Christ and his reign in human life. The Holy Spirit gives us gifts and abilities to do so. These *charismata* require education and maturation for strengthening and effective use so that we can use them most effectively in love for the benefit of others. The posture of a servant, reflecting Christ, is formed deeply in us as we practice self-denial in service of the kingdom and others.

Glorification is absolute human perfection. As Protestants, we believe that whatever sanctifying work is left undone in a Christian finds completion in physical death. Wesleyan-holiness theology expects the full restoration of the moral image as part of the normative Christian life. The natural and political image, however, while progressively renewed through sanctification, is not completed until death.

At physical death, our souls experience "paradise," the intermediate state of the righteous, the "ante-chamber" of heaven, awaiting the day of bodily resurrection at Christ's second coming. There, as John Wesley describes, our "physical" sense of sight and hearing are heightened; memory and understanding are freed from the limitations of the fallen world; will and affections are made incorruptible; new senses are given to perceive the imperceptible in the created order; and continued growth in knowledge and love occurs in the presence of God. We enjoy the "intermediate" expressions of our full destiny.[57]

While we are ushered into God's presence, it is still a state of physical death, where sin and Satan have the last word over our lives. Physical death remains the consequence of sin. While our soul is saved, our body is not. We exist apart from our bodies, which makes us only partially and not fully human. The Father's redemptive work in the Son through the Holy Spirit is incomplete. To be fully human in "the life everlasting" means we must experience bodily resurrection as Jesus did. The Holy Spirit must raise us to incorruptible life at Christ's second coming. When this happens, sin's last curse will be defeated. The intermediate heaven will transition to a final heaven, the "new creation."[58]

In the new creation, we will share fully in God's glory as the *imago Dei*. We, along with the rest of the transformed created order, will be brought into full union with God—Father, Son, and Holy Spirit. Ultimate union with God anticipated in Genesis, described in Revelation, is realized. We will experience true liberty—thinking and acting only in accordance with holy love of God, others, and creation, truly living to the glory of God. As actualized persons, we will reflect divine goodness in the "life everlasting" in a different and individuated way. Thomas Oden writes in this regard, "Though each individual shares in the same salvation, the refracted glory will not be monotone, but varied."[59] Glorification will not be static. Humanity's physical, intellectual, rational, social, and spiritual abilities will transcend what was experienced in Adamic perfection and be directed to the everlasting love of God, others, and creation. We will know absolute human perfection through union with the divine. All praise be to God—Father, Son, and Holy Spirit.

---

[57]Wesley, "On Faith," 6-7.
[58]Wesley, "The New Creation," *WJW* 5:288-96.
[59]Oden, *Classic Christianity*, 838.

Conclusion

In summary, through the redemptive work of the Father, through the Son, in the Holy Spirit, we can experience Christian perfection in this life. Through justification we are absolved of the guilt of sin, and through regeneration, in which the moral image of God is partially restored, we are liberated from the power of sin. We are set free from sin as an act, so that we are empowered to walk in obedience to God. Through Christian perfection, the moral image is completely renewed in us, setting us free from the condition of sin. As we continue to mature in perfecting grace, the natural and political image experience ongoing transformation, enabling us to address more adequately the infirmity of sin. Finally, in glorification, the full image of God is redeemed, and we realize absolute human perfection, becoming fully like God through participation in his life.

12

THE WHEN AND HOW
OF HOLINESS

WESLEYANS DO NOT THINK uniformly about Christian perfection.[1] While we share common theological language and concepts, diverse perspectives exist. The purpose here is to explore crucial differences in the Wesleyan understanding of Christian perfection, also called entire sanctification, based on 1 Thessalonians 5:23 ("May the God of peace himself *sanctify* you *entirely*," NRSV; emphasis added). We will begin by outlining the three major Wesleyan positions on Christian perfection and then argue for the strength of one of them.

THE THREE MAJOR POSITIONS ON CHRISTIAN
PERFECTION IN THE WESLEYAN TRADITION

Expressed in the most general terms, sanctification addresses the entire work of transformation in human lives by the Holy Spirit from the moment individuals are born again until they are glorified in death. The ultimate end of the Spirit's work is to restore the full

---

[1]This section is adapted from Christopher T. Bounds, "What Is the Range of Current Teaching on Sanctification and What Ought a Wesleyan to Believe on this Doctrine?," *The Asbury Journal* 62 (2007): 33-53.

image of God in humanity, making humanity like Christ, thereby glorifying God in creation.

When the Spirit takes residence in humans, he begins to transform our attitudes, interests, and actions, while confronting the internal principle of selfishness and sin that stubbornly persists in us. This is often called "initial" and "progressive" sanctification. While this principle may be described in different ways, there is a consensus among Wesleyans that the Spirit can conquer this condition and enable believers to love God entirely, to live in complete obedience to his revealed will, and to serve others in love.[2] Within the Wesleyan tradition, this work of the Spirit has been called "Christian perfection," "perfect love," "baptism of the Holy Spirit," "entire sanctification," and "fullness of the Spirit." The work of sanctification does not end here. Over time, as Christians continue to submit to the Spirit, their love deepens, and their knowledge and understanding of God's will increase, thereby bringing them into greater conformity with Christ until they reach "final sanctification" in the moment of glorification.

Wesleyans generally agree on "what" Christian perfection is, albeit with some important nuances. Major disagreements, however, arise in answering the question of "how" a believer experiences it in life. These nuances in understanding and differences on means have led to three major positions on Christian perfection in the Wesleyan tradition.

The "shorter way"—Christian perfection now by total consecration and faith. The most optimistic view on holiness teaches that believers can experience Christian perfection now, in the present

---

[2]There are a number of ways the deliverance from inward sin has been described in the Wesleyan tradition: an "eradication of the sin nature," a "cleansing from inward sin," "freedom from all inward rebellion," "the full restoration of the moral image of God," "the removal of the principle of sin," etc. Regardless of how it has been described, the Wesleyan tradition has taught that Christians can be freed from the inner propensity to sin, the drive to assert personal will, and the desire against God's will. As such, the Christian can be freed from the constant struggle between "the flesh" and "the Spirit," where the basic orientation of the Christian's life is obedience to and love of God.

moment, through an act of entire consecration and faith, whereby believers surrender their lives to the lordship of Christ and trust God to purify and empower them. Christian perfection is a simple synergism in which the work of consecration and faith by a Christian is met immediately with deliverance from the inner propensity to sin by the Holy Spirit.

J. A. Wood, in the American holiness classic *Perfect Love*, illustrates this perspective in his instructions on the exercise of faith necessary to appropriate entire sanctification. To be perfected in love, he states that we must (1) believe that God has promised it in the Scriptures; (2) believe that what God has promised, God is able to do; (3) believe that God is willing to do it; (4) and believe that God has done it in us. He then asks, "Are you now committing all, trusting in Christ? If you are, it is done."[3]

What makes this position unique in the larger Wesleyan tradition is its understanding of Christians' ability to consecrate themselves and to exercise faith. Every believer has an inherent power, either as a gift of prevenient grace, regenerating grace, or as an uncorrupted part of the moral image, to do the grace-enabled human work required in the experience of Christian perfection.[4] From the moment of conversion any Christian can appropriate perfection. Because the Holy Spirit is always ready to respond to a personal act of consecration and faith, ignorance on the part of a believer, an unwillingness to surrender fully to the Lord, or a lack of will to believe become the root causes for not experiencing entire sanctification.

This teaching makes a distinction between Christian perfection and spiritual maturity. It is possible for a person to be set free from inward and outward sin and perfected in love but not to have the

---

[3]John Allen Wood, *Perfect Love*, 87-88.
[4]Charles Finney is an example of a holiness evangelist in the nineteenth century who denied original sin and taught that this power to exercise faith is naturally inherent in each person apart from grace.

wisdom, experience, and knowledge necessary for Christian maturity. In other words, one can be fully renewed in the moral image of God yet lack significant restoration of the natural and political image. Yet, a Christian cannot become fully mature without the experience of entire sanctification. A believer can know what to do in each situation but not have the power or proper motivation to execute it in a way fitting for spiritual maturity. Holiness is ultimately a dynamic experience that intensifies and grows throughout the life of a Christian, continuing beyond Christian perfection and enabling us to address more fully sins of infirmity in life.

Traditionally, this view has been termed the "shorter way" for its emphasis on the immediacy of the experience of Christian perfection; one does not have to wait any significant length of time to experience it after conversion. Primarily associated with the teaching of Phoebe Palmer and the holiness movement, this position can be seen in Allan Brown's "How to Be Entirely Sanctified in Four Easy Steps." It is a possible interpretation of the Church of the Nazarene's Articles of Faith and seems to be implied by the expectation of Christian perfection for those seeking ordination. Nazarenes require all their ordained ministers to testify to the experience of entire sanctification.[5]

The "middle way"—Christian perfection by seeking until you receive. The next view on holiness in the Wesleyan tradition affirms with the "shorter way" that entire sanctification is realized in a Christian's life through personal consecration and faith. Also like the "shorter way," it makes a distinction between Christian perfection and spiritual maturity. Perfection is what

---

[5]Allan P. Brown, "How to Be Entirely Sanctified in Four Easy Steps," *God's Revivalist*, September 2012, 1-4; "Article of Faith VII: Prevenient Grace," in *Manual of the Church of the Nazarene 2017–2021* (Kansas City, MO: Nazarene), ¶ 7. A close reading of this article indicates that the prevenient grace given to all of humanity empowers a person to exercise saving faith, needing no additional grace, making possible the exercise of faith for salvation an inherent power within an individual. If this is true for conversion, it would appear to be true for entire sanctification as well. See also ¶ 502.2 which stipulates all Nazarene ministers "must have peace with God through our Lord Jesus Christ, and be sanctified wholly. . ."

makes growth toward spiritual maturity optimal. However, unlike the "shorter way," it does not believe that faith necessary to appropriate Christian perfection is a power inherent at any given moment in a believer's life. Rather, sanctifying faith is seen as a gift of grace, a grace with which a Christian can choose to cooperate or not. The grace capable of creating this faith is more than what one receives at conversion.

John Wesley's teaching on levels or degrees of grace and faith is at the heart of this holiness teaching. Wesley taught that a person is totally dependent on God's grace for the work of salvation. At each stage or level of progression in the way of salvation, more grace is needed to move forward. For example, Wesley taught that prevenient grace given to every person enables a person to respond to grace, but that prevenient grace does not have within itself the power to exercise faith to appropriate the new birth. God must give more grace beyond prevenient grace to create the possibility of saving faith. This grace is communicated through the various means of grace, most notably through the preaching of the gospel, but also through other "instituted" and "prudential" means, such as prayer, Bible reading, fasting, and holy Communion. Through participation in these means of grace, saving faith can be communicated, with which a person can choose to cooperate or not. In the same way, to the grace made available at conversion, more grace must be added in order to make possible the creation of faith necessary for salvation and sanctification.[6]

From this perspective, believers actively seek Christian perfection, availing themselves of the various means of grace, waiting for God's grace capable of creating faith to appropriate it. Thus, a person cannot be entirely sanctified at any given moment, but only in those times and places in which God's grace is being made available that can create such faith. For example, while Wesley describes faith that

---

[6]Wesley, "The Means of Grace," *WJW* 5:185-201.

sanctifies entirely as a trust that "God hath promised it in the Holy Scripture," that "God is able to perform" it, that "He is able and willing to do it now," and "that He doeth it," he makes clear that it is "a divine evidence and conviction"; it is a faith that God creates and enables through the means of grace.[7]

To be clear, the "middle way" teaches that a person can be sanctified in the moment a believer asks for it. It can happen immediately, or over a shorter or longer period. The premium here is placed on God's timing. From this perspective, we cannot determine how God wants to move in any given moment; we can only either cooperate with or resist what God is doing. Among the various Wesleyan models, this teaching may be called the "middle way," rejecting the simplicity of the "shorter way," while refusing to succumb to the arduous nature of the "longer way," addressed below. The "middle way" is seen in John Wesley's "The Scripture Way of Salvation," in Steve DeNeff's *Whatever Became of Holiness?*, and can also be argued as a possible position taken in The Wesleyan Church's Articles of Religion, but more particularly with its candidates for ordination.[8]

The "longer way"—Christian perfection by a long process of continual growth. In contrast to the previous two positions, the third Wesleyan view on holiness emphasizes that Christian perfection is realized most often in a believer's life after a long journey of dying to self, following many years of spiritual development. There will be some Christians who will realize entire sanctification in the present

---

[7]Wesley, "The Scripture Way of Salvation," *WJW* 6:43-54.

[8]Wesley, "The Scripture Way of Salvation," *WJW* 6:43-54; Steve DeNeff, *Whatever Became of Holiness?* (Indianapolis: Wesleyan, 1996), 125-37; "Article of Religion XIV: Sanctification: Initial, Progressive, Entire," in *The Discipline of the Wesleyan Church 2000*, ¶ 238. A close reading of this article affirms a progressive sanctification leading to the experience of entire sanctification. Progressive sanctification is described as a daily growing in grace. While not explicitly stated, this growing in grace may indicate the need for more grace to be added to the grace given in conversion for a believer to fully surrender to Christ and exercise faith to appropriate entire sanctification, pointing to the "middle way." The Wesleyan Church's middle way approach is clearly seen in ¶ 5566, where candidates for covenant membership are asked, "Have you the assurance that you have experienced the deeper grace of heart cleansing? If not, do you propose to diligently seek this grace?"

life, but most will not experience it until just before death or at the point of death. A belief in the persistence and stubbornness of original sin forms the heart of the doctrine. This recalcitrance can only be overcome gradually over a lifetime through significant growth in grace, personal denial, and spiritual development.

The analogy of a slow death is one of the most well-known descriptions of this view, an analogy that emphasizes the complementary nature of process with an instantaneous moment. In a slow death, there is a long process leading to the point of death, often a painful and arduous process. Nevertheless, there is a point at which a person dies. While this view does not deny the possibility of a short process and early death, or the exercise of personal faith in appropriating entire sanctification, its focus is on the long progression. While the moment in which a Christian dies completely to self is always the goal in the present life, the process leading to the goal takes preeminence.

Furthermore, while there are exceptions, many who adhere to this doctrine of holiness equate Christian perfection with spiritual maturity or closely link them. John Wesley's high view of Christian perfection comes to the fore, a perfection in which a believer has "the mind of Christ" in speech, saying what Christ would say, and in action, doing what Christ would do.[9] The movement toward this state of perfection can only be brought about by growth in grace, knowledge, wisdom, experience, and the practice of spiritual disciplines. As such, entire sanctification is not really seen as a possibility for new converts but only for those who have diligently followed Christ for many years.

In the Wesleyan tradition this view has been called the "longer way," because of its focus on an extended process in the realization

---

[9]Wesley, "The Character of a Methodist," *WJW* 8:341-44. If a Wesleyan holds to this as a definition of entire sanctification, the person must realize that this goes beyond the common understanding of entire sanctification as defined here. It must also be noted that Wesley at times defines Christian perfection in ways that encompass Christian maturity and at other times in ways that do not.

of Christian perfection. The "longer way" is described and embraced in John Wesley's more pessimistic writings, such as "Brief Thoughts on Christian Perfection," where he states, "As to the time, I believe this instant generally is the instant of death, the moment before the soul leaves the body. . . . I believe it is usually many years after justification."[10] Denominationally, this position represents the United Methodist tradition and expectation for people seeking ordination, where they are asked, "Are you going on to perfection?" and "Do you expect to be made perfect in love in this life?" The expectation is that no one at the time of ordination can testify to the experience of entire sanctification.

THE EXERCISE OF FAITH IN THE EXPERIENCE OF CHRISTIAN PERFECTION: TWO CONTRASTING PARADIGMS

The relationship between divine grace and personal faith in Christian perfection is one defining difference among Wesleyans. All Wesleyan traditions in their doctrinal statements affirm salvation "by grace through faith." A question arises: "Is faith primarily a gift of grace, or a power residing in humanity through prevenient grace or the human will?" Stated differently: Is the faith that saves and sanctifies principally a human work or a gift of divine grace? Do we have the power within ourselves "to believe" at any given moment, or must God impart it to us?

How Wesleyans answer these questions determines our conception of salvation and influences how we understand the experience of new birth and, more importantly for our discussion, Christian perfection. It guides, in turn, what counsel is given on the experience of Christian perfection. Theologically, Wesleyans adhere

---

[10]Thomas C. Oden, *Life in the Spirit*, vol. 3, *Systematic Theology* (San Francisco: HarperSanFrancisco, 1992), 226-57; Randy Maddox, *Responsible Grace: John Wesley's Practical Theology* (Nashville: Kingswood, 1994), 176-90, 201-15; Wesley, "Brief Thoughts on Christian Perfection," *WJW* 11:446. In these thoughts, Wesley states, "As to the time, I believe this instant generally is the instant of death, the moment before the soul leaves the body. But I believe it may be ten, twenty, or forty years before. I believe it is usually many years after justification; but that it may be within five years or five months after it, I know no conclusive argument to the contrary."

to two contrasting paradigms, determined by (1) their respective understandings of original sin and (2) the relationship between divine grace and human action. Historically, these differences are rooted in the Pelagian-Augustinian debates over the centuries of the church and the various nuanced positions that have developed from them.[11]

Christian perfection when we decide. The first paradigm focuses on immediate experience. We can exercise sanctifying faith at any moment we decide. The moment of entire sanctification is determined largely by us. Wesleyans ground their understanding here in either the image of God in humanity, in its remaining vestiges, or in a robust view of prevenient grace.

To begin, a small minority of Wesleyans reject the doctrine of original sin and hold to a form of Pelagianism. They argue that people are born into this life like Adam and Eve before the fall in the garden. This aligns them with Pelagianism. What sets them apart is their belief that humanity inevitably sins, as Adam and Eve did, and requires the application of Christ's atoning work to their lives. They teach that humanity retains the free will enjoyed by our first parents in the garden or one similar to it. Therefore, people have the internal resources within themselves to begin to move toward God, repent, and exercise faith to believe the Gospel. They believe as human beings we have an inherent ability to see the truth of the Gospel and act accordingly. The same holds true for Christian perfection. Once understanding comes of the truth of entire sanctification, we have the power to meet the conditions necessary to experience it.[12]

---

[11]The four major historical positions from the most optimistic view of humanity in the work of salvation to the most pessimistic are (1) Pelagianism, (2) semi-Pelagianism, (3) semi-Augustinianism, and (4) Augustinianism. There also exist important differences and nuances among these major positions. For a more detailed and extensive discussion of these contrasting paradigms, see Christopher T. Bounds, "How Are People Saved? The Major Views of Salvation with a focus on Wesleyan Perspectives and Their Implications," *Wesley and Methodist Studies* 3 (2011): 31-54.

[12]Charles G. Finney represents this view. See Finney, *Systematic Theology* (Minneapolis: Bethany House, 1976), lectures 35 and 55.

Another minor group of semi-Pelagian Wesleyans acknowledge original sin and its impact on us. Semi-Pelagians believe every person arrives at birth with a propensity to rebellion, disobedience, and selfishness, contributing to human sinfulness. We nevertheless retain vestiges of the moral image of God and the ability to will the good. We have some measure of free will to contribute to salvation's work. It remains in our power to recognize our alienation from God because of sin and to turn to Christ for salvation. The same is true for the experience of Christian perfection. Believers have the power to exercise sanctifying faith once they have knowledge of it.[13]

Finally, many Wesleyans are semi-Augustinian. They acknowledge "total depravity" and the state of "natural humanity" as spiritually dead to God, thoroughly corrupt, and dependent on God's initiative in the work of salvation. They teach that God has taken that initiative through prevenient grace given to all. However, in sharp contrast to John Wesley's teaching, they hold to an expansive, robust view of prevenient grace. They have softened Wesley's strong semi-Augustinian theology. Prevenient grace given to every person makes repentance and faith operative within every person. As such, we have the ability in any given moment to believe the truth of the gospel and appropriate salvation. These "soft" semi-Augustinian Wesleyans also believe we have the power to determine the moment of Christian perfection once we have adequate knowledge of what it is and how it is experienced.[14]

Regardless of differences, each of these Wesleyan understandings believe that we can hear the message of Christian perfection, weigh

---

[13]Nazarene theologian A. M. Hills is an example of this view. See A. M. Hills, *Fundamental Christian Theology: A Systematic Theology*, 2 vols. (Pasadena, CA: C. J. Kinne, 1931), 2:179-80.

[14]Examples of Wesleyan theologians holding to a soft semi-Augustinian theology include Daniel D. Whedon, "Doctrines of Methodism," in *Essays, Reviews and Discourses* (New York: Phillip and Hunt, 1887), 110. See also "Article of Faith VII: Prevenient Grace," in the *Manual of The Church of the Nazarene 2005-2009* (Kansas City, MO: Nazarene), which states, "But we also believe that the grace of God through Jesus Christ is freely bestowed upon all people, enabling all who will to turn from sin to righteousness, believe on Jesus Christ for pardon and cleansing from sin, and follow good works pleasing and acceptable in His sight" (33).

the strengths and weaknesses of its arguments, decide to believe in the fullness of salvation expressed in teaching on entire sanctification, exercise sanctifying faith in Jesus Christ, and be sanctified. Our act of faith is principally what we do. We can experience entire sanctification at any moment we decide because we have the power to appropriate the fullness of Christ's redemptive work through faith.

This Wesleyan model places emphasis on human initiative in one way or the other. God does not determine when people are entirely sanctified; it rests entirely on us. Once knowledge comes, the door to Christian perfection is before us, and we can decide to go through it at any time. The Holy Spirit then imparts entire sanctification. This human-divine synergism pervades evangelical Wesleyan churches in general and Wesleyan-holiness denominations in particular. While hopeful because it promises an immediate experience, it leads people to think they can have Christian perfection when they decide.

Christian perfection by seeking until God decides. The second paradigm focuses on seeking Christ for grace until the Holy Spirit imparts sanctifying faith. In contrast to the first model, Wesleyans here teach that actions attributed to us in salvation are not inherent powers; rather, they are gifts of grace. When God gives grace to repent, and when God bestows grace to believe, only then is Christian perfection possible. Through prevenient grace granted to all, humanity can receive God's grace and choose to embrace or resist it. We play a role in what happens with grace in our lives once given, but we cannot determine it.

Until God moves to bring awareness, repentance, and sanctifying faith, Christian perfection cannot happen. People, therefore, who have been awakened to the "sin that remains after new birth" and desire entire sanctification must seek God for grace in the appointed means of grace, until God moves to make it happen. The testimonies to entire sanctification found in John Wesley's *Arminian Magazine* illustrate this model well. In testimonies of entire sanctification people had to wait an average of six years between the time they began to ask God for entire sanctification and the experience of it.[15] Some had shorter periods, while others had longer.

At the heart of this second Wesleyan model is a particular understanding of grace. Unless the Spirit is working in a way that makes entire sanctification possible, people cannot experience it. Only in moments in which the Holy Spirit enables sanctifying faith are people entirely sanctified. This model, therefore, places the premium on the divine initiative. God ultimately determines when people can be entirely sanctified. Then, and only then, can people decide whether they want to submit to or resist the grace God makes available. God opens and closes the doors of opportunity to experience entire sanctification, and humanity chooses whether to go through the doors or not. Humanity, however, cannot go through the door if it is not opened by God.

This is a divine-human synergism and the full expression of Wesley's full semi-Augustinianism, which has a more limited view of prevenient grace. While contemporary Wesleyan theologians express a clear semi-Augustinian view of salvation, their discussions of the implications of this theology have been shallow or absent, leading to the preeminence of the first paradigm today.[16] As a result, the Wesleyan paradigm for the experience of Christian perfection is missing in Wesleyan churches, and one of the key insights of Wesleyan theology has a diminished voice in contemporary Christianity.

A Neo-Holiness "Middle Way" Understanding of Christian Perfection

At the heart of John Wesley's theology is the doctrine of Christian perfection or entire sanctification.[17] Wesley believed that there is a

---

[15]Mark Horton, "Research on Revival," *The Arminian Magazine* 21, no. 2 (2003): 11-13.

[16]See H. Ray Dunning, *Grace, Faith and Holiness: A Wesleyan Systematic Theology* (Kansas City, MO: Beacon Hill, 1988), 431, 439-41; J. Kenneth Grider, *A Wesleyan-Holiness Theology* (Kansas City, MO: Beacon Hill, 1994), 351-55, 362-65, 405-8; Kenneth J. Collins, *The Theology of John Wesley: Holy Love and the Shape of Grace* (Nashville: Abingdon, 2007), 14-15, 73-82.

[17]John Wesley famously called Christian perfection "the grand depositum which God has lodged with the people called Methodists; and for the sake of propagating this chiefly He appeared to have raised us up" (*WJW* 13:9).

work of divine grace available to all that can liberate human life from the guilt, power, and being of sin, empowering a Christian to fulfill the two greatest commandments. Through God's justifying grace, sin is forgiven. Through God's regenerating and sanctifying grace, bondage to sin is broken, enabling believers to walk in obedience to the known will of God, and the "propensity toward sinning" is corrected, making the love of God and neighbor the natural response of human hearts.

John Wesley left little ambiguity about *what* entire sanctification is. His theological heirs have embraced almost universally Wesley's definition. This can be seen in the Articles of Religion and Confessions of Faith of Wesleyan denominations and in the theological treatises and texts written by Wesleyan theologians.[18] However, because Wesley and the eighteenth-century Methodist revival wavered in their understanding of *when* Christian perfection takes place in life, their heirs followed in one of two basic trajectories: the more optimistic "shorter way" or the more pessimistic "longer way."[19]

No place better expresses John Wesley's equivocation here than his sermon "The Scripture Way of Salvation" and his "Brief Thoughts on Perfection," a brief addendum to *A Plain Account of Christian Perfection*. In his sermon, Wesley concludes a discussion of Christian perfection with a confident exhortation to experience it in the present moment:

> But you shall not be disappointed of your hope: it will come, and will not tarry. Look for it then every day, every hour, every moment! Why not this hour, this moment? Certainly you may look for it now, if you believe it is by faith . . . expect it by faith; expect it as you are; and

---

[18]For an example in a Wesleyan denomination, see "Article of Religion XIV: Sanctification: Initial, Progressive, Entire," in *The Discipline of the Wesleyan Church 2000* (Indianapolis: Wesleyan, 2000), ¶ 238. For an examples of Wesleyan theologians, see Grider, *A Wesleyan-Holiness Theology*, 367-468; Oden, *Life in the Spirit*, 226-57. For examples of popular Wesleyan writers, see DeNeff, *Whatever Became of Holiness?*, 125-37; Keith Drury, *Holiness for Ordinary People* (Indianapolis: Wesleyan, 1983), 71-88.

[19]These two different views about the timing of entire sanctification in Wesley establish one of the distinguishing marks between Wesleyan denominations.

expect it now! . . . Do you believe we are sanctified by faith? Be true then to your principle; and look for this blessing just as you are, neither better nor worse; as a poor sinner that has still nothing to pay, nothing to plead, but "Christ died." And if you look for it as you are, then expect it now.[20]

However, "Brief Thoughts on Perfection" gives a striking contrast. Wesley portrays the typical experience of entire sanctification as the culminating experience in a long process of gradual growth, taking place in most Christians just before the moment of death. He states, "As to the time, I believe this instant generally is the instant of death, the moment before the soul leaves the body. But I believe it may be ten, twenty, or forty years before. [However], I believe it is usually many years after justification."[21]

Denominations generally following Wesley's "longer way" include the United Methodist Church, the British Methodist Church, and the African Methodist Episcopal Church. Churches traditionally championing the "shorter way" include the Wesleyan Church, the Free Methodist Church, the Church of the Nazarene, the Churches of Christ in Christian Union, and the Salvation Army.[22]

---

[20]Wesley, "The Scripture Way of Salvation," *WJW* 6:53.

[21]Wesley, "Brief Thoughts on Perfection," *WJW* 11:446.

[22]One of the clear ways to distinguish between denominations holding the "longer" and "shorter" ways is to examine the questions asked of ministerial candidates. Churches holding to the "longer way" ask the historic question John Wesley posed to his preachers, "Do you expect to be made perfect in this life?" The assumption is that candidates have not realized it yet but would expect to do so before death. In contrast, denominations holding to the "shorter way" require their prospective ministers either to testify to the experience of entire sanctification for ordination or ask their candidates, "Have you been entirely sanctified?" The expectation is that ministers have already experienced Christian perfection or are near it.

For examples of the "longer way," see the doctrinal statements on sanctification from The United Methodist Church, *The Book of Discipline of The United Methodist Church 2004* (Nashville: Abingdon, 2004); The British Methodist Church, *The Constitutional Practice and Discipline of the Methodist Church 2012: Volume 2* (Peterborough, UK: Methodist, 2012); The African Methodist Episcopal Church, *The Doctrines and Discipline of the African Methodist Episcopal Church 2008* (Nashville: AMEC Sunday School Union, 2009).

For examples of the "shorter way," see the doctrinal statements on sanctification from *The Salvation Army Handbook of Doctrine 2010* (London: Salvation, 2010); *Manual of The Church of the Nazarene 2009-2013* (Kansas City, MO: Nazarene, 2013); *The Free Methodist Church of North America 2007 Book of Discipline* (Indianapolis: Free Methodist, 2007); *What We Teach: A Summary of the Doctrine of the Churches of Christ in Christian Union* (Circleville, OH: Advocate, 1974).

Historically, the latter bodies are called "holiness" denominations because their appropriation of Wesley's "shorter way" theology was forged in the nineteenth-century American holiness movement. Through revivals, camp meetings, accountability groups, hymnody, and print media, they made the doctrine and experience of Christian perfection accessible to the common masses across the United States and the world.[23] The holiness movement's message of the "shorter way," however, has fallen on hard times and is almost totally eclipsed in Wesleyan circles today by the "longer way."[24] Theologically, there is much to embrace in the holiness movement's "shorter way," but there are also some glaring problems in need of correction.

Advantages of the holiness movement's "shorter way" over the "longer way." There are important differences and modifications in thought that set apart the American holiness movement's teaching from its sibling. First, Holiness theology believes that an entirely sanctified life is the normative Christian experience. While the "longer way" believes every Christian should experience perfection in this life, most will not until death or just before death. Yes, there will be a few believers who walk in perfection long before death, but this is the exception rather than the rule. The general expectation is to see it as the culmination of a long process of gradual sanctification. Focus is placed on a life that is slowly dying to sin.[25] In contrast, the "shorter way" believes freedom from the power and condition of sin should typify the basic life of every Christian. Entire

---

[23]For historical treatments and descriptions of the American holiness movement's substantial influence in society and the church in the nineteenth century, see Melvin Dieter, *The Holiness Revival of the Nineteenth Century* (Lanham, MD: Scarecrow, 1996); and Timothy L. Smith, *Revivalism and Social Reform: American Protestantism on the Eve of the Civil War* (Nashville: Abingdon, 1957).

[24]See Keith Drury's famous address to the Christian Holiness Partnership, "The Holiness Movement Is Dead," in *Counterpoint: Dialogue with Drury on the Holiness Movement,* ed. Larry D. Smith (Salem, OH: Schmul, 2005), 17-27.

[25]For examples, see United Methodist theologian Stephen Long's discussion of this "longer way" issue in *Keeping Faith: An Ecumenical Commentary on the Articles of Religion and Confession of Faith in the Wesleyan Tradition* (Eugene, OR: Cascade, 2013), 73-84; Maddox, *Responsible Grace,* 176-90, 201-15.

sanctification is an experience that should happen soon after becoming a Christian, not after a decades-long process of growth.[26]

Second and closely connected, holiness theology makes a clear distinction between entire sanctification and Christian maturity. It is possible for a person to be set free from inward and outward sin and perfected in love but not to have the knowledge, wisdom, and experience necessary for Christian maturity. Yet a Christian cannot become fully mature without the experience of entire sanctification. A believer may know what to do in each situation but not have the power or purity of heart to execute it in a way fitting with spiritual maturity. Holiness theology understands that Christian perfection sets the foundation and enables the movement toward Christian maturity.[27] By contrast, the "longer way" often conflates entire sanctification and maturity, seeing perfection as the ultimate expression of Christian maturity. John Wesley's high view of Christian perfection comes to the fore, a perfection in which a believer has "the mind of Christ" in thought, speech, and action—thinking, speaking, and doing only as Christ would.[28]

Third, while the "shorter way" and the "longer way" share the same definitions of entire sanctification, they nuance their respective understandings of (1) salvation from sin's condition and (2) perfection in love. The "longer way" has the tendency to raise its understanding of perfection, while the "shorter way" lowers it. The "longer way" sees perfected Christians as always joyful, always giving thanks, and always loving to the full extent to which they can love.[29]

On the other hand, the holiness tradition's bias is to recognize limitations in the experience of perfect love at times. People who

---

[26]See Phoebe Palmer, *The Way of Holiness* (New York: Piercy and Reed, 1843), pref., 10-14; and Daniel Steele, *Love Enthroned: Essays on Evangelical Perfection* (New York: Richard Dickerson, 1883), 55-70, 352-63.

[27]For examples, see Donald S. Metz, *Studies in Biblical Holiness* (Kansas City, MO: Beacon Hill, 1971), 238-39; J. A. Wood's *Purity and Maturity* (Chicago: Christian Witness, 1913), 180; and Phoebe Palmer, *The Way of Holiness*, 32-48.

[28]See United Methodist theologian Stephen Rankin, *Aiming at Maturity: The Goal of the Christian Life* (Eugene, OR: Cascade, 2011), 48-60; Wesley, "The Character of a Methodist," *WJW* 8:341-44.

[29]The classic expression of this view is Wesley, "The Character of a Methodist," *WJW* 8:341-44.

have been entirely sanctified may have love as the natural reigning disposition of their hearts, and yet love may not always be actualized fully in their lives. They may not always love God to the full extent of their "heart, soul, mind, and strength" and may not always love their neighbors with their complete capacity. While the fruit of the Holy Spirit is abundantly manifested in their lives, there may be fluctuation in expression. These limitations have several possible causes: ignorance (lack of self-awareness regarding cultural bias), physical limitations (lack of sleep, food), emotional trauma (due to poor modeling of love), and so on.[30]

Fourth, what the "longer way" makes implicit in its teaching on Christian perfection, the holiness tradition makes explicit: empowerment for ministry. One of the few distinctive differences between Articles of Religion and Confessions of Faith in the American holiness and "longer way" traditions is that the "shorter way" denominations have added a specific statement on ministry empowerment.[31] When a Christian's heart has been perfected in love, then obedience to God and loving neighbor become the normal response. Christians no longer must "force themselves" to evangelize the lost or reach out in service to people in need. Spirit-infused love for neighbor naturally compels and enables witness and service, even in the most difficult and trying of circumstances. While "longer way" theology would agree, it has not focused on this benefit as much as the holiness tradition.[32]

Finally, the "longer way" often leads to a practical problem: If Christians must wait a lifetime before they can hope to be entirely

---

[30]See Grider, *A Wesleyan-Holiness Theology*, 464-68; Metz, *Studies in Biblical Holiness*, 221-43; John N. Oswalt, *Called to Be Holy: A Biblical Perspective* (Nappanee, IN: Francis Asbury, 1999), 185-200. In this regard, the American holiness movement's understanding is closer to Thomas Aquinas' definition of Christian perfection. See Aquinas, *Summa Theologiae*, 2a-2ae, Q. 184.

[31]See Article of Religion XIV: "Sanctification: Initial, Progressive, Entire," in *The Discipline of the Wesleyan Church 2000*, ¶ 238; Grider, *A Wesleyan-Holiness Theology*, 388.

[32]See The United Methodist Church's Confession of Faith on "Sanctification and Christian Perfection" in *The Book of Discipline of The United Methodist Church 2012*, ¶ 104.

sanctified, they have little expectation for the power and condition of sin to be broken in their foreseeable future. There is an increased temptation to acquiesce to a life in which they try to manage their sins and become satisfied. The "shorter way," however, when it has been expressed well, leads to expectation and earnest seeking, confident that the holiest longings of the human heart can be realized in life, sooner rather than later.

In the end, these are strengths only if they comport with the gospel of Jesus Christ. Obviously, many inside and outside of the Wesleyan tradition would question whether they do. Skeptical Wesleyans, however, should note that the "shorter way's" nuanced understanding of entire sanctification as the normative Christian life captures well historic Wesleyan exegesis of Matthew 5–7, Romans 6–8, Galatians 5, and 1 John.[33] Those outside the Wesleyan tradition, who may see the "shorter way" as novel and outside the bounds of historic Christianity, would do well to recall that the "shorter way" resonates with the earliest post-New Testament view of Christian perfection found in the ante-Nicene church (the apostolic fathers, Irenaeus, and Origen) and in later Greek and Latin fathers from the fourth and fifth centuries.[34] Furthermore, the holiness movement's basic understanding of entire sanctification echoes Thomas Aquinas' teaching on the type of Christian perfection every believer should expect to experience in the present life. He states that it is a removal of "whatever hinders the mind's affections from tending wholly to God."[35]

---

[33]For an example of early Wesleyan exegesis of these passages, see Wesley, *Explanatory Notes on the New Testament*; and Adam Clarke's *Commentary on the Whole Bible*, 6 vols. (Nashville: Abingdon, 1977). For a more recent treatment from a Wesleyan perspective, see the *Asbury Bible Commentary* (Grand Rapids, MI: Zondervan, 1992).

[34]For the ante-Nicene fathers' treatment of Christian perfection as a normative experience, see Christopher T. Bounds, "The Doctrine of Christian Perfection in the Apostolic Fathers," *Wesleyan Theological Journal* 42, no. 2 (2007): 7-27; "Irenaeus and the Doctrine of Christian Perfection," *Wesleyan Theological Journal* 45, no. 2 (2010): 45-60. Even Augustine believed the normative Christian life was one in which the love of God reigns in the human heart, enabling a Christian to walk in full obedience to God. See Christopher T. Bounds, "Augustine's Consistent Belief in a Christian's Victory over Sin," *Asbury Theological Journal* 44, no. 2 (2009): 20-35.

[35]Thomas Aquinas, *Summa Theologica* (Notre Dame, IN: Christian Classics, 1981), 2a-2ae, Q. 184, art. 2.

The "Achilles' heel" of the "shorter way." The American holiness movement's "shorter way" captures well the biblical and early Christian vision of the normative Christian life. However, it has been hampered and stifled by an inadequate understanding of the divine-human synergism in Christian perfection.[36] As the holiness tradition has proclaimed, taught, and counseled people about how to experience entire sanctification, it has fallen victim at times to forms of Pelagianism or semi-Pelagianism. More often, it has softened Wesley's semi-Augustinianism and given too much credit to prevenient grace given to all. This has often been done unwittingly, but at other times in full knowledge of the facts.

Holiness theology teaches that Christians can experience Christian perfection now through an act of entire consecration and faith, whereby believers surrender their lives to the lordship of Christ and trust God to purify and empower them. Entire sanctification is a simple synergism in which the work of consecration and faith by a Christian is met immediately by the grace of the Holy Spirit, bringing deliverance from the inner propensity to sin and empowerment to walk in love of God and neighbor.[37]

The human part of this synergism is represented in the three "easy steps" to sanctification first formulated by Phoebe Palmer and enshrined in the holiness tradition: First, Christians are to "present [themselves] to God in full surrender," that includes the "spirit," "soul," and "body." Second, they are "by faith [to] ask the God of peace to sanctify [them] and believe that He does it." Third, they are to "testify to others that [they] by faith believe God has received [their] full surrender and has entirely sanctified [them]."[38]

---

[36] While there are other theological problems with the holiness movement's theology of the "shorter way" that could be addressed, such as the tendency at times to "sell short" the work of regeneration and to overly simplify sin, I believe their understanding of operant grace is most problematic.

[37] For a few examples, see Brown, "How to be Entirely Sanctified," 25-27; Virgil A. Mitchell, "How to be Entirely Sanctified," *Vista* (Indianapolis: Wesleyan, 2009), 2-4; Leslie D. Wilcox, *Be Ye Holy* (Cincinnati, OH: Revivalist, 1965), 110-40.

[38] See Brown, "How to be Entirely Sanctified," 25-27; Phoebe Palmer, *The Way of Holiness*, 1-38. Brown teaches at God's Bible School and College in Cincinnati, Ohio, a school that epitomizes nineteenth-century American holiness theology.

At this point, what makes holiness teaching unique in the larger Wesleyan-Arminian tradition is its understanding of Christians' ability to consecrate their lives and exercise sanctifying faith. Every believer has the inherent power, either as a gift of prevenient grace, regenerating grace, or as an uncorrupted part of free will to do the human work required in Christian perfection.[39] From the moment of conversion, any Christian can appropriate entire sanctification. Because the Holy Spirit is always ready to respond to a personal act of consecration and faith, ignorance on the part of a believer, unwillingness to surrender fully to Christ, or a lack of will to believe become the root causes for an inability to achieve Christian perfection.[40]

The holiness movement places the focus squarely on human initiative and power to consecrate and believe. God does not determine when people are entirely sanctified (or converted); this rests entirely on humanity. Once people begin to see the truth of holiness, the door to Christian perfection is before them, and they can choose to open it, go through, and enter the sanctified life. When they choose to go through the door, God bestows this work of holiness.

---

[39]Charles Finney, *Systematic Theology* (Minneapolis: Bethany House, 1976), lectures 35 and 55, is an example of a nineteenth-century holiness evangelist who almost holds to pure Pelagianism through his denial of original sin (he is a soft semi-Pelagian) and teaches that the power to exercise faith is naturally inherent in each person. An example of a true semi-Pelagian view is Nazarene theologian A.M. Hills, who in his influential systematic theology (the first in the holiness tradition), *Fundamental Christian Theology: A Systematic Theology*, 2 vols. (Pasadena, CA: C. J. Kinne, 1931), 2:179-80, recognizes the debilitating influence of Adam's sin on humanity but argues for humanity's free will and natural capacity "by virtue of creation" to recognize the truth of the gospel, repent of sin, and exercise saving faith and sanctifying faith. While semi-Augustinian in his theology, Wesleyan theologian R. Larry Shelton unintentionally communicates a semi-Pelagian theology with his chapter "Initial Salvation: The Redemptive Grace of God in Christ," in *A Contemporary Wesleyan Theology: Biblical, Systematic and Practical*, ed. Charles Carter (Grand Rapids, MI: Zondervan, 1984), 496-99, by treating repentance and faith that appropriates salvation in a way that makes it seem like an inherent power all humanity possesses. An example of a Wesleyan theologian who explicitly teaches that the power to consecrate and exercise sanctifying faith is given to all through prevenient grace (a form of soft semi-Augustinianism) is nineteenth-century Methodist theologian John Miley, who in his influential *Systematic Theology*, 2 vols. (New York: Hunt and Eaton, 1894), 2:301-15 grounds humanity's freedom to repent and exercise faith in Christ's gift of prevenient grace given to all. See also "Article of Religion VIII: Personal Choice," in *The Discipline of the Wesleyan Church 2000* ¶ 224.

[40]Brown, "How to be Entirely Sanctified," 25-27.

However, there are several problems with this Pelagian, semi-Pelagian, and soft semi-Augustinian holiness perspective from a biblical, historical, and theological perspective.[41] Because of the fall in the garden, humanity does not have the ability to recognize the truth of the full gospel unless enlightened by the Holy Spirit, does not have the ability to have true sorrow over remaining sin, turn completely from sin, consecrate themselves fully to God, and have the faith to believe that God can sanctify them wholly unless the Holy Spirit gives this grace. Ultimately, total consecration and sanctifying faith are a gift of divine grace and not an innate ability.[42]

The holiness movement's confidence in human ability to fulfill the requirements to experience entire sanctification has led to many practical problems. For example, when the holiness tradition taught that people must be converted and sanctified to have a "ticket to heaven," many sincere seekers despaired of being "saved" at all after experiencing repeated failure to enter the sanctified life by its easy-to-follow formula. Many gave up on Christianity altogether as a result. Some Wesleyans simply conceded to the "longer way" after unsuccessful attempts to get "the victory." Many fellow seekers eventually rejected any Wesleyan teaching on holiness, embracing more Reformed or Lutheran understandings of sanctification. Others, after testifying to the experience of Christian perfection publicly to show their exercise of sanctifying faith, settled into bifurcated lives: giving public face and witness to a life of holiness while being plagued by a deeply divided heart and a persistent struggle to keep their sinful actions hidden from the church. Still others reduced heart holiness to entire consecration, whether sin

---

[41]See Thomas C. Oden's discussion of historic Christianity's rejection of any form of Pelagian or semi-Pelagian theology and the church's embrace of semi-Augustinianism in *The Transforming Power of Grace* (Nashville: Abingdon, 1993), 93-124, 206. See also Oden, *Classic Christianity: A Systematic Theology* (New York: HarperCollins, 2007), 567-77, 603-7.

[42]See Steve DeNeff, *The Way of Holiness* (Indianapolis: Wesleyan, 2010), 61-75, for a description of true grace-empowered repentance. See Wesley, "The Scripture Way of Salvation," *WJW* 6:53, for a description of the grace-created faith necessary to appropriate entire sanctification.

still reigned in their lives or not, or they condensed holiness to a certain list of behavioral rules that became the primary criteria by which a sanctified life was judged. If people could keep the rules, they would be judged to be perfect.

Ultimately, the holiness movement's "shorter way" works well when Christians immediately experience entire sanctification at the moment they seek and ask for it. However, it has limited theological and practical resources to offer seekers who do not genuinely experience it straightaway.[43] While the Holy Spirit used this theology in the nineteenth and twentieth centuries to bring many into the experience of entire sanctification, it has led too many seekers to settle for something less than true sanctification or to despair of the experience.

A "middle way" perspective: A neo-holiness theology of Christian perfection. The American holiness movement has captured well Scripture's vision of the normative Christian life and the expectation that entire sanctification should happen sooner, rather than later, in the Christian life. Its greatest weakness, however, arises from its belief that Christians have the ultimate power in determining when and where perfection occurs. It fails to understand the finer nuances of God's grace and it erroneously gives too much power to humanity in the synergistic work of salvation and sanctification.

To correct this problem, the holiness tradition must recover John Wesley's semi-Augustinian understanding of grace. He believed that because of the fall and transmission of original sin, humanity is destitute of all natural ability to move toward God at any point in salvation; people are impotent to perform even the normal

---

[43]This does not mean that the holiness tradition is without any sound advice for seekers of holiness. However, the advice given is often inconsistent with their semi-Pelagian theology. Ultimately, when Christians experience entire sanctification at the moment they ask and exercise faith, as it happens at times in the holiness tradition, it is only because God has given them the gift of sanctifying faith and given them this moment to be sanctified.

actions assigned to humanity in the work of salvation: repentance and faith.[44]

Wesley believed all human beings are "naturally" dead to God spiritually, thoroughly sinful, under divine condemnation, helpless to change themselves, ignorant of their present condition, and are incapable of grasping their true predicament in life. Therefore, if salvation is going to happen, God must take the initiative. If people are to awaken from their spiritual sleep of death, experience conviction of sin, repent, and exercise faith in Christ for salvation, then God must do the work.[45]

Wesley taught that God takes initiative by giving humanity prevenient grace. This grace makes possible the reception of additional grace and a response to it.[46] As God's grace comes at different times and in various ways in life, prevenient grace enables people to receive it and then empowers them to decide whether to cooperate with what God is doing in the moment or not.[47] In any positive human action in the way of salvation, there is first God's grace, followed by human reception and cooperation.

For example, when God brings illuminating and convicting grace into a person's life, prevenient grace enables the individual to receive it and to choose whether to embrace or resist it. When God gives grace to believe the gospel, prevenient grace makes it possible to receive and respond. Heart conviction and saving faith are impossible without God giving grace in the moment for each. As such, Wesley's understanding of grace is a divine-human synergism, with priority given to God's work.

---

[44]See Wesley, "On the Doctrine of Original Sin—Part II," *WJW* 9:261-88. In his treatise Wesley defends propositions on original sin given in response to questions 22-27 in The Westminster Larger Catechism; "On Original Sin," *WJW* 6:60; "On the Fall of Man," *WJW* 6:223-24.

[45]Wesley, "Journal," *WJW* 1:214; "The Spirit of Bondage and Adoption," *WJW* 5:99, 101, 108-9; "Wandering Thoughts," *WJW* 6:24; "Original Sin," *WJW* 6:58-59, 63; "The New Birth," *WJW* 6:70.

[46]At this point, it might be helpful to give a basic definition of grace. Grace is the unmerited work of God for us, in us, and through us. It is any work of God on our behalf.

[47]See Collins, *The Theology of John Wesley*, 14-15, 73-82.

At this point, the differences between Wesley's conception of grace and the holiness tradition are evident. Wesley believed that prevenient grace only restores humanity's capacity to receive and cooperate with further works of grace, while holiness teaching believes it reinstates everyone's ability to see the truth of the gospel, to repent of their sins, and to believe in Christ without further grace. The former view of prevenient grace is more modest, the latter more expansive. For Wesley, the possibility of illumination, amendment of life, and the exercise of saving faith requires more grace than what is given preveniently.

Wesley's semi-Augustinian conception of grace has ramifications for the experience of Christian perfection. He believed that Christians cannot recognize the truth of holiness unless *the Spirit brings* this recognition. They cannot begin to really despise their sin unless *the Spirit empowers* them to do so. They cannot turn toward God in total consecration unless *the Spirit enables* them. And they cannot exercise sanctifying faith, even if they see the truth of the "full gospel," unless *the Spirit creates* such faith in them. Prevenient grace only enables them to cooperate with sanctifying grace as the Spirit works in divinely appointed times and ways.

Therefore, people cannot choose when they are entirely sanctified. The experience of entire sanctification can only happen in the moments in which God gives grace to make total consecration possible and to create sanctifying faith.[48] Once awakened to the truth of Christian perfection and empowered to make a thorough surrender of their lives, Christians can only seek more grace until they are given personal faith to believe in the Spirit's cleansing work and to exercise that faith for sanctification.[49]

---

[48]Steve DeNeff states this explicitly in *Whatever Became of Holiness*, 53-63. To clarify, "moments" does not mean any specific duration of time. These moments can last for minutes, days, weeks, or months. It only means a period of time in which God is at work bringing a person to entire sanctification.

[49]Wesley, "Letter to Isaac Andrews, January 4, 1784," in *Letters of John Wesley*, ed. John Telford, 8 vols. (London: Epworth, 1931), 7:202.

If people are completely dependent on God's grace for even the human work in Christian perfection, a question arises: "How does God give this grace to people?" The answer: God works through appointed channels, or means.[50] As people are exposed to the means of grace, or as they place themselves in the means of grace (as they hear the gospel, partake in baptism and holy Communion, participate in the body of Christ, study the Bible, pray, fast, hear testimonies, listen to sermons, etc.), the Holy Spirit works to awaken people to the possibility of salvation from sin's power and being, to empower repentance and consecration, to create sanctifying faith, to perfect in love, and to move them to Christian maturity.

At this point, it is important to clarify that Wesley did not believe that participating in the means of grace necessarily means that someone will receive the specific grace they are seeking in the moment.[51] Christians cannot control how God works; they can only receive and respond to the grace God makes available to them at any given time. For example, when the truth of entire sanctification is preached, God may only be planting in one Christian the seed that with more grace will overcome the hardness of their heart to the possibility of holiness. In another believer, God may only be giving grace to bring conviction and repentance of remaining sin, but not sanctifying faith. Other people may respond to the truth of Christian perfection and seek it but not yet have sanctifying grace given to them; they may only be experiencing a deeper level of consecration, but not full consecration. From a human perspective, the Spirit may be doing very little, while at other times, God ordains the message to draw, convict, convince, and give sanctifying faith.

---

[50]Wesley, "The Means of Grace," *WJW* 5:185-201.

[51]Wesley, "The Means of Grace," *WJW* 5:185-201. Wesley states, "We know that there is no inherent power in the words that are spoken in prayer, in the letter of Scripture read, the sound thereof heard, or the bread and wine received in the Lord's Supper; but that it is God alone who is the Giver of very good gift, the Author of all grace; that the whole power is of Him, whereby, through any of these, there is any blessing conveyed to our souls" (188).

CONCLUSION

Historically, the holiness tradition's "shorter way" paradigm for the experience of entire sanctification has been shaped by different forms of semi-Pelagianism and soft semi-Augustinism, leading to the erroneous belief that Christians have the power to determine when they experience perfection. The problems arising from this model unfortunately have caused many Wesleyans to forsake the "shorter way."

The "longer way," while embracing Wesley's semi-Augustinian theology, offers no real expectation of Christian perfection early in believers' lives. While it exhorts Christians to seek perfection in love in the means of grace, few will experience it until just before or at the point of death. This view has discouraged many from earnestly seeking Christ for entire sanctification.

In this last chapter, we have tried to make the case for a "middle way" between the "shorter" and "longer way." The "shorter way's" vision of the normative Christian life and the expectation of entire sanctification happening toward the beginning of the Christian life and not the end need not be abandoned. Rather, holiness theology must embrace John Wesley's semi-Augustinian doctrine of grace, leading to a more theologically sound and helpful "middle way" model: actively seeking Christian perfection until the Spirit gives it, with the confidence it will happen sooner rather than later.

CONCLUSION

In this book, we have argued that the Wesleyan doctrine of entire sanctification / Christian perfection is well-grounded in Scripture (parts one and two), well-represented in the Christian tradition (part three), and consistent with classic Christian teaching (part four). We ended part four by outlining what we believe to be the most biblically faithful and theologically coherent version of the doctrine: a neo-holiness "middle way."

Our goal in this concluding chapter is to summarize and clarify our overarching argument and to reflect on its implications for the Christian life. We begin by offering a brief catechism on holiness that provides short, memorizable answers to five of the most important questions about entire sanctification / Christian perfection. We then address a series of frequently asked questions that require more extended answers. Finally, we discuss how to experience entire sanctification.

Holiness: A Brief Catechism

What is entire sanctification / Christian perfection? It is loving God with all your heart, soul, mind, and strength, and loving your neighbor as yourself (Deut 6:5; Lev 19:18).[1] Entire sanctification is something that God does in our lives after we believe in Jesus. It frees us *from* the power and condition of sin and frees us *to* live like Jesus by the power of the Spirit.

---

[1]This answer is inspired by Wesley, "Minutes of Some Late Conversations," *WJW* 8:279.

In what sense can Christians be perfect? Christians can be perfected in love so that they love God and neighbor with a whole heart.

In what sense can Christians not be perfect? Christians are not free from ignorance, error, infirmities, or temptation.[2] God will perfect us in these ways at the final resurrection.

Can an entirely sanctified person sin? Yes. Entirely sanctified people are able not to sin, but they are also able to sin and even to fall away from the faith.

How can I be entirely sanctified? By giving everything to God and seeking him expectantly until he sanctifies you entirely.

Frequently Asked Questions

The doctrine of entire sanctification / Christian perfection often raises many questions, especially for those who are hearing about it for the first time. Below we provide answers to some of the most common questions about entire sanctification that we have encountered in our preaching, teaching, and conversations.

Can all Christians be entirely sanctified? Yes, broadly speaking. However, there are a few caveats. On the human side, Christians must consecrate themselves to God and seek him expectantly as they await his work of entire sanctification. If a Christian refuses to do this, then they will likely not be entirely sanctified. On the divine side, entire sanctification is an act of God, so it ultimately depends on God's will and timing. First Thessalonians 4:3 and 5:23-24, however, give us confidence that entire sanctification *is* something that God desires to do in the life of every believer.

If an entirely sanctified person sins, do they "lose" their entire sanctification? It depends on the nature and extent of the sin. If an entirely sanctified person commits an isolated sin, is convicted by the Spirit, repents, and renews their relationship with God, we do not think it necessary to say that they have "lost" their entire

---

[2]Wesley, "Christian Perfection," *WJW* 6:2–5.

sanctification (a brief "lapse" might be a better way of describing this). As an analogy, when a believer (entirely sanctified or not) sins and responds in the way indicated above, we do not usually say that they have "lost" their status as a Christian and require them to receive Jesus as Lord again or be rebaptized. Rather, we tell them, "Be who you are." We suggest that the same is true for those who are entirely sanctified. If, however, an entirely sanctified person engages in a pattern of unrepentant sin, then it is certainly possible for them to lose their entire sanctification and to need to consecrate themselves and seek God for entire sanctification once again.

Do you have to believe in entire sanctification to be entirely sanctified? Not necessarily. We believe that many Christians who do not believe in entire sanctification have nonetheless experienced it, and that others can. Yet we would also suggest that a Christian is far less likely to experience entire sanctification if they reject that it is a possibility. If, for example, a Christian believes that they will sin daily in word, thought, and deed, it is less likely that they will open themselves to the full extent of the sanctification that God wants to accomplish in them.

Do you have to be entirely sanctified to be saved? We first need to clarify the question. In Wesleyan theology, entire sanctification follows justification and regeneration, so we take "saved" above to refer to ultimate salvation—that is, whether a Christian must be entirely sanctified to receive eternal life. God is the one who judges, and we do not presume to know precisely how much one must be sanctified to receive eternal life. What we do know is that "without holiness no one will see the Lord" (Heb 12:14), so we would encourage brothers and sisters in Christ to withhold nothing from God but to give him everything and to seek him expectantly in hope of entire sanctification.

Does being entirely sanctified mean you've "arrived" or have hit a "glass ceiling" where no more growth is possible? No. Entire sanctification is a state of dynamic perfection in which believers can grow and be perfected further as the Spirit empowers them to live like Jesus. For example, a believer who is entirely sanctified at age twenty-five is freed from the power and state of sin, but she will still have many ways in which she can become more like Jesus as she walks with him through the joys and trials of life. Work, marriage, singleness, parenting, health challenges, deaths of loved ones, and so on, may all provide her with opportunities to walk by the Spirit in ways that she has not had to before. As she submits to the Spirit's leading in this uncharted territory, she will become more of what she already is—entirely sanctified.

If entire sanctification is a biblical concept, why don't more Christians believe in it? We would first like to note that a significant number of Christians *do* believe in the Wesleyan doctrine of entire sanctification (or something close to it). The Wesleyan tradition constitutes a significant movement within global Christianity, and while not all Christians in Wesleyan-Arminian churches affirm entire sanctification, many do. In addition, some churches outside the Wesleyan tradition affirm or are open to the doctrine of entire sanctification, even if they do not emphasize it. The charismatic movement, for example, emphasizes the gifts of the Spirit rather than his sanctifying work, but some charismatics would affirm entire sanctification or something very close to it. And whatever the situation may be in modern Christianity, part three of this book has shown that numerous theologians throughout Christian history have taught Christian perfection in ways that resonate with the Wesleyan doctrine of entire sanctification.

But the question stands: Why don't more Christians believe in entire sanctification if it is biblical? We would note at least three factors. First, entire sanctification is inconvenient to our sin. We are all born corrupted by sin, and since this is the only existence that we have ever known, it is hard to believe that God could deliver us from the power and condition of sin. Indeed, to believe this would mean that we could no longer sin comfortably, using the excuse that "I'm just human." Entire sanctification thus comes at a high existential cost. It means that we must give our all to God (even our favorite sins), and this is not an easy thing to do.

Second, many fail to see evidence for entire sanctification in Scripture because of doctrinal biases. We all read Scripture with presuppositions, and sometimes those presuppositions cause us to filter out or tone down certain elements of what the Bible says. As noted in chapter four, when Jesus says, "Be perfect . . . as your heavenly Father is perfect" (Mt 5:48), many people assume that he is laying down an impossible ideal or a command for some special class of Christians, even though according to our reading this is not the case. In some cases, our Bible translations tame the text for us. The muting of perfection language in numerous translations is a prime example of this.[3] We do not say this to cast doubt on Bible translations but simply to emphasize that translations are produced by people, and people (even well-intentioned ones) have doctrinal biases. We would advise readers to use multiple Bible translations to help overcome this difficulty.

Third, Wesleyans have not always been good witnesses for entire sanctification—the doctrine that John Wesley believed God had raised up his movement to proclaim.[4] At times, we have failed to communicate entire sanctification well, neglecting its biblical foundations or promoting unbiblical expectations for when or how it should occur. But most of all, we have failed to live out the reality of entire sanctification. Too often we have substituted mental assent to entire sanctification for fervently seeking God. Too often we have treated entire sanctification as a badge earned or a box checked rather than a grace-given reality to grow in. Too often we have received entire sanctification, sinned, and refused to repent to others because of a desire to save face. Such shortcomings have understandably led believers both inside and outside the Wesleyan

---

[3]See chapter five on Philippians 3:12, 15 and chapter six on perfection language in Hebrews.
[4]Wesley, "Letter to Robert Carr Brackenbury (September 15, 1790)," *WJW* 13:9.

movement to question whether entire sanctification is really possible. We have written this book to show the biblical and theological basis for entire sanctification, but it is important to remember that many people will evaluate the doctrine based not on our words but on our lives.

Have you been entirely sanctified? If so, what is your testimony? Yes, by God's grace. Below are our individual testimonies.

Matt. I lived and served in Haiti as a career missionary with my family for thirteen years. Haiti is a hard place to live for most non-Haitians. It is a beautiful place in many ways, and is filled with beautiful people, but it takes a lot of effort just to carry out day-to-day tasks due to the lack of infrastructure that most Americans are accustomed to. Adding language and cultural barriers to the sometimes insurmountable challenges of carrying out daily life will humble anyone attempting to do effective ministry in Haiti. For me, the depth of the sin condition *quickly* surfaced when serving in this sort of ministry context. I thought I was patient until I was faced with sitting through lengthy worship services at over 100 degrees with no water. I thought I was equipped and trained for ministry until I sat on the edge of an emaciated man's bed who was suffering and dying from a treatable disease. I thought I had compassion and lived sacrificially until I witnessed people living on $700 a year sharing their resources with one another to survive. These sorts of conditions forced me to face my sinful condition *daily.* One of the greatest challenges for me was not being resentful toward the people I was serving. I was guilty of giving in to the temptation to blame my own struggles on the people and culture I was serving. This manifested itself through thoughts like, *This all wouldn't be so hard if Haitians could just get their act together!* I carried resentment in my heart for many years for the people I was called to serve. I saw in my wife, however, a pure, holy *love* for the people she too was called to serve. She genuinely loved (and loves) *them, the other,* more than herself. She had endless patience, grace, charity, compassion, and strived—with success—to demonstrate the unconditional love of God to the Haitian people without faltering. She had pure, Jesus love. Her witness further revealed my own inadequacies and selfishness. I prayed, waited, and strived for a love that was perfect like hers. It took many years, but eventually God *completely purified my heart of all resentment and bitterness toward the people I was called to serve,* even my enemies. To this day, I have a love for my Haitian brothers and sisters that is so pure, holy, and inexplicably unwavering that I would stop at nothing for the redemption of that nation.

Chris. I had not been a Christian for very long when I began to recognize the disparity between my internal motivations, outward actions, and the holiest desires of my heart. While I wanted to love God with all my heart and give myself in loving service to others, I knew the frustration of not being able to walk fully in that love. Because of my sinful condition, the natural bent or proclivity of my heart was to love myself more than God and neighbor. While I had the desire to love and serve God, the desire to please myself was stronger. Even when I tried to be unselfish and walk in obedience to Christ in difficult circumstances, I failed more than I succeeded. Holy love did not come easily to me.

In those early years of Christian life, I found myself in a frustrating predicament. Part of me longed to give myself completely to God and to others in love, while another sought my own selfish end. I discovered that I did not have the internal power to follow Christ. I had the desire to be a Christian but did not have the power to live the life to which I had been called. The question arose from my heart: Can Christ liberate the holiest longings of my heart? As a student in a Wesleyan-holiness college, I learned that he could.

I began earnestly to seek the Lord for this work. After pursuing for four years, unexpectedly, I experienced a breakthrough. As a former professor prayed over me, the Spirit came and liberated the holiest desires of my heart, setting me free from the power and state of sin. While this experience was not like my conversion experience, it has been far more transformative. I have walked in an abiding victory, experiencing greater depths of divine love, and grown to Christian maturity. While I cannot testify to always loving God and others to the fullest extent in every moment of my life, I can say that my heart has been established in the love of God, with the Spirit's fruit reigning in my life. Thanks be to God: Father, Son, and Holy Spirit.

Caleb. I initially received Christ as Lord at age five. I grew up in a strongly Wesleyan home, so I was exposed to the idea of entire sanctification at an early age. However, while I believed that God could make people holy in this life, I tended toward a "longer way" view of entire sanctification. I was committed to following Christ faithfully and growing in sanctification, but I did not expect to receive entire sanctification soon.

In 2011, I began graduate studies at Wesley Biblical Seminary and accepted a pastoral position at my home church—a Nazarene congregation. I soon started to pursue ordination in the Church of the Nazarene. This created a tension for me because on my minister's license application every year I had to answer the question, "Are you entirely sanctified?" For years I answered, "No." In my application for 2016, I explained that while I had no persistent sin in my life, "God has not yet brought me to a point where I can say that my every thought and action are animated by perfect love." In essence, I held the doctrine of entire sanctification in high regard and did not want to be a poor witness for it by claiming to have experienced it before I was living it.

The following spring, however, the Lord began to challenge me on my "No." I felt him leading me to ask myself, "Am I living the entirely sanctified life? If not, why not?" As I prayed, the Lord revealed that in order to experience the entirely sanctified life, I would have to depend on the Holy Spirit daily in a new and deeper way. I began to walk in this dependence, and after a season the Lord gave me an assurance that he had entirely sanctified me. God has filled me with his Spirit and his love so that Spirit-empowered obedience to him is the overarching and consistent pattern of my life.

What are the most important biblical passages for understanding entire sanctification? Some of the clearest and most explicit passages are Deuteronomy 6:4-9, Leviticus 19:18, Isaiah 6, Jeremiah 31:31-34, Ezekiel 36:25-29, Matthew 5:43-48, Romans 6–8, 1 Thessalonians 4:3 and 5:23-24, Philippians 3:12-15, 1 Peter 1:14-16, and 1 John 2:28–3:10. However, it is important to note that the doctrine of entire sanctification rests not on these texts alone but on the entire witness and metanarrative of Scripture (see parts one and two of this book).

HOW TO EXPERIENCE ENTIRE SANCTIFICATION

The doctrine of entire sanctification, like all theology, must be lived out to be truly meaningful. All the biblical and theological thought in the preceding chapters means little if we do not live the holy life ourselves. We therefore conclude this book with some reflections on how to experience entire sanctification. As noted in the preceding chapter, entire sanctification is a gift that God gives us. All we can do is receive it. How do we enter this normative Christian life, intended for every believer? It is not like "three easy steps" as portrayed in the "shorter way," nor is it as difficult and "near impossible" as implied by the "longer way." What follows is biblically and theologically informed advice. It should not be taken as law, but only used as a guide. We frame this counsel around the two points offered in the final question of the brief catechism above.

Give everything to God. If we desire to experience entire sanctification, we must fully surrender our lives to God, holding nothing back. We need to give everything to God—our time, talents, treasure, dreams, fears, emotional wounds, strongholds of sin, divided heart, pride, and so on. We must be willing to go anywhere and do anything for God. We must consecrate to God all areas of our lives over which we have control, as well as those over which we have no control. Christ must have it all. If we are unwilling or unable to do this, the possibility of entire sanctification is impeded, and we must seek Christ for the power to make a total consecration.

John Wesley captures this attitude of full surrender well in his Covenant Prayer:

> I am no longer my own, but yours. Put me to what you will, rank me with whom you will; put me to doing, put me to suffering; let me be employed for you or laid aside for you, exalted for you or brought low for you; let me be full, let me be empty; let me have all things, let me have nothing; I freely and heartily yield all things to your pleasure and disposal.
>
> And now, O glorious and blessed God, Father, Son, and Holy Spirit, you are mine and I am yours. So be it. And the Covenant which I have made on earth, let it be ratified in heaven.[5]

Seek God expectantly until he sanctifies you entirely. If we desire to experience entire sanctification, we must seek God expectantly until he accomplishes this work. It is important that we seek *God*, not just an experience. People can sometimes become more focused on experiencing entire sanctification than on knowing God, which ironically hinders them from receiving entire sanctification. But if we are seeking God, we must also do so expectantly, asking him in faith to sanctify us entirely and eagerly anticipating his response. Three elements are key to this expectant seeking.

First, we must *believe* that God makes people holy in decisive moments and that he wants to do this *in our lives*. To believe this is no easy thing, for there is a deep and pervasive skepticism about the possibility of entire sanctification in the American church. Even in Wesleyan-holiness denominations, one can find cynical attitudes about the possibility of entire sanctification. If we find ourselves skeptical of the idea that God can sanctify entirely, we must ask the Spirit to open our hearts to this possibility.

Second, we must *ask* Christ in faith to sanctify us now. Because entire sanctification is an act of God, we cannot do it for ourselves but must receive it in faith. John Wesley describes sanctifying faith

---

[5]Wesley, "A Service for Such as Would Make or Renew Their Covenant with God [A Modern Adaptation]," in *John and Charles Wesley: Selected Prayers, Hymns, Journal Notes, Sermons, Letters, and Treatises*, ed. Frank Whaling, Classics of Western Spirituality (New York: Paulist, 1981), 387.

as a divine evidence and conviction, "First, that God hath promised it in the Holy Scripture. . . . Secondly, that what God hath promised he is able to perform. . . . Thirdly, . . . that he is able and willing to do it now. . . . To this confidence, . . . there needs to be added one thing more . . . a divine evidence and conviction that he doeth it."[6]

Third, if entire sanctification does not occur when we initially ask for it, we must *wait* actively and persistently in the means of grace. What does this look like? Here are some examples of how Christians can seek God for entire sanctification in the means of grace:

- Study and memorize the Scriptures, especially key passages about holiness.
- Pray and fast regularly, asking God for entire sanctification.
- Invite other believers to hold you accountable in areas where you are vulnerable to temptation.
- Listen to the testimonies of believers who have experienced entire sanctification and ask them (and others) to intercede for you.
- Ask God to sanctify you entirely at appropriate moments during corporate worship (e.g., Holy Communion, altar calls).
- Serve the needy and ask God to perfect your heart in love as you serve.

By actively seeking God for entire sanctification through these and other means of grace, we can position ourselves to receive his sanctifying work when he brings it.

CONCLUSION

We hope that every person who reads this book comes to experience entire sanctification. But as noted above, receiving entire sanctification does not mean that we have "arrived" or hit a "glass ceiling" where no more growth is possible (or necessary). Entire sanctification,

---

[6]Wesley, "The Scripture Way of Salvation," *WJW* 6:52-53.

while it is a decisive point of in our walk with Christ, is more the beginning of a journey than the end of one. Entirely sanctified believers must persevere in the grace that they have received, loving God and neighbor with a whole heart. Indeed, love of God and neighbor is the heartbeat of holiness. We should not seek entire sanctification merely because it benefits us (though it certainly does). We should seek entire sanctification because it enables us to love God completely and to bring maximum glory to him, as we bear his image in the world in the fullest way possible this side of the new creation. And when we do this, the world encounters the holy One who alone can satisfy the deepest desires of their hearts. The world is hungry for God. May they find him when they meet us. *Soli Deo gloria.*

APPENDIX

RECOMMENDED READING ON HOLINESS

PRIMARY SOURCES

Ambrose of Milan. *Jacob and the Happy Life*. In *Saint Ambrose: Seven Exegetical Works*. Translated by Michael P. McHugh. The Fathers of the Church 65. Washington, DC: Catholic University of America Press, 1971.

Bernard of Clairvaux. *On Loving God*. In *Bernard of Clairvaux: Selected Works*. Translated by G. R. Evans. Classics of Western Spirituality. New York: Paulist, 1987.

De Sales, Francis. *Introduction to the Devout Life*. Translated by John K. Ryan. Image Classics. New York: Image, 1966.

Law, William. *A Treatise on Christian Perfection*. Edited by Erwin Paul Rudolph. Carol Stream, IL: Creation, 1975.

Palmer, Phoebe. *The Way of Holiness*. New York, 1854.

Teresa of Avila. *The Way of Perfection*. Translated by Kieran Kavanaugh. Washington, DC: Institute of Carmelite Studies, 2000.

Thomas Aquinas. "On the State of Perfection in General." In *Summa Theologica*, 2a 2ae, Q. 184. Art. 1. Translated by the Fathers of the Dominican Province. New York: Benziger Brothers, 1947.

Wesley, John. "Christian Perfection." *WJW* 6:1-22.

———. "A Plain Account of Christian Perfection." *WJW* 11:366-446.

———. "The Scripture Way of Salvation." *WJW* 6:43-54.

SECONDARY SOURCES

Bassett, Paul M., and William Greathouse. *The Historical Development*. Vol. 2, *Exploring Christian Holiness*. Kansas City, MO: Beacon Hill, 1985.

Collins, Kenneth J. *The Theology of John Wesley: Holy Love and the Shape of Grace*. Nashville: Abingdon, 2007.

DeNeff, Steve. *The Way of Holiness*. Indianapolis: Wesleyan, 2012.

Drury, Keith. *Holiness for Ordinary People*. Indianapolis: Wesleyan, 1983.

Greathouse, William M. *From the Apostles to Wesley*. Kansas City, MO: Beacon Hill, 1979.

Grider, Kenneth. *A Wesleyan-Holiness Theology*. Kansas City, MO: Beacon Hill, 1994.

Leclerc, Diane. *Discovering Christian Holiness: The Heart of Wesleyan Holiness Theology*. Kansas City, MO: Foundry, 2010.

McCall, Thomas H. *Against God and Nature: The Doctrine of Sin*. Foundations of Evangelical Theology. Wheaton, IL: Crossway, 2019.

Noble, T. A. *Holy Trinity: Holy People: The Theology of Christian Perfecting*. Eugene, OR: Cascade, 2013.

Oswalt, John N. *Called to Be Holy: A Biblical Perspective*. Nappanee, IN: Francis Asbury, 1999.

NAME INDEX

SCRIPTURE INDEX